HYDE: FROM DISSOLUTION TO VICTORIAN SUBURB

Christine Grover

Front Cover: Engraving of Hyde Abbey by Tracey Sheppard.
Reproduced by kind permission of the artist.

Back Cover: Flint and brick houses in Hyde Street built by William Barrow Simonds.

ISBN: 978-0-9564701-8-8

Published 2012 by Victorian Heritage Press www.victorianheritagepress.co.uk

Email: victorianheritagepress@gmail.com

Printed by Sarsen Press, 22 Hyde Street, Winchester SO23 7DR

Contents

Figures vi

Tables ix

Acknowledgements...x

Foreword xi

Part 1: The Dissolution of Hyde Abbey and the Aftermath 1

  Chapter 1: The Dissolution of Hyde Abbey 3

    The establishment of Hyde Abbey in 1110 3

    Landownership in Hyde...7

    Monastic rise and downfall...9

    The disposal of Hyde Abbey's lands 13

    Wriothesley and his descendents 21

    Conclusion...24

  Chapter 2: Papacy and Plots 25

    Hyde in the sixteenth and seventeenth centuries 25

    The Bethell family at Hyde Abbey Farm 1546-1592 28

    The Clerke family at Hyde Abbey Farm 1592-1693 35

    Walter and Thomas Chaundler at Abbots Barton c1540-1564.................39

    Roger and Mabel Corham at Abbots Barton 1564-1615 41

    George & Thomas Chaundler at Abbots Barton 1615-1650 43

    Ownership in Hyde Street...44

    Conclusion...46

Part 2: The Agricultural Revolution, the Knights and the Duke.................47

  Chapter 3: Custodians of Abbots Barton and Hyde Abbey Estates........49

    Abbots Barton and the Mynnes, Lewkenors and Martins 49

    Abbots Barton and the Knights 57

    Hyde Abbey and the Duke..62

    Reunification of the Abbey farms and the end of the Knights' ownership 66

    Conclusion...71

Chapter 4: Abbots Barton and Hyde Abbey Farms............................**72**

Farming at Abbots Barton in the eighteenth century..72

Hop production 76

Water Meadows 79

Abbots Barton and Hyde Abbey Farms 87

Sale of the Abbey site, its farm and Abbots Barton 103

Conclusion 105

Chapter 5: Hyde Street in the eighteenth and nineteenth centuries..........**106**

Turnpikes 106

Hyde Street 109

Education 116

Reform 119

Industry 125

Conclusion 132

Part 3: The Making of the Modern Suburb **133**

Chapter 6: William Simonds, the farmer **135**

The law suit 135

The coming of the railway 138

Early land releases 142

Hyde Street 145

The brewery and the Simonds 149

The death of William Simonds 156

Conclusion 157

Chapter 7: William Barrow Simonds, the developer **158**

The Simonds' family 158

The decline in agriculture and the fragmentation of Abbots Barton Farm.......161

The Old Hop Garden Development..167

The Limekilns Development 171

The Gallows Hill Development: Park Road West 173

The Gallows Hill Development: Park Road East 176

Worthy Road Development 183

Conclusion 185

Chapter 8: Suburban Estates for the Mass Market **187**

The house building process 187

The closure of the Bridewell 190

North Walls and the Refuge 194

Hyde Abbey Road 196

Eagles Field Estate..201

Conygary Estate..208

The Oxlease Estate 214

Other developments 218

Conclusion 220

Chapter 9: Barrow Simonds' Hyde – then and now **222**

Hyde Street 222

The breweries 227

House ownership in 1912 233

Hyde 2012...235

Nine hundred years of changing ownership................................**240**

Appendix **245**

Endnotes...**249**

References...**270**

Index...**278**

Figures

Figure I: Winchester's Northern Suburb – Hyde in 1750 xiii

Figure II: Winchester's Northern Suburb – Hyde in 1909 xiv

Figure 1a: St Bartholomew's Church c.1870 2

Figure 1b: Capital from Hyde Abbey...2

Figure 1.1: Speed's Map of Winchester in 1611 4

Figure 1.2: Schematic plan of Hyde Abbey and its precincts 5

Figure 1.3: Nuns Walk...6

Figure 1.4: Hyde Abbey Gateway in the eighteenth century 15

Figure 1.5 Hyde Gateway in Victorian times and today 16

Figure 1.6: The Abbot's bridge over the Mill Stream 17

Figure 1.7: Hyde Abbey remains..18

Figure 1.8: Houses in Hyde Churchyard 20

Figure 1.9: Window detail in Hyde Abbey Gateway 22

Figure 1.10: The Wriothesley-Russell Family Tree 23

Figure 1.11: Durngate Mill from the south c.1870......................................24

Figure 2.1: Hyde House and Gardens...30

Figure 2.2: Layout of Hyde House 31

Figure 2.3: The extension to Hyde House 33

Figure 2.4: The Abbey's water meadows..38

Figure 2.5: Godden's house - later called Hyde House or Hyde Abbey 45

Figure 3: Durngate Mill c.1870 48

Figure 3.1: Lady Anne Mynne, wife of Sir John Lewkenor 52

Figure 3.2: Mynne Family Tree..52

Figure 3.3: Lewkenor Family Tree..53

Figure 3.4: Knights of Chawton Family Tree 54

Figure 3.5: Elizabeth Martin Knight and Bulstrode Peachey Knight.....................56

Figure 3.6: May Family Tree..60

Figure 3.7: Thomas (Broadnax May) Knight (1701-1781)................................61

Figure 3.8: Austen Family Tree..67

Figure 3.9: Thomas Knight (1737-1794)..68

Figure 3.10: Edward Austen Knight (1767-1852).......................................68

Figure 4.1: Water meadows near Abbots Barton farmhouse 81

Figure 4.2: Neglected water meadows – the Abbey Mill Stream 81

Figure 4.3: Abbots Barton Dairy 86

Figure 4.4: Abbots Barton Farmhouse from the east 87

Figure 4.5: Part of Barton Farm and Hyde Abbey Farm 1753 88

Figure 4.6: Abbots Barton Uplands rising above the water meadows 94

Figure 4.7: Survey of Abbots Barton Uplands 1769 95

Figure 4.8: Survey of the Abbey Lands, Abbots Barton 1769 96

Figure 4.9: Survey of Barton Meadows, Abbots Barton 1769 97

Figure 4.10: Old cottages in King Alfred Place 105

Figure 5.1: St Bartholomew's Hyde 109

Figure 5.2: Hyde Street about 1750 110

Figure 5.3: Hyde Abbey House, No. 23 Hyde Street 112

Figure 5.4: Rear wall of No. 23 Hyde Street 112

Figure 5.5: No. 33 Hyde Street 113

Figure 5.6: No. 58 Hyde Street 114

Figure 5.7: Kingston House 114

Figure 5.8: Sloane's new schoolroom 117

Figure 5.9: Hyde in the late 1790s 124

Figure 5.10: Malthouse No. 2 in the north of Hyde Street 128

Figure 5.11: Swan Lane c.1875 130

Figure 5.12: Malthouses No. 1 (Hyde Street) & No. 3 (Swan Lane) 131

Figure 5.13: The White Swan and Northfield House in Hyde Street 132

Figure 6.1: Georgian terraced houses in Hyde Street 134

Figure 6.2: Barton Farm and the remnants of Hyde Garden 137

Figure 6.3: Hyde Lodge 143

Figure 6.4: The northern part of Hyde Vicarage 146

Figure 6.5: Nos. 31 and 32 Hyde Street 148

Figure 6.6: The Counting House next to the Swan Inn 150

Figure 6.7: Knight's Cottage and Mr May's house (later Hyde Tavern) 154

Figure 6.8: Hyde Tavern and adjacent Georgian houses 154

Figure 6.9: Nos. 61 to 65 Hyde Street 157

Figure 7.1: Abbotts Barton House 1858 159

Figure 7.2: The Barrow Simonds Family Tree 160

Figure 7.3: Index of agricultural rents 1850 to 1914 161

Figure 7.4: Barrow Simonds' Plan for Park Road 166

Figure 7.5: The Old Hop Garden and Park Road East 168

Figure 7.6: Northlands, Worthy Road 169

Figure 7.7: Salcot Lodge, Worthy Road 170

Figure 7.8: Limekilns, Gallows Hill and Park Road West 172

Figure 7.9: Rosslyn, Park Road 175

Figure 7.10: Arts and Crafts design in Micklam's houses, Park Road 175

Figure 7.11: Lynton, Park Road 177

Figure 7.12: St Waleric, Park Road 177

Figure 7.13: Brendon, Park Road 178

Figure 7.14: Valentio 182

Figure 7.15: Abbots Acre 182

Figure 7.16: Selborne Lodge, Worthy Road. 184

Figure 7.17: William Barrow Simonds 186

Figure 8.1: No. 68 Hyde Street...190

Figure 8.2: King Alfred Place 1873 192

Figure 8.3: King Alfred Place 193

Figure 8.4: The Refuge and its extensive grounds 196

Figure 8.5: Hyde Abbey Road...197

Figure 8.6: Houses in Hyde Abbey Road...200

Figure 8.7: Eagles Fields 202

Figure 8.8: Eagles Field Estate 204

Figure 8.9: Old and new houses in Hyde Close 207

Figure 8.10: Conygary and Oxlease Estates..209

Figure 8.11: Conygary Estate 213

Figure 8.12: Exterior Design on the Oxlease Estate 215

Figure 8.13: Interior Design on the Oxlease Estate..............................216

Figure 8.14: No house the same 217

Figure 8.15: King Alfred Terrace 218

Figure 8.16: Alswitha Terrace 219

Figure 8.17: Victorians at leisure 221

Figure 9.1: Hyde Parish Hall..226

Figure 9.2: Hyde Brewery 1873 & 1897 229

Figure 9.3: West side of Hyde Street looking north..............................231

Figure 9.4: The King Alfred...232

Figure 9.5: No. 26 Hyde Street...234

Figure 9.6: Hyde Abbey Remembered...243

Tables

Table 2.1: Owners of Hyde Abbey to 1693 27

Table 2.2: Owners of Abbots Barton to 1650 27

Table 2.3: Hyde House 32

Table 3.1: Owners of Abbot Barton Farm 1650 to 1811 51

Table 3.2: 1765 Bill of works for repairs to Barton Farm 65

Table 4.1: Expenditure per acre from setting up a hop field 77

Table 4.2: Income and expenditure from established hop production 78

Table 4.3: Annual income and expenditure per acre on an established water..........

meadow 82

Table 4.4: Details of proposals agreed in May 1738 by the owners and tenants of ....

Abbots Barton and Hyde Abbey Farms. 85

Table 4.5: Abbots Barton Farm in 1726 90

Table 4.6: Hyde Abbey Farm in 1767 92

Table 4.7: Description of Hyde Abbey Farm in 1767 93

Table 4.8: Survey of the Uplands Abbots Barton by Henry Hogben 1769 98

Table 4.9: Freehold Estates of Thomas Knight 1769 – the Abbey Lands.................99

Table 4.10: Freehold Estates of Thomas Knight, 1769 – Barton Meadows 100

Table 4.11: Abbots Barton Estate in 1811 104

Table 5.1: Income and expenditure for proposed Winchester Turnpikes 108

Table 5.2: Tradesmen's bills for Hyde Abbey School 1824 118

Table 5.3: Offences of Bridewell prisoners in 1819 122

Table 5.4: Key events in the history of Hyde Brewery 1770 – 1807 126

Table 6.1: The Hinton and Baverstock claim to legal title of Abbots Barton...........136

Table 6.2: Inventory of casks at the Hyde Street brewery 1843 151

Table 7.1: Abbots Barton Farm 1858 164

Table 7.2: Inventory of Park House for Capt. Radford 1914 180

Table 7.3: Details in Inventory of Park House for Capt. Radford 1914 181

Table 8.1: Hyde Abbey Road development 1881 to 1888 198

Table 8.2: Eagles Field development 1879 to 1883 205

Table 8.3: Architects of the Conygary & Oxlease Estate 1896 to 1911 211

Table A1: Details of property ownership on the former Uplands 1912 245

Table A2: Main Property Owners in Hyde in 1912 247

Acknowledgements

- A special thanks to Richard Knight for permission to use his family's portraits.

- Thank you to Stephen Lawrence at Chawton House.

- Hampshire Record Office for the use of maps and images:
  COPY/562/ 18 & 19, 13M85W/48, 76A03W/7
  O.S. Maps of Winchester – 1st Edition (1873), 2nd Edition (1897) and 3rd Edition (1909).

- Winchester City Council for the use of the following images:
  W/F5/1/10, W/C5/10/23/71/1, W/C5/10/23/71/3, W/K4/1/15/1 and W/C11/2/563.

- Winchester City Council Museums for the use of PWCM2707. PWCM2737, PWCM2738 and PWCM3793.

- Neil Jenkinson for permission to use the image of William Barrow Simonds from his book.

- Professor Tom Beaumont James for his continuing support in my endeavours over the last decade

- The University of Winchester for their support.

- Colleagues who have provided valuable feedback and advice.

- Margaret and Tony for proof reading

- Finally to Richard Grover for his expertise and comments on numerous drafts over the four years of research and writing.

I hope the reader is as fascinated by the history of Hyde as I have been researching it.

Chris Grover, August 2012

Foreword

All that now stands above ground of this wealthy foundation is the entrance to the abbot's house. This is a noble stone archway with some flanking passages still left, but it now serves as the entrance to a farmyard, and the side buildings are used as stables. Happily, the owner of the property, Mr W. Barrow Simonds, has given the place to the City, and it will now be rescued from its ignoble use, and be properly preserved. The Corporation has also bought some 35 acres adjoining, which included the whole site of the Abbey, and are going to turn it into a park named after the national hero. They have already begun making excavations, and have found portions of the walls of the choir, which show that the building was not in the position hitherto assigned to it by antiquaries. Strong hopes are entertained that some relic of the great Alfred's tomb may be found during these excavations, for he was known to be buried near the head of the church. Unfortunately, the Puritans, in their contempt for mouldering bones known as relics, and the County Magistrates in past times, when they built a now vanished Bridewell on the site, have probably made the discovery of Alfred's tomb impossible.

T. W. Warren (ed.) (1903)

Hyde, the northern suburb of the Cathedral City of Winchester, was the home of Hyde Abbey, the final resting place of King Alfred the Great. The main thoroughfare, Hyde Street, lies outside the City's North Gate. The City ditch, or North Walls as it was later known, separated Hyde from the City. To the east of Hyde, the extensive river system, which provided rich agricultural land, hindered urban expansion.

Hyde: From Dissolution to Victorian Suburb follows the history of the northern suburb of Winchester, in the south of England, starting just prior to Henry VIII's edict to members of his inner court to inspect and then destroy all the monasteries, including the rich Abbey of Hyde. Henry VIII's most trusted royal courtiers included Thomas Wriothesley who sought to ingratiate himself with the King. Wriothesley was in the enviable position to benefit from the destruction by purchasing the former Abbeys' extensive lands in Hampshire.

Although Wriothesley retained many of these properties and manors, he relinquished the site of Hyde Abbey and the home (Abbey or Barton Farm) and the grange (Abbots Barton) farms. The new occupiers, men also associated with the King's court, were in the prime position to take on the lease and subsequently the freehold of the land. These new owners were royalists and were comfortably ensconced on their new estates which passed down to their children. Unfortunately during the Civil War, these families found that royalist allegiances threatened their peaceful enjoyment of the property. Sequestration (the seizure of properties) and swingeing fines ended their tenure and the courtier families lost control of the former Abbey's properties.

The derelict site and the home and grange farms passed into the hands of gentry families. Abbots Barton was sold to a rich widow, Anne Mynne, whose father had been Lord Mayor of London in 1634. Her wily husband survived the political turmoil to become an MP in the early 1600s. The next 150 years saw the estate pass between members of her extended family as successive owners failed to produce heirs. Anne Mynne's daughter married into the Lewkenor family who had extensive estates in Sussex and a presence in Parliament.

When the Chawton estate in Hampshire was inherited by Elizabeth, the daughter of Frances Lewkenor, a stipulation was that she changed her name to Knight. This condition saw the Knight family name survive as the Abbey's former lands, along with Chawton, passed to distant cousins. However, as Jane Austen's readers know, inheritance law is a minefield. The entail set up in Elizabeth's will was to prove a challenge to Jane's brother Edward when he inherited the Hyde Abbey's farms, Chawton, and Godmersham, outside Canterbury.

Meanwhile, Thomas Wriothesley's descendants still held the Hampshire manors belonging to Hyde Abbey. One of these, the Duke of Bedford, purchased the Abbey site and farm. He held them for a short period before financial troubles on his London estates forced him to cut the family's long link and sell out to the Knight family.

In the final part of the story, modern Hyde was formed. Edward Knight was forced to sell the reunited Abbey Farm and Abbots Barton to a local farmer, William Simonds, in order to pay off his debts. Farming provided a respectable income until, first the railways and then the importation of cereals and frozen lamb, opened up distant markets and threatened the livelihoods of William and his son, Barrow Simonds. The railway cut through the farm and slowly, over 100 years the former fields were developed, as Barrow Simonds replaced unprofitable crops and livestock by lucrative housing developments.

This story of Hyde does not just trace those that held the land, but explores farmland management, in particular the importance of water meadows in raising sheep. It explains why this type of farming became unprofitable, leading to the fields being covered with urban development. Many large families, especially those who had been long-term residents, were instrumental in changing the face of the suburb. Manufacturing businesses, like breweries, flourished and then died as they were taken over and their premises became surplus to requirements. Reforming institutions – the prison and the Refuge - and schools served the local community and, like the Abbey before, made Hyde known throughout the nation.

The final chapter provides an overview of how Hyde has changed since the Great War to become a desirable suburb for those moving from London whilst still providing the services required by the modern City of Winchester.

Figure I: Winchester's Northern Suburb – Hyde in 1750

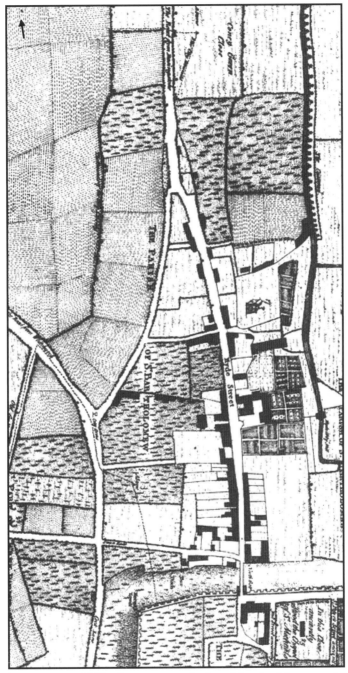

Part of Godson's Map of Winchester commissioned by the Mayor and Corporation
The map shows the agricultural suburb which had changed little since the 1550s.

Figure II: Winchester's Northern Suburb – Hyde in 1909

Ordnance Survey Map 3rd Edition 1909
The map shows Hyde in 1909 when urbanisation had taken hold.

Part 1: The Dissolution of Hyde Abbey and the Aftermath

Derek Wilson in his book, *In the Lion's Court: Power Ambition and Sudden Death in the Reign of Henry VIII*, describes the economic climate and the behaviour of the 'wheeler-dealers' at the time of the Dissolution in terms that would be recognised today:

> The 1530s, like the Thatcherite 1980s, were years of sanctified greed. When Cromwell flooded the property market with consecrated church lands, buildings, furnishings and building materials, he gave government encouragement to speculation, profiteering and personal empire-building on a massive scale. The sixteenth century equivalent of yuppies and fat cats besieged his office and the Court of Augmentations, clamouring to buy or rent.

The Dissolution of Hyde Abbey and the Aftermath tells the story of the events leading to the reform of the Church, the destruction of Hyde Abbey and the fate of its land in the suburbs following the religious unrest in the sixteenth century.

Chapter 1 provides the background to the establishment of Hyde Abbey in 1110, the extent of its lands and wealth, and examines the reasons for the Abbey's closure in 1538. The men whose descendants were influential in shaping Hyde after the Abbey was destroyed are introduced.

Chapter 2 traces the fate of the Abbey lands in Hyde during the sixteenth and seventeenth centuries. The majority of these lands passed through several generations of three families - the Bethells and Clerkes at Hyde Abbey Farm and the Chaundlers at Abbots Barton Farm. Meanwhile the residents of Hyde sought to survive the loss of earnings and security that a large and prosperous institution had provided.

Figure 1a: St Bartholomew's Church c.1870

Source: WINCM:PWCM 2707

Figure 1b: Capital from Hyde Abbey

Located at St Bartholomew's Church

One of several surviving artifacts made of oolitic limestone. More images can be found at
http://www.mondes-normands.fr/angleterre/archeo/Angleterre/sculpture-index.htm

Chapter 1: The Dissolution of Hyde Abbey

The establishment of Hyde Abbey in 1110

In the eleventh century, Winchester had two competing centres of worship situated in the current Cathedral grounds. Winchester's first church, built in about 648 and subsequently upgraded in 662, was later known as Old Minster. There was also New Minster, founded by King Edward the Elder in 901, which was built adjacent to Old Minster.[1] Charters declared that the purpose of New Minster was to serve the spiritual interests of the King and his ancestors by the daily delivery of prayers. New Minster became the royal mausoleum in 902 when the remains of Alfred and his wife Ealhswith were transferred from Old Minster.[2] Buildings crowded the precinct and the area around the service buildings, which stood next to a watercourse, was dank and fetid.[3]

New Minster's extensive lands brought immense wealth and influence. There were royal grants in the tenth century and many other people also bequeathed land.[4] In 1086, Domesday Book recorded that New Minster's land amounted to 400 hides and extended beyond Hampshire to the neighbouring counties of Berkshire, Dorset, Surrey, Sussex and Wiltshire. A hide is often taken to be 120 acres, though others argue the area was not a fixed amount.[5] In Hampshire, holdings included 100 hides within the Micheldever Hundred (Northbrook, Southbrook, Popham and East Stratton), 15 at Abbots Ann, 9 at Stratton, 8 ½ at Popham and 10 at Woodmancote.[6] Such assets placed the Minster amongst the top ten wealthiest monasteries in England.[7]

In 1110 New Minster's community moved north beyond the City walls to Hyde Moors in order to escape the confines of the original site. Speed's Map shows the relative positions of the Cathedral and Hyde Abbey (Figure 1.1). The River Itchen flows on the eastern side of the walled City; the Minster is in the southern part of the City; and the castle is outside the walls in the south-west corner. The Saxon layout of the City still dominated. North of the Minster, the main thoroughfare extended from West Gate to East Gate. In the north-west corner of the City stood North Gate which led to Hyde Abbey and the church of St Bartholomew. The relocation was probably part of a long term plan to combine the religious functions of Old and New Minster into a single institution.[8] King Aethelred had granted Hyde Moors to Bishop Aelgar in 983. This irregular piece of land was approximately 60 hectares in size, covering most of modern day Hyde.[9] The site probably stretched from the River Itchen in the east across to the Hyde Abbey stream in the west.[10] The land adjacent to the river was low lying and flood-prone. The new buildings stood in the south-west corner, close to the modern Hyde Street and away from the meadows. Even so the monks had to secure the foundations by importing clay, which was compacted to a depth of four feet. By

1110 the building at Hyde was ready for occupation and the monks, with the remains of King Alfred, processed through the North Gate to the new site.

Figure 1.1: Speed's Map of Winchester in 1611[11]

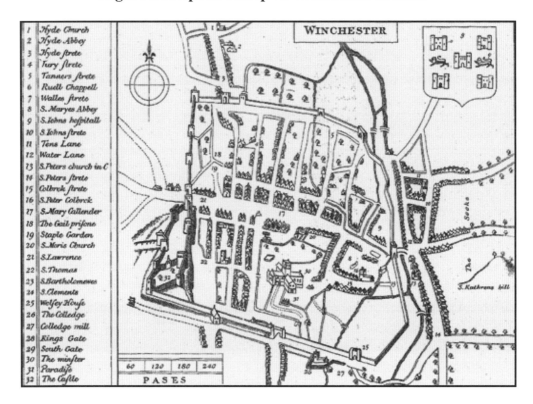

How the Abbey looked and its layout is a matter of supposition, but most Benedictine Abbeys were built to a standard plan. Figure 1.2 shows the extent of the Abbey's buildings and cloisters superimposed on the 1909 Ordnance survey map. The outer court or forecourt which surrounded the church of St Bartholomew was accessible to all. In the inner courtyard, reached through Hyde Abbey gateway, were the service functions of the Abbey. These included accommodation for travellers, stables for their horses, and a brewhouse and bakery to provide succour to both visitors and the monks. The inner courtyard led to the monastic compound - the spiritual centre and hub of the site. The main church consisted of the chancel with altar at the eastern end, the choir and then, separated by a screen (or pulpitum) the nave. The chapter house, where monks assembled each day, and the cloisters stood on the south side of the Abbey. The cloisters were built here to ensure sunlight penetrated into the garth (or garden). South of the cloisters were the refectory and the kitchens. West of the cloisters, overseen by the cellarer, was the cellarium, where food and drink were stored. The Abbot was provided with a separate residence while most monks slept in the dormitory above the chapter house. Beyond the dormitory was the infirmary.

The community was to a degree self-sufficient. On the home farm (Abbey Farm) there was a dairy, granary, malthouse, smithy, stables and animal pens, and a slaughter house. To the south of the complex, were a water mill to grind corn and fishponds providing dietary variation. The home farm was operated by the Abbey's employees, whereas the grange farm (Abbots Barton) was tenanted.

Figure 1.2: Schematic plan of Hyde Abbey and its precincts

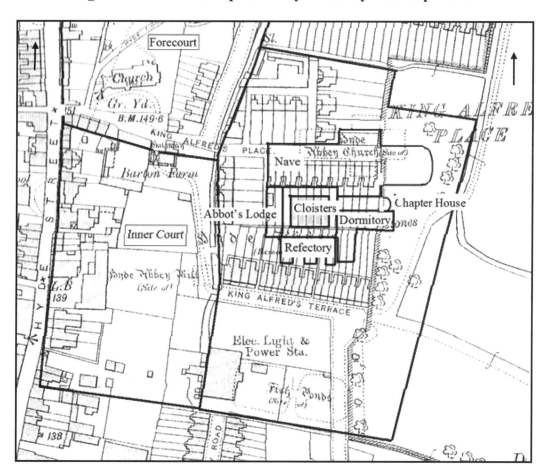

Base map: O.S. Map 3rd edition 1909. Adapted from the Hyde 900 exhibition[12]

In 1114, New Minster's move to Hyde was finalised with an exchange of land between Old and New Minsters to give each exclusive possession over the lands in their respective locations. This took a form of a declaration by Henry I, with the agreement of Bishop William Giffard and Abbot Geoffrey of New Minster, for the removal of the monastery to Hyde. The Bishop surrendered the site of the Abbey, land and houses nearby and the manor of Worthy, its church and parochial rights, to Hyde Abbey. The land formed the boundary of the Bishop's Easton estate which stretched from the northern edge of the City to Micheldever. Those worshipping at St Gertrude's Church, north of Abbots Barton,[13] were brought under the Abbey's leadership. In return the Abbot relinquished both his interest in New Minster's former site and the estate of Durley in Micheldever. In 1148, the Abbey's holding included most of the northern suburb with the exception of land just outside North Gate. [14] The houses in Hyde Street were worth 7s. p.a. in rent and, no doubt, the arrival of the Abbey increased their value and spurred further developments along the street. [15] In 1148 the Abbot owned 94 tenements - nine per cent of the City's properties.[16] This brought in £11 4s. 3½d. p.a. – three per cent of the City's total rental income. [17] The amount was small compared to the Bishop's 34 per cent share of City's properties, equivalent to a 16 per cent share of the rental income.[18]

Figure 1.3: Nuns Walk[19]

This causeway ran alongside the Abbey Mill Stream from Hyde to St Swithun's Church at Headbourne Worthy. It was, sometimes, more appropriately named Monks Walk. The walk marked the start of the Pilgrims' Way to Canterbury.

Landownership in Hyde

Landownership is a social construct whereby society has built a system which manages access to land and the rights over it. These range from informal to formal tenures. Informal tenures consist of customary tenure and rights of common, while legal and formal tenures include freehold and leasehold.[20] The rights can be amalgamated into different packages with the result that those who may be thought of as the owners of one particular property may have different rights from those owning neighbouring properties. Abbeys were granted or endowed with land usually with an obligation to perform religious services, such as to pray for the donor. As lord of the manor, an abbey could transfer home farms and sites to new owners without any manorial encumbrances.

Freehold land held in fee simple allowed the owner to sell it, bequeath it, give it away, or to mortgage it. Legal transfer was achieved by different methods according to period: by feoffment or by quitclaim (12th to 19th centuries), by bargain and sale or by lease and release (16th to 19th centuries), by final concord or by common recovery (up to 1833), and in modern times by deed of covenant or by conveyance. Freeholders might have rights of common, such as grazing rights, over land that belonged to the lord of the manor.

Copyhold land was held from the manor and could be sold, inherited or mortgaged only with the permission of the manorial court. The lord of the manor was entitled to an annual rent, as fixed by custom, fines on the renewal of the copyhold, and heriot on the death of the holder. Copyhold was not converted into freehold until the Law of Property Act, 1922. Although copyholders faced some restrictions on what they could do with the land, such as cutting timber, overall they had considerable freedom.[21]

Leasehold involves the temporary conveyance of property subject to conditions in return for an annual payment. As in modern practice, land tax and local rates assessors treated long leaseholders as the owners and the freeholder as the ground landlord.[22]

Keene's epic *Survey of medieval Winchester* provides a detailed history of land parcels in the neighbourhood of Hyde.[23] These land parcels are of prime importance since they determined the subsequent layout of the modern suburb of Hyde. The Abbey's lands stretched from the River Itchen in the east to the Mill Stream in the west, and northwards from the City ditch. The Mill Stream dated from the thirteenth century, when the water from a spring at Headbourne Worthy was canalised to supply the Abbey's mill and replenish the monastic fishponds which lay to the south. The area of land outside the north-east section of the City walls (the site of Durngate Mill) belonged to the Bishop.[24]

Godson's map of 1750 gives a good idea of the main thoroughfares in medieval times (Figure I p.xiii). Hyde Street ran from North Gate to the Abbey and beyond to London and the north. At this time, the City ditch formed an impenetrable barrier extending from West Gate to east of North Gate. Just outside the gate, Beggar Lane (Swan Lane) ran westwards, crossing the road to Oxford (Andover Road), which started at West Gate and continued on to Stockbridge. Bone Street (now Worthy Lane) connected Andover Road to the top of Hyde Street where it became Worthy Road.

Prior to the Dissolution, the Abbey held extensive lands along these thoroughfares. With very few exceptions, all the east side and lands north of the Soke on the west side of Hyde Street fell under the Abbey's control. The Soke was land falling under the Bishop's jurisdiction. The northernmost part of the Soke appears to have been just south of the present day Hyde Close and stretched from the south wall of No. 23 to the junction of Andover and Worthy Road. The arrow between the H and Y in Hyde Street in Figure II (p.xiv) shows the likely boundary. The parish church, vicar or parishioners, owned rights to some plots of land, which may have been bequeathed by thankful parishioners.

On the west side of the present day Worthy Lane and Worthy Road, a large slice of land stretched west to the suburban ditch (Figure II). Although mainly under the control of Hyde Abbey, St Bartholomew's parishioners had rights over a large parcel adjacent to the top of Hyde Street. Hyde Abbey had rights over two out of three parcels on the north side of Swan Lane whilst the south side was held by the Bishop. Most of the land in the Soke between Hyde Street, Swan Lane, Andover Road and Worthy Lane was controlled by the Cathedral Priory. The triangular piece of land lying between Andover Road, the suburban ditch and Stockbridge Road, was divided into five parcels (clearly seen in Figure I). The ownership of the northern parcels at this time is unclear, although it is likely that the Cathedral Priory and Winchester College had rights over these two large plots. Hyde Abbey owned the two western plots along Stockbridge Road, while St John's Hospital had rights to the eastern piece. More detailed information can be found in Keene's book. However it should be remembered that property rights were transferable and sources usually only recorded the occupiers of the land.

The Abbey's manor or grange was known by several names including Abbey Barton or Hyde (Hide) Barton. Immediately prior to the Dissolution the farm was leased to John and Margaret Barnabe for 40 years at an annual rent of £21 5s. 8d. Rent could be money or payment in kind. This charge included:[25]

Site of manor, lands and pastures	£5	2s.	
Tithes (payable in money or kind)	£5		
12 quarters of wheat	£3	8s.	
12 quarters of malt	£4		
12 quarters of oats	£1	4s.	
2 cartloads of wheat straw and 2 cartloads of barley		6s.	8d.
12 gallons of milk and 3 gallons of cream		5s.	

In addition there was an annual charge of transporting eight cartloads of food or other goods from Southampton (or any other place within ten miles) to Hyde or a payment of £1 6s. 8d..

Monastic rise and downfall

In 1530, approximately one in 375 people in England and Wales was a member of a religious community.[26] Other sources put the number as high as 1 in 50 adult males.[27] Hampshire's religious houses were amongst the largest landowners in the county. The largest and richest of Winchester's institutions, the Cathedral Priory, had 45 monks and an annual income of over £1,500.[28] In comparison, Hyde Abbey had an income of just £860, but it was more than twice as wealthy as other Hampshire monasteries such as Christchurch, Beaulieu or Titchfield.[29]

A religious community, which included servants and an extensive household, was dependent on the income from its landed estates. Local gentry and landowners often carried out the administration of the larger estates on behalf of abbeys. Hyde employed 30 estate officers (stewards, receivers and bailiffs) and over 100 domestics.[30] Apart from being a source of employment, the monastery had administrative and quasi-legal functions, which attracted visitors and trade from tenants, petitioners and local officials into the City.

Abbey estates were complex and their management required well-developed skills from surveyors, rent collectors and bailiffs, who earned an income from the monastery. Abbeys needed to defend their possessions from neighbours and were involved in legal proceedings about tenure and leases. Abbeys leased out much of their demesne land to local gentry and yeoman rather than working the land themselves.[31] These were able to take advantage of their position as sitting tenants after the Dissolution and purchased tithes and land on favourable terms. Leases were typically issued for three lives or 40 years with a fixed annual payment. Additional income came from any changes to the lease. When a named person died, another life, usually that of a young child, was added to the lease in return for an entry charge (fine). Fixed term leases could be extended by paying a renewal fee. Copyholders (the successors of the medieval serfs and villeins) held their land from the Abbey in its capacity as lord of the manor and paid it quit rents and entry fines. Any change of tenant had to be approved and recorded by the lord of the manor in the court roll. The lord benefited from charges on new tenants and heriots, a charge payable on a tenant's death. Given that only one-third of monastic income came from leases of demesne land, the importance of income from quit rents and entry fines cannot be ignored.[32] Economic pressures meant that better estate management was a priority to ensure that income did not fall.

There is continuing debate as to why monasteries were dissolved. Smaller houses were unable to satisfy all the demands of religious life, for example choral display. Recent commentators cite three main reasons: the irreligious behaviour of the monks, the need for the King to raise money to protect his borders - both land and sea - and, most importantly, to assert his power.[33] Indeed, the abbots' support for the papacy during Henry VIII's divorce proceedings appeared a challenge to him. However, the influence of men like Cromwell within Henry VIII's inner circle, who as Protestants did not support the religious tenets of monasticism, should not be ignored.

There was some rationalisation of religious houses as early as the 1480s in order to endow educational establishments. This strategy accelerated in the 1520s when Cardinal Wolsey, the Lord Chancellor, aided by his administrator Thomas Cromwell, was responsible for the closure of 29 religious houses to provide the capital to establish both an Oxford college and a grammar school in Ipswich.

After two weak abbots, Hyde Abbey was in a poor position to resist the assault on the monastery by Henry VIII and Cromwell. John Salcot was appointed abbot in 1530 after the community had failed to find a suitable internal candidate. Salcot was then aged 50 and, at that time, the Abbot of St Benet's monastery in Norfolk. With a career in the Church spanning 28 years, Salcot was well known to Henry VIII and Cromwell. He had been an active supporter of Henry in his divorce from Catherine of Aragon, pressurising the University of Cambridge to recognise the divorce. Salcot's legal arguments in support of the divorce caused Henry to exclaim that 'the Abbot of Hyde is a great clerk and singularly learned in divinity.'[34]

The Act of Supremacy 1534 gave Henry VIII the power to conduct visits to monastic houses and correct the abuses of the Church.[35] A few monks and friars were executed for refusing to accept Henry's ecclesiastical supremacy.[36] The Act of the First Fruits and Tenths (1534) allowed the raising of monies by taxing Church bodies one-tenth of their net annual income. To ensure the successful adoption of this act, four commissioners were appointed in January 1535 to carry out a national survey of clerical incomes. The *Valor Ecclesiasticus* of Hyde Abbey listed the income received, for example, the tithes from the parish church, fixed rents, income from lands and tenements, sale of woods and profits from manorial courts. From these were deducted a range of allowances, including rents paid, pensions and stipends, alms distributed to the poor, and the fees and wages of officers (stewards, receivers, auditors and bailiffs). The Abbot and senior officials were rich and powerful. The revenues of the incumbents totalled £993 9s. 5d. gross (or £865 1s. 6d. net) and the prime obedientaries were listed as follows:[37]

	Gross			Net		
	£	s.	d.	£	s.	d.
Abbot	617	13	6	523	17	11
Prior and Cellarer	345	17	10	316	19	7
Sacristan and Hospitaller	18	18	2	16	18	8
Bowser or Vintner	5	2	2	3	3	6
Chapel Master				1	11	8
Surveyor or Monk Bailiff				0	19	9
Infirmarer				1	13	11

Cromwell replaced his former mentor, Cardinal Wolsey, as Henry VIII's chief minister. In 1535, in his role as vicar-general, he appointed commissioners to obtain evidence of monks' misdemeanours - evidence of sexual irregularities and the retention and veneration of saintly relics. A file of so-called evidence concerning such corruption was accumulated. The commissioners appointed were usually local gentry, who were also tasked with reporting on the state of the buildings and whether the monks or nuns intended to remain in holy orders. There were, of course, conflicts of interest as many of the commissioners stood to benefit personally from the closure of a religious house. Evidence from the north of England indicated that less than ten per cent of monks admitted any sexual wrong doing and problems were usually centred on the smaller monasteries.[38] The local gentry appeared to be satisfied with the spiritual and pastoral leadership provided by the monasteries and those in the north were active in showing their displeasure with Henry's actions.

Henry issued injunctions in 1535 and 1538 against the veneration of relics and the making of pilgrimages to the shrines of Our Lady at Walsingham and St Thomas à Becket in Canterbury. Royal visitors, led by the chief commissioner - Thomas Wriothesley - were sent to Winchester. They reported to Cromwell on the removal of all 'abominations of idolatry' described as the rotten bones or relics from the Cathedral Priory, Hyde Abbey and Nunnaminster (St Mary's Abbey). Their task was an easy one since Salcot had prepared the way for his friend Wriothesley and Gardiner, then Bishop of Winchester, seems to have welcomed the removal of St Swithun's shrine.

The strategy for closure of the monasteries changed after the Pilgrimage of Grace uprising in north-east England in 1536. Cromwell's nominated candidates filled abbey vacancies. If needed, incentives were offered and where persuasion and bullying failed, for example - the resistant Abbot of Glastonbury - the Tower of London was the alternative.[39] No new acts were introduced - Parliament was only required to confirm the closures. The signing over was deemed purely voluntary.

The campaign of 1535 intended only the partial dissolution of smaller abbeys. The government established the Court of Augmentations of the Revenues of the King's Crown in 1536 to handle the process. A distinction was drawn between the smaller abbeys, with an annual net income of less than £200 (and usually less than twelve members), which were suppressed, and the larger ones which survived.[40] However, a new campaign in 1538 targeted the larger houses and they surrendered over the next two years. The confiscation of the monastic lands by the Crown was a successful money raising exercise. For example, between April 1536 and Michaelmas 1538, the treasurer of the Court of Augmentations received £27,732. Of this, £1,099 came from Richard Paulet, the receiver for South Hampshire, Wiltshire and Gloucestershire. The sale of gold and silver raised a further £6,987, of which £588 was from Paulet. In addition, £5,948 was raised by way of fines for exemption from suppression. Nunnaminster was saved from immediate closure by the payment of just over £333. The monies raised was not all profit for the King as the process of dissolution generated various costs, including running the Court of Augmentations, wages of surveyors, visitors and other officials as well as the need to pay pensions to the monks.[41]

It can be argued that if the purpose was to raise immediate finance, the dissolution of the monasteries was a short-sighted strategy. Although £1.5m was raised by the sales, if the lands had been kept under the Crown's ownership, then a future guaranteed income would have accrued. Estimates put the revenue of religious houses at over £130,000 p.a., in excess of twice that of Crown lands. Those that benefitted from the land grabbing would have remained loyal supporters of the King whatever his future actions. In the light of opposition, Henry felt a need to assert his authority.[42] However such concerns were overtaken by the demands of war.

At Hyde, Abbot Salcot was ambitious. Correspondence in 1533 with both Cromwell and his 'friend Master Thomas Wrythysley' gave a glimpse of the intrigues leading up to the Dissolution.[43] As a reward for Salcot's support during the King's divorce, Archbishop Cranmer presented him with the Bishopric of Bangor in 1534. Salcot remained Abbot of Hyde and, in 1538, he persuaded the monks to hand over the monastery. The Deed of Surrender contained 21 monastic names and signatures. Salcot's final reward was the Bishopric of Salisbury in 1539, where he became a zealous Protestant reformer.

Thomas Wriothesley, like Salcot, was an opportunist and an expert at promoting himself at Court. He had a favoured upbringing: he was a childhood friend of Leland (the writer), and he studied at Trinity Cambridge under Stephen Gardiner (later Bishop of Winchester), with whom a beneficial relationship was nurtured. He was closely allied with Cromwell throughout the ten years of his reforming ministerial role. In 1534 Wriothesley was admitted to Gray's Inn and after two years he became coroner and attorney of the King's Bench. With Cromwell's support, he was elected to the House of Commons and retained the position in the elections of 1542. Chapuys, the Imperial Ambassador to England, described him as 'one of the two people who enjoy nowadays most authority and have the most influence and credit with the King.' Wriothesley was appointed Lord Chancellor in 1544 and was elevated to Earl of Southampton in 1547.[44]

Before the Dissolution in 1537, Salcot granted Wriothesley a 61-year lease on the parsonage tithes out of Abbey lands at Micheldever. At the same time, Wriothesley also obtained a lease to the manor of Prior's Barton in St Cross from the prior of St Swithun's. The manor included land in St Faith's, Teg Down, St Catherine's Hill and St Giles Hill, all outside the City.[45] The tithes were valuable and the long lease minimised renewal fines. In today's terms this could be regarded as insider trading. Wriothesley is an example of how those close to the King benefitted from the monastery closures. He obtained 32 per cent of the monastic land grants in Hampshire. The King rewarded him with the small Quarr Abbey on the Isle of Wight in 1537. He was promised both Titchfield Abbey near Southampton and Beaulieu Abbey in the New Forest, and had set his sights on other Hampshire monastic lands besides those of Hyde Abbey.

The disposal of Hyde Abbey's lands

Within four years all monasteries in Hampshire were dissolved. Over the next decade the lands were mostly sold, with the peak year being 1543. Some lands were also given away. The closure of Winchester's four friaries and three monasteries took place between May 1538 and November 1539. The Cathedral (but not the Cathedral Priory) and Winchester College escaped dissolution. In 1541 the new Dean and Chapter were endowed with most of the manors and the related rights belonging to the Cathedral Priory, the rectories of Hyde Abbey, and various properties in Winchester. These included both tangible assets, such as houses and buildings in the City and suburban parishes like St Bartholomew, and rights, such as rents, tithes and reversions.[46] Winchester College benefitted from the closure of the lesser monasteries, gaining the sites of the Carmelites in Kingsgate Street, the Austin Friars in Southgate Street, the Dominicans in Eastgate Street, and the Franciscans in Middle Brook Street.

Valuable gifts were made to the King's minsters and servants as a reward for their services and continuing support. Over many generations, these land-owning families continued to dominate society and mould the landscape. The social environment of the time is summed up in an article about Thomas Wriothesley:

> One observes immediately in the correspondence of the time the fever of avarice that set in - the greedy grasping for church land, the jostling and pushing, the buying and selling, the pulling down and building up, the accumulation and dispersal of fortunes: features conditioning much of social life for the remainder of the century.[47]

In Hampshire the initial beneficiaries employed at the royal court or in government included William Paulet and William Sandys, both of whom were well established in the county.[48] The old West Country Catholic family of Paulet (Paulett, Pawlett or Poulet) had acquired land in Somerset, Devon, Wiltshire and Hampshire through a series of marriages. Sir John Paulet married his cousin Alice Paulet and resided at Basing House. Their descendants played an important part in the history of Hyde Abbey's lands after the Dissolution. Paulet's elder son William, who later took the title of Marquess of Winchester, had a distinguished career and was a close associate of Wolsey and friend of Cromwell. He was a steward to the Bishop of Winchester - Richard Fox - joint Master of the King's Wards and Comptroller of the Royal Household. He held the post of sheriff of Hampshire on three occasions and served as Lord Treasurer until his death in 1572. As reward for his services to the Henry VIII, he received eight per cent of the Hampshire grants including Netley Abbey which he converted into a country mansion.[49] Sir John and Alice Paulet's younger son, George, was married three times and had nine children. One daughter, Mabel, married Thomas Chaundler and, on his death, married Roger Corham, both of whom became owners of the former Hyde Abbey's land.

In April 1538, Hyde Abbey was transferred to the King. A pension of £13 6s. 8d. p.a. was awarded to the prior, £10 p.a. each to three senior monks, and either £8 p.a. or £6 p.a. for the rest. The closure of the Abbey did not eliminate the monks' influence in Hyde or the City. Of the 20 monks expelled from the Abbey, many stayed in religious service close to Winchester: two remained in Hyde as vicar and curate of St Bartholomew's, two became curates in City parishes, one moved to the Cathedral, another became the keeper of the charnel chapel, and a further five monks were appointed to parishes within Hampshire.[50]

Although Cromwell received some annuities out of the Abbey funds, Wriothesley was the prime beneficiary, receiving valuable manors, including Micheldever and Stratton along with the lease of the Abbey site. His residence at Micheldever was short lived and in 1538 he moved to Titchfield. However he retained the manorial rights. After Cromwell's execution in 1540, the rate of disposal of monastic lands was rapid as the government was in dire need of finance to support wars with Scotland in 1542 and France in 1543. The estimated cost of these was £2 million - equivalent to eleven times the annual value of all monastic properties. To raise these sums, two-thirds of monastic estates were sold over the period 1543 to 1547.[51]

Since the aim was to destroy the abbeys and to appropriate their property, any valuable parts of the buildings were stripped and claimed by the Crown. Bells were sent to the foundry at the Tower of London to be melted down for cannons and lead was systematically stripped and melted down for transportation. The roof timbers were used to fuel the fires. If anything valuable was left on the site, the new owners had to pay extra for it. There was a difference between the treatment of fixed assets and those which could be readily disposed of. The real estate consisted not only of the monastic buildings but also gardens and orchards, demesne lands, urban plots, outlying granges and manors, some of which were let on long leases. The assets more readily disposed of included the stock of crops collected as tithes, monastic furnishings, vessels, plate and ornaments, and agricultural equipment and stock. The latter were offered to the new farmers irrespective of whether their tenure was leasehold or copyhold.

Wriothesley's short tenure of the Abbey enabled him to dismantle it and sell the materials. His lease clearly stated the royal claims on the estate:

> The stone, tymber, slates, iron and glasse, remayning within and upon the Church cloister, chaptre house, dormytery, frater, the Convent Hall, with the lodgings adjoining and the Gatehouse, deemed by the King's Comyssioners to be superfluous houses, to be rased and taken to thuse of the kinge his majestie. And likewise of all the leade, remayning upon Thabbotts Hall, the Chapell, the Treasurer, the new Chamber and oder houses assigned to remayne for the fermour. To be reserved to the use of the Kinge his Highness.[52]

This destruction contrasts markedly with former abbeys like Titchfield and Mottisfont that became the country seats of those who purchased them.

This desecration of Hyde Abbey is recorded by many writers. [53] Leland in 1539 wrote 'In this suburb stood the great Abbey of Hyde and hath yet a parish church.' In 1695 Camden found the site as 'deformed with heaps of ruins, daily dug to burn lime.' All that remained were 'some ruinous outhouses, a gateway and a large barn supposed to have been the abbot's hall.' In 1723 William Cole describes the Abbey as 'a close with pits and holes of foundations.' The barn (thought to be the refectory) was still standing and 'good houses have been built' with the stone being recycled. Even in 1788, following quarrying and institutional use, the foundations were still clearly marked.

Little of the Abbey buildings have survived except St Bartholomew's Church (the parish church) and the Abbot's Gatehouse. The gatehouse, built in the fifteenth century, was a rectangular north-facing building. The entrance was on the west side whilst the east side consisted of a two-storey building accessed from the Abbey's precincts.[54] Figure 1.4 gives an artist's impression of the south side of the gateway in the eighteenth century and Figure 1.5 show the building in the Victorian era and today. There are remains of several walls in the vicinity; some have survived intact but are hidden between recent developments; and some foundations have been added to or strengthened with brick corners and tops (Figures 1.6 and 1.7). The scattered stones were ideal for the construction of cottages in nearby Hyde Churchyard (Figure 1.8). Although remaining stones continued to be used as building materials, the site remained undeveloped for 300 years.

Figure 1.4: Hyde Abbey Gateway in the eighteenth century

Source: Warner (1795)

Figure 1.5 Hyde Gateway in Victorian times and today

Source: Warren (1903) and author.

Figure 1.6: The Abbot's bridge over the Mill Stream

Source: Warren (1905) and author.
The strong construction survives another century.

Figure 1.7: Hyde Abbey remains

The Almoner's Hall and the Inner Courtyard, hidden walls and reconstructed wall by the guest house

Where monastic properties were sold freehold it was usually at 20 year's purchase. That is the cost was set to 20 times the net annual value or a yield of 5 per cent. Often the purchaser also acquired the right to rectorial tithes. Purchasers were usually local landowners adding to their estates, younger sons trying to establish themselves, or yeoman farmers seizing the opportunity to buy freehold land. Many already leased the land or had a local connection.[55] The extensive lands of an old abbey site and its demesne (the home farm) were attractive, and some new owners, like Wriothesley at Titchfield, saw an opportunity to use the remnants of the buildings as the foundation for a new palatial residence. But no such development took place in Hyde.

At the time of the Dissolution the lease of the demesne land of Abbots or Hide Barton (known at various times as Abbotts or Hyde Barton) was granted by Wriothesley to Walter Chaundler, a local merchant. The estate included the manor, grange and three meadows, St Audrey's Mead, Wildmore and Connyngar, and, with them, the great and small tithes.[56] The great tithes, usually in the form of corn, were due to the Abbey whilst the small tithes benefitted the vicar. Chaundler also received the grant of a limekiln near Wayeward Marks and the right to dig clay at Connyngar for an annual payment of 42s. 7d.. He was unhappy with the state of the property and complained that the supply of wood was not adequate to maintain the house or fences as required by the lease.

In 1546, the Hyde Abbey site and its demesne lands (known at various times as Abbey Farm or Barton Farm) were bought by Richard Bethell, a cloth merchant. The property, which was valued at over £100 p.a., had been previously stripped by Wriothesley. The land included the tenements, gardens, meadows and land in the Soke.[57] The buildings consisted of a dwelling house (formerly the Abbot's lodgings) with a barn and two stables, two granaries, a dove-cote and malthouse, an orchard and garden, a dwelling house (the prior's lodgings), two parcels of meadow adjoining, the burial ground and parcels of vacant land within the circuit and precinct. The location of the prior's house is not known. However the adjoining meadows may be those to the east of the church. The lands attached consisted of sixteen meadows called Sexterymede, Dyersmede, Midelmede, Bartonmede, Chalkesmede, Littleoxelease, Greateoxelease, Arrowmede, Rogersacre, Le Parke, Little Shepewikeclose, Great Shepewikeclose, Denmarkeland, Brodemeade, Pymoremede and St Gertrudesmeade.[58] Some of these meadow names or their derivatives, like Little Oxlease and Great Oxlease, Arrow Mead, Chalk Mead, the Park and Danemark, were retained by future owners and their locations are known. Figure 2.4 shows the location of the water meadows and Figure 4.5 provides an eighteenth century map of Hyde.

Details of property rights from 1550-1590 are provided in Keene's *Survey of medieval Winchester*. With the purchase of the Barton Farm, Bethell received the Abbey's properties on Hyde Street and former lands in the area, which included the site of the Swan Inn just outside the North Gate. The parcels of land north of Hyde Church Lane are clearly marked on Godson's map of 1750 (Figure I). The southernmost plot is described as belonging to William Lane and the large plot adjacent, to William Godden, who had built a large property on it. The exact nature of their tenure is unknown. The parish church or the vicar continued to own the rights to the parcels, which were in their remit prior to the Dissolution. One of these small plots can be seen north of Godden's house. The land owned by the Cathedral Priory transferred to their successors, the Dean and Chapter. They also gained the parcels along the north side of Swan Lane. John Purdew leased the L-shaped plot which connected Hyde Street with Swan Lane. Purdew built a malthouse on it and by 1589 had gained the freehold of the adjacent corner plot.

West of Worthy Lane and Worthy Road, Bethell was the major landholder. St Bartholomew's parishioners leased their land to Roger Corham, who was described as the landlord and tenant of the adjacent plot to the north. The Abbey's land in the triangular area west of Andover Road passed to Bethell. He also leased the adjacent field from Winchester College. The ownership of the Cathedral Priory's land transferred first to the City and then to St John's Hospital.

Figure 1.8: Houses in Hyde Churchyard

These cottages, built before 1790, were probably constructed using stones from the Abbey site. The newer Victorian properties in Monks Road can be seen in the background.

Wriothesley and his descendents

Thomas Wriothesley was the main determiner of what happened to Hyde Abbey's lands after the destruction of the buildings. Although it appears that Wriothesley's link to the Abbey had ended and he had relinquished all control over the Hyde Abbey site, he retained the lordship of many of its manors. Wriothesley accumulated manors and their lands in the years following the Dissolution. The manor of Abbots Worthy was part of the endowment of Hyde Abbey. In 1542, Henry VIII granted Abbots Worthy and other manors to his physician Augustine de Augustinus. He was one of four physicians who administered to the King during his long illness prior to his death in 1547. In 1545 Henry VIII allowed Augustinus to sell the manor to Wriothesley. In 1544 Wriothesley purchased the Abbey's manor of Micheldever from the Crown and two years later added the manor of East Stratton from Edmund Clerke.[59]

As Wriothesley's descendants were important in future changes to Hyde, it is necessary to examine his political ascendency and his family tree. Wriothesley's standing and power continued to grow not only in Hampshire but also in government. His upwards trajectory continued and, in 1544, he became Lord Chancellor. In this role he announced Henry's death to Parliament in 1547. As Henry VIII's heir Edward was not yet eighteen, Wriothesley took an active role in looking after Edward VI's interests and, of course, his own. Henry left him £500 and the wish that Wriothesley, along with other loyal supporters, should be elevated to the peerage. Misuse of powers was normal and Wriothesley, now Earl of Southampton, gained a further £300 in lands.

Wriothesley's fate changed when Edward VI dismissed him from his role as Chancellor. His role in Parliament remained untenable until his foe, the Protector (the King's uncle, the Duke of Somerset) was sent to the Tower.[60] Wriothesley's health was affected by the political upheavals and he died in 1550. Titchfield, Micheldever and almost 20 other manors in Hampshire passed to his heirs. As was her legal right, his widow received one-third of the estate for her life. The estate passed to Thomas' son Henry, second Earl of Southampton, and then in 1581 to his grandson, also Henry, the third Earl of Southampton (best known as the patron of Shakespeare). Finally (in this history of Hyde) it passed to Thomas, fourth Earl of Southampton in 1624.

His great-grandfather's interest in politics was inherited by Thomas, the fourth Earl. Initially he was a Parliamentarian, but reversed his interest following atrocities carried out by them. He became a staunch supporter of Charles I and, as a result, was forced to pay the Commonwealth a fine of £6,000 for this misdemeanour. During the reign of Charles II, he rose to the role of lord high treasurer. Although he married three times, he only had two surviving daughters. The eldest, Rachel, married William Russell who, when his father-in-law died, in 1667, inherited all his lands. William and Lady Russell resided at Stratton. When William was beheaded for treason for his part in the Rye House plot against Charles II and his brother James (the Duke of York), the estate passed to his son. He was known as Lord

Russell from 1683 to 1695, and then Marquess of Tavistock until 1700. When his grandfather on the Russell side died, he became the second Duke of Bedford. Figure 1.10 traces the Wriothesley-Russell family tree.

The Hampshire manors, which included Abbots Worthy, Micheldever, and the Strattons, were passed down through the Wriothesley family - the Earls of Southampton. When there were no further male descendants, they passed by marriage into the Russell family and to the Dukes of Bedford. The Micheldever estate was eventually sold to Sir Francis Baring of the Baring banking family in 1801. His great-grandson, Thomas George Baring, became Earl of Northbrook in 1876 and was active in Winchester's suburban development both in Hyde and on St Giles Hill, where the family were commemorated in the road names – Baring Road, Stratton Road and Northbrook Avenue. [61]

Figure 1.9: Window detail in Hyde Abbey Gateway

Figure 1.10: The Wriothesley-Russell Family Tree [62]

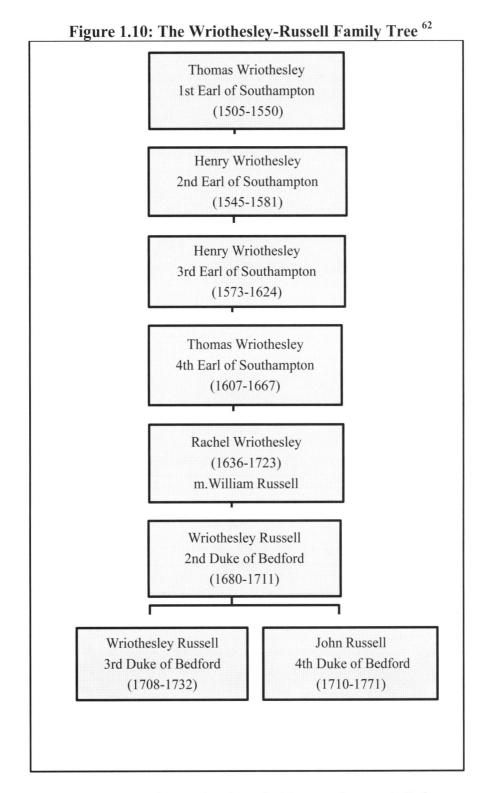

The family is only traced to the end of their involvement in Hyde.

Conclusion

The Dissolution of the monasteries led to one of the most far reaching redistributions of land ownership in England. Many of those purchasing monastic lands already owned estates or manors in the area. By buying, or in the few cases receiving, monastic land, families were able to achieve upward mobility and aspire to membership of the gentry. In Winchester, the dissolution of Hyde Abbey and the fragmentation of its lands released the northern suburb from ecclesiastical ownership. This was not true in the other suburbs of Winchester where the medieval plots and fields were transferred from the Cathedral Priory to its successor, the newly-created Dean and Chapter. The Bishop held on to his Soke and Winchester College retained land adjacent to the college and water meadows in the south.

Whereas new ownership opened up Hyde for more fragmentation and development, the Dean and Chapter saw no need or reason, with a few exceptions, to change the agricultural tenure of their lands until forced to do so by legal changes in the nineteenth century. Winchester College gained land from the closure of the small religious institutions but apart from selective sites that were later sold for development, were wealthy enough to retain the ownership of undeveloped land. [63] The demise of Hyde Abbey opened the way to the eventual urban development of Hyde. Thomas Wriothesley did not prevent the bifurcation of the Abbey site and farm and the Abbot's farm or barton, though one of his descendants was to enable them to be reunited.

Figure 1.11: Durngate Mill from the south c.1870

Source: PWCM2737

Mills not worked by an abbey were leased to wealthy citizens for a substantial rent. A mill belonging to the Bishop stood on this site from c.1213. For many centuries the owners of Abbots Barton leased the mill but the option to buy was finally taken up in 1811 by the new local owner.

Chapter 2: Papacy and Plots

Hyde in the sixteenth and seventeenth centuries

After the Dissolution, the City of Winchester did not immediately prosper and there was little urban growth.[1] Winchester's population in 1520 was about 1,500 within the walls and 1,300 in the suburbs. In 1603, the respective figures were 1,600 and 1,500. Hyde mirrored the City's population stagnation.[2] The City was split into six Aldermanaries, one of which was Northgate Street (Hyde). In 1416, the Aldermanry of Northgate had consisted of 66 cottages and 21 tenements giving a possible population of 370 inhabitants. In 1604, although the number of tenements remained stable at 20, many cottages and small houses had disappeared with the sites, by then, just garden plots. Often one new tenement was built on the site of two or three cottages.[3]

By 1611 Hyde Street had been extensively built up on both sides from the junction with Swan Lane up to St Bartholomew's Church and Hyde Church Lane (see the top of Speed's map Figure 1.1). There was a continuous row of tenements stretching from North Gate. North of the Swan Inn, was a row of small cottages with an annual ground rent of only 3d. or 4d.. Beyond these, near the churchyard, were the ruins of nine cottages which contributed only 1d. to the City's coffers.[4] These were in the area where the Abbot had altered the doorways on to the Abbey's lands in order to defray the rent charged by the City. To the west of Hyde Street there were a few distinguishing features: the junction of Worthy Lane and the road to Oxford (Andover Road) was marked by a cross; the church of St Mary in the Vale was sited north of the junction of Swan Lane with Worthy Road; and the gallows stood on land close to the future railway sidings in Andover Road.[5]

In the early seventeenth century, Hyde and its inhabitants suffered economic turmoil along with the rest of Winchester. This was a time marked by plagues, food shortages, high prices, unemployment, industrial depression, impressments into the army and heavy taxation.[6] Speed's map of 1611 shows the City suffering decline with large areas of open spaces within the walls. Plague hit Winchester in the latter years of the sixteenth and the early seventeenth centuries, notably in 1593, 1603, 1625 and 1637-8. In 1583 the Corporation built a house for the infected in the Hyde meadow known as the Town Ponds. The house was leased to each mayor to use as a pest house (place of quarantine) according to need. The house was demolished after the initial epidemic, but was rebuilt in 1593 and 1603. In the 1620-30s, 40 per cent of Winchester's population experienced serious financial hardship.[7] The owner of Hyde Barton reported to the county's Justice of the Peace (JP) that vagrants often sheltered in his outhouses 'putting the fear into him and his household'. The parish baptism records cite that, in 1629, two babies were born in the cowshed there.[8]

Winchester was not a desirable place to live during the Civil War. Initially the City supported King Charles I and Royalist troops were garrisoned in the City. However events caused the City to change its allegiance. After Portsmouth fell to the Parliamentarians in 1642, Winchester and Basing came under attack. In 1642 Winchester returned two MPs: John Lisle, a friend of Cromwell, and Sir William Ogle, a staunch Royalist. The Parliamentarian, Sir William Waller defeated the royal garrison in 1642, which resulted in the looting of the City. Ogle recaptured the City in 1643 and Royalist troops were briefly stationed in the City again. Further looting and destruction occurred when the City was recaptured by the Parliamentarians in 1644 and when the castle was attacked and destroyed by Cromwell in 1645.[9] Cromwell's troops were encamped just south of the City, at what became known as Oliver's Battery, from where he led the assault on Winchester Castle. Contrary to popular belief, the cannons of the day would not have reached the City from this outpost.

It is not known to what extent residents in Hyde took an active part in the defence of the City. Leading citizens were ordered by Parliament to seize any horses, arms, ammunition, money and provisions that they suspected might be used to make war against Parliament. Sir John Lewkenor whose kin were to become owners of Abbots Barton suffered a common fate of Royalist supporters, illustrating the dangers of being on the wrong side. Lewkenor was Recorder for Chichester and served as an MP in both the Short and Long Parliaments of 1640 until barred as a Royalist. Subsequently he was involved in the siege of Portsmouth in 1642 and declared guilty of treason to the Commonwealth ending up, in the next year, imprisoned in Windsor Castle. Finally in 1651, Lewkenor's lands were ordered to be sold.

The Corporation suffered financial losses during this period, trading decreased, many houses were demolished and the City's finances were not adequate to help the two hundred poor families in dire need. Those involved in the City's affairs were small landowners and merchants, not wealthy enough to go unscathed. However the picture was not bleak for the richer inhabitants during the years when Winchester developed as a social centre for local gentry. In Hyde, the wealth of the few, for example Thomas Clerke, Roger Corham and George Chaundler, was reflected in their inclusion in the subsidy list (a tax payable to the King). Another wealthy resident was Sir John Powelett (Paulet), the illegitimate son of the third Marquess of Winchester and Jane Lambert, who lived in Hyde Street with his wife Elizabeth. When he died in 1632 his property was left to his widow during her lifetime. In 1682 when his nephew died, the large house with gardens, meadows, orchards and lands along with houses in Hyde Street were sold.

Only two families owned the Abbey's lands in Hyde during the sixteenth and seventeenth centuries. The site and home farm passed through three generations of the Bethell family before being sold to the Clerkes who also held the land for three generations. At Abbots Barton, the Chaundlers retained the property for four generations. Tables 2.1 and 2.2 provide details and dates of these families' ownership.

Table 2.1: Owners of Hyde Abbey to 1693

1546-1570	Richard Bethell (1489-1570)	Married Avice Roby
From 1570	William Bethell	Married (1st) Elizabeth (Isabel) Meux Married (2nd) Alice widow of Owen Hobbes Married (3rd) Elinor Edmunde Married (4th) Elizabeth Manfield
c1592	Zachary Bethell	Married Alice Hobbes Left land but unable to take possession
c1592 to 1629	Thomas Clerke	
c1631 to 1642	Sir Henry Clerke	
1642 to 1693	Edmund Clerke	

Table 2.2: Owners of Abbots Barton to 1650

Dates	Owners	
1537 or 1541 to 1546	Walter Chaundler (c.1486-1546).	Married Cecily Skeich (d.1552) Four children
1546 to 1552	Estate passed to Walter's widow Cecily Chaundler (d.1552).	Cecily re-married to Roger Massam in 1546
1552 to 1564	Thomas Chaundler (1524-1564)	Married Mabel, daughter of Sir George Paulet of Crondall, Hants (d. 1615) Five children
1564 to 1615	Estate passed to Thomas' widow Mabel.	Mabel married Roger Corham (d.1600) in 1564
1615 to 1633	George Chaundler (d.1633)	Married Josina Van der Hagen Four children
1633 to 1650	Thomas Chaundler	Married Mary daughter of Sir William Lisle Three children

Rosalie Pennell, in researching her book *Account of the Parish of Hyde* written in 1909, was able to draw on the family histories of the Bethells and Chaundlers through Richard's and Walter's descendents – W. Wood Bethell and Capt. Chaundler.

The Bethell family at Hyde Abbey Farm 1546-1592

After the Dissolution the seven-acre site of Hyde Abbey along with 70 acres of surrounding meadows were leased to Thomas Wriothesley and sub-let to Richard Bethell. Wriothesley was probably acting as an agent since he held on to the land for only a short period. This was his apparent strategy when he purchased the site of St Elizabeth's College, which he then transferred one month later to Winchester College, where he was employed as a steward.[10]

Richard Bethell was a mercer from Flintshire, who moved to Hampshire with his wife Avice in 1520. He was employed by the Abbot, moved to Hyde in 1526, and served as a churchwarden at St Bartholomew's in 1553.[11] Bethell made his living trading in cloth. It is known that in 1544, he sold a quantity of cloth to Winchester College for servants' aprons. He was described as a man of great substance who was rising in society and had many friends. He was a freeman of the City in 1551 and Member of Parliament in 1553.[12] His brother, Richard was an MP in 1559.

There was little opportunity for interested purchasers in Hyde as monastic land was obtained either by Bethell, the newly formed Dean and Chapter, or the Corporation. The situation was not so restrictive elsewhere in the City. Although by 1604, 40 per cent (out of 281) monastic properties were now in the hands of small investors, 25 per cent had been claimed by the Corporation, including those that belonged to St John's Hospital.[13] Bethell already had other interests in land when he took over the Abbey site. In 1536 he took on the Abbey's lease of Woodmancote for 99 years for £11 12s. 8d. p.a.. In 1544, under an exchange of certain manors and parsonages, Woodmancote was assigned to Winchester College. Bethell's tenancy was unaffected, although he was awarded the right to fell timber.

In 1546 the Crown sold the Hyde estate to Bethell at 20 years purchase along with some of the Abbey's properties elsewhere in the City. He seems to have obtained these properties at only seven years purchase, a very low price, but the high yield of 14 per cent is possibly explained by the poor condition of these tenements. It is likely that he employed some of the Abbey's former servants.[14] Bethell's estates not only included the Abbey site but also the Abbey's gardens and meadows in the parish and the Soke. Little is known about his land management. He retained his properties in St Bartholomew and sold those in the City. He sold a meadow near the Town Ponds to William Laurens in 1564. There was no access from North Gate and Laurens was allowed to make 'a sufficient gate for a cart to pass through the town wall where never yet hath gate or door been.' Although Laurens had freedom of movement, he was required to keep the gate in good repair and 'shut the same gate at all times at command of the mayor for the safety of the Queen's City.'[15] Such a breach in the City's northern defences was an important stage into easing access to the former Abbey's lands. At this time Elizabeth had enjoyed six years on the throne.

Bethell's contribution to the urban landscape of Hyde was the building of the substantial Hyde House on the east side of Hyde Street. The construction date is not known, but the style suggests it was built during the second half of his residence in Hyde, perhaps in the 1560s. Stone blocks and carved features from the Abbey were recycled. In 1565 he sold stone from the Abbey ruins to Winchester College for various repairs, including the kitchen oven. Assuming this stone was surplus to Bethell's own requirements, Hyde House had probably been completed by this date.[16]

Bethell's new house overlooked the River Itchen and the hills to the east, and was surrounded by gardens and courts on three sides. The property's entrance utilised the remains of Hyde Abbey gateway, which may explain why this and adjacent buildings survived. There was a coach house on the east and a large barn with animal stalls on the west. A back entrance adjoined Hyde Street in the west. Figures 2.1 and 2.2 and Table 2.3 give an idea of the house's extent and how its design reflected the desire for space, comfort and heating seen in the proportions and appearance of numerous chimneys. These would cost the household 2s. p.a. for each fireplace when the Hearth Tax was introduced in 1662 to support Charles II after the restoration of the monarchy. To the left of the entrance was the Great Hall, which at a height of 13 feet 3 inches, featured three sets of east facing windows. The hall led to the Great Parlour and the main stairway up to the dining room and chambers. To the right of the entrance was the butler's pantry with stone vault below and a passage to the kitchen and other offices. There were two courtyards within the office area. A domestic courtyard on the north side of the building gave access to Hyde Street.

On the east side of the house there was a substantial upper courtyard leading to a lower courtyard some three times larger (Figure 2.1). The footprint of the house and these courtyards extended to ¾ acre. Three similar sized gardens adjacent on the south and north covered a further acre, and yards and barns extended to another acre. Three areas - a garden (1 rod 21 perches),[17] the little orchard (18 perches) and an area near the entrance - had been converted to hop gardens.[18] As water was not pure enough to drink, beer was an important commodity. There may have been remnants of the Abbey's brewery buildings that Bethell easily restored for his own use.

Over the last 200 or 300 years the buildings on the site of Hyde House have undergone substantial demolition, rebuilding and conversion. The stone part of the original house on the eastern side was demolished during the eighteenth century, but brick additions, which sit on a stone base, have survived. A brick wing, still in existence, was added during the seventeenth century. Although there was no shortage of stone, the use of brick reflected the fashion at the time. The extension added servants' accommodation, a desirable feature at this time for the more affluent citizen. The Dutch gable at the west end abutting the road, reflected the owner's standing in the community (Figure 2.3). In the eighteenth century the Abbey's home farm and its grange farm were reunited and there was no need for a second residence, so the main house was demolished.

Figure 2.1: Hyde House and Gardens

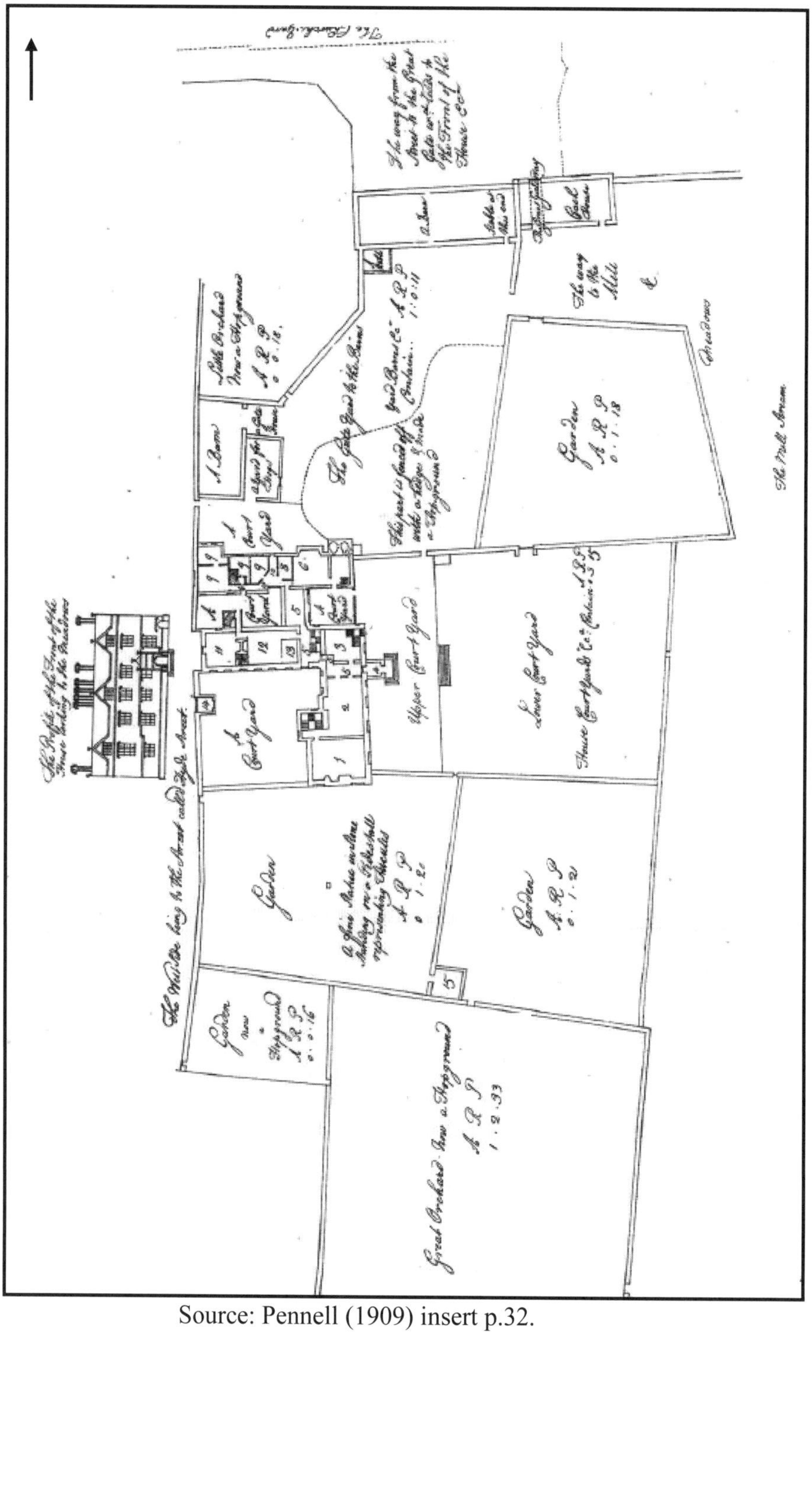

Source: Pennell (1909) insert p.32.

Figure 2.2: Layout of Hyde House

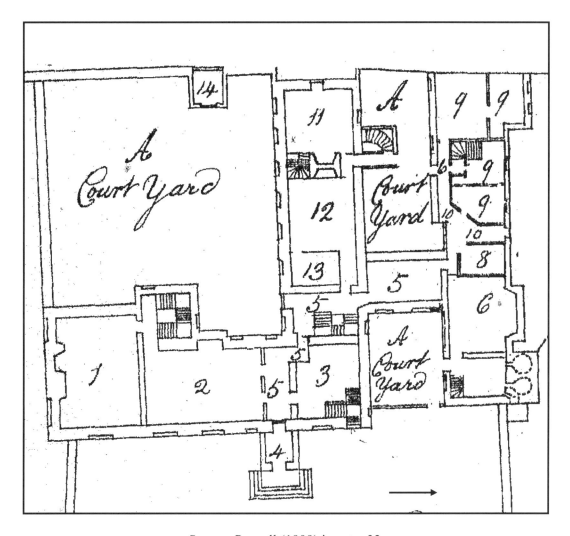

Source: Pennell (1909) insert p.32.

Table 2.3: Hyde House

Area	Description	Height		Length	Breadth	Height
1	Great Parlour	10ft	Over it dining room.	31ft 8in.	21ft 10in.	13ft 2in.
2	Great Hall	13ft 3in.	Over hall & pantry are three chambers: North & Middle Chambers	20ft	17ft 6in.	10ft 6in.
3	Butler's Pantry with fire vault	13ft 3in.	South Chamber	21ft 8in.	20ft	10ft 6in.
4	Stone Porch					
5	Passage by the street of the hall to the kitchen & other offices		Over the passage is a closet to North Chamber & three little rooms	8ft	6ft	
6	Large Kitchen	9ft	Over it a nursery chamber			
7	Bake house	8ft	Over it a chamber			
8	Well house		Over it a chamber			
9	Old Buildings for a farmer. Kitchen, pantry, cellar & milk house		Over it a two large chambers			
10	Passage from the out-yards to the house buildings					
11	Servants' Hall	9ft	Under is good cellar & over it a chamber	19ft 10in.	17ft 6in.	9ft 4in.
12	Parlour	9ft	Over it a chamber	19ft 10in.	19ft 3in.	9ft 10in.
13	Pantry	9ft	Over it is a chamber	15ft 5in.	10ft	9ft 10in.
14	Porch to street					
15	Banqueting House					
16	Gallery running whole length of house 85ft by 12ft	8ft 6in.	At the south end of this gallery is a Chamber on the west side	15ft	10ft	8ft 6in.

Adapted from Pennell (1909) insert p.32.

Sections 11 to 13 are part of the seventeenth-century brick extension.

Figure 2.3: The extension to Hyde House

After the demolition of Hyde House, only the later wing survived.

The farm site was used as agricultural premises, and a malthouse and barns were erected. Substantial evidence exists that the stone was again recycled. The stone sections of the surviving building display decorative medieval stones and, during renovations and alterations of surrounding walls, column segments of Caen stone and Purbeck limestone were found.[19] Non-uniform blocks, including Quarr stone, had been used in one of the barns. The walls of the courtyard of the present Hyde House contain a mixture of flint, brick and architectural fragments from the Abbey, including two complete and one partial torso of monkish figures.

William Bethell inherited the estate in 1570, although his father seems to have retired to Woodmancote several years earlier leaving William effectively in charge. Like his father he was political and served as mayor in 1577 and MP in 1582. William's business acumen was not as sharp as his father's and he did not benefit from being widowed four times and claiming property through marriage. He fell into financial difficulties necessitating a loan from John Ward, a leather seller of London. Although the estate was given as security, he made it over to his son Zachary (or Zachariah), whose wife, Alice, was William's second wife's daughter by her first marriage. What followed were years of legal wrangling in which Ward took the case to the Court of Chancery.[20] Ward paid off £2,000 to William's creditors before seizing the estate. Zachary supported by William attempted to get Ward out of the property by threatening and menacing behaviour. Ward was granted a writ of injunction that gave him peaceful ownership until the matter was heard by the court. Eventually in 1592 the Court concluded that Ward should restore the manor and monastery for the sum of £1,840. William was asked to re-pay the £2,000 of debts immediately. Ward was barred from any profit from selling stones, glass or wainscot from the monastery site.

Zachary did not enjoy the return of ownership. Prior to the judgement, his wife died and he sold the property to Thomas Clerke.[21] In spite of his family problems, he retained his political connections which enabled him to become MP for Lyme Regis in 1593. Zachary had the patronage of the third Marquess of Winchester, who during the minority of the third Earl of Southampton (Henry Wriothesley) was Lord Lieutenant of Dorset.[22] The Bethell family's connection with Hyde Abbey's lands had ended although the family flourished and survived.

Flouting the court's ruling, Ward made a final attempt at redress and sent a servant to carry away several loads of stone. Sir Walter Sandys (Sands), the high sheriff of Hampshire, was also owed money by William and he carried away 90 loads worth of stone, 100 loads of burrs and flint, 40 loads of sand and 9 loads of chalk, with a total value of over £66.[23] In 1610 Sandys owned considerable property in Tanner (Lower Brook) Street in the City. This included a large house on the west side of the street, which was originally three tenements, and another large house on the east side, which had been built on the site of three smaller houses and two cottages.[24] Some of these properties were the likely destination for the remaining stones from Hyde Abbey.

The Clerke family at Hyde Abbey Farm 1592-1693

Financial matters had not been resolved for Thomas Clerke, the new owner of Hyde Abbey Farm. He was forced to honour his predecessor's debts to the church and vicarage. In 1597 the new vicar, Thomas Caule, found that not only was the stipend in arrears during Ward's occupation, but that the annual tax on church livings was also unpaid. Clerke was unwilling to pay these dues and, on investigation, Caule discovered that he had a right to enter Clerke's land and seize property in recompense. Agreement was reached by way of payment of £33 5s. and the granting of life-long leases on certain lands worth 21s 8d.. This may have been the two meadows which lay beyond the churchyard and described as glebe land. The length of this lease is unknown but may have been for three lives or for 40 years. Clerke's attempt to gain redress from Ward's widow for both these sums and the removal of stone was not successful.

The Abbey site remained a source of local building material during Clerke's ownership. A house in the north part of Hyde Street, later to become the Parish Hall, has the inscription: 'William Wickham built this ston house Ano Domyni 1596 Th. Clerk'.[25] Similar to Hyde House, there is little of the original structure remaining but, during later building works, many carved stone fragments were revealed. In 1607 a hundred loads of freestone (used in moulding) were purchased from Clerke by the Corporation for the construction of Christ's (or Peter Symond's) Hospital in Symonds Street, adjacent to the west wall of the Cathedral precinct. Stone made strong foundations, especially for brick buildings, and although some of this material is visible, most is now hidden by brick cladding.[26]

Thomas Clerke died in 1629 and was buried in the Cathedral. He left a house with an annual rental value of 26s. to St Bartholomew's to enable a weekly payment of 6d. of bread to six poor people who attended the morning service or waited in the porch. Thomas' property was left to his children. His elder son was left tenements for a maximum period of 80 years on the condition he provided his widowed aunt with a room in his house and an annual income of 20s.. Part of this income was to be distributed to the poor as she saw fit, with the proviso that she was to spend half the day looking after Thomas' children. Although his second son, Henry, appears not to have been provided for in the will, he was in possession of Hyde Abbey two years later. Henry was at that time involved in a lawsuit with the Corporation over non-payment of a quit-rent of 13s. 4d. on land and ditches which had belonged to the Abbey.[27] He had also allowed tenements on the north side of the Abbey to fall into decay and the land to be subsumed into his gardens.[28] Henry died in 1642 and the farm passed to his heir Edmund (or Edmond) Clerke.

The identity of individuals from within an extended family is often difficult to trace as the same forenames are used both in different generations and branches. Thomas Clerke was described as a wealthy man owning property in the north of Hampshire including Popham, the Oakelys and several other manors.[29] He was related to Sir Thomas Clerke who, for a short period, was the unpopular lord of the manor of Hursley. In 1613, they purchased the manor of

Headbourne Worthy (or Worth Mortimer) - which extended across the parishes of Headbourne Worthy, Kings Worthy, Abbots Worthy, and Otterbourne - for £950 from the bankrupt Earl of Salisbury. Sir Thomas Clerke settled both the manor of Headbourne Worthy and Worthy Pauncefoot on his son Henry in 1625, several years before he died in 1630.[30] Henry died without children and the owner of the manor in 1652 was Edmund Clerke, grandson and heir of Edmund Clerke of South Stoneham. The parallels with the owners of Hyde Abbey Farm suggest that these were the same persons.

The continued success or demise of a family rested on circumstances. A good marriage brought in a dowry, and possibly additional land. However, for those with daughters, marriage was an expense on the estate. Sons were provided for by the estate when they reached 21, but the use of primogeniture meant that only the eldest would inherit the land. A marriage settlement ensured that an estate was passed intact from one generation to the next and that claims of jointure, portions and annuities could be met. Jointure was the provision for the widow, usually a dower house and regular income. By common law, a widow would hold one-third of the estate for life. This could become a considerable financial burden. A portion was the settlement to younger sons and daughters not otherwise inheriting. This was payable at 21 for sons or on a daughter's marriage. An annuity was an annual payment to an heir raised by the estate. The inheritance by a minor was often a time when estates could be nursed back to financial health by trustees since the heir had no power and few demands for income.

When Edmund Clerke married Martha Ford in 1674,[31] the terms of the marriage settlement specified the lease and release of property and lands in Hyde.[32] A lease and release was a form of conveyance used from the seventeenth century up to 1841 when the Conveyance by Release Act took away the necessity of the lease part. This process of conveyance was used for sales, mortgages and settlements and featured two stages - a lease was granted for a year for a very small consideration, in this case 5s.; and usually the next day the lessor's rights of ownership were released in return for the full consideration. The agreement involved three parties: Edmund Clerke of Hyde, John Ford Esq. with John Webb (gentleman of Winchester), and Martha Ford of Winchester (spinster daughter of John Ford).

A daughter entered marriage with a dowry or lump sum. If the sum was large it allowed her some choice of potential suitors. However when a man had several daughters, the provision of a dowry was a financial burden and daughters often remained unmarried. It was expected that the older daughter should be married first. If a suitor was hard to find, younger sisters had to wait, and some never married. In return for the dowry, the settlement specified a regular allowance made by a husband to his wife and the jointure she could expect if widowed. This was often set as a percentage of the profits of the estate.

On marriage, a settlement was drawn up to clarify inheritance rights. Simple settlement would state Person A has the use of estate for life before it passed to his or her heirs. A more complicated settlement defined the inheritance pathway in case of the demise of the beneficiary. Martha's marriage portion, provided by her father and John Webb, was £1,000.

We do not know whether John Webb was a relative or a money-lender. The estate was described as:

> The abbey and monastery of Hide, houses, edifices, barns, stables, orchards, gardens, courts, yards, messuages, lands, tenements, cottages, meadow, land floodings, castings, commons, waste grounds, mill ponds, streams, fishings, ground rents, royalties, franchise, privileges, profits and hereditaments. [33]

It was conveyed by the method of Bargain and Sale to John Ford and John Webb.[34] Their status is not clear, although it was likely that they were trustees of the marriage settlement and Clerke had beneficial, but not legal, ownership of the property.

The extent of the property was summed up as:

> The house and site of the late monastery, 92 acres of meadow, eight acres of ground called Conyger,[35] 21 pieces of land (the tenants are named), an orchard within the walls of Winchester, two orchards and closes occupied by Symon Blake, two closes totalling sixteen acres outside Hyde gate and quit rents from six messuages in Hyde (the occupiers are named) amounting to 10s. 1d..[36]

Figure 2.4 shows the extent and names of the meadows.

The settlement allowed Edmund to enjoy the estate for the remainder of his life, whence it then was to pass to Martha for the remainder of her life and thereafter to the first and later sons of the marriage. If there were no sons only daughters, Edmund Ford - son of John living in London - was entitled to the property for 21 years, after which it passed to any daughter of Edmund and Martha. If there were no daughters it went to Edmund. It appears that there were no children and Martha must have died because neither were mentioned when Edmund made his will in 1693. It commenced 'Being sick of body but of perfect sense and memory' and continued:

> First I commend my soul into the hands of Almighty God and my body to be decently buried. And for my estate land and personall I dispose these as follows: One-third of property to sister Lucy Mackadam and her son Christopher Johnson and their heirs; one third to kinsman James Morecroft and his heirs and one third to kinsman Henry Colpes and Anne his wife and their heirs.[37]

Lucy, James and Henry acted as executors and inherited all his goods and chattels. Edmund also left £10 to Charles Colpes, £5 to his servants Mathius Ecton (one of the fields is named Ecton's piece), Susan Dickson and Anna Bull, and 40s. to be distributed to the poor. Little is known of the management of the estate over the next 40 years except that a house, garden and orchard lying between the churchyard and vicarage lane was leased in 1695 to John Kernott, a bricklayer, for 30 years.

Figure 2.4: The Abbey's water meadows

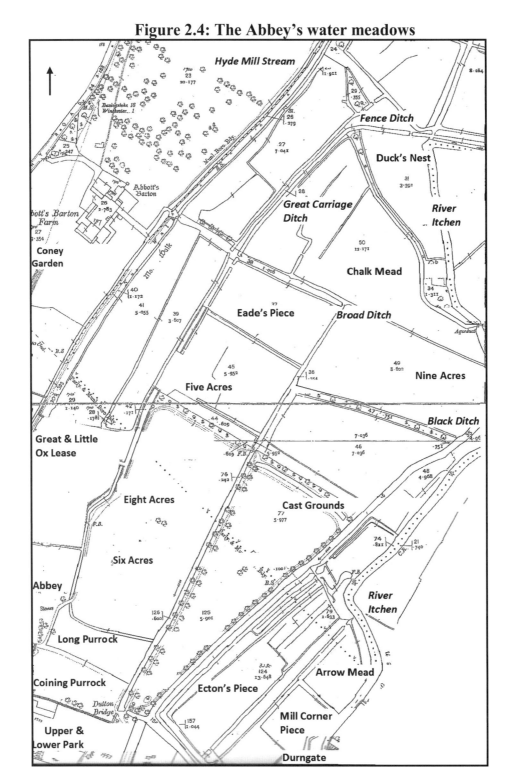

Adapted from W/K4/1/15/1 and superimposed on the 1909 Ordnance survey map

Walter and Thomas Chaundler at Abbots Barton
c1540-1564

Walter Chaundler, a mercer, and his wife Cicely had dealings with Hyde Abbey before the Dissolution. The Chaundlers were an established Winchester family who can be traced back to the early fourteenth century. Walter's father John, described as a baker, stood as mayor in 1503. There is evidence that John purchased the lease of Barton Farm in 1499 from the Abbey after the death of the previous tenant William Carpenter, a yeoman.[38] The Abbey's estate was run by William Reeve (or Ryve) until his death in 1521, when the position passed to Reeve's son, who was described as a 'Deputy to Mr Wrysle' (who later elongated his name to Wriothesley).[39]

Walter took an active role in local affairs as both a bailiff (1521 and 1524) and mayor (1530). He married Cecily Skeich and they had four children. They had a house on the High Street and, when his father died in 1505, inherited property in the City and Soke as well as elsewhere in Hampshire. [40] When the vicar, Gilbert Fraunce (or Francis), died in 1541 he left the Chaundlers the whole of his property. Walter's wealth was assessed as £45 in 1524. In 1531 he became the lessee of the manor of Segensworth from Viscount Lisle and had property in Titchfield.[41] In 1536 he and two others had the grant of presentation of the vicar of St Bartholomew.[42]

Wriothesley probably intended to hold on to Abbots Barton in an extensive portfolio of Hampshire lands; but saw the opportunity to expand his holdings in Titchfield for little cost. As Lord Lisle's tenant in Titchfield, Chaundler held leases to three manors that were attractive to Wriothesley (the owner of Titchfield Abbey) and he proposed a part-exchange with the Hyde Abbey Farm lands. Wriothesley promised to intervene with the King on Walter's behalf. Permission was needed from the King to pass on the manors. Walter, although acquainted with Thomas Wriothesley, did not receive any preferential treatment in his dealing with him. Although the deal was agreed in June 1537, Walter was prevented from accessing the land. He made the mistake of appealing to the King, who had little interest in such minor affairs, and instead he roused Wriothesley's wrath. Resorting to legal means was not fruitful as Wriothesley was the secretary to the privy council and so able to manipulate any outcome in his own favour. After apologising publicly to Wriothesley for any slur against him, Walter eventually gained access to the land and was able to move his family to Abbots Barton in 1541, but only after Wriothesley secured a further £383 on top of the land exchanged.

Walter Chaundler accumulated a number of properties in Winchester and was one of the richest men in the City during the early 1500s. He was described, by a servant of Lisle, as a 'very crafty fellow'. He died in 1546 leaving the manor and grange to Cicely during her life time, which then passed to his son Thomas in 1552. An inventory taken at his death gave his worth as £607, third only to the warden of Winchester College (£811) and the keeper of Wolvesey Palace (£793).[43] Details of the Abbots Barton's property and contents are given.

On the ground floor was a hall and two parlours, one at the north end and the other near the street door. Upstairs were four bedrooms and a study. The kitchen was set apart. The dairy cottage was built on twelfth or thirteenth century foundations. Outhouses included a corn sifting house, linen and brewing houses, a milk house, a wool loft, a carter's room, a malthouse, two stables and a large barn.

Marriage often resulted in amalgamation of estates and it was not only first marriages which benefited. Cicely married Richard Massam, who, when he died in 1550, left her copyhold land in Otterbourne and Selborne, along with a share of the parsonage and one hundred acres of arable land at Basingstoke.[44] Cicely died in 1552 and Abbots Barton passed to Thomas, Walter's and Cicely's son. After the death of his first wife, Jane, Thomas married Mabel Paulet, whose uncle was the Marquess of Winchester. The marriage consolidated Thomas' social standing within the community.[45]

Thomas Chaundler's estate was not limited to Abbots Barton, but included leasehold property let for 30 or 40 years. The parsonage of Hurstbourne and St Mary Bourne was held on lease from St Cross Hospital at an annual rental of £33 and payment in kind of 40 quarters of pure clean wheat, and 60 quarters of barley. If resident, the vicar was to receive four quarters of wheat and four quarters of barley malt, otherwise the produce went straight to St Cross Hospital. Further monies were payable for tithes (20s.) and rent on two tenements and land (6s. 8d.) in the location.[46]

The exact state of the farm buildings at Abbots Barton at that time is not known, but during Walter's ownership he either renovated or built the four-bay timber lodge. The medieval south grange was probably in a derelict state. Thomas is thought to have rebuilt the north wall, removing the oriel window and adding a much needed chimney to provide the family with heating.[47]

When Thomas died at the young age of 40 in 1564, his wife Mabel was left with five young children. She quickly married her husband's co-trustee and close friend - Roger Corham - who was a barrister at Lincoln's Inn Fields. The estate consisted of the site of the manor and grange, one messuage, 700 acres of land, 100 acres of meadow, and 40 acres of pasture in the parish valued at over £20 p.a.. Also included were a messuage and three gardens within the City. Mabel held the property for her life and, with Corham, received the profits from the parsonage until Thomas' and Mabel's eldest child William was 24. William was also to receive £400 on reaching 30. Their other son George was to receive £100 and their three daughters £100 each at their coming of age or marriage. Roger Corham received the lease of the manor of Penynton and £200. A £10 loan was made available to the local poor when needed, and £40 sent to the Mayor and Commonalty of Winchester to be used to provide wood and fuel for the poor of the City. The will stipulated that this was to be at cost and without profit for the City.[48]

Roger and Mabel Corham at Abbots Barton 1564-1615

Roger Corham, whose family came from Ottery St Mary in Devon, was a landowner in his own right having purchased the manor of Brown Candover near Alresford in 1571. The manor, originally part of the Hyde Abbey lands, was granted to Sir William Paulet by Henry VIII in 1539. Corham and his wife Mabel (formerly Chaundler) let the land to a series of tenants. Roger also held a 99-year lease on the tenement and mills at Abbots Worthy, from the Wriothesley family.[49]

During Roger and Mabel's time at Abbots Barton, England went through several years of religious turmoil and both Catholics' and Protestants' lives were upended. The second year of Elizabeth's reign, 1559, saw the start of a series of Parliamentary Acts which restricted Catholics' ability to own land and take part in public life. As a result many Catholic families in Hyde, such as the Corhams, suffered financial insecurity and lost their position in the community.[50] In 1564 a list of 'mislikes of religion' was drawn up and included the mayor Robert Hodson, the town clerk John Potinger, and Richard Bethell. Roger Corham, who had been expelled from Lincoln's Inn because of his Catholicism, was surprisingly listed as a 'favourer'. In 1585 a list of recusants in the County of Southampton was drawn up and in Hyde, Mabel Chaundler (now the wife of Roger Corham), Dorothy Chaundler (daughter of Mabel) and Robert Willie were named. Following various plots and conspiracies, punishments became more severe in the latter part of Elizabeth I's reign. Winchester's Catholics did not escape execution with seven, including two priests, meeting this fate.[51]

The Catholics represented all social classes and many were of high standing including Sir Walter Sandys' wife, Lady Mary West. Recusant rolls were produced in 1590 and yearly thereafter. In the first year Mabel, described as resident at Hide Barton, was charged £20 per month over two years totalling £480. Initially the fines were trivial but were later enormous. Those unable to pay the fines were liable for the confiscation of up to two-thirds of their lands and goods whilst those who attended private masses faced imprisonment. Mabel and Roger were fined for their allegiance to the Pope. Even with the inheritance to pay such fines, financial problems increased and land had to be leased out. Financial pressures were already an issue in 1579, when Mabel's occupancy was reduced to 210 acres, and peaked in 1598 when some 500 acres were leased to William Cooper to cover financial shortcomings.[52]

By the end of the sixteenth century most of the gentry conformed to the new religion but there were fourteen recusants listed in St Bartholomew's in 1598. Although Roger Corham appears to have conformed to the Anglican religion, Mabel's son William Chaundler was listed as a recusant convict in 1628. From 1699 Catholics were no longer able to purchase land or inherit it. Various subterfuges were necessary to get around this law including the passing of their lands over to a friendly Protestant. It was another 79 years before this Act was repealed but the freedom to hold office and stand for Parliament was not given until 1829.

Roger Corham died in 1600 and, in his will, left his lands to his son William and instructed that the lands and tenements in Hyde Street, which he had brought from the church, should be returned and profits should be used for the repairing the chancel and the church.[53] William lacked the moral integrity of his father. In 1654 he was subpoenaed by the Mayor, Bailiffs and Commonalty of Winchester on two charges. First he did not carry out his father's instruction to pay the City £40 for fuel for the poor within a year of his death. Second he failed to pay rent, maintain or produce his lease for the property he rented from the Corporation.[54]

William Corham's son, Roger, was noted as a papist during the Civil War, when he was besieged in Basing House and sent to prison. In 1648 he was named on a list of excluded royalists of Winchester Corporation and described as 'a delinquent and in arms against the Parliament.'[55] In 1641, Roger Corham conveyed the Brown Candover estate to Henry Sandys and others, who were believed to be holding it in trust for John, fifth Marquess of Winchester (a descendent of Sir William Paulet).[56] The subterfuge undertaken by both recusants and those supporting the royalists in the Civil War reflected the political situation at the time. Little is known of the details, but most properties were returned to their rightful owners by the reign of Charles II (1660-1685). Some, for example, Thomas Chaundler, were not so fortunate with irreversible consequences.

The Catholic presence in Hyde did not disappear. Richard Warner in his *History of Hampshire* notes:

> Hide or Hyde House, in the northern part of Winchester, is an undemolished piece of an old monastery, where some Roman Catholic gentry are still tolerated with residence, and where it is said, they have an oratory and live according to the rules of St Benedict. [57]

George & Thomas Chaundler at Abbots Barton 1615-1650

Thomas Chaundler favoured his younger son George as heir to Abbots Barton over the elder William. In the event William predeceased his brother at the age of 28 in 1585. On the death of Mabel (Thomas' wife) in 1615, George - then a draper residing in London - returned to take over the estate. At this time the farmhouse was a brick building with stone features. The stone chimneys were a dominant feature and had a chequer-board breast of mixed stone and bricks. This effect is seen elsewhere during the period, for example, the Tudor house in St Johns Street. The original chimneys were rebuilt in the twentieth century in the same style. George and his wife Josina Van der Hagen had four children. On George's death in 1633, Abbots Barton passed to his son, Thomas, who generously compensated his younger brothers, even though they appeared comfortable in their own careers - William Chaundler was Rector of Stopham in Sussex and George was a merchant adventurer. [58] Thomas was Deputy Lieutenant of Hampshire and married to Mary, daughter of Sir William Lisle. He was well connected and secure in his tenure until political events led to the end of the Chaundler family's custodianship of Abbots Barton.

The execution of Charles I in 1649 saw the establishment of the Commonwealth until 1653, followed by the protectorate under Oliver Cromwell, which lasted until 1659. Thomas Chaundler along with the City of Winchester had supported the King in the Civil War. As a result Thomas suffered a similar fate to fifteen other royalists in the locality and was fined heavily for his royal support. Although he sought redress from the county court, seeking a revaluation of his estate, his liabilities wiped out his assets. He was forced to mortgage his property for £2,000 with Thomas Hussey, a Wiltshire landowner and at one time MP for Whitchurch. Thomas leased out part of his estate to local yeomen - Ellis Webb of Kingsworthy, John Page of Abbots Worthy and Henry Wade of Weeke. The three year lease raised £270 p.a. [59]

The lease details give a valuable picture of Abbots Barton at this time. Thomas retained the larger part of the farmhouse, garden and orchards, stables, malthouse and pigeon house, along with the hawking, hunting, fishing and fowling rights. The tenants had use of the bakehouse, dairy, meat cellar, wool loft, chambers above the dairy and two further chambers suitable for the servants, the middle orchard and kitchen garden. Thomas retained the area called Limekilns, giving an allowance against the rent of the tenants of 8s. per acre, with the right to pasture two horses, two cattle, two hogs, two pigs and poultry. In addition, he paid £1 per ton of hay from Ox Lease to feed his horses. The usual restriction prevented the tenants from changing the husbandry, for example new ploughing, or depriving the land of nutrients by failing to recycle plant debris and dung. Thomas prudently retained his residence and land to ensure he could be self-sufficient. Such actions gave short term relief and three days before he died in 1650, he decided to sell the farm to meet debts of £4,500. The estate was purchased for £5,500 by Anne Mynne (or Mynn), widow of George Mynne of Woodcott, Epsom. Thus came to an end four generations and 110 years of Chaundler family tenure and the direct link to those who benefitted from the Dissolution. [60]

Ownership in Hyde Street

At the beginning of the sixteenth century, Hyde Street was a busy thoroughfare and service area for those visiting Hyde Abbey and for pilgrims making their way between the shrines of St Swithun and St Thomas à Becket in Canterbury. The closure of the Abbey initially brought austerity to the inhabitants of Hyde as plots passed to the Abbey lands' new owners. The majority of the east side of Hyde Street passed first to Richard Bethell, then to his son William, and then in 1592 to Thomas Clerke.[61] Godden's map, commissioned by the Mayor and Corporation in 1750, shows the location of the plots whose history is traced below. Used in conjunction with Figure I and Figure II, it will allow the reader to locate these holdings.

On the north side of Hyde House and its grounds were a group of tenements let out to tenants, the last of which formed part of the Abbey's gatehouse. The plots between the former entrance to the Abbey and the future Egbert Road were also let to tenants. Most of the land south of Hyde House also belonged to the Bethells.[62] In addition, Richard Bethell owned land on the west side of Hyde Street, north of the future Hyde Close up to the junction of Hyde Street and Worthy Road. South of Hyde Church Lane was a plot containing three tenements with gardens and orchard.

At the southern end of Hyde Street, was the Swan Inn, which is thought to date from the fourteenth century. This was leased to Edmund Poore in 1590 and Anthony Bethell in 1604. There were several plots under individual ownerships just north of the Swan Inn. One of these was owned by Roger Corham and contained two cottages, one of which was in a state of decay.[63]

The triangular piece of land lying between Hyde Street and Worthy Lane and north of Hyde Church Lane, was leased to William Godden who, sometime before 1590, built a large property on the 1½ acre plot.[64] Confusingly, during Victoria's reign, several properties in Hyde Street were known by similar names to former properties. Godden's house was later known as Hyde House and then Hyde Abbey. Whilst the interior of houses were retained and modernised, façades were rebuilt and reflected the current fashions in architecture. The current house was built on slightly elevated ground; it has red bricks with a grey string course, and a brick dentil cornice under the brick parapets. Parapets were an architectural feature that hid the roof and particularly the dormer windows in the servants' rooms.(see Figure 2.5) [65] Bethell still owned land to the south of Hyde Church Lane but the land immediately north of the lane appears to have been sold.

The area north of the junction of Hyde Street with Worthy Lane, known as Coney Green Close, was part of Abbots Barton and owned by the Chaundlers. Roger Corham was named as the tenant in 1590, by which date he had married Mabel, Thomas Chaundler's widow. The Chaundlers also owned a plot on the west side of the street, later the site of No. 23 Hyde Street.[66]

Figure 2.5: Godden's house - later called Hyde House or Hyde Abbey

Ownership had changed little in the south of Hyde since the Dissolution. The Dean and Chapter owned a substantial contiguous area on the north side of Swan Lane, fronting Hyde Street and along the east side of Andover Road. One of the Hyde Street tenements was leased to Edmund Cooper, a labourer, for 40 years at a yearly rent of 4s.. The large plot with a frontage in both Hyde Street and Swan Lane was still leased to John Purdew for an annual rent of 11s. 4d.. The tenement had decayed and been converted into a malt house by 1649. John Purdew still held the freehold of the plot on the corner of Hyde Street and Swan Lane. The Bishop owned most of the south side of Swan Street with the exception of a large plot owned by Winchester College. This was held on a 40-year lease by Edmund Poore of the Swan for a charge of 1s. and a bushel of malt each year. [67]

The land on the west side of Worthy Road was undeveloped and its ownership was often disputed. William Bethell was in possession of the most northerly plot, which was later let to William Godden. There is evidence to suggest that surrounding plots had been acquired by the City, but by 1590 Roger Corham was in possession of the land, and his son William claimed ownership in 1604. Adjacent plots were farmed by Roger Corham, but belonged to the parishioners of St Bartholomew's. The large parcel which stretched down to Andover Road was used as arable by William Bethell, and later let out by Clerke. [68]

The large triangular plot bordered by Andover Road on the east and the suburban ditch on the west, was owned by St John's Hospital and Winchester College. The Bethells leased the land from Winchester College; subsequently the lease was transferred to Clerke. Sometimes ownership was not clear. Along Stockbridge Road two plots belonged to Richard Bethell in 1558, but the tenant John Purdew claimed the landlord was the parish. At a later date Corham took over the tenancy. This is feasible if Bethell left the land to the church. [69]

Conclusion

After the Dissolution, the newly formed Dean and Chapter, Winchester College and the City gained or retained land in the south of Hyde. The main changes in tenure concerned the Abbey site and its meadows. These had passed fairly intact from the Bethells to the Clerkes. The Bethell and Clerke families and Roger Corham farmed the land and supplemented their holdings by renting additional land from Winchester College. However some plots had moved into individual ownership and the process of fragmentation had begun with the first of the new mansions built in Hyde Street. At the close of the seventeenth century, Edmund Clerke died and ownership of the former Abbey site was split between three of his relatives. The Chaundlers only kept their hold on Abbots Barton until the mid-seventeenth century, when financial necessity forced a sale to a rich widow looking to increase her estates. The Abbey's home farm and grange were no longer controlled by local people who lived on and farmed the land.

Any building stones or embellishments remaining on the site of Hyde Abbey after the Dissolution were slowly recycled for their owners' new abodes. Some surplus to use were sold off but other materials were seized by the creditors of those who over extended themselves or fell-foul of religious or political machinations. Some of the ancient stones travelled little distance and have survived in the foundations of properties in Hyde Street. Others were sold to charitable organisations and the keen observer can identify their reuse in other buildings in Winchester.

There was little change in the ownership of the former Abbey lands during the sixteenth and seventeenth centuries. The site of Hyde Abbey with its farm and Abbots Barton Farm were under separate ownership. The former were held by Richard Bethell and his heirs from 1546 until 1592 when they were sold to Thomas Clerke to meet Richard's son, William, mounting debts. Abbots Barton was owned by Walter Chaundler and his heirs from 1537 to 1650. The estate passed into the hands of his widow for her life and then to their son Thomas. Mabel, Thomas' widow, married Roger Corham and she held the property until it passed to her son George Chaundler on her death. Political upheaval brought the end of the Chaundler's custodianship when George's son, Thomas, failed to pay his debts and was forced to sell to an investor living outside of Hampshire.

Part 2: The Agricultural Revolution, the Knights and the Duke

Each year thousands of visitors flood to the village of Chawton, 16 miles north-east of Winchester, to see the house where Jane Austen lived and Chawton House which she regularly visited. In the Church of St Nicholas where her sister and mother were buried, tourists may read this epitaph on a memorial stone:

> Lyes the body of William Knight only son of Edward Woodward of Fosters Surry by Elizabeth elder daughter of and coheir of Christopher Lewkenor of West Dean who assumed the name Knight upon marriage to Elizabeth only daughter of Michael Martin gent of Eynsham Oxford (whose mother was a Knight of this place) by Francis the other coheir to Sir Richard Lewkenor whereby were united the several estates of the Lewkenors Knights Woodwards and Martins.

It is a little known fact that for over 160 years, the Knight family were also owners of the former Hyde Abbey's lands in Winchester. The ownership of Abbots Barton, along with the main estates in Chawton and Godmersham, passed between the generations of one extended family. When periodically faced with a lack of a male heir, they perpetuated the Knight family name and kept estates intact by importing heirs from amongst remote cousins, one of whom was Jane Austen's brother, Edward.

Although the Knights lived in their country seats far removed from Hyde, they still took an active part in the running of the Abbey and Abbots Barton Farms. Sheep farming and hop production produced a healthy income, but the management of the water meadows, on which prosperity depended, provided a challenge.

The Agricultural Revolution was marked by the enclosure of open fields and common lands and changing methods of farming. Yields increased as crop rotation was widely adopted and greater mechanisation was introduced. The move from arable to pasture, along with selective breeding changed the face of the downland farms. Machines replaced agricultural workers and people left the countryside to work in the expanding towns.

Chapter 3 traces the history of Abbots Barton through generations of the Knights, the Abbey site and farm under the stewardship of the Duke of Bedford, and the eventual reunification of the Abbey's farms in 1767.

Chapter 4 explores Hyde's farming practices and agricultural output in the eighteenth century and the management challenges to the Knights and the Duke of Bedford from the users of the water meadows.

Chapter 5 looks at the development of Hyde Street and its environs during the eighteenth and nineteenth centuries; the economic and social importance to the inhabitants of the educational and reform institutions; and the burgeoning brewing industry.

Figure 3: Durngate Mill c.1870

Source:WINCM:PWCM2738

This view from the north was taken after the owner of Abbots Barton had purchased the freehold from the Bishop of Winchester. The waters of the Durngate River were divided to work the two wheels. The nineteenth century extension is clearly visible on the right side of the photograph.

Chapter 3: Custodians of Abbots Barton and Hyde Abbey Estates

Abbots Barton and the Mynnes, Lewkenors and Martins

Anne Mynne, who purchased Abbots Barton from a financially-ruined Thomas Chaundler in 1650, came from a respected family. Her father, Sir Robert Parkhurst, became Lord Mayor of London in 1634. Her husband, George Mynne, has been described as a merchant, draper, clothier, royal servant, politician, ironmaster, moneylender, clerk in Chancery, and extortionist.[1] Although a royalist supporting the King with a loan of 6,000 lbs. of iron and several financial contributions, evidence suggests that he also supplied the Parliamentarians.

George died in 1648 without a will and his son, also named George, died four years later leaving no heirs. Sir John Baker and Richard Parkhurst, George Mynne's trustees, managed his estate on behalf of Anne, the sole beneficiary. In 1649 she brought the reversionary interest of the Manor of Steventon in Hampshire from Thomas Brocas, who in 1635 had raised a mortgage from George Mynne's trustees.[2] In 1650 she purchased Abbots Barton and the manor belonging to Edward Darcy in Epsom.

Anne Mynne's ownership of the Hyde estate was marked by financial troubles. In 1652 she leased (or extended the lease) of the farm to Thomas Hussey, who as tenant was responsible for both repairs and taxes. Thomas Hussey retained the tenancy until he died in 1671, by which time he had substantial rent arrears, accumulated at a rate of £130 per half year. His executor, Mr Phillips, was sued for payment in 1672. The property had been neglected and substantial repairs costing over £148 were needed. Carpentry and masonry work on the house and the repair of walls and fences of the courts and garden cost £56 10s.. Repairs to the outbuildings, including stone and woodwork for the barn, cart and hay house and re-thatching of the barley barn and malthouse, amounted to £54 10s.. The farmland had also been neglected and misused. The hedges, ditches and sluices were in a poor state and trees and bridges had been removed for firewood. Repairs to these cost a further £37 10s.. As the estate was sub-let to tenant farmers, these repairs were urgently needed to realize any profit. How many of these tenants were local is not known.[3]

To appreciate the successive ownership at Abbots Barton during the seventeenth and eighteenth centuries, an understanding of inheritance law is helpful. Primogeniture, whereby inheritance of land passed to the eldest son and thereafter to the male descendants, was dominant. The system prevented the fragmentation of estates, a feature often seen in other societies. Property and land would be passed to the first son of the marriage and then to the heirs of his body. If the first son had died and there were no grandsons (born or still living) the estate passed to the second son and so on. This was known as tail male; daughters could only inherit if tail general had been set up. In the absence of a son, daughters would inherit as 'tenants in common'. Daughters would take an equal share in the estate and if they married their share passed to their husband. In the unlikely event of no children, the remainder would go to 'right heirs' of the tenant in possession. If the mother survived her husband, the estate would pass into her family.

On Anne Mynne's death in 1663 her estates passed to her daughters - Elizabeth (wife of Richard Evelyn) and Lady Anne (wife of Sir John Lewkenor of West Dean, Sussex). The Epsom estate passed to Elizabeth, Abbots Barton to Lady Anne, and Steventon was shared between them. Under the law at that time, John Lewkenor was seen as the owner of all Lady Anne's wealth and property. Table 3.1 gives a list of owners of Abbots Barton from 1650 to 1811. A portrait of Lady Anne is given in Figure 3.1 and the relevant parts of the Mynne and Lewkenor family trees are given in Figures 3.2 and 3.3 respectively.

Lady Anne was well-connected. Her husband's uncle was Sir Christopher Lewkenor - MP for Midhurst (1628) and Recorder of Chichester (1640). Sir John died in 1669 (aged 46) and Lady Anne (then aged 35), as was common for a young widow, soon married again. Her second husband, Sir William Morley of Halnaker, Sussex, was also a rich and respected member of the gentry.[4]

Infant mortality was high. Epidemics struck regularly and where there was a predominance of cousin marriages, genetic traits may have led to a higher illness and mortality in children than expected. Elizabeth Evelyn died in 1691 without surviving heirs. She had four sons who died in infancy and a daughter Mary Ann who died heirless in 1688. Mary Ann was unfortunate in marriage. Her husband, William Montagu, was described by her uncle John Evelyn, the writer, gardener and diarist (a contemporary of Samuel Pepys), as a man 'who ruined both my niece and himself by his scandalous life'. Elizabeth's inherited estates passed to her sister.

Lady Anne died in 1704 and all her estates, including Abbots Barton and the lease of Durngate Mill, passed to her son John Lewkenor. Durngate Mill, which lay to the east of St Bartholomew's alongside North Walls, was leased from the Winchester Bishopric Estate. John Lewkenor was a public figure sitting as MP for Midhurst in 1661 and from 1681 to 1705. He died in 1706 with no legitimate heirs and Abbots Barton passed to Elizabeth Knight (formerly Martin) through her parents Michael and Frances (née Lewkenor). Elizabeth already owned extensive property when she inherited lands at Chawton in 1702 after the deaths of her brothers Richard and Christopher. As a requirement of this inheritance she changed her name to Knight as her brothers in their turn had done. The marriage links between the Lewkenor and Knight families can be seen in their respective family trees in Figures 3.3 and 3.4.

Table 3.1: Owners of Abbot Barton Farm 1650 to 1811

1650 to 1663	Anne Mynne	Two daughters Elizabeth and Anne.
1663 to 1704	Lady Anne Lewkenor	
1704 to 1706	John Lewkenor	No legitimate heirs.
1706 to 1737	Elizabeth Knight (née Martin)	Married (1st) to William Woodward (1667-1721). They both changed their names to Knight. Married (2nd) Bulstrode Peachey (c.1681-1736). He changed his name to Knight. Neither marriage produced an heir. Left estate to cousin Thomas Broadnax.
1737 to 1781	Thomas Broadnax of Godmersham Park, Canterbury	Changed name to May (1727) Changed name to Knight (1738).
1767		Purchase of Hyde Abbey Farm from Duke of Bedford.
1781 to 1794	Thomas Knight	Married Catherine Knatchbull. No children. Adopted Edward Austen, brother of Jane.
1794 to 1798	Catherine Knatchbull (d.1812)	Inherits from husband.
1798 to 1811	Catherine Knatchbull & Edward Austen	Estates are managed by Edward Austen. Edward changed name to Knight on inheritance in 1812.

Figure 3.1: Lady Anne Mynne, wife of Sir John Lewkenor

Courtesy: The Knight Collection, Chawton House

Figure 3.2: Mynne Family Tree

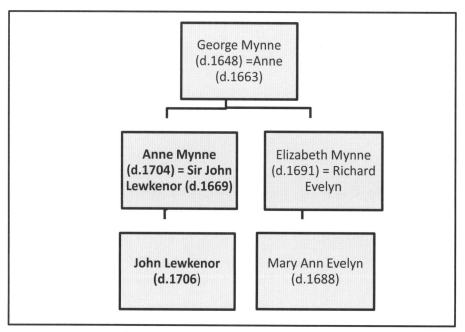

Sources: Burke (1835) and Leigh and Knight (1911)
Those who inherited Abbots Barton are emboldened.

Figure 3.3: Lewkenor Family Tree

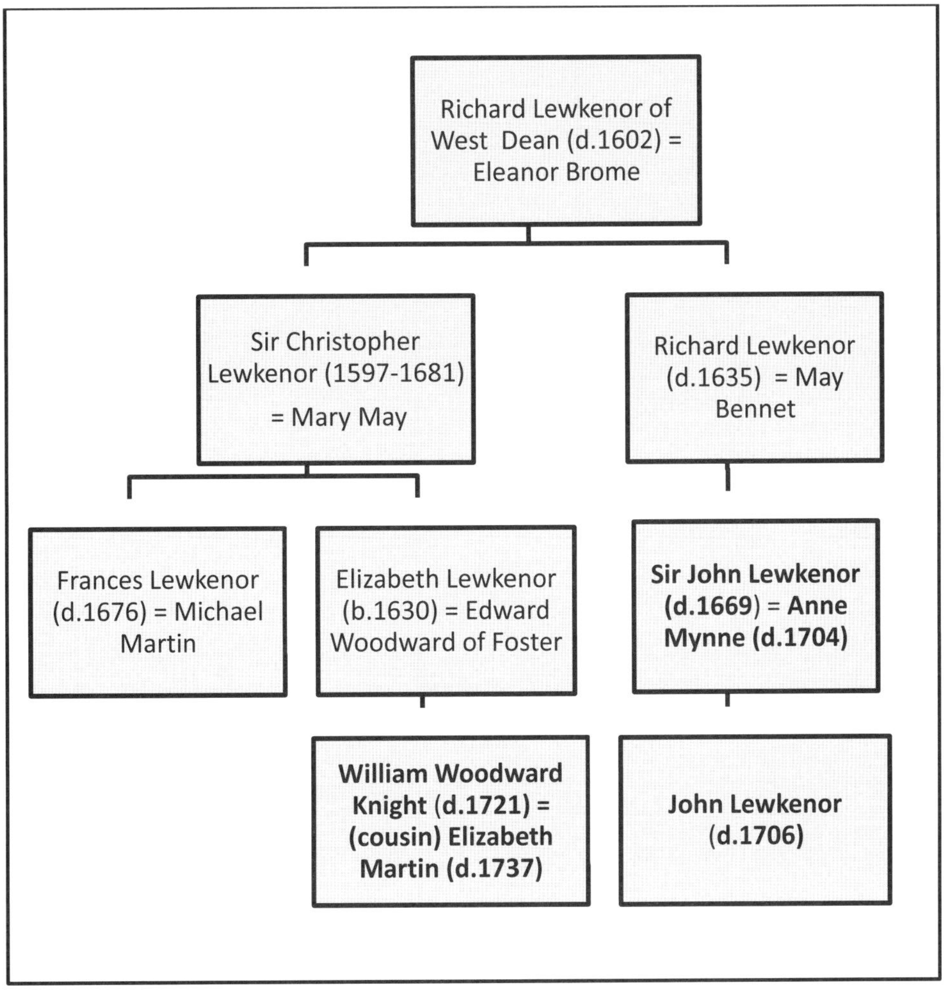

Richard Lewkenor of West Dean (d.1602) = Eleanor Brome

Sir Christopher Lewkenor (1597-1681) = Mary May

Richard Lewkenor (d.1635) = May Bennet

Frances Lewkenor (d.1676) = Michael Martin

Elizabeth Lewkenor (b.1630) = Edward Woodward of Foster

Sir John Lewkenor (d.1669) = Anne Mynne (d.1704)

William Woodward Knight (d.1721) = (cousin) Elizabeth Martin (d.1737)

John Lewkenor (d.1706)

Sources: Burke (1835) and Leigh and Knight (1911)
Those who inherited Abbots Barton are emboldened.
n.b. Date of death can vary between different sources.

Figure 3.4: Knights of Chawton Family Tree

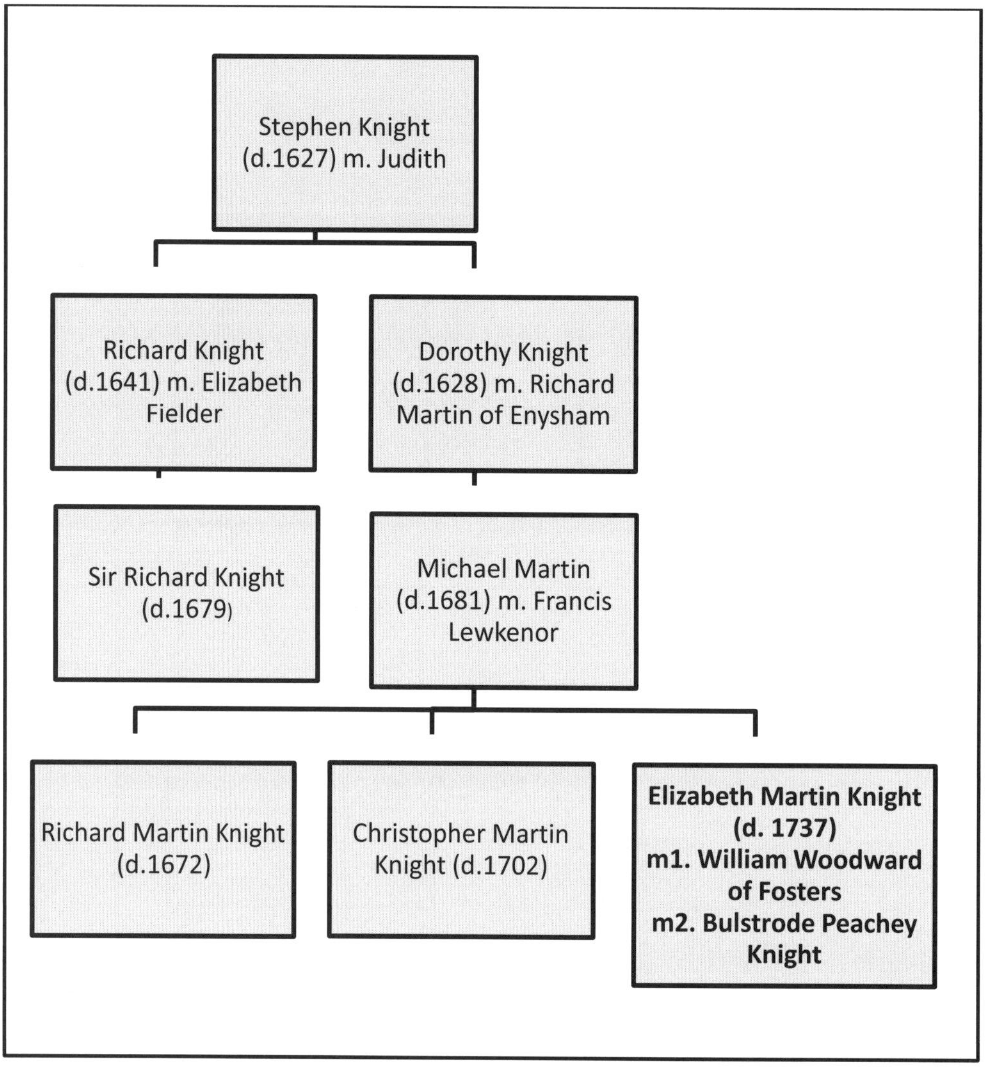

```
                    ┌─────────────────────────┐
                    │     Stephen Knight       │
                    │   (d.1627) m. Judith     │
                    └─────────────────────────┘
          ┌──────────────────────┴──────────────────────┐
┌──────────────────────┐              ┌──────────────────────┐
│    Richard Knight     │              │    Dorothy Knight     │
│ (d.1641) m. Elizabeth │              │ (d.1628) m. Richard   │
│       Fielder         │              │  Martin of Enysham    │
└──────────────────────┘              └──────────────────────┘
          │                                      │
┌──────────────────────┐              ┌──────────────────────┐
│  Sir Richard Knight   │              │    Michael Martin     │
│      (d.1679)         │              │ (d.1681) m. Francis   │
│                       │              │       Lewkenor        │
└──────────────────────┘              └──────────────────────┘
                    ┌──────────────────┼──────────────────────┐
┌──────────────────────┐  ┌──────────────────────┐  ┌──────────────────────────┐
│ Richard Martin Knight │  │  Christopher Martin  │  │ Elizabeth Martin Knight  │
│      (d.1672)         │  │   Knight (d.1702)    │  │       (d. 1737)          │
│                       │  │                      │  │ m1. William Woodward     │
│                       │  │                      │  │     of Fosters           │
│                       │  │                      │  │ m2. Bulstrode Peachey    │
│                       │  │                      │  │       Knight             │
└──────────────────────┘  └──────────────────────┘  └──────────────────────────┘
```

Sources: Burke (1835) and Leigh and Knight (1911)
Those who inherited Abbots Barton are emboldened.
Not all children are included in family trees.

Families sought to protect the future of their estates, to expand them through favourable marriages and to prevent their breakup through dissolute living or inheritance. The desire was strongest when the family was long-established in the county. Inherited estates from distant relatives were of less concern and usually the ones to be exchanged for financial or geographical advantage.

Elizabeth married her cousin William Woodward (he was the son of Elizabeth Lewkenor, her mother's sister). On marriage William changed his name to Knight thus perpetuating the Knight family name even though the last direct heir had died in 1679.[5] Four years after William Knight (Woodward) died in 1721, Elizabeth married Bulstrode Peachey who was at one time MP for Midhurst. He also changed his name to Knight becoming known as Peachey Knight. The portraits of Elizabeth Knight and Bulstrode Peachey are shown in Figure 3.5.

A second marriage was not to be lightly entered into, especially when both parties owned considerable real estate inherited from their respective families. Lawyers were involved in drafting the terms of a marriage settlement that would allow protection for the heir of Elizabeth Knight's estates once her husband had rights over his wife's property.[6] The marriage settlement between Bulstrode and Elizabeth detailed their separate estates. Elizabeth was not entirely happy with the settlement. The rents of Elizabeth's estate, settled on her for life, and other rents paid her £4,000 a year. She remarked that 'she accepted for the sake of peace as apprehending that if she insisted to have received the whole of such rents it would have occasioned a break or separation between them.'[7] There was some doubt of whether Peachey was happy to go through the legal process to separate out the two interests to ensure the profits from Elizabeth's estates went to her and for her lands to be passed to her heirs rather than to his family. If such an agreement had not been reached the future of Abbots Barton would have been very different. Bulstrode died in 1735 and as his brother had predeceased him, his lands were left to his nephew Sir John Peachey for his life.[8]

Even as a distant landowner, Elizabeth certainly took an active interest in Abbots Barton and repairs were carried out to the house's roof timbers whilst it was under her stewardship. In his will Bulstrode had noted that he had laid out 'considerable sums of money in repairs and lasting improvement of Mrs Knight's separate estate and of her other estates all with repairs and improvements.'[9] As was a recurring fate in this family, especially amongst those marrying their cousins, Elizabeth died in 1737 leaving no surviving heirs and no immediate relatives. On her memorial stone in St Nicholas Church, Chawton, the owner of Abbots Barton is described thus:

> She lived with affectionate Tenderness to her Husbands, a courteous Affability to her Friends and charitable Liberality to the Poor. In the true Faith & Fear of God. In a constant Practice of Piety, a christian Charity: and an Example of the true Religion, and Virtue.

Figure 3.5: Elizabeth Martin Knight and Bulstrode Peachey Knight

Courtesy: The Knight Collection, Chawton House

Abbots Barton and the Knights

Property inheritance followed a well-defined pathway: father (the current entail) to son (the new entail), and then to the heir of the son's body (future entail). Entails were added or refreshed in each generation. The widow inherited for her lifetime. The current landowner had a life interest being either a 'tenant for life' or 'tenant in possession.' Fee-tail limited inheritance of the estate to a specified heir or heirs by means of a settlement or will. Usually inheritance was restricted to legitimate male heirs described as 'of the body', and so excluded adopted children. Males took precedence over females (as is common in royal lineage). Strict entail in tail-male barred an estate passing to more distant relatives such as cousins. The line could not pass through the mother or a wife.

The employment of good lawyers and trustees was an essential requirement to the survival of a family's wealth and lands, and detailed settlements were set up to preserve the estate. A strict settlement, which could last for a century, was a device which ensured land was kept in the family and was essential to prevent loss during religious or political upheaval or extravagant living. Land could not be sold or exchanged without the agreement of all parties involved in the settlement, including those with an interest in the remainder. The potential damaging behaviour of a new heir to the future viability of the estate needed careful management. Cash flows were threatened by the undertaking of expensive building projects such as house extensions and landscaping, by speculating in stocks and shares, by gambling, or just being incompetent.

If land was sold it was likely to be outlying sections of the estate or preferably land some distance away, which had recently come into the family ownership. However money could be obtained fairly safely by mortgages, which were a secure and a low cost way of raising capital. With any luck a wayward heir, addicted to the gentlemanly pleasures to be found in Bath and London, would have been seen by them into an early grave before his own son attained majority. The trustees would then be able to pay off his debts without interference.

There were significant risks for purchasers of land under the prevailing deeds system. The owner in the common law system was the person who currently had the greatest claim to title. The danger was that a claimant with a better claim than the seller could emerge later to challenge the purchaser's title. It was important that purchasers secured the agreement of all potential claimants to a sale, including those whose claims might arise only under certain conditions, such as the failure of distant cousins to produce male heirs.

Elizabeth Knight died just after the court ruling of 1736, which made it unlawful for land ownership to be protected for more than a life-in-being plus an additional 21 years. Entails had to be broken and set up again for every generation, usually when the entail reached 21 or was married. Such settlements, especially when revised at the time of marriage, detailed how much income or settlement younger brothers and sisters should receive from the estate. This was a liability and often quite a burden, requiring mortgages to meet these claims.

Settlements could only be broken by an Act of Parliament unless no further entails had been added. When the last son reached 21, the settlement ended. Therefore families took care for each father to tie his son into a settlement to prevent the spendthrift heir from dispensing with the family's assets.

Elizabeth took sound legal advice when making her will. She had no children or close relatives since she inherited her estates following her brothers' demise. Under Elizabeth's will, Abbots Barton and her other estates passed in tail-male to a distant relative; in this case a second cousin related three generations back. By her will the estates were put into the hands of trustees - William Guidott of Lincoln's Inn, John Baker and Edward Munford (both deceased before she died) and their heirs on trust. Trustees, who were lawyers or friends, were used to ensure that the settlement was executed correctly. Trustees performed a role whereby estates were conveyed to them for the use of a third person. Thus the legal ownership of the estate was in different hands from the beneficial owner who received the income. The family had an equitable estate, which prevented its sale for two generations. This overcame the weakness of an entail, which, if set up say on marriage, and hence before an heir was born, could be broken.

The will set up an entail naming Thomas May of Godmersham, William Lloyd of Newbury and Rev. John Hinton of Chawton and their descendants successively as the heirs.

> Manors of Lordships, messuages, farms, land, tenements, hereditaments and premises were given to the use of Thomas May of Godmersham for his life without impeachment of waste, remainder to the use of William Guidott, John Baker and Edward Munford and their heirs during the life of Thomas (May) Knight in trust to preserve the contingent remainder and after the death of Thomas Knight to use of the first and every other son of the body of Thomas Knight lawfully to be begotten successively in tail-male remainder to the use of William Lloyd of Newberry, gent for his life with the provision for supporting the contingent remainder and after his decease to use of the first and every other son of his body lawfully to be begotten successively in tail-male. Remainder to John Hinton of Chawton, clerk for his life without impeachment of waste with like limitation to preserve the contingent remainder and after his decease to use of the first and every other son of his body lawfully to be begotten successively in tail-male. Remainder to the right heirs of the testatrix Elizabeth forever.[10]

A proviso or condition was that Thomas May, his sons and the heirs of their respective bodies who came into possession of the premises, were to change their surname to Knight.

Although this was the age of the gentry, there have been continual debates among academics about the nature of the gentry. The consensus is there are no sole criteria and those that are used can be unreliable. Ownership of freehold land and property set at a minimum value assumes reliable data, clarity on the value of urban as opposed to rural holdings and an appreciation of upward mobility. The requirement of position of duty to the Crown also raises issues of both the willingness to undertake these and the availability of positions.

Different stratifications have been proposed: the proper gentry – the knights and esquires – and the gentlemen and others; or the county elite and parish gentry; or the upper, middling and inferior. A recent view proposes the gentry can be recognised by the following: membership of the lesser nobility; ownership of land and property (including urban) and the recognition of its accumulation by professional endeavours; public authority, power and social standing.[11] Typically, the gentry of the eighteenth century resided in their country houses and derived most of their income from farm management, either by direct involvement or by means of rental income.[12] The families frequently inter-married so strengthening the bond in successive generations. Thomas was the son of Anne May and William Broadnax. His mother's aunt, Mary and her husband, Sir Christopher Lewkenor, were the grandparents of both Elizabeth Knight and her first husband William Woodward. The family relationship can be traced in Figure 3.6: May family tree.

The custodianship of the Abbey's lands moved to a new family, albeit related paternally in a web of threads. The new owner of Abbots Barton, Thomas Knight, was well respected, highly educated and active in politics. He was educated at Balliol College, Oxford, studied law, acted as High Sherriff of Kent and became MP for Canterbury. A portrait is given in Figure 3.7. Born a Broadnax, Thomas had changed his name to May in 1727 after inheriting the estates of Sir Thomas May of Rawmere, near West Dean in Sussex. This inheritance was not straightforward as family members often saw the death of relatives who lacked heirs as an opportunity to promote their positions.[13] After his death in 1718, Sir Thomas May's estates passed to his widow for her life and when she died in 1726, Rawmere passed to the Broadnax family, whose seat was at Godmersham outside Canterbury, Kent. Thomas married Jane Monk in 1729 and they had many children but only five survived to adulthood, a son and four daughters, who died spinsters. On Elizabeth's death, Thomas once again was compelled to change his name as a condition of inheritance - this time to Knight.

Each change of name required a private and expensive Act of Parliament and one MP commented:

> This gentleman gives us so much trouble that the best way would be to pass an Act for him to use whatever name he pleases.[14]

Even before the days of ease of travel the gentry formed a compact society, often related by marriage and keen to keep in touch by gossiping at the numerous social occasions. Positions in Parliament provided opportunities to network and discuss potential business deals. Thomas Knight took the opportunity to expand and consolidate his land holdings. He sold Rawmere, the ancestral home of the Mays, and in 1744 he exchanged some of Lewkenor's West Dean estate with land close to Chawton, now in the ownership of Sir John Peachey. As the two estates had almost identical values, Sir John Peachey and Thomas Knight for 'their mutual convenience and accommodation and for the improvement of their several estates in two counties have proposed to make exchange.'[15]

Figure 3.6: May Family Tree

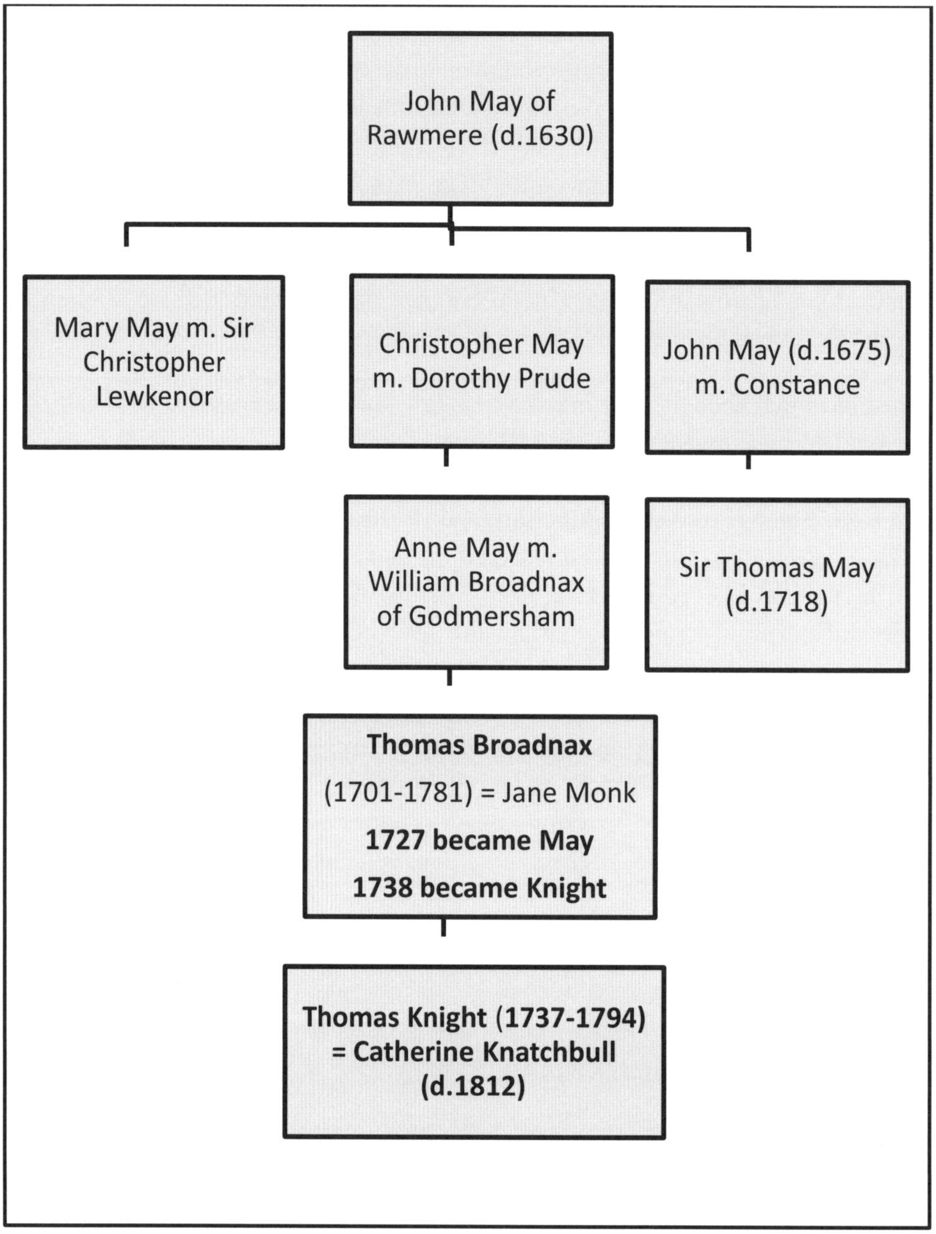

```
                    ┌─────────────────────┐
                    │    John May of      │
                    │  Rawmere (d.1630)   │
                    └─────────────────────┘

┌──────────────┐    ┌─────────────────┐    ┌─────────────────┐
│ Mary May m.  │    │ Christopher May │    │ John May (d.1675)│
│   Sir        │    │ m. Dorothy Prude│    │  m. Constance   │
│ Christopher  │    │                 │    │                 │
│  Lewkenor    │    │                 │    │                 │
└──────────────┘    └─────────────────┘    └─────────────────┘

                    ┌─────────────────┐    ┌─────────────────┐
                    │  Anne May m.    │    │  Sir Thomas May │
                    │ William Broadnax│    │    (d.1718)     │
                    │ of Godmersham   │    │                 │
                    └─────────────────┘    └─────────────────┘

                ┌──────────────────────────┐
                │   **Thomas Broadnax**    │
                │ (1701-1781) = Jane Monk  │
                │   **1727 became May**    │
                │  **1738 became Knight**  │
                └──────────────────────────┘

              ┌──────────────────────────────┐
              │ **Thomas Knight (1737-1794)**│
              │  **= Catherine Knatchbull**  │
              │         **(d.1812)**         │
              └──────────────────────────────┘
```

Sources: Burke (1835) and Leigh and Knight (1911)
Those who inherited Abbots Barton are emboldened.
Not all children are included in family trees.

Figure 3.7: Thomas (Broadnax May) Knight (1701-1781)

Courtesy: The Knight Collection, Chawton House

The exchange required the agreement of all those with an interest in the properties, namely those named in the two respective entails - James Peachey and William Lloyd, John Hinton and Martha Hinton – the potential heirs of Elizabeth Knight, and her surviving trustee William Guidott.[16]

The inheritance allowed further improvements to be made at Godmersham which became a fine country seat befitting a member of the gentry. Although Thomas Knight's main residence was a long way from Hampshire, this did not mean he neglected Abbots Barton or failed to visit regularly, especially when there were management issues with the water meadows (Chapter 4).

Hyde Abbey and the Duke

When Edmund Clerke died in 1693 the Hyde Abbey site and buildings were divided into three equal parts; one part to his sister Lucy Mackadam and her son Christopher Johnson, one part to James Morecroft, and one part to Henry Colpes. The three parties appear to have managed the estate jointly. Colpes, described as a gentleman living in Hyde, left his property to his kinsman, Christopher Johnson in 1702. However he must have upset another relative because in January 1704 there was a lawsuit between Christopher Johnson and Charles Colpes, defendant. Three years later in July 1705 Christopher, who lived in St John's in the Soke east of St Bartholomew, left this share to his cousin Francis Wickliffe. [17]

The co-heirs sought to release capital from the estate without selling their shares. Sums of money were regularly needed to meet inheritance dues, such as portions to children or marriage settlements. The property was used as collateral to raise money on several occasions by way of a mortgage. In February 1702, James Morecroft raised a £300 mortgage for a period of 2,000 years on his share of the capital messuage with 20 acres, the site of Hyde Abbey, and 150 acres of land, from Thomas Randall, a yeoman of Otterbourne. [18]

There were two types of mortgage. A mortgage by demise involved the transfer of property for a period, often in excess of 1,000 years. Although the repayment date may have been given as within a year, the loan was intended for a longer period since the process was a method of investment for the mortgagee (lender). The interest was stated in pounds, for example £5 meant five per cent, and due dates for payments, usually twice yearly, were given. If the charges were not met or the mortgagor (borrower) failed to repay the loan, then the mortgagee could re-claim the debt or property. Further borrowing often occurred as this was a straightforward means of raising money when needed. A mortgage by conveyance, also known as a 'mortgage by fee', involved the conveyance of the property to the lender and its equitable re-conveyance when the loan and all the interest had been repaid.

On Christopher Johnson's death, his mother Lucy Mackadam, a resident in St John's became sole owner of the joint one-third share. In March 1709, just prior to her death, she initiated a lease and release of the Hyde Abbey site and the messuages and appurtenances in St John's, which put ownership in the hands of a trustee and raised a sum of money for inheritance This document mentioned the love and affection Lucy felt for her nephew James Morecroft. Richard Cobb Esq. of St Michael's parish (on the south side of the City), was appointed the trustee for Lucy's life, and then for a further 2,000 years, in order to raise £450 for James and his heirs. Following probate the £450 was distributed to Morecroft's children as follows: James £50, Thomas £100, William £50, Elizabeth Crabtree £50, Martha Grover £50 and Mary £100. A few months later James assigned his £50 to Elizabeth's husband, Palmer Crabtree, who resided in London. [19]

On Lucy Mackadam's death, James Morecroft controlled two of the three shares in the property. In October 1709 his eldest son, James, married Elizabeth Riley. Elizabeth's father presented £500 to the couple and James' father sought to match this. He did this by raising a mortgage for £500 from Rev. Dr. Robert Eyre of Winchester and John Colson of North Stoneham, using a lease and release. In August 1715 a further mortgage, by demise for 500 years secured against a one-third share, raised £160 from John Penton.[20]

Mortgages were commonly paid off at several dates, releasing the equity of redemption. £515 was paid off in March 1712 to Randall's executors and legatees, Thomas Broadway and his wife living in Winnall. A further £960 plus interest was paid to Broadway in 1724. When a lender wanted to reclaim his money and the borrower was unable or unwilling to repay it, the mortgage could be assigned to another lender for the remainder of the term. In 1727 Broadway sought to raise £100 and assigned a remaining mortgage on the property to William Baker, a clerk living in Sparsholt who was paid back in June 1728.[21]

After 40 years, the Morecroft family's ownership of the Hyde Abbey estate came to an end. Nothing is known about how the land was managed, whether James was active in farming the land or if the different parties merely took their share of the profits. The estate remained in the hands of trustees, with Richard Chalenor Cobb taking on the role from Amy, the daughter of Richard Cobb. Many of James Morecroft's children no longer lived in the City – Thomas resided in Hampstead and William and Martha (now married to Samuel Tiggell) lived in Portsmouth, but Mary, still a spinster, stayed in Winchester.

John, Duke of Bedford sought to purchase the Hyde Abbey estate in the early 1730s. Whether there was any relationship with the Morecroft family is not known but it should be remembered that Bedford was a descendent of Thomas Wriothesley. He had thus inherited several manors in the vicinity, which had passed down through the Wriothesley family into the Russell's hands. As mentioned, the land was subject to several mortgages which were paid off in 1732 and 1733. In December 1732, Bedford paid £1,167 13s. 4d. for the one-third share which Ambrose Wickcliffe (living in County Durham) had inherited from his father Francis Wickcliffe. In the same month Bedford paid £299 to Deborah (widow of John Penton) in order to discharge the mortgage taken out in 1715.

Heirs had an interest in property and to ensure a good title to the land all interested parties, including those with a potential claim on the remainder, were asked to sign a quitclaim and promise not to bring any future legal actions. In January 1733, Thomas Morecroft for consideration of payments renounced his interests in the property sold by James Morecroft to the Duke of Bedford. In February, Bedford purchased by lease and release Morecroft's two-thirds share in the Hyde Abbey land for £2,333 6s 8d. However this money did not all go to James Morecroft or his son James's widow - Elizabeth - as the various mortgages had to be discharged. These included the sum to John Colson (Robert Eyre left his estate in law to Colson) borrowed on Elizabeth's marriage. By February 1733 both James Morecroft (the elder) and Elizabeth (his daughter-in-law) had died. Bedford paid further amounts to discharge payments, which included £247 to Jane Baker (widow of William) who had bought from Thomas Broadway part of the mortgage he had inherited from Thomas Randall.[22] It should be noted that purchase of the property also involved the liability to pay the annual stipend to the vicar of St Bartholomew.

Eventually by two legal processes in February and April 1733 between James Morecroft for two-thirds and Ambrose Wickcliffe for one-third of the estate, the Duke of Bedford gained legal title to the messuage, watermill, three gardens, three orchards, 40 acres of land, 160 acres of meadow and 10 acres of pasture with appurtenances in St Bartholomew, Hyde, which cost him a total of £3,350.[23]

 The Duke of Bedford played an active part in the management of his estates, particularly when Thomas Knight found the Duke's tenants' misuse of the water meadows impeded the smooth running of his Hyde estate in 1738. However, because of financial problems on his main holdings in London, the Duke was forced to sell his Hampshire estates including Barton Farm.

In 1765, prior to sale, substantial repairs were carried out on Barton Farm. The tenant, who had responsibility for repairs, had neglected the property over a long period. The bill of works, which totalled £147, gives an indication of the extent of the farm buildings and their condition, as well as providing a valuable insight into the cost of building work at that time. The breakdown of the repair costs are detailed in Table 3.2. The house consisted of a kitchen, two cellars, a little parlour, a new study and chamber on the lower floor, and two further chambers upstairs. This was a working abode – entertaining was not important. Outbuildings consisted of a granary, brewhouse and extensive array of animal accommodation, a cart house and barns. Lathe and plaster was used in the construction of walls which were often filled with straw or horsehair to create a firm surface. The repairs suggest that both ceilings and walls were in much need of maintenance. Great effort was made to spruce up the buildings with new stone floors in the kitchen and outbuildings, and the replacement of rotten window frames and the hanging off doors in the cow shed. The roof also needed attention. Of particular interest is the £6 cost for a master stonemason to repair the walls which were 'broken and bad'. A master craftsman was needed to mend the old walls of the Abbey.

Table 3.2: 1765 Bill of works for repairs to Barton Farm

	£	s.	d.
About 48 square of tiling lathes. Lathes be 12 f. square round.	28	16	
Ceiling lathering and plastering in all at least 100 yards at 12d.	10		
Fence wall in the front and about the offices broken and bad. Stone master work.	6		
Kitchen new paved with Purbeck or Newcastle stone 20 by 18.5 is 370 f. at 8d.	12	6	8
Brewhouse new laid with both the old stone, 20 by 18.5 is 370f. at 1d.	1	10	10
2 cellars to be new paved with bricks about 70 yards. Sand & brick & work.	3	10	
7 stone steps wants turning or new cut.	1		
Granary to be (?) and paved, new built where necessary 5.5 at 12 p. square.	3	6	
Paving the stable about 64 yards at 12d. Stone & work. *Not to be done*	3	4	
Some brick pannell in stable granary & offices to repair.	2		
	71	13	6
1 chamber floor may be covered with white (?) deal. 20 by 16 is 220 f. Work & deal	3		
15 timber steps & 2 half spaces & head of stayers all covered as above.	3	2	
12 front transom window frames may be shortened & new sills & putting in again.	1	16	
1 chamber white deal plain door and hanging.		5	
1 lower floor now a chamber & new study 16 by 13 new inch oak 208f.	4		
The old study 8 by 8. 64f. Oak inch board & joist. Paved with brick.	1	16	
Little parlour before the sd old study 12 by 13 is 156f. Oak inch board.	2	4	
6 rafters over the old study. 12f. long & a tye beam in granary 18f. long. Work.		18	
Furring the main roof of the house & several gang beams to support the roof. Work.	5		
A garden door case cull shorten & a new sill etc.		5	
A new paver of barn doors & by 12 yards. Deal and putting up.	2		
A new floor of oak in the stable 20 by 14 is 280f. Boards & work.	3	18	
A turret or floor over the horses 48 by 20. 960f. 4 boards will do.	5	10	
5 bays to the cart house. Some posts broke & sunk. Raising & a stable door case new.	3	5	
7 cow stall door hanging & about 1000f. of 4 board in all wanting.	8	10	
5 barn floors wanted in 5 years, 2400f. of plank at 36 p. 100 & work 4d.	19	13	
Timber (except the carriage of all materials) about for post rail gate etc.	10		
Elms to be cut for boards.	75	2	0
In all	**£146**	**15s**	**6d**

Source: HRO:18M61/BOX20/27COPY

Reunification of the Abbey farms and the end of the Knights' ownership

The residue of Thomas Wriothesley's Hampshire estates came under the Bedford family's control through the marriage in 1669 of Rachel, the second daughter and co-heir of the last of the Wriothesley line - Thomas, 4th Earl of Southampton - to Lord William Russell. The Wriothesley-Russell family tree is given in Figure 1.10. Families of the gentry often survived financial difficulties by selling outlying estates and in 1768, the fourth Duke of Bedford was forced to sell his Hampshire estates due to the heavy charges on his London estates.[24] Bedford appears to have initiated the sale in the previous year. In June 1767 the Duke of Bedford sold Abbey Farm to Thomas Knight owner of the adjacent Abbots Barton for £5,000. The property consisted of a house with outbuildings and 20 acres, the site of the Abbey, the mill and buildings and 80 acres of land and meadows. The Abbey site and its farm and Abbots Barton were reunited after 230 years and the echo of Thomas Wriothesley in the downfall of Hyde Abbey was finally extinguished.

When Thomas Knight died in 1781, his son Thomas inherited his estate. As his father was 80 when he died, the son may have had control of the management for some years. Edward Hasted writing in 1798 described how Thomas':

> Eminent worth is still remembered by many now living; whose high character for upright conduct and integrity, rendered his life as honourable as it was good, and caused his death to be lamented by everyone as a public loss.[25]

Like his father, Thomas Knight was highly educated and also active in Kentish society and Parliament. He was educated at Eton and Magdalen College, Oxford. He was MP for New Romney in Kent and a Baron of the Cinque Ports. He married Catherine Knatchbull in 1779. However, like many of the families who owned the Abbey lands, there were either no children born or none surviving, and so no direct heirs to the estate. The newly married Thomas and Catherine visited Jane Austen's family at Steventon. They took a fancy to Jane's twelve-year old brother Edward, the third son of the Reverend George Austen and his wife Cassandra Leigh. George Austen shared a great-grandfather with Jane Monk (Thomas Knight's mother). Edward Austen accompanied the Knights on the remainder of their wedding tour of their estates (Abbots Barton must have been on their itinerary) and they asked for him to spend his summers with them in Kent. The relationship flourished and, since they produced no children, Edward was soon regarded as their son. It is not surprising that in 1783 at the age of 16, they officially adopted him.[26] The Austen family tree is given in Figure 3.8. A portrait of Thomas Knight is given in Figure 3.9 and of Edward (Austen) Knight in Figure 3.10.

Figure 3.8: Austen Family Tree

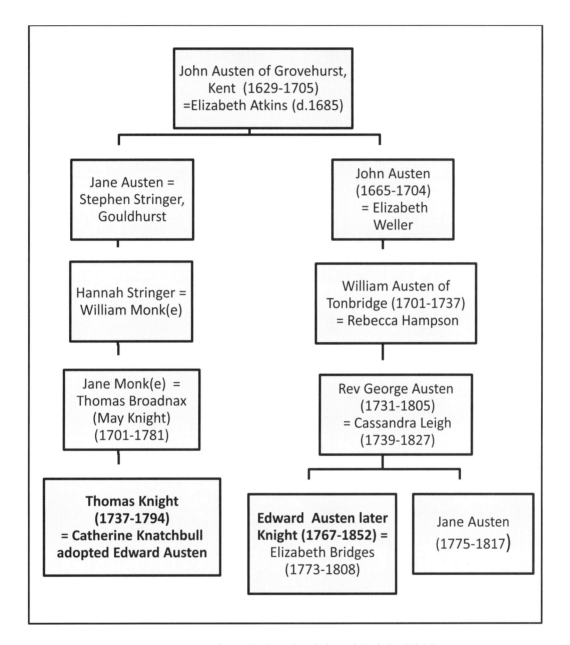

Sources: Burke (1835) and Leigh and Knight (1911).
Those who inherited Abbots Barton are emboldened.
Not all children are included in family trees.

Figure 3.9: Thomas Knight (1737-1794)

Figure 3.10: Edward Austen Knight (1767-1852)

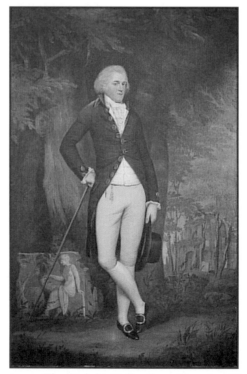

Courtesy: The Knight Collection, Chawton House

Thomas Knight died in 1794 and in his will he left Godmersham and his other estates, which included Abbots Barton, to his widow, Catherine, and confirmed Edward as his adopted heir.[27] He added the clause that if Edward did not have any children, then the estates should pass to his brothers in succession. Four years after her husband's death Catherine decided that the estate was best passed over to Edward and his family to run, than for him to wait for her to die before inheriting. When Mrs Knight died in 1812, Edward as a long standing condition of the inheritance changed his name to Knight. In a letter to Jane Austen, Edward's daughter Fanny comments 'We are therefore all Knights instead of dear old Austen, How I hate it!!!'[28]

Thomas Knight's estates had been tied up in trust between William Deedes (the elder and younger) and Nicholas Cage, of whom only William Deedes (the younger), was still alive.[29] However:

> Catherine Knight out of her love and affection for Edward Austen and in order to advance him to their present possession of the estates which were settled on him and his issue in remainder under the will agreed to convey all the estates unto and to the use of Edward Austen during the joint lives of him and her Catherine Knight subject to a rent charge or clear annual sum of £2,000 clear of all deductions and taxes to be reserved and made passable.[30]

Jane Austen did not hold back in her opinions of her brother's benefactor and in a letter to her sister Cassandra in 1798 comments:

> Mrs Knight giving up the Godmersham estate to Edward was no such prodigious act of generosity after all it seems, for she has reserved herself an income out of it still; this ought to be known, that her conduct may not be over-rated. I rather think Edward shews the most magnanimity of the two, in accepting her resignation with such encumbrances.[31]

There are no details of Edward Knight's involvement with Abbots Barton which continued to be let out to tenants. Edward visited Hampshire often and moved his family there when Godmersham was being redecorated. Edward and Elizabeth had eleven children before she died in 1808. Edward's sons attended Winchester College and Edward made frequent visits to his mother and sisters, who had moved into a cottage on the Chawton Estate after Rev. George Austen's demise. Possibly Edward visited the Hyde estate when he took his sons to school. As the nearest city, the family was likely to have visited Winchester frequently for shopping excursions, although the only mention in Jane's letters is in 1800 when her brother James went to the Winchester fair and bought a horse. The Austens purchased books from Burdon's bookshop (now Wells) in College Street and Jane may have combined a visit to her nephews with a browse at Mr Burdon's.[32]

Winchester residents did feature in the Austens' circle of friends and acquaintances. In a letter to Cassandra in 1778 Jane tells how her father, George Austen, had applied to Mr May, a brewer of Basingstoke and Mr Deane of Winchester for an alehouse on behalf of John (known as Robert and the husband of Nanny Hilliard, née Knight). Jane continues:

> This was my mother's idea, who thought he would be proud to oblige a relation of Edward in return for Edward's accepting his money. He sent a very civil answer indeed, but had no house vacant at present.[33]

Catherine Knight still had an interest in Abbots Barton although she had left the management to Edward. Catherine had moved to Canterbury leaving Edward the pleasure and worries of Godmersham Park. Thomas Knight's trustees who included William Deedes (the younger) still monitored the legalities. Edward's stewardship lasted for 13 years before the decision was made to sell this more remote part of the Knight's lands and his future inheritance.

The economy was buoyant during the earlier part of the nineteenth century. Edward was able to release capital to meet financial demands and cut costs by selling land which was expensive and difficult to maintain. In February 1811 Abbots Barton Farm, extending to 501 acres of uplands and water meadows, was sold for £33,670 to William Simonds of Priors Barton Farm in St Cross. The Simonds were a Reading malting family, whose main outlet in the late 1700s was the London markets. The Hampshire branch of the family had moved into farming and taken the tenancy of Priors Barton Farm from the Dean and Chapter in the 1760s.

To meet the cost, Simonds raised a mortgage of £10,000 from his relative William Blackall Simonds.[34] There was a quit rent due for £2 2s. 7d. p.a. to the manor.[35] This was payable to the Bedford family who still owned the manorial rights of Abbots Worthy, part of which - Bullbridge meads - was included in the sale to Thomas Knight in 1767.

Deeds often contain the history of the estate to provide legal provenance of title. Before compulsory land registration, proof of title required details of the chain of conveyance from the initial grant. A challenge to any link in the chain could undermine the title. The owner was merely the person in possession with the best claim to title, who could at any time be ousted by a superior claimant. The schedule of the land provides key events and dates of transfer. Commencing in 1659 when Anne Mynne died, ownership is traced through the Lewkenors, Elizabeth Knight and her two husbands, then to Thomas (Broadnax) May, his son Thomas, and finally to the adopted Edward Austen. The right to sell was reiterated. Whereas the estates of Godmersham and Chawton could not be sold or exchanged because of a deed of trust, this stipulation did not apply to Abbots Barton. Simonds was required to pay 10s. to Deedes to surrender the remainder of the 99-year lease created in 1798 in order to merge it with the freehold of the property.

Conclusion

Abbots Barton changed little under the custodianship of the name-changing descendants of the Knight family - the Austens, Broadnaxs, Lewkenors, Martins, Mays, and Woodwards. Through rigorous use of entail male, successive inheritors were required to change their name to Knight. The surname continued down the generations even though the estate passed to distant cousins when the current owner of the estates failed to produce an heir.

The Abbey site and home farm eventually passed to the Duke of Bedford, a descendent of Thomas Wriothesley - the man who played a major part in the Abbey's demise. Bedford had ownership for only 34 years before, faced with financial difficulties on his London estates, he was forced to sell Hyde Barton to the neighbouring landowner - Thomas Knight. Some 250 years after the dissolution of Hyde Abbey, this sale reunited the two parts - the ancient and now ruinous site of the Abbey and farm with the Abbots Barton.

Following Thomas Knight's death, his widow and his adopted son, Edward Austen, sought to release capital from their estates. As the Godmersham and Chawton properties were protected from sale, the only land that could be sold was Abbots Barton. After seven owners and 160 years the age of the gentry in Hyde was over.

The story of Abbots Barton is intimately connected to that of Chawton House. Visitors to St Nicholas Church in Chawton, at the entrance gates of the great house, can find the vaults or memorials to Elizabeth Knight (née Martin) and her brothers Richard Knight (born Martin) and Christopher Knight (also born Martin) as well as the pretenders to the Knight estate - Jane Baverstock and John Hinton Knight - who tried to wrest Abbots Barton from the new owner by claiming the estate under Elizabeth Knight's will (See Chapter 6). Displayed at Chawton House are portraits of Elizabeth Knight along with her two husbands - William Knight (born Woodward) and Bulstrode Peachey Knight, Thomas Knight (Broadnax - May) and his wife Jane (née Monk), their son Thomas Knight and, of course, Edward Knight (born Austen), as well as the famous silhouette scene in which the twelve-year old Edward is first presented to his benefactors Thomas and Catherine Knight.

Chapter 4: Abbots Barton and Hyde Abbey Farms

Farming at Abbots Barton in the eighteenth century

Many of the established great landowners were conservative in their estate management. Those that prospered most had a more flexible business-like approach both to the management of their tenants and their directly farmed demesnes. Marriage settlements brought together several estates and, as in the case of Edward Knight, the largest property and that closest to his wife's family, became the main residence. Absenteeism among landowners led to a decline in demesne farming. This was often unavoidable as inherited land was often hundreds of miles from the main estate and travel between parts was time consuming. In 1738 Thomas Knight appointed Edward Randall from Canterbury to be the steward of his farms, lands and tenements on his Hampshire, Surrey and Sussex estates. Randall was told to travel by Dartford, Bromley and Croydon to Guildford or alternatively via Cobham, a journey of three days on horseback.[1]

Absent landowners may have been involved in parliamentary business, in colonial or military service or living abroad. Sometimes when the owner was absent for a short time, was ill or had died, the wife or widow and daughters took an active part in the management roles. Property and farmland was rented to tenant farmers and stewards or agents were employed to oversee the landowner's interests. Sometimes large tenant farmers also acted as stewards over smaller neighbouring properties. The lesser gentry were less likely to be able to afford a steward and took a more active role themselves or employed an attorney or other farmers to collect rents and undertake regular inspections.

Tenancy came with responsibilities to the owner and obligations on the tenant. The landowner provided the land, farmhouse and outbuildings. The land tax was payable by the tenant but potentially recoverable from the landlord. The tenant was responsible for the parish rates. The landowner was concerned with the long term value of his property and was keen to see that the land and buildings were not neglected. For example, on the Barton and Abbey Farms, the state of the water meadows and hatches were of great importance to the fertility of the land. A good landowner sought to undertake improvements that would benefit the property and also advised the tenants how to maximise efficiency by better practices, use of common or waste land and drainage.

Leases often detailed how the land was to be farmed. Tenants were carefully screened to ensure that the valuable assets were protected from damage and neglect. There was a sharp fall in agricultural prices in the late seventeenth century and into the eighteenth century. The net return on land rented to tenants was as low as three per cent. Other forms of investment, for example, in mortgages or in trading and financial companies, were attractive as they were more secure, had a high liquidity, and were easily available.

Surviving letters between Thomas Knight and his steward Randall give an insight into his involvement in the daily running of the Hampshire estates. This must have been challenging as the quickest time for a letter to arrive was several days. Letters dated 1740, 1742 and 1757 show Thomas Knight was fully aware of the issues on his estates and the need for financial acumen. There were instructions on tenancy matters including heriots (payment on the death of a manorial tenant) and the adding of further lives to leases:

> As to the heriot which you have seized off the widow Prowting you may take six shillings for it. Don't care to take five shillings as before because in time they may claim a custom of paying five shillings for a heriot.[2]

He kept up to date with the value of his stock:

> I would have you go to John Budd as soon as you can and desire him to inform you the price of my ewes and ewe lambs. They are all very healthy and in good order, and the lambs just now weaned. The ewes are all of Forder's breed and some have four teeth and some six teeth, none of more, and my shepherd says, they will weigh from eleven to twelve pounds a quarter and the lambs will be of the same sort and size.[3]

Since lamb's teeth grow at a rate of two per year, these animals were two to three years old.

He was aware of market economics:

> Nicholas should not sell anymore corn for present and I would have him still continue to keep it back, till the Act is past for taking the prohibition upon exportation, which will probably be in a week or ten days, of which I will give you notice.[4]

Abbots Barton was not left to be run by the tenants and there were strong links with the Hyde community. Thomas was not a distant landowner but showed concern about his workers. In 1742 his (Chawton) gamekeeper John Gunner appears to have been involved in an affray and was due to stand trial at Winchester Assizes. He asked Randall to write to Mr Sheppard (a tenant at Barton Farm) or anybody at Winchester.[5]

Randall's stewardship included responsibility for Barton Farm and its tenant Mr Waldron, and for carrying out negotiations with the owner of Hyde Abbey Farm, the Duke of Bedford, over the operation of the water meadows whose functioning affected both estates. Randall reports:

> Friday 18th. I was at Mr Sheppard and met Mr Davis, the Duke of Bedford's steward, and Mr Gatehouse and viewed all the work in the mead and they seemed very agreeable and gave order for the doing of everything that Mr Sheppard could propose which would be for any advantage to either. Waldron seemed not to be satisfied but stayed but a little part of the time which they were in the mead with us. And they both declared they would from that time take no notice of this mischief and Mr Davis declared if he made any further disturbance he should leave the farm.[6]

Details of the farming practices and financial information at Abbots Barton or the Abbey Farms are sparse. However, Vancouver's survey of 1810, which was drawn up for the Board of Agriculture and Internal Improvement, gives a detailed picture of agriculture in Hampshire at the start of the nineteenth century following radical changes which had taken place over 200 years. Hampshire was traditionally a sheep and corn area. The ideal farm allowed for mixed agriculture utilising both downland and water meadows. Vancouver sums it up thus:

> And hence rises the favourite idea among the down farmers, that no farm can be advantageous disposed for the general circumstances of that county, unless it has water-meadows at one end and maiden down at the other.[7]

Vancouver noted that most farmhouses and offices, like the Barton house and farm, were sited near the river or streams and rarely were there any outposts on the downs.

Hampshire was a sheep breeding region. Ewes were deemed a sound investment, not only for the production of lambs and wool but for producing manure to improve fertility. There were challenges to keeping ewes as they were susceptible to harsh winter conditions, required high quality feeds during lambing and needed better care than rams. Although the wool industry had declined in Winchester, sheep husbandry was an important part of the farming balance with the yield of arable land being dependent on the size of the flock. Apart from their meat sheep were valuable as 'the only dung-carriers to distant parts'. Flocks were limited by the shortage of fodder during the winter and at lambing time. The construction of the water meadows in Hampshire in the late 1600s improved the supplies of sheep feed. The flooding of the meadows protected them from hard frosts allowing the early development of young shoots of grass. There was little change in some practices over the centuries. In an interview recorded in 1969, John Barrow Simonds (a descendent of William Simonds who purchased Abbots Barton from the Knight family) talks about the importance of shepherds for the hurdled flocks on Barton Farm in St Cross. Like Abbots Barton, the farm had large flocks of sheep kept on the arable fields and water meadows. The early succulent grass provided nutrition for the pregnant ewes from January. John Barrow describes how his great, great grandfather had imported merino lambs to cross with the Hampshire Down sheep to improve the wool. [8]

As wheat prices rose in the late eighteenth century, arable farming increased and farmers adopted a range of rotation practices. Wheat crops were followed by spring corn, then grass and clover ley. The latter was best left for two years, providing a mowing for hay in the first year and then grazing thereafter. Leases usually contained covenants to ensure that tenants looked after the land. Conditions restricted the ploughing of pasture without permission. Initially there was a stipulation that all useful by-products, such as hay, straw, stubble and dung were used on the farm and not sold, but this was later waived when feeds and fertilisers became more easily and cheaply available. Even rape and malt dust nourished crops. Another condition ensured that the land was fully utilised or fertilised by setting a minimum size for sheep flocks. The stipulated details of rotations were to ensure a mix of grain and other crops to protect the fertility of the land. However, when tenancies were coming to an end there was nothing to prevent the more reckless tenant from forgoing good practices to maximise possible yields, leaving the land in a poor state for the owner and subsequent tenant. [9]

Vancouver praised the farmers as:

> Generally a smart, active, intelligent set of men, well educated, liberal and inspired with a general education emulation for the improvement of their stock, particularly their flocks, on the success of which their very all depends. [10]

This was the era of advances in crop management. An experiment was carried out by the South Hants Agricultural Society on a 200-acre downland arable farm in Clanfield (in east Hampshire) to compare the profitability of the use of drill and broadcast husbandry. [11] Fisher's experiments on agricultural yields were still 100 years away in the future so the results of these early experiments were unlikely to have had adequate controls for confounding factors, though they indicated an improved system of broadcast management to be the most beneficial. Other evidence from several efficient farms provided a full breakdown of costs and benefits under different rotation regimes. The small sample of five gave an annual profit per acre of between £1 and £2. The values of the crops have a small variance: wheat from £12 to £15, barley from £8 to £11, turnips from £4 to £6 and clover and grass £7 or £8 per acre. Costs deviated considerably notably for wheat, with a range from £5 6s. to £13 10s., and turnips, from £4 to £11 9s.. The chief factor was the cost of manure, which added £4 or £5 to the cost of turnip production and a little less for wheat. Where sheep were used, this cost was saved. The use of sheep folds led to a more even application of manure. [12]

Rentals, which formed the basis of much of the tithes and other taxation which landowners were subjected to, varied considerably according to the type of land. Typical annual rentals per acre given by Vancouver for the mid Hampshire downland (District II) were: the old downs and sheep walks - 5s. to 10s.; high land with thin soils - 12s.; more fertile tillage land - 17s.; upper meadows and good pasture land - 32s.; water meadows - between 40s. and 60s.; and accommodation land (noted as in the neighbourhood of Winchester) - £3 to £5. [13] The value Vancouver put on water meadows is consistent with other evidence. The advantage of Winnall Mead was put at over £30 per year in 1752 and the extensive 1,271 acres of water meadows that stretched from Winchester College's mill to Swaythling (near Southampton) was assessed in 1808 at £4,050, that is £3 12s. per acre. [14] Un-watered meadows were worth only one-third of this. The accommodation land close to the City was not farmed but was a lucrative source of income as it could be rented to butchers for drove animals awaiting slaughter or for horses. The rent for an entire farm was typically between £200 and £800 p.a. depending on size. [15]

Hop production

Winchester had several breweries, many of which were situated in Hyde. Their origins went back to the monastery and were an important adjunct to farming on the Barton and Abbey Farms. The exact output from hop production is not known though legal documents and estate maps give some indication of land use. In 1726 Barton Farm had two hop areas of 13¾ acres on the uplands and ¾ acre nearer to the farmhouse. By 1771, the large hop growing area on the downs was described as the Old Hop Garden, but whether this indicated a mature plot or that hops had been grubbed up is not known. In 1767, the Abbey Farm had a small hop garden of ½ acre close to the house as well as a malthouse. The farm had a large malting with two floors and a cistern and kiln to wet and dry 20 quarters of malt at one time. Grain was measured in quarters of a hundredweight (cwt.). One quarter is equivalent to 12.7 kg.

Hop production was lucrative to farms in close proximity to a city like Winchester. There was heavy demand for fertiliser but proximity to a town kept the costs of transporting nutrients to the fields to a minimum. A ready supply of night soil or privy manure and urine was available along with manure from the stables. Vancouver enthused 'and too much pain cannot be used in collecting them together.'[16] The best class of manure came from carnivorous animals, then in order of desirability: birds which had been fed on pulses and grain, horses, sheep, grazing bullocks, and finally milch cows and rabbits. [17] Vancouver's survey gave a detailed breakdown of the costs involved based on a six-acre hop field - see Tables 4.1 and 4.2.[18] These estimates are very detailed and the cost of finance at 10% is included along with taxation.

Hop fields were valuable and subject to both parish rates and tithes based on the rack or market rent. The establishment of hop fields required cleaning and manuring the land. Although the use of the farm's own dung would not necessitate a cash outlay, it was still valued at market cost as it could have been used elsewhere. As Abbots Barton's hop field was adjacent to the Andover Road, the delivery of the manure would not have been a problem. Costings assumed that the ploughing, harrowing and tillage was performed by the farmer at three-quarters of the market rate for a labourer and no account was made for the construction or maintenance of the hop kiln. Over the first three years, the set up costs amounted to £53 per acre; however in the third summer the first hops valued at £20 reduced this cost to £33. There were considerable on-going costs in running the hop fields including labour, replacement poles and charcoal used in the drying process. Once established the hop grounds generated an income of £52 per acre. Barton Farm's hop garden could have provided an income of over £700 p.a..

Table 4.1: Expenditure per acre from setting up a hop field

	£	s.	d.
Four ploughings at 9s. per acre each.	1	16	0
Harrowing, dragging, rolling and cleansing the ground at 5s. each time.	1	0	0
15 carts of home or town dung of 30 bushels each, cost and carriage included.	7	10	0
Barrowing, spreading etc.	0	6	0
Parochial levies 6s. in £ on the rack rent.	0	15	0
Tithe great and small compounded crop and fallow, at one quarter of the rack rent.	0	12	6
Rent.	2	10	0
Gripping and fencing.	0	1	0
Expenses accruing per acre in the first year.	**£14**	**10s.**	**6d.**
Interest on capital.	0	14	6
4,300 nursery plants at 6d. per 100.	1	1	6
Labour per contract per acre.	4	0	0
Sticks to mark the hills.	0	6	0
Planting.	1	10	0
Rent, tithe, taxes, gripping and fencing as above.	3	18	6
Expenses accruing per acre in the second year.	**£26**	**1s.**	**0d.**
Interest on this sum.	1	6	0
Dressing of manure, as above stated.	7	16	0
Labour per contract.	4	0	0
3000 small poles for training the young plants at 5s. per 100.	7	10	0
Rent, tithe, taxes etc. as above.	3	18	6
Expenses accruing per acre in the third year.	**£50**	**11s.**	**6d.**
Interest on this sum.	2	10	6
Total expenditure per acre up to the close of the third year, from the time plantation was begun.	**£53**	**2s.**	**0d.**
Hops in the third summer on an average of 2¼ cwt. and after deducting the expenses of gathering, drying, duty and sending to market.	20	0	0
Balance chargeable on the expenses of establishing the hop-ground.	**£33**	**2s.**	**0d.**

Source: Vancouver (1810) pp. 201-4.

Table 4.2: Income and expenditure from established hop production

Expenditure (per acre)	£	s.	d.
Interest on set up costs £33 2s.	1	13	0
3900 full sized poles, 16 ft in length, cost and carriage 22s. per 100 amounts to £33, the annual interest is:	1	13	0
500 new poles, annually required per acre for keeping up the stock at 22s. per 100.	5	10	0
Annual dressing of manure.	7	16	0
Labour per contract.	4	4	6
Picking 630 lbs of hops, the average produced over 7 years, at 1½d. per bushel green hops which weighs 1½ lb when dry.	2	12	6
Pole pulling.	0	7	6
Measuring hops and attendance on the pickers.	0	11	0
Carting to kiln.	0	12	0
24 sacks of charcoal for drying at 1s. 9d. per sack	2	2	0
Attendance at drying.	0	4	6
Bagging 9d. per cwt.	0	4	9
Carriage to fair and market charges.	1	5	3
Interest on first cost of ladder, surplices, hair-cloths, bags and small implements exclusively belonging to the hop-ground and kiln, and valued at £5, ten per cent interest.	0	10	0
Allowance of middlings or beer and rolls.	0	3	6
Supper at end of gathering, amounts per acre.	1	2	6
Duty on 630 lbs. of hops at 2d. per pound.	5	5	0
Rent, tithe and taxes as above.	3	18	6
Total expenses accruing on an acre of hop ground when in full plant.	39	15	6
Annual balance per acre in favour of hop husbandry.	12	5	9
	£52	1s.	3d.
Income			
630 lbs of hops (average produced over 7 years) and selling at average price of 19½ p. per pound.	51	3	9
Value of refuse poles.	0	10	0
Value of hop-bines.	0	7	6
Total value of an acre of hop ground in full plant.	**£52**	**1s.**	**3d.**

Source: Vancouver (1810) pp. 201-4.

Water Meadows

Water meadows, also described as water mead or wet mead, were an important part of farming in the chalk valleys of Hampshire and neighbouring counties over 300 years. Several books, detailing landowners' experiences in Hertfordshire and Dorset were published in the early 1600s, promoted their use.[19] Over time the systems became more complex, making the construction expensive, and, because water meadows were a permanent improvement, the expense fell on the landowner, although tenants were often asked to contribute. [20] The landowners in Hyde were proactive in minimising the operational costs by preventing potential problems from mismanagement or neglect of their water meadows. Management costs were an increasing liability on the meadows just south of Winchester: Marsh Moors cost £3 6s. per acre in 1670-72 and Otterbourne Mead cost £6 per acre in 1730-31 to maintain. Prices were little changed in the early nineteenth century at between £5 and £6 per acre, but had risen to £25 to £40 per acre by the middle of the century.[21] Expertise was needed to ensure that the land was carefully levelled and the network of channels, drains, weirs and hatches constructed to allow the meadow to be fully flooded and the water to flow continuously rather than stagnate. Otterbourne Mead is an example where bad design, inadequate supply of water and poor drainage, with lack of overall management and little collaboration between neighbours lead to disaster. Initially, the water meadows were efficiently operated leading to a doubling of cattle on the land. However, by 1740, their condition had deteriorated and even alterations costing £163, did not alleviate the problems. Investors saw little return and by 1800 any benefit was marginal.[22]

The operation of the water meadows required the employment of experts (watermen, meadmen or downers) who followed a strict timetable subject to weather conditions. Preparation of the land included: smoothing and levelling, especially when it had been used by cattle who had 'poached' the marshy soil, and the cleaning of the main and smaller channels. The meadows were flooded weekly between late November or early December to the beginning of March, thus protecting the land from frosts and allowing the nutrients in the water to fertilise the land. It was essential that the water continually flowed, described as in at a trot and off at a gallop, otherwise the grass would be damaged and weeds and rushes would take over. [23] Water extraction had to be paid for and on-going maintenance was essential. Renewing a hatch was expensive and required securing firm foundations by piling the river bed, building walls some 48 feet long and 8 feet high to contain the river, and the installation of heavy wooden hatches.[24]

The flooding of the meadows produced an early growth of young succulent grass. This facilitated early lambing and increased the viability of larger flocks. The ewes and lambs were kept on the meadows for five or six weeks. The use of hurdles increased efficiency and they were so designed to let lambs through to feed on fresh grass ahead of their mothers. One acre accommodated four hundred couples (ewe with lamb) and the value on the rental market was put at 6d. to 8d. per couple per week. The sheep were fed on the meadows during the day (8a.m. to 6p.m.) and at night they were taken to the downs, where they were kept in a fold using wicker gates. This ensured a rich and easy application of manure to land, which was then used for spring-sown barley.[25] Sheep were taken to the higher pastures once the warmer weather ensured grass growth. This avoided the dangers of liver fluke and foot-rot on the damp pasture. The meadows were left for hay. The watered meadows produced twice the yield of un-watered ones with the difference more marked in years of drought. The hay crop was mown in mid-June. Second crops were unusual as the land was utilised for cattle and was particularly beneficial to milch cows.

Vancouver itemised the costs of the various tasks on an established water meadow (see Table 4.3). The most important tasks were to keep the water flowing by removing weeds, keeping the sluices in good repair and ensuring the meadows are level. Income allowed for 400 couples at 7d. per couple per day and a hay crop weighing 30 cwt., although this may have been as low as 22 cwt.. The estimated annual profit of over £3 per acre may be an over-statement as it was based on taking a second hay crop and afterwards grass.[26] However such value is difficult to assess if the farmer was also offering use of his land on the open market. Those with extensive meadows rented them out for grazing with the additional benefit of enriching the land.

Water meadows were seen as a safe investment with a good return in excess of 35 per cent using Vancouver's estimates. His calculations gave all costs, including tithes and other parochial charges, and allowed for interest payments on setting up costs. The (simple) interest was equivalent to 5 per cent on the setting up costs of £5 per acre. Although the benefits far outweighed the costs, the operation of the water meadows required clear agreements between neighbouring landowners, tenants and users downstream, and legal disputes were common. Owners sought to defend their rights and ensure the viability of their meadows.[27] The problem was that there was no central management of the water meadows binding all the owners and tenants, with each contributing to the costs through rates as tended to happen with salt marshes and sea defences.

There were continuous disagreements between the landowners and tenants on the different parts of the water meadows between Abbots Worthy and Winchester. In 1675, when Edmund Clerke was owner of Abbey Farm, he took legal proceedings to issue a bond with a penalty of £50 against Henry Dymock the tenant of Abbots Barton Farm. Dymock, described as a bounder, had committed 'several trespasses & drainage' on Clerke's land. He had opened several hatches at the same time out of the Great River to flood his land at Winnall, Kings Worthy and Hide (sic) Barton with the result that the river no longer ran its course. The bond required Dymock not to use hatches, bays or sluices for taking or conveying water into his meadows, except from two small hatches at the town end of Winnall Mead. Neither was he to break down or spoil any banks, bays, bridges or hatches belonging to Clerke. Other bonds were issued against Guy Badcock (a tanner) and Joan Fifield of Abbots Worthy for £30 and they were required to open only one hatch at a time. Action was taken by John Primmer (the tenant of Abbey Farm) against Thomas Cooper (the tenant at Barton Farm). Cooper had drawn so much water into the Black Ditch it resulted in flooding and damage to Primmer's meadows.[28]

Figure 4.1: Water meadows near Abbots Barton farmhouse

Figure 4.2: Neglected water meadows – the Abbey Mill Stream

Table 4.3: Annual income and expenditure per acre on an established water meadow

Expenditure	£	s.	d.
Interest on money expended in forming water meadows.	0	5	0
Keeping sluices, stop-gates weirs etc. in repair.	0	7	6
Scouring the principal carriages, trimming, cleaning out the smaller branches, smoothing, levelling and righting the surface of the meadow, preparatory to its receiving winter watering.	0	5	0
Trimming and cleansing out all the conducting branches after the spring feeding.	0	0	6
Ditto after the hay crop.	0	0	6
Mowing.	0	4	0
Making.	0	4	6
Carting and stacking.	0	8	0
Thatching.	0	3	6
Rent.	2	10	0
Tithes on a rack rent, commutation for the whole occupation.	0	12	6
Parochial assessments.	0	15	0
Hurdles for penning off and dividing the meadow, with expense of removal.	0	2	6
Total expense per acre per year.	5	18	6
Net profit per acre per year.	3	4	10
	£9	3s.	4d.
Income			
400 couples (ewe and lamb) for one day at 7d. per couple weekly.	1	13	4
30 cwt. hay at 3s. 3d. per cwt.	4	17	6
Value of second crop and after grass until shut up for watering.	2	12	6
Total value of produce per acre per year.	**£9**	**3s.**	**4d.**

Source: Vancouver (1810) pp. 276-277.

Water from the river was valuable to the tenants, who claimed a right to take it without payment since the practice was established from time immemorial. In 1729 Thomas Broadway (a currier) and others faced court proceedings accused of pilling up 20 cwt. of stone, extending to 12 feet in length and 3 feet in breadth. This obstructed the water courses of Itchen River and prevented its flow into Winchester. They were found guilty and made to restore the Carriage Bridge and fill and make good where the ground was washed away.

The problem of the flooding of Hyde Abbey meadows by the tenant of Barton Farm did not stop. In 1738 a survey of the state of river and meadows at Hyde Farm was undertaken for the Duke of Bedford. Bays had been made to facilitate the diversion of water on to the 50 acres of meadows at Barton Farm. The water was then thrown back into the Black Ditch, which did not have the current for draining the Barton meadows. The banks had overflowed and the Hyde meadows were damaged. Although the Durngate River was 8 to 10 feet in width, the overgrown sedges obstructed the water flow in many places. Even though the Black Ditch was widened from 14 to 28 feet, it was still not adequate to cope with the water put back into it. Mr Sheppard (the tenant at Barton Farm) had erected a carrier which drew on four single hatches on the Durngate River to water 15 acres of meadow, which when it was returned to the river, drowned the Duke's land.

The only way to resolve the problem was for the various landowners and tenants to reach an agreement. Mr Knight put forward his proposals, which of course were advantageous to him.

> Mr Knight is to give leave to tenant at Durngate Mills to let the Duke's tenant have water at all times when they can spare it paying an acknowledgement and to let his tenant or workmen come upon Barton Farm to cut the weeds and clean the Abbey Mill Stream as often as they think fit not doing any damage and in view there of Mr Knight's tenant at Barton to have liberty of making a bay at the head of the City Ditch as hath been usual and to have the liberty of taking of water out of the Abbey Mill Stream to water Chappel Mead as is usual and to have the liberty of coming upon the grounds to cut the weeds and cleanse Black Ditch, not doing any injury and to have the liberty of cutting the weeds and cleansing the Fence Ditch that runs between Barton Farm and Hide Meadows for the draining of the water from the meads called Home Meads belonging to Barton Farm. If everything is settled as here proposed it would be much to the advantage of both the estates especially to his Grace.[29]

The locations of the waterways are shown in Figure 2.4.

By the sixteenth century there was a fulling mill (thought to be on the site of the Willow Tree pub) and a corn mill at Durngate.[30] The wide rectangular corn mill straddled the main stream of the Itchen, which was divided into two races. The original mill house was on the south side and access across the river clung to the north of the three-storey building. The upper floor lay under the steeply pitched roof (Figure 1.11 and Figure 3).

The Duke of Bedford was described as 'a man of excellent parts, thought deficient in common sense, was in the highest degree passionate, but perfectly good natured.'[31] He had 'a keen sense of his own importance, and his pride and arrogance frequently caused offence.'[32] The Duke's reply to Mr May (not addressed as Mr Knight) was more extensive, advantageous to himself, and carefully listed Knight's responsibilities. The letter gave a further insight into the operation of the water meadows. The Duke stated that it was an advantage for the tenant of Hyde (Abbey) Farm to have water out of Durngate River when the miller could spare it. Previously the tenant had to request it and the miller could hinder the tenant. The tenants of Barton Farm were responsible at their own expense to clear the weeds and were required to cleanse the Abbey Mill Stream. If they failed to do so, they were obliged to pay 30s. p.a. for the work to be done. The issue was identified as follows:

> By working a bay at the head of the City Ditch there is five times the quantity of water thrown down into the Ditch as usually would ... and which run through the tenant of Barton Farm meadows and empty itself into Black Ditch which overflows the Ditch into Hyde Meadows. Tenants of Hyde Farm always had the benefit of the Mill Stream water to themselves if they were to part with any it would be a great prejudice to them.[33]

The Duke proposed that the bay at the head of City Ditch be pulled down and the Durngate River cleansed so the current and water had final courses. The tenant of Hyde Farm would have the right to open one hatch when he pleased, and two hatches when the miller could spare it, in order to water 20 acres lying near Durngate Mill. Furthermore he had the right to open three hatches at the upper end of Hyde Meadows to carry water on to the Carriage Bridge. He was to cut weeds in the Black Ditch only after the weeds in the Durngate River were cut. He could drain the meadows into Black Ditch making an unspecified payment, provided he had not allowed the water to overflow the banks and flood Hyde Meadows.

These proposals were made under the advice of their respective lawyers. The water rights between Kingsworthy Mill and Durngate Mills, with the exception of the City's claim for water in the City Ditch and water flowing through Arrow Hole hatch to Abbey Mill, belonged to Knight as the head lessee of Durngate Mills. The owners of the land bordering the Durngate River had a duty to maintain the banks of the river and cut weeds against their respective land. Maintenance of the banks of the Abbey Mill Stream running through Barton Farm was the responsibility of the owner of the Hyde Abbey lands but the owner of Barton Farm was responsible for cutting the weeds.

A meeting held on the 23rd May 1738 ratified the final proposals. These were very detailed and give a full appreciation of the complexity of operating water meadows that crossed several farms operated by many sub-tenants (See Table 4.4). Present were Mr Knight (himself), Mr Davis (steward of Duke of Bedford), Mr Sheppard (tenant of Barton Farm), Mr Waldron (tenant of Hyde Abbey Meads), and Mr Drewett and Mr Barney (tenants of Durngate Mills). All present consented to the proposals. Mr Knight and the tenants of the mills raised the issue of whether there was enough water for the mills when the proposals were executed. However they were 'desirous that things may be tried and banks and hatches made good and weeds cut.' The lawyers and the miller were appointed to view the mill working when the hatches were opened and the miller agreed not to draw his flood hatches, thus preventing the watering of the lands above, when he was not grinding.

The many landed interests in Hyde and Winnall moors, showed the need for the distant landowners of Abbots Barton and the Abbey Farms to be aware of both the operational practices of their tenants, and the behaviour of the neighbouring landowners' tenants. Even though lawyers formed a crucial part of the negotiations, site visits were necessary to ensure everyone recognised the problems and were amenable to the resolution proposed. It was commendable that Thomas Knight had travelled from Canterbury to deal with the matter, but not surprising that the Duke of Bedford delegated to his steward.

Table 4.4: Details of proposals agreed in May 1738 by the owners and tenants of Abbots Barton and Hyde Abbey Farms.[34]

Knight's tenants take as much water at the head of the City Ditch as the city have right to take in at that place and at Bullbridge Knowle too.

And Duke of Bedford or his tenant shall not obstruct Mr Knight's tenant in his making a bay across the river at the head of the City Ditch which he shall have liberty to make except between 1st June to 1st November each year.

And for convenience of watering the meads between Kingsworthy Mills and Durngate Mills proposed that Mr Knight shall give liberty for Duke of Bedford tenants of Hyde Abbey Mead to take water out of the Durngate River at two of the three hatches at the Carriage Bridge being 2 feet 10 in. wide each and at the second hatch being not above 3 feet wide the paying an acknowledgement of forty shillings p.a.. And all other hatches now standing against Hyde Abbey Mead shall be damned up.

And Mr Knight to give liberty to Mr Waldron's tenant to take water out of Durngate River at one hatch less than 2 feet wide paying an acknowledgement of eleven shillings p.a.. And all other hatches now standing in Mr Waldron's mead shall be damned up.

And Mr Knight's tenant at Barton shall take water out of Durngate River at two hatches less than 4 feet 6 in. in whole for watering part of Barton Meads next to Durngate River and all other hatches damned up.

And Mr Knight shall give liberty for Bedford's tenant at Bullbridge Meads to take water out of Durngate River by one hatch less than 3 feet paying thirty-five shillings p.a. and other hatches damned up.

And Mr Knight shall give liberty for tenant of City Meads to take water out of Durngate River by one hatch less than 2 feet paying ten shillings p.a. and other hatches damned up. And no water shall be taken out of Durngate River at hatches from 1st June to 1st November.

And the owners of such land which takes water out of the Durngate River shall maintain the banks and hatches belonging to several lands from leaking and shall twice in each year (at ten days' notice given to these by the miller at Durngate Mills) and cleanse weeds out of Durngate River against their respective lands.

And in case any owner of such lands shall after such notice neglect or refuse to repair his banks or hatches or cut and cleanse the weeds out of the river the miller shall have the power to repair, cut and cleanse and stop up hatches belonging to such land till he shall be paid his full cost for so doing.

And the Duke of Bedford tenant shall give liberty for Mr Knight's tenant at Barton to take water out of the Abbey Mill Stream for a fortnight in year (which time the Duke's tenant shall allot) for watering Chappel Mead. Mr Knight's tenant to pay one shilling.

And whereas weeds in Black Ditch ought to be cut and cleansed twice a year by persons whose land adjoins and Abbey Mill Stream ought to be cut and cleansed by the tenant at Barton Farm, Fence Ditch between Hyde Abbey Meads and Barton land ought to be cut by the tenants of lands. It's agreed by Mr Sheppard and Mr Waldron tenants of the land. It will be most convenient that the tenants of Barton Farm shall cut and cleanse such ditch and part of Barton Ditch running through the meads and the tenants of the meads shall cut and cleanse Abbey Mill Stream for which the tenant of Barton Farm shall pay five shillings p.a..

Figure 4.3: Abbots Barton Dairy

Abbots Barton and Hyde Abbey Farms

Legal documents and surveys give some insight into the extent and value of the farms from the early 1700s onwards. With enclosures, land exchanges to consolidate estate ownership, and steps to avoid legal disputes over boundaries, the employment of surveyors to undertake an accurate survey of land was a common occurrence. Maps ranged from simple sketches to more detailed and colourful works of art.

Maps were also commissioned by the Mayor, Bailiffs and Commonality of Winchester. These included the 1753 map of part of Barton Farm and Hyde Abbey Farm, drawn by William Godson (Figure 4.5). The extent of the River Itchen, ditches and water meadows are clearly portrayed. The water from the Black Ditch and meadows was channelled into the City via the Upper, Middle and Lower Brooks. To the east of these were Durngate Mills and beyond the River Itchen, the parish of Winnall, and the houses in Wales Street. The land lying beyond North Walls belonged to the City. Abbots Barton farmhouse stood isolated alongside Barton Causeway. Alongside the stream marked Upper Brooks, Nuns Walk took foot travellers from St Bartholomew's Church to the Worthys.[35]

Abbots Barton farmhouse was a large house with the stone-built range at right angles to a timbered framed wing. Timbers in the wing have a felling date of 1491.[36] The timber-frame with brick infilling was built on stone foundations. The house and outbuildings were renovated in the eighteenth century. There is a two-storey dairy cottage, a barn built in 1799 which was converted from stables, and a dovecote (Figure 4.4). The dairy cottage is just visible on the south side and the dovecote on the north side.

Figure 4.4: Abbots Barton Farmhouse from the east

Figure 4.5: Part of Barton Farm and Hyde Abbey Farm 1753

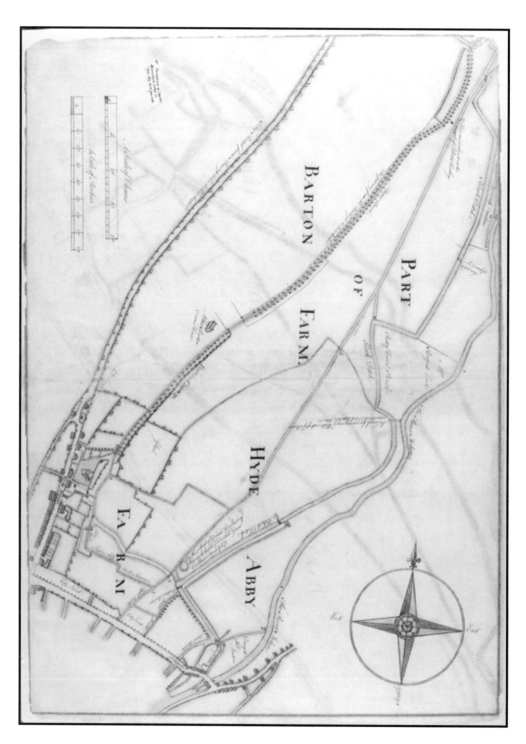

Source: HRO:W/F5/1/10. Reproduced with permission of Winchester City Council.

In 1726 Bulstrode Peachey Knight (the second husband of Elizabeth Knight) commissioned Meridith Jones to value Abbots Barton Farm in order to set a rent. It is not known if this involved a survey or if known field sizes were used. Jones appears to have been employed at Peachey's other estate in West Dean, Sussex. He recommended the tenant should be responsible for further work.

> Thirteen acres of hop ground which is now planted I throw in with the neighbouring arable as it must shortly be converted to that use. Upon the whole I think the farm a good bargain all £300 a year, the price I have set being much short of what land goes at with us at West Dean. If you let a lease t'would be very proper to oblige the tenant to plant a hedge against Andover Road and Worthy Common field which in time will be a considerable advantage to your farm. ... Forward of which there's above 20 acres more which I take notice of that is not very prosperous, of last year's sowing.[37]

The field names and their extent are given in Table 4.5. Some of the locations are not clearly specified.[38] The first nine fields - Lime Kilns, Hop Garden, Gallows Field, Round Field, Banks Field (later called Hangar), Upper, Middle and Lower Bottom Field, and the Down - are described later as the Uplands and lay between the Andover and Worthy Roads. The remaining fields lay east of the Worthy Road and stretched down to the River Itchen, with the last four fields being water meadows. Locations can be discerned from a later survey carried out in 1769 (Figure 4.6 and Table 4.8).

The rental cost of £300 for the 496 acres listed gave an average value of 12s. per acre. Not all the land was productive. Some 105 acres of down was deemed in a poor condition. There were 59 acres of land close to the water and 11½ acres were given over to hops. Furthermore there were 17 acres of waste land, 10 acres of hedges and 27 acres of what are described as rivers but may have included the water meadow system.[39]

A detailed description of the Hyde Abbey Farm estate was given in the lease and release document dated 1733 between James Morecroft and the Duke of Bedford. The fields are named and extent given.

> Also all houses, outhouses, barns, stables, edifices, buildings, bank sides, orchards, gardens, lands, meadow pastures, fording ways, water, water streams, easements, woods, under-woods, commons, (?), advantages, privileges, hereditaments and appurtenances to the great or capital messuage and site of the Abbey of Hyde, mill, meadows and land belonging to have and to hold of the great or capital messuage and site of the Abbey of Hide, mill meadows and land.

> Great or capital messuage, outhouses, stable, garden, orchards estimated at 20 acres. The site of the Abbey of Hide and water corn mill with outhouses, water streams and appurtenance and meadows called the Parks, Mill Mead, Flag Mead and the Banks, Dutton and Arrow Hole Mead, Great Dutton Mead, Rogers Acre Mead, a meadow called Five Acres, a meadow called Thirteen Acres, a meadow called Ten Acres, a meadow called Seven Acres, a meadow called Nine acres, Chalk Mead, a meadow

called Ten Acres, a meadow called Eight Acres, a meadow called Six Acres, Miller's Mead, Drews Purrock, another purrock adjacent containing five acres.[40]

These can be located by reference to Figure 2.5, 4.8 and 4.9, and Tables 4.9 and 4.10.

Table 4.5: Abbots Barton Farm in 1726

	acres	rods	perches
Lime Kilns	8	1	12
Hop Garden	13	3	9
Gallows Field	55	2	8
Round Field	54	1	34
Banks Field	12	0	31
Lower Bottom Field	12	2	7
Middle Bottom Field	6	1	1
Upper Bottom Field	6	1	1
Down	136	2	16
Coney Garden	13	2	32
Hop Garden	0	3	1
Orchard	1	3	24
Causeway	2	0	9
Lower Causeway	1	2	13
Gate room & garden	1	2	15
Broad Close	10	1	7
Dell Close	14	3	9
Waterside Close	33	2	34
Mill Lane Furlong	24	2	5
Bunting Mead	1	2	35
Mead beyond Black Ditch	12	1	2
The Lays	3	2	24
Home Mead	5	1	22
More meadow	62	1	14
Total[41]	496a.	1r.	5p.

Source: 39M89/E/B560/1-11

Samuel Waldron was tenant-at-will, occupying Hyde Abbey house (the manor house) with outhouses and buildings adjoining, and just over 107 acres of good meadow and 10 acres of very good pasture land. This commanded an annual rent of £120. The value of the farm was given as £3,100, equivalent to about 25 years' purchase. Samuel Tewkesbury took over the lease from Samuel Waldron for eleven years from Michaelmas 1753. Also included was the malthouse in Hyde Street (vacant after the death of Allen Pyott) valued at £700 and rented at £35 p.a.. This was described as a messuage and large malting with two floors, and a cistern and kiln to wet and dry 20 quarters of malt at one time. Tewkesbury also leased 22½ acres on Bedford's Abbots Worthy manor (passed down from Thomas Wriothesley), which included Bull Bridge, Badcocks, Out Hooks and Jenny Creeks, for £20 p.a..

As a preliminary to John, Duke of Bedford selling the estate in 1767, a map of the Manor of Hyde was produced, probably by William Godson. Bedford had purchased the estate in 1733 from the Morecrofts. Apart from financial problems with his London estates, he suffered personal loss with the deaths of his son (the Marquess of Tavistock), who was thrown from a horse, and his daughter-in-law soon afterwards.[42]

The map, measuring 30 inches by 25¾ inches showed Hyde Abbey house and attached lands.[43] Hyde Street is described as the road to Stratton. The crest, at the top of the map, consists of three shells or escallops and a rampant lion, and belonged to the Russell family, whose seat was at Stratton.[44] The map details field names and their acreages were given both on the plots and in a table, but these are faded and illegible in places. Annotations provide information on land ownership: the terrace of tenements just outside the North Gate was sold off and Taylor had use of the City ditch lying outside the City walls. The eastern prospect of Hyde House and gardens are shown in detail. To the south of the house was Hercules' Garden depicted with a statue. East of this, but not adjacent to the house, was the Kitchen Garden. On the eastern side of the house was Green Court and north of this the Rose Garden. Table 4.6 details the estate as accurately as can be discerned from the map. The fields all lay on the eastern side of Hyde Street and benefitted from the system of water meadows.

Hyde Abbey Farm, consisting of a house with outbuildings and 20 acres, the site of the Abbey, the mill and buildings and 80 acres of land and meadows, was sold to Thomas Knight in June 1767 for £5,000. The full legal description is given in Table 4.7. Many of the field names are consistent with the 1733 details. There is reference to the erection of a malthouse, kilns and a cistern on the Abbey foundations, built using the Abbey stones. In addition, the sale included land at Bullbridge Meadows in Kingsworthy, which were part of Bedford's manor of Abbots Worthy.[45] As they were leased to the same tenant as Abbey Farm it was prudent to annex them to the sale. Their inclusion made the management of the water meadows system an easier task for Thomas Knight.

Table 4.6: Hyde Abbey Farm in 1767

	acres	rods	perches
Abey (sic)	11	0	30
Black Ditch	1	1	?
Broad Ditch	1	9	19
Cast Ground	22	2	10
Chalk Meadow	14	0	30
Coining Purrock	1	1	0
Drews Purrock	0	2	16
Eades Peice (sic)	11	2	10
Ectons Peice	6	1	20
Eight acres	9	0	38
Five acres	5	1	9
Flag Meadow	3	2	0
Gate to house	0	1	12
Great garden & peice	1	2	38
Green Court	0	1	38
Great barn & coach house	0	0	13
Hercules Garden	0	1	17
Hop garden & waste adjacent	0	2	0
Hog pen & low barn	0	0	35
Kitchen garden	0	1	12
Long Purrock	3	3	5
Lower three halves	1	2	20
Manor House, Nursery & Court	0	0	35
Middle Three Halves	2	2	20
Mills Corner Piece	7	2	10
Nine Acres	9	0	7
Out waste near Churchyard	0	0	7
Park Upper	2	1	0
Park Lower	3	0	28
not readable	?	?	?
Rose Garden	0	1	14
Six Acres	6	2	35
Upper Three Halves	2	0	15
Waste	0	1	17
Total accountable	134a.	1r.	0p.

Source: W/K4/1/15/1

Table 4.7: Description of Hyde Abbey Farm in 1767

All that great of capital or messuage and outhouses, stables, gardens, orchards, 20 acres situated and lying and being in the parish of St Bartholomew and also the site of the Abbey of Hyde, mill with outhouse and water streams and appurtenances and meadow and lands called the Parke, Mill Mead, Flagg Mead and Bottom Dutton and Arrow Mead, a meadow 5 acres, a meadow 13 acres, a meadow 10 acres, a meadow 7 acres, a meadow 9½ acres, a meadow 10 acres, a meadow 8 acres, a meadow 6 acres, Millers Mead, Drews Purrock, another purrock adjoining, 5 acres all which meadow rounds in whole about 7 score and 10 acres and also all that and those the ... erected malthouse, two kilns and a loaden cistern on the old foundations of the Abbey and built with the material and also a small messuage or tenement or cottage near the Malthouse now or late tenure or occupation of John Edwards, labourer and small piece of land leading from the street to the bottom of the sloping bank in the east 140 feet length and 127 feet breadth – occupied by Samuel Tewekesbury by lease by John Duke of Bedford at a rent of £155 p.a.

Also a piece or parcel of meadow called Bull Bridge Mead 7a 1r 25p and a mead called Outhookes Mead 2a 30p and a mead called Bullbridge Mead 7a 3r 27p. Jenny Creeks Mead 5a 2r (?)p plus meadows and meads in Kingsworthy occupied by Samuel Tewekesbury and all houses, edifices, buildings, barns, stables, dovecotes, gardens, orchards, yards, barn, sides, lands, meadows, pastures, profits, commodities, emoluments, hereditaments and appurtenances.[46]

Source: W/K4/1/15/1

Although Thomas Knight resided at Godmersham in Kent, he took an active interest in Abbots Barton, which continued to be leased to Samuel Tewkesbury for over 35 years. In 1765, extensive repairs costing £146 15s. 6d. were carried out. Work included: re-timbering and tiling the roof, re-laying floors with oak downstairs and deal upstairs, bricking the study floor, repaving the kitchen in quality stone, and bricking two cellars and re-cutting the access. Manufacture of malt and brewing were important aspects of farm production and outhouses needed careful maintenance to maximise returns. The brewhouse had a new stone floor, the barns were given new doors and floors, the stable had oak flooring, and beams were replaced in the granary.[47]

After the two farms were reunited under his ownership, Thomas Knight employed Henry Hogben, a surveyor to carry out surveys in 1769 of the downland and the lower lying lands in the Itchen valley. These provided a detailed measure of the extent of the lands and a location map. The estate had four well defined areas. The Uplands extended to 118 acres and included the higher arable land west of the Worthy Road, the pasture land east of the Worthy Road and Abbots Barton farmhouse. The Abbey lands included Hyde House and substantial water meadows. There were a further 111 acres of water meadows, of which 88 acres belonged to the Barton Farm and 23 acres called Bullbridge Meads, which lay just north of the parish boundary.[48] The Uplands are shown in Figures 4.6 and a description of the fields given in

Table 4.8. The former Abbey lands and Barton Farm consisted primarily of low lying fields and water meadows. These are shown on the maps in Figures 4.8 and 4.9 and details provided in Tables 4.9 and 4.10.

The land to the east of Worthy Road consisted of a 61-acre field and two closes of about 11 and 14 acres. The land rose steadily from Nuns Walk. Abbots Barton farmhouse with its outbuildings, garden and orchard lay at the lowest point. To the south was Coney Garden stretching to 14½ acres. Lying in a triangular area between the Andover and Worthy Roads were several large arable fields in excess of 50 acres, along with several smaller fields. In the southern part were Gallows Field (55 acres), the Old Hop Garden (13 acres) and Limekilns (8 acres). These three areas were to become prime development land. The tip of the triangle was occupied by Young and Doswell.[49]

Figure 4.6: Abbots Barton Uplands rising above the water meadows

Figure 4.7: Survey of Abbots Barton Uplands 1769

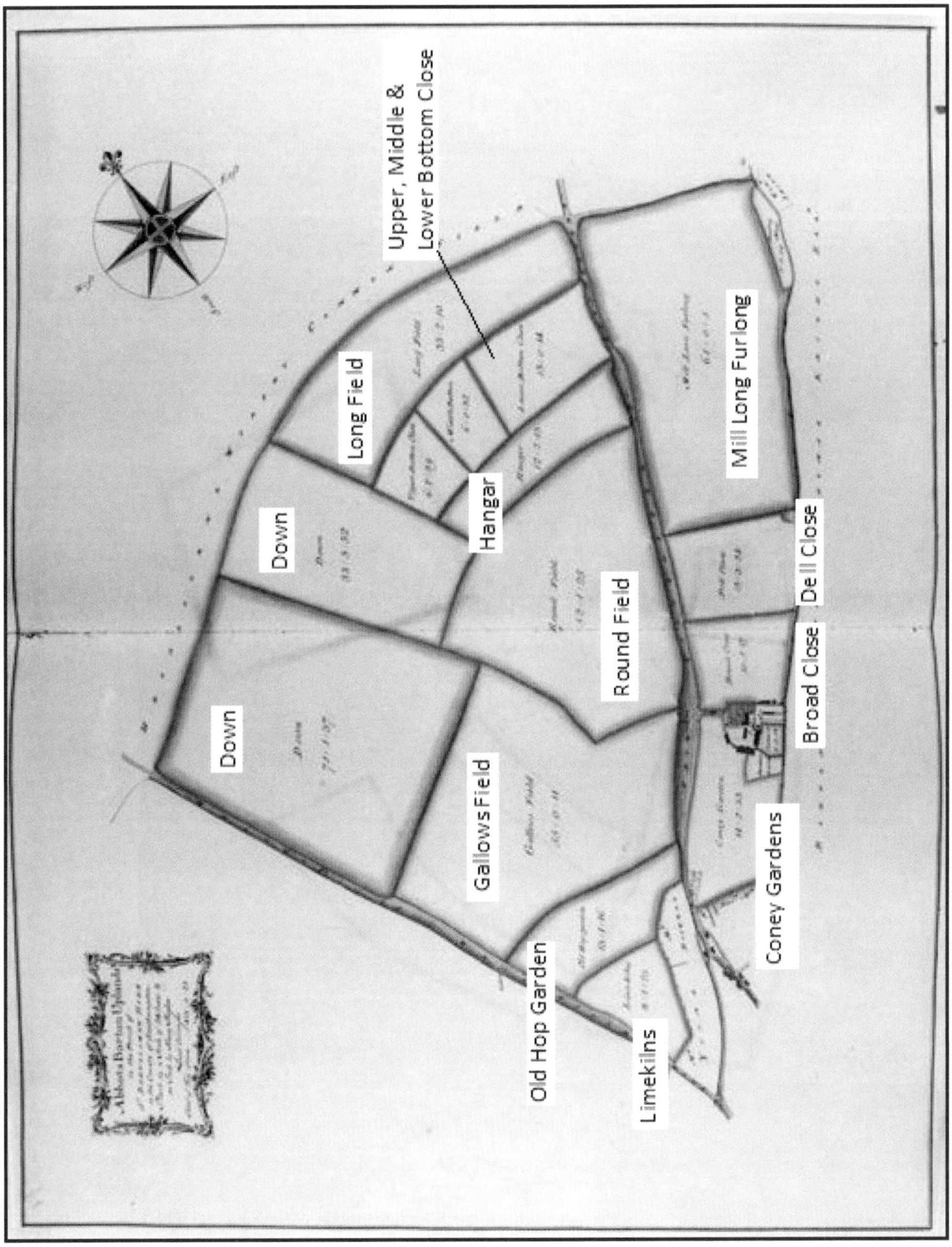

Annotated copy of HRO: COPY/562/18. See Table 4.8 for details.

Figure 4.8: Survey of the Abbey Lands, Abbots Barton 1769

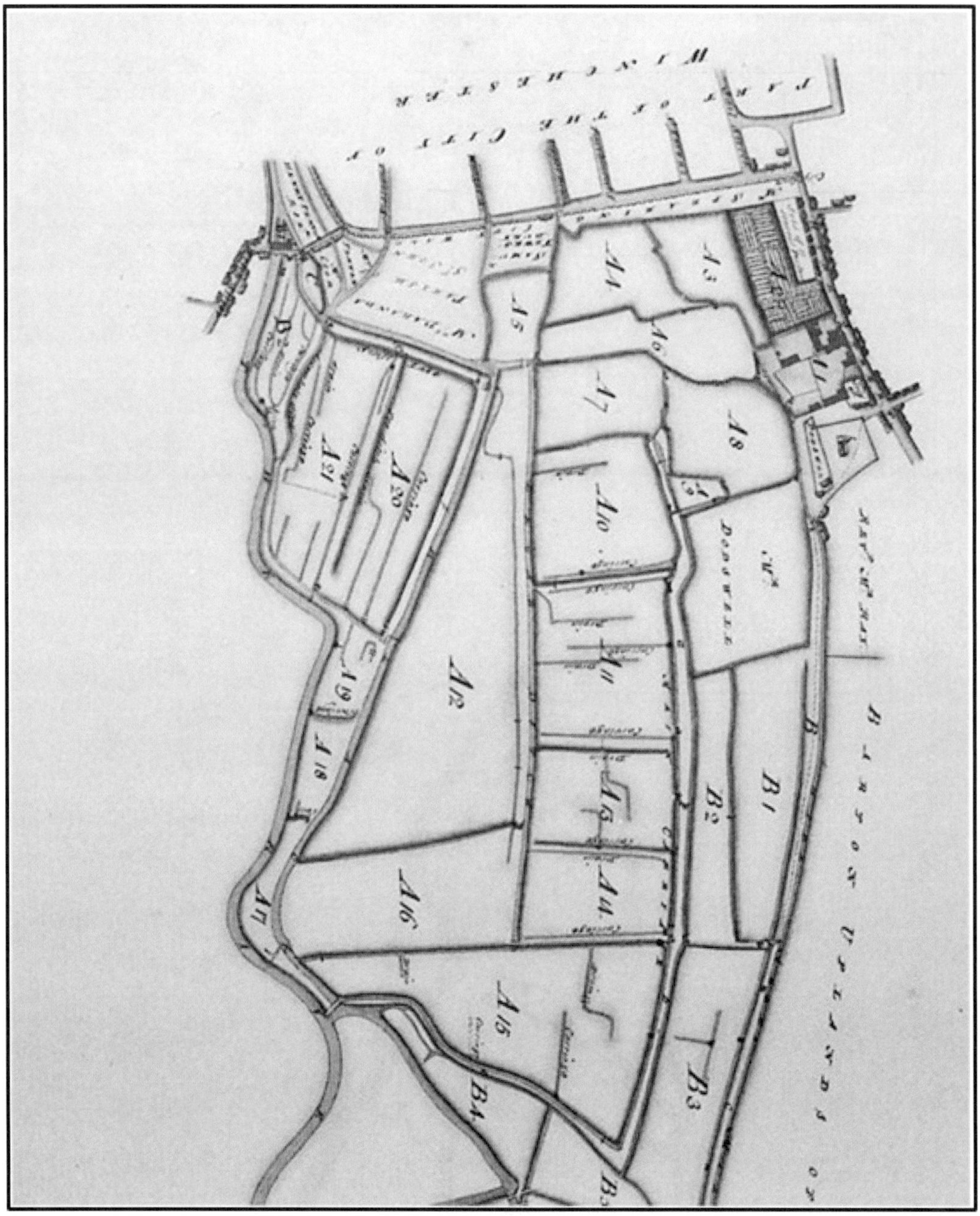

Part of HRO: COPY/562/19. See Table 4.9 for details.

Figure 4.9: Survey of Barton Meadows, Abbots Barton 1769

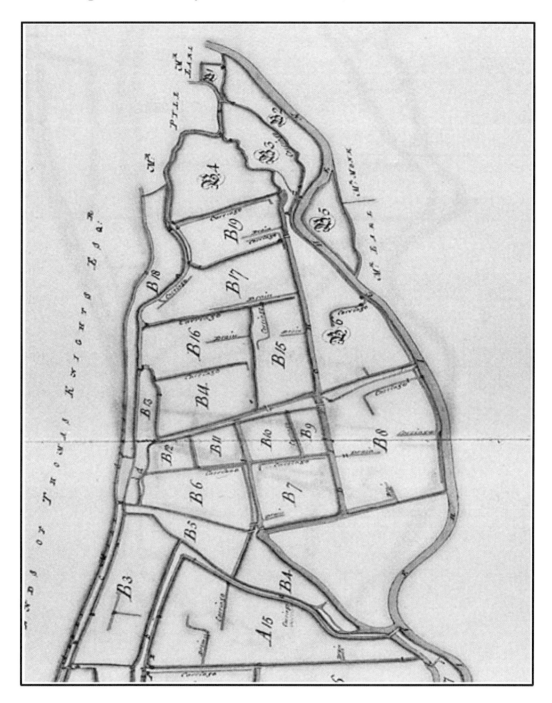

Part of HRO: COPY/562/19. See Table 4.10 for details.

Table 4.8: Survey of the Uplands Abbots Barton by Henry Hogben 1769

	acres	rods	perches
Down	71	1	37
Down	33	3	32
Long Field	33	2	10
Upper Bottom Close	6	2	39
Middle Bottom Close	6	0	32
Lower Bottom Close	13	0	14
Hangar	12	2	13
Gallows Field	55	0	11
Round Field	52	1	25
Old Hop Garden	13	1	16
Lime Kilns	8	1	23
Mill Lane Furlong	61	0	1
Bunting Mead	1	3	25
Dell Close	13	3	24
Broad Close	10	2	17
House	2	0	30
Orchard	0	3	18
Garden	0	3	24
Coney Garden	14	2	33
City Liberty	0	1	29
	413a.	1r.	13p.

Source: HRO: 13M85W/33

Table 4.9: Freehold Estates of Thomas Knight 1769 – the Abbey Lands

		acres	rods	perches
A1	House barn & garden etc	2	2	1
A2	Three gardens	2	1	39
A3	Upper Park	2	3	18
A4	Lower Park	3	3	17
A5	Flagg mead	1	3	21
A6	Corning Purrock	3	2	25
A7	Long Purrock	3	3	31
A8	Abbey	4	2	12
A9	Drews Purrock	0	2	22
A10	Six Acres	6	2	1
A11	Eight Acres	8	1	15
A12	Cast grounds	20	1	35
A13	Five Acres	4	3	24
A14	Eades Piece	5	0	10
A15	Chalk mead	12	0	26
A16	Nine Acres	8	2	39
A17	Upper Three-halves	1	3	0
A18	Middle Three-halves	1	2	15
A19	Lower Three-halves	1	2	19
A20	Ectons Piece	7	0	34
A21	Mill Corner Piece	8	0	6
a	Castway	1	2	27
b	Castway	1	2	3
e	Castway		2	19
f	Castway		3	34
g	Castway		2	24
Summary Abbey Lands		**118a.**	**0r.**	**37p.**

Source: HRO:13M85W/32

Table 4.10: Freehold Estates of Thomas Knight, 1769 – Barton Meadows

		acres	rods	perches
	Castway	1	3	23
B1	Lower Home Mead	5	3	33
B2	Course leeze	4	0	3
B3	Upper Home Mead	6	3	33
B4	Ducks Nest	3	1	30
B5	Ducks Nest	2	3	0
B6	Chalkdell Four Acres	5	0	15
B7	Ducks nest Four Acres	5	0	2
B8	Ten Acres	12	3	39
B9	Acre	1	1	18
B10	Two Acres	2	0	30
B11	Three halves	1	3	0
B12	Acre	1	1	7
B13	-	1	1	11
B14	Lower Five Acres	4	3	39
B15	Blackditch Four Acres	4	3	16
B16	Middle Five Acres	4	3	37
B17	Upper Five Acres	5	3	9
B18	Chapple Mead	4	1	25
B19	Four Acres	3	3	15
c	Castway	1	0	34
d	Castway	2	0	12
	Summary Barton meadows	**88a.**	**0r.**	**31p.**

1	Bullbridge meads	0	1	32
2	Bullbridge meads	3	0	5
3	Bullbridge meads	3	2	11
4	Jenny Creeks	5	1	28
5	Out Hooks	2	1	36
6	Badcocks and Bank joining	8	1	33
	Summary Bullbridge meads	**23a.**	**1r.**	**25p.**

B1	Mill House Gardens & Water	0	0	31
B2	Durngate Mill Mead	2	2	23
	Sum of lease and lives	2a.	3r.	14p.
C	Stable & orchard		1	23
	Lease from City for 40 years			
	Total	**233a.**	**0r.**	**10p.**

Source: HRO: 13M85W/32

The maps of Barton Hide and Bullbridge meadows are very detailed and show small plots divided by water meadows.[50] Many of the meads retained earlier names, although some names were just descriptions of their extent and location, for example, Middle Five Acres. The acreage of these areas is consistent with earlier conveyances. Dell Close was an artificial hollow left from quarrying chalk. The nearby houses were called Chalk Pit Cottages. At the Lime Kilns, lime and sand were made into mortar, plaster and stucco. Flagg Mead would have been a source of reeds and rushes used for thatching. A purrock was a grassy enclosure. Chappel Mead was the likely site of St Gertrude's Chapel. The City's gallows were not sited on the Abbey land. The name - Gallows Field - may have originated from the fourth or fifth century cemetery sited there. The name - Old Hop Garden - speaks for itself.[51] There is some debate when hops came to England although a well-known couplet states 'Hops, reformation, bays and beer - came into England all in one year.'[52] Hops were used as winter fodder, as a dye and for medicinal uses.

All the land was freehold with three exceptions sited at the north-east corner of the City walls: the Durngate Mills with the miller's house and garden, Durngate Mill Mead which stretched northwards along the Durngate River, and an adjacent plot on the west side of the mead described as a stable and orchard. The river divided above the mill providing two races. The Durngate Mill complex belonged to the Bishop of Winchester and was on a lease for three lives, whilst the small orchard belonged to the City and was on a fixed 40-year lease.[53] All of Winchester's mills, except one, were owned by the Bishop who charged a substantial rent to the wealthy landowners who then sub-let or installed their own millers. Durngate was in a good position as the first City mill on the River Itchen or Durngate River as called locally.

Structurally mills were a liability. The timber base provided poor foundations and was subject to rot, and the mill itself was subject to ingress from floods. The vibrations of the machinery, weight of the grain and risk from fire all added to the potential risks of damage, giving mills a short life span, especially in pre-industrial times. The last mill and house was built in the late eighteenth century, possibly when Thomas Knight inherited Abbots Barton in 1781. Maintenance of machinery was a continual process. The tenant's lease gave him 'the liberty and license to fell, cut and carry away yearly during the term in and out of the wood of the Lord Bishop of Winchester and his successors.' The tenant was allowed to cut down two loads of beech from the Bishop's woods to make 'cogs, floats and wrungs' and 'grete timber' by agreement. This material was essential to replace worn parts such as the gear wheel teeth and the wheel floats.[54] The miller supplemented his income by trapping eels. The traps were set during the winter storms at a full moon. The eels were harvested from the grating in the morning and collected by the local fishmonger. Later, after the railway had reached the City, they were dispatched to Billingsgate Market in London. No doubt these rich pickings also attracted otters who have recently returned to the City Mill and the Winnall Moors to the north. By the end of the nineteenth century the traditional process of low milling, whereby the grain was crushed into flour by a single transit through the mill stones, had fallen out of favour. Demand was for purer white flour, which was harder to produce. New imported varieties of wheat were used rather than local ones and the continental methods of grinding using rollers were adopted. Milling moved away from local production centres to the major sea ports where wheat was imported.

In 1799 Abraham Knight, a yeoman, took on the 14-year lease of Abbots Barton and Hyde Abbey Farm, the land at Bulbridge, Kingsworthy and Durngate Mills at a yearly rent of £550 from the owners, Edward Knight of Godmersham and Thomas Knight's widow Catherine. It is not known if Abraham was related to the Knight dynasty. The land had previously been leased to William Burge, who had sub-let to Thomas Pink. The description of Hyde Abbey Farm was similar to that in the 1767 sale document. The lease included the water grist mills known as Durngate Mills and adjoining land, described as marsh or moor ground, and a six-foot way from the street to the mills and Durngate, all sited in the parish of St John. The mill equipment supplied by the owners was itemised:

> The use of four pairs of French mill stones, two water wheels, two waterwheel shafts, two cog wheels, two spur wheels, two upright shafts, two spur willows, four pairs of nuts to the stones, four hoops, four horses, four bins, four hoppers, two sets of bolting tackle, two bolting mills, two machines for flour, four leather straps, two sets of hoisting tackle with ropes, two hursts, four spindles, four centre irons, four feeders to the four pairs of stones, and other utensils.[55]

The land and rights are finally summed up as:

> Together with all other lands, meadows, pasture, headings, houses, outhouses, barns, stables, edifices, buildings, backsides, gardens, orchards, common ways, paths, passages, water, water courses, bridges, hatches, carriage, sluices, trunks, light easement, privileges, hereditaments and appurtenances.[56]

Abraham Knight's lease did not include the walled Hyde Garden, which had recently been sold freehold with the rights to take timber (trees, saplings, pollard willow, bark etc.) to Thomas Deane and Rev. Charles Richards. Thomas Deane had been the former tenant. Abraham Knight did not have the right to take timber from the premises or fish in the Durngate River, except from the brickwork of the mills, or to take water from the river.

Sale of the Abbey site, its farm and Abbots Barton

There was a boom in Hampshire's economy from 1793 to 1815, especially during the Napoleonic Wars, which resulted in farmers expanding their business and borrowing in the expectation of continuing high prices. Although sheep and corn husbandry was still prevalent, in contrast to 100 years previously, farming reflected a focus on grain production and the sale of sheep products with wheat, lamb and mutton all commanding high prices. The ownership of a large freehold estate would have been very attractive to William Simonds when he purchased 500 acres of farming land in Hyde in 1811. This supplemented his leasehold estate in St Cross, which had been held by his family for many decades.

There was a clear demarcation between the former Abbey's two farms. Barton Farm was described as the 'great or capital messuage, buildings and yards, garden and orchards.' The Abbey site and farm was described as:

> The capital messuage called Abbey Farm with all appurtenances and 20 acres of land and site of Hyde Abbey with 117 acres and malthouse, two kilns etc. and 23 acres in Kingsworthy.'

Table 4.11 gives the details of the acreage.[57] Although the estate's boundaries had changed little since the 1769 survey, undertaken by Thomas Knight, several pieces of land had been sold:

> The piece or parcel of Thabbots gardens and ground of two acres part of the site of the Abbey sold and recovered by Thomas Knight the younger to the County of Southampton for the purpose of building a House of Correction and likewise the same and except all the piece or parcel of garden ground two acres and three rods part of the said Hyde Abbey Garden and sold and conveyed by the Trustees of Thomas Knight to Charles Richards clerk together with all ways, paths, passages, water courses etc. woods profit etc.[58]

On the same date Simonds purchased Durngate Mills for £1,500. This is described as the:

> Bargain and sale of water mills and fulling mills known as Durngate Mill in the parish of St John with rights, messuages and appurtenances, houses, edifices, buildings, liberties, customs, services and emoluments. And also the parcel of marsh or moor ground near the mills in the north part of void plot or ground and way six feet wide leading from Durngate into the marshland.[59]

The land was held by lease for three lives from the Bishop of Winchester. The lessee was entitled to the reversion or remainder fee simple, which meant the freehold could be purchased for a multiple of the yearly rent, commonly between 20 and 28.[60]

Table 4.11: Abbots Barton Estate in 1811

	acres	rods	perches
Down	71	1	37
Down	33	3	32
Long Field	33	2	10
Upper Bottom Close	6	2	29
Middle Bottom Close	6	0	32
Lower Bottom Close	13	0	14
Hanger	12	2	13
Mill Lane Furlong	61	0	1
Dell Close	13	3	24
Broad Close	10	2	17
Round Field	52	1	25
Gallows Field	55	0	11
Old Hop Garden	13	1	16
Lime Kilns	8	0	18
Site of house, yards	2	0	20
Road		2	27
Bunting Mead	1	3	25
Castway	1	3	23
Lower Home Mead	5	3	33
Course Leeze	4	0	3
Upper Home Mead	6	3	3
Ducks Nest	3	1	30
Another piece called Ducks Nest	2	3	0
Chalk Mead	4	5	15
Ducks Nest Four acres	4	5	2
Ten Acres	12	3	39
One Acre	1	1	18
Two Acres	2	0	30
Three halves	1	3	0
Not named	1	1	7
Another piece called Once Acre	1	1	11
Lower Five Acres	4	3	9
Black Ditch	4	4	9
Austen Prior	10	1	7
Middle Five Acres	4	3	37
Upper Five Acres	5	3	9
Chapel Mead	4	1	25
Four Acres	3	3	15
Castway	1	20	4
Castway	2	0	12
Total	**500a.**	**1r.**	**12p.**

Source: HRO: 13M85W/36-38

Conclusion

Abbots Barton was typical of downland farms in Hampshire where sheep provided the main income. Both Abbots Barton and the Abbey Farm benefitted from water meadows which provided early spring pasture for the ewes and their lambs. However the management of these was a challenge to Thomas Knight and the Duke of Bedford and an expense both in time and lawyers' fees.

Thomas Knight's survey of 1769 provides both a map and details of the meadows of Abbots Barton and Abbey Farm. It is not known what percentage of the Abbey Farm's 118 acres were flooded regularly to provide the lush spring grass, but many of the fields had a network of drainage ditches. The low lying fields covering 88 acres on Abbots Barton Farm were hemmed in by a grid of drainage ditches which indicate these were all water meadows.

Financial data suggests that although the establishment of hop fields took three years and cost £53 per acre, once they were in production annual income per acre could reach £52 per acre. Similarly the annual expense of maintaining the water meadows amounted to £5 18s. per acre. The benefits to the sheep farmer with an intensity of 400 couples (ewe and lamb) per acre was £9 3s. per acre giving a healthy profit. These farms benefitted from close proximity to the City where a constant source of rich manure was available for the hop fields. The hops that were sold to the local brewery provided some extra income, but those that were kept went into beer for the consumption of the family and workers.

Figure 4.10: Old cottages in King Alfred Place

After surviving for centuries, these cottages in the former Bridewell Lane were demolished in the slum clearances of 1955.

Source: W/C5/10/23/71/3

Chapter 5: Hyde Street in the eighteenth and nineteenth centuries

Turnpikes

During the 1700s road transport was slow and roads were muddy and rutted. Roads from Southampton to London passed through Twyford and Bishops Waltham skirting the City several miles to the east. For the owner of Abbots Barton, this made the control of the outlying estates difficult and the use of the estate manager's time was eroded by the hours spent travelling between Kent and Hampshire. Around 1720, during Elizabeth Knight's ownership of Abbots Barton, a detailed computation of the potential annual revenues from the proposed Winchester Turnpike was put together. Turnpikes were the toll-motorways of their age, ensuring that roads between towns were kept in a usable condition by raising tolls rather than relying on local taxes.

The proposal gives an insight into Winchester's importance - the level of transport to the ports of Southampton and Gosport and the popularity of the medieval local fairs still held on St Giles and Maudlin (or Morn) hills. The plan was for five toll gates though locations were not specified. Regular trade was expected to include wagons and stage coaches. The weekly wagons from Winchester could be charged 4s. and those from Gosport or Southampton 6s. for each journey. Stage coaches operated thrice weekly with a charge to passengers of 8s. from Winchester and 6s. from Southampton. Smaller coaches, carts and chaises would pay according to the number of horses and in terms of the distance they could cover. The total annual income was estimated at nearly £539. A further £70 was expected from the trade generated by the fairs - people, goods and animals (Table 5.1). [1]

The turnpike's setting up costs were £3,000, which included an Act of Parliament (£325), the erection of the gates and toll houses (£175), and most expensive, the laying out the roads covering 40 miles, at a cost of £62 10s. a mile (£2,500). The labour costs to collect the tolls were estimated at 7s. a week for four toll gates and 5s. for the fifth one. A further sum of £65 p.a. was added for salaries. These most probably accounted for the legal and financial costs. The roads had to be kept in good condition at an annual estimated expense of £160. This gave a total of £416, which as the report stated:

> If these calculations turn out to be right there will be near £200 for a sink fund to pay off the principal money borrowed. [2]

A very basic calculation, not allowing for any discount factor, gives a return of 6 per cent, a very profitable investment at a time when agricultural tenancy might only return 3 per cent.

In 1759, during Thomas Knight's ownership of Abbots Barton, the Act for 'Repairing and widening the roads from Oxdown Gate, in Popham Lane, to the City of Winchester' which passed through Hyde was made law. The trustees included Sir Charles Powlett (the Marquess of Winchester), Sir Thomas Heathcote (a large landowner to the south of Winchester), the Archdeacon of Winchester and the Warden of Winchester College. Although Thomas Knight was not named in the list of Trustees, his interests would have been looked after by a solicitor. John Gatehouse, the Duke of Bedford's legal representative was named. The fourth Duke of Bedford, John Russell (1710-1771), who owned Hyde Abbey Farm, was a politician with an interest in promoting turnpike bills.[3] Trustees were required to have a high level of financial standing and satisfy one of four criteria. The first was to have possession of rents or profits of land, tithes or hereditaments (which could be freehold, leasehold or copyhold), or to be the heir apparent to these. If this condition was not satisfied an estate-in-law of £100, a rectory valued at £50 p.a., or a personal estate of £1,000 was sufficient.

The Act proposed the erection of gates or turnpikes across the road within 500 yards of the north end of Hyde Street and on Andover Road just north of the junction with Worthy Lane. These were known as the Hyde Street and Swan Lane toll gates. The type of transport was fully listed and costs given. Coach, chair (various types were described) or hearse drawn by four horses, geldings, mules or other beasts, caravan, wagon, cart, dray or other carriage were charged 1s.. If they were drawn by fewer horses a charge of 3d. per horse was made. For horses whether laden or not, the cost was 1s.. Droves of oxen and cows were charged at 10d. per score (or pro rata) whereas calves, hogs and sheep and lambs were cheaper at 5d. per score.[4] The toll gates were advertised for rent in the local Hampshire Chronicle. The small cottages provided a suitable home for a small family. However there was gender equality - in 1861 the Andover Road toll was run by an unmarried woman.

There is evidence that the turnpikes were not operational in Winchester until 1810.[5] In the 1820s there were ten coach companies offering seven destinations including London, Romsey, Reading and Salisbury. By 1830 Oxford and Newbury were added to give 150 services per week.[6] Coach fares depended on whether the seats were inside or outside. In 1825, Collyers charged £1 4s. (for inside) and 15s. (for outside) to Basingstoke. The coach to Portsmouth, perhaps to link to the ships travelling to distant lands cost just 9s. inside. Fares further afield to Oxford and Cheltenham cost £1 8s. and £1 18s. respectively but those willing to bear the elements paid only 14s. or £1 3s..

Hyde's community benefitted by these major transport improvements. The toll roads not only improved the access through Winchester's northern portal but facilitated the growth of trade and communications with ports like Southampton and Portsmouth and other country towns like Guildford. Trading opportunities increased for William Simonds, the new owner of Abbots Barton, as more distant markets became reachable. However, trade with far flung colonies brought the looming threat of competition.

Table 5.1: Income and expenditure for proposed Winchester Turnpikes

	£	s.	d.
2 wagons for Winchester (go up and down) once a week and pay 4s. toll each journey which is 16s. a week.	41	12	0
2 wagons from Gosport and Southampton (go up and down) once a week and pay 6s. toll each journey which is 12s. a week.	31	4	0
1 stage coach from Winchester (go up and down) thrice a week and pay 8s. toll each journey which is £1 4s. a week.	62	8	0
1 stage coach from Southampton (go up and down) thrice a week and pay 6s. toll each journey which is 18s. a week.	46	16	0
Other coaches and wagons and carriages with four or more horses.	182	0	0
Coaches, carts chaises etc. with two horses ten miles a day, 3650 @ 6d.	91	5	0
Single horse chaises and carts 5 miles a day at 3d.	22	16	3
Single horse 40 miles a day. 14600 p.a. at 1d.	60	16	8
Sub total:	538	17	11
Maudlin and Giles Hill Fairs. If 1,000 wagons with four or more horses go from Winchester to Maudlin Hill and back again, and come for east of the county to Giles Hill and back again. If throwing in a single horseman and carriage less than four horses that will amount to:	50	0	0
Drove cattle.	20	0	0
Subtotal:	70	0	0
Total	**£608**	**17s.**	**11d.**
A computation of the previous experience for which money must be borrowed:			
Erecting five gate and toll houses at £35 each.	175	0	0
Expenses of Act.	325	0	0
To be laid out on the roads being £62 10s. a mile.	2,500	0	0
	3,000	**0**	**0**
Computation of subsequent annual expense:			
Interest of £3,000 at 3½ per cent.	105	0	0
Four gates at 7s. a week each.	73	0	0
One gate at 5s. a week if found pays.	13	0	0
Annual expense of mending roads after being made good 40 miles. beside the statute work.	160	0	0
Salaries.	65	0	0
	£416	**0s.**	**0d.**

Source: HRO: 39M89/E/B614/8,9

Hyde Street

Just off Hyde Street is the church of St Bartholomew which dates from the twelfth century and was built to serve the lay community of Hyde Abbey. Although Walter Chaundler made the presentation in 1541, the advowson was passed to the Crown in 1546. After the Dissolution the church was neglected and the graveyard was used for grazing cattle. Although the parishioners sought to repair the church in the early 1700s with the help of the Bishop, the sheer quantity of timber needed hindered attempts.[7] Figure 5.1 shows the state of the Church's chancel in the late 1700s. There was one aisle and the chancel had collapsed. In contrast, the Abbey gatehouse behind appears in good condition.

Figure 5.1: St Bartholomew's Hyde

Source: Warner (1795)
The church has a chequered stone and flint tower with pyramidal roof.

The parish had 500 inhabitants in 1801. Increased prosperity may have improved the state of the church. However the rebuilding of the chancel on the original foundations in 1838 suggests the church had been in a poor condition since the Dissolution. The parsonage, an old brick and timber building was also in need of renovation. Rev. Charles Richards was the vicar from 1797 to 1833 with the additional responsibility for the chapel at the Bridewell (County prison). Richards had been educated at Corpus Christi College, Oxford and graduated with a B.A. in 1781 and a M.A. in 1783. He took over as headmaster of prestigious Hyde Abbey School on the death of his father-in-law in 1779.[8] He was ordained in 1797 and became prebendary of Winchester in 1827, holding these posts until his death in 1833.[9]

After the Restoration in 1660, Hyde Street recovered from the economic stagnation and religious unrest which followed the turmoil of the Civil War. Sizeable inns like the Swan attested to Hyde Street's importance at the entrance to the City. The street provided housing for workers on the Duke of Bedford's Abbey Farm and those involved in the developing brewery industry. Many of Winchester's rich had built houses there and it was a centre for education, as an alternative to Winchester College, for those that could afford to send their sons to receive a classical schooling.

Godson's map of 1750 illustrates the houses in Hyde Street (Figure 5.2).[10] In the south (to the right of the map) the Swan Inn and outbuildings are clearly shown.[11] A terrace of houses stretched northwards towards Hyde Garden.[12] The large plot behind with frontage on to Hyde Street was void. Hyde House and its gardens dominate the rest of this section of the street until the old Abbey gateway and farm buildings are reached. The church stood alone with no evidence of any nearby cottages.

Figure 5.2: Hyde Street about 1750

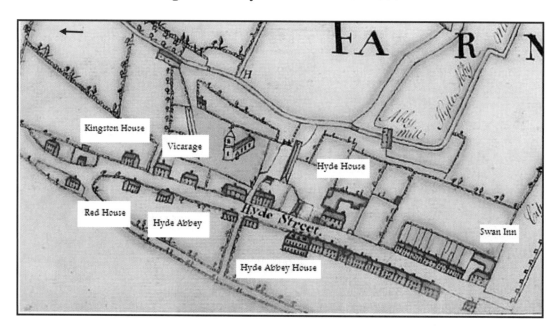

Annotated section of Godson's map (HRO:W/F5/1/10)

On the west side of Hyde Street, there was a single freehold property next to the City Ditch (on the corner of the later Swan Lane), an undeveloped plot and then a continuous row of houses which culminated in Hyde Abbey House. The majority of this land, up to the site of Hyde Abbey House, belonged to the Dean and Chapter, whose ownership continued into Victorian times. Hyde Abbey House (No. 23 Hyde Street) was built in about 1700, probably on earlier foundations. The building was re-fronted later in the eighteenth century. Built of red bricks, the grand frontage supports a Georgian doorway with fanlight, classical pillars and pediment.[13] There are seven windows on the first floor. The hipped roof had five dormer windows (Figure 5.3).

One owner, probably Rev. Richards, had a passion for Elizabethan and Jacobean decorations and statues. These included a pair of figures set in shell-headed niches underneath a pediment. This stone feature, set into the flint and brick garden wall, was a popular manifestation of the Italian Renaissance. The remains of an elaborate rear doorway, composed of different architectural elements, can be seen in Victoria Road.[14] The stone doorway, which originally had a wooden door, is now bricked up. Over time the road has been raised leaving only part of the former access visible. Above the doorway, on top of the garden wall, is a heavy stone decorative crest with a large scallop shell (See Figure 5.4). The family crest of the Russell family who owned the Abbey site and farm, contained three scallops.

The antiquities and other internal features found in Hyde Abbey House probably originated in Hyde House. The house and gardens were part of Abbey Farm purchased by Thomas (Broadnax May) Knight from John Russell, fourth Duke of Bedford in 1767. The owner of Hyde Abbey House, Rev. Charles Richards, had purchased part of Hyde Garden from Edward Austen in 1799, the year after Thomas Knight's death. By this time, Hyde House, with the exception of the later extension and barns, had been demolished as it was surplus to requirements. Richards probably seized the opportunity to buy the historic decorative features from either Thomas Knight or Edward Austen. Hyde Abbey House's antiquities were interesting enough to feature on a postcard in the early twentieth century.[15]

There were two similar properties - No. 33 (later known as Magdala House) and No. 34 - either side of Hyde Church Lane, which leads through to Worthy Road (Figure 5.5). Although this part of Hyde Street appears undeveloped in 1750, it was not green-field land. Keene's survey describes the many tenements that existed at the time of the Dissolution.[16]

On Godson's map two substantial houses can be seen at the north end of Hyde Street. The most southerly was initially called Hyde House and then Hyde Abbey; the other was known as the Red House. Without archaeological evidence, it is difficult to know whether any of the properties were later knocked down and rebuilt or whether later facades were added to older foundations and structures. The Red House was built with red bricks, has a hipped roof and a double drive. When sold in the early twentieth century by Miss Gudgeon for £6,000, it was set in a quarter of an acre. Although much smaller than Hyde Abbey the reception rooms were palatial. There was a lounge (24 ft. 9 in. by 19 ft. 10 in.), a sitting room (22 ft. by 16 ft.), a dining room (17 ft. 4in. by 16 ft.) and a study.[17]

Figure 5.3: Hyde Abbey House, No. 23 Hyde Street

Figure 5.4: Rear wall of No. 23 Hyde Street

Before the Dissolution, the land north of Hyde Abbey Gateway was owned by the Abbey, the church or the parishioners. There are three almost identical Georgian houses – Nos. 58 to 60 Hyde Street (Figure 5.6). Further north only the properties' foundations have survived.[18] The new vicarage, built in 1835, replaced an old brick and timber parsonage. Near the junction with Worthy Road stands Kingston House which can be seen on Godson's map (Figure 5.2 and 5.7). Unusually for Winchester the building was constructed with grey bricks. It had a hipped roof over a wide cornice and two ground floor windows in recessed elliptical arches.

Another map of Winchester, covering Hyde, was produced by John Milner in c.1800 (Figure 5.9).[19] There were some notable changes from Godson's map of 1750. In the east of the suburb and dominating the area was the New County Gaol and Infirmary, which was better known as the Bridewell. Swan Lane is clearly marked with buildings at the eastern end and new houses had been erected at the bottom of Hyde Church Lane and beyond the Church on the north side of Hyde Church Path. Several farm cottages and buildings had appeared on Hyde Street after the reunification of the two former Abbey's farms. This consisted of an L-shaped block on the corner of what became King Alfred Place and barns at the back of the severely reduced Hyde House. At the end of Hyde Church Path, by the Abbey Stream, stood a row of cottages of which only two survived into nineteenth century Saxon Road. Also clearly marked are the new toll gates on the roads to Basingstoke and Whitchurch.

Figure 5.5: No. 33 Hyde Street

Figure 5.6: No. 58 Hyde Street

Figure 5.7: Kingston House

The extensive grounds can be seen in Figure 5.10.

At the time of Thomas Knight's death in 1794, Hyde Street was a mix of old tenements, brewery buildings, public houses, schools. Information on the properties, their owners and tenants in the first half of the nineteenth century can be gleaned from several sources including parish rates and land taxes. Many families were long established in the parish by 1800 and have featured already in this history of the Abbey's lands; their descendants were to play an important part in Hyde's suburbanisation.

The occupiers of Hyde Street are recorded in several documents. Land tax records cover 1794 to 1830 and the poor relief rate books from 1794 to 1817.[20] Unfortunately there is no way to determine from these sources if the occupiers were also the owners of the houses and land. Most proprietors, including long leaseholders, were also occupiers. Tenants were responsible for paying the land tax, although formally it was a charge on the proprietors, and in theory rent was reduced to reflect this liability. In 1801, the land tax became a permanent rent charge. Landowners were able to pay the government for the right not to pay the tax. This was achieved by the purchase of government stock that was then surrendered. The land tax for St Bartholomew's raised £8 14s. in 1815 but until 1817 no description of the properties was given. Revs. Charles Richards (father and son) were the largest holders of land and property in Hyde Street with three large properties, seven further houses, tenements and two plots described as 'stables etc.'. Ownership of Rev. Richards' house, the Gentleman's Academy (Hyde Abbey School), malthouse, stables and part of Hyde Garden (which he had purchased in 1799 from Thomas Knight), generated a land tax liability of £3 5s. (37 per cent of the total raised in the parish).

The parish rate book of 1800 provides details of properties and occupiers.[21] The total rate levied was £54 5s. 10d.; of this Abraham Knight (the tenant at Abbots Barton) paid £24 7s. 4d.. The poor rate contribution provides a measure by which to compare the size of the holdings. Knight's payment was 45.1 per cent of the total raised by the parish which reflected both the extent and the farm's economic importance to the local community. The Richards' liability amounted to £5 10s. 6d. (10.8 per cent of the total). Another affluent inhabitant and substantial landowner was the brewer Thomas Deane who had considerable holdings. He paid £7 19s. 4d (14.6 per cent of the total raised) for his house, field, four tenements and a malthouse in Hyde Churchyard. He also had property in Swan Lane, which included houses or tenements and another malthouse, which were occupied by Mr Money. The butcher John Doswell was liable for £2 13s. 8d. (five per cent of the total). He had rights over land near the church, Long Close which lay at the top of Hyde Street (later held by the dairyman William Wigg), as well as a house and several tenements. Other residents who contributed were William Young, a woolstapler and one of the overseers of the poor, the Bridewell keeper, Richard Page, who was liable for his own property and eight tenements, and Mrs Tewkesbury.[22] Page may have been liable due to his position rather than having any tenurial rights.

Education

Hyde Street had many large properties built in the late 1700s and early 1800s. Some provided luxurious accommodation for the prestigious residents of Winchester and their families, but others were used as schools or academies for young gentlemen. Before the extensive provision of state education, private establishments for the rich and church and other voluntary schools for the poor were the only source of community education. With a private school's success, the property was extended or altered and neighbouring plots and properties purchased.

Hyde Abbey School, described as 'one of the first classical schools of the kingdom,' was founded in about 1760 by Mr Cotton when Abbots Barton was owned by Thomas (Broadnax-May) Knight and the Abbey site and farm by the Duke of Bedford. On Cotton's death in 1799 the school passed to his son-in-law Rev. Charles Richards. A rare insight into the school can be gleaned from an article in Household Words in 1850 which at that time was edited by Charles Dickens.[23] An ex-pupil, who began school in about 1826, provided a humorous account of his school named as 'Rood Priory' or 'Old Bob's', but clearly meant to be Hyde Abbey School. The writer described how Rood Priory was named after the monastery and was in the same Cathedral town as the 'College of St Joseph' (a reference to Winchester College), which generated some rivalry between the two institutions. The school was described as a large detached building of red bricks with a slate roof and tall arched windows. The refectory was housed in another building. Pupils lived at Rev. Richard's house or adjacent buildings.[24]

The school room had dark oak wainscot on the lower part of the walls, and, at the risk of flagellation, was carved with the names of pupils. Each pupil was assigned a compartment (a scob) of the desk. There were two fireplaces, one for seniors and the other for juniors, and lighting was supplied by candles, the responsibility of the youngest boys. In attendance were three masters placed at either end of the room and in the middle, between the fireplaces. Although a private school it was conducted as a public one. Rev. Richards was described as good tempered, patient and forbearing, and not punishing without fair warning. He was attentive to the health and comforts of the pupils. However he was a traditionalist who administered the flogging system, not for the love of flogging, but with a belief in its virtue. Such punishment was the result of a series of offences or shortcomings, such as being caught out of bounds, misconduct or idleness. The whip would be applied six times over a five minute period out in the porch, witnessed by any boys who were in need of a warning. It was claimed that troublesome boys were sent to watch a public hanging to learn the consequences of bad behaviour and mend their ways. The linchpins of the curriculum were Latin and Greek. A chapter of the New Testament was read and prayers said in the morning and evening.

In 1796, expansion necessitated opening a new schoolroom designed by John Sloane, the eminent London architect (Figure 5.8). By this date Abbots Barton and the Abbey Farms had been reunited and the Abbey's site sold for the Bridewell, Thomas Knight had died, and his wife Catherine managed the enlarged estate with the help of Edward Austen.

Figure 5.8: Sloane's new schoolroom

In 1820 there were 90 scholars, whose ages ranged from 6 to 18 - most being 14 or 15.[25] The school was nationally renowned and with the increasing ease of access via the new toll roads, attracted scholars from a wide area. The homes of the 93 scholars in 1824 (where identified) were as follows: Winchester - 14, elsewhere in Hampshire - 22, counties west of Hampshire - 26, and London and the Home counties - 20. Only six scholars had homes further afield; one came from Ireland and two from Trinidad. Many families had more than one child at the school. New boys in 1826 included Henry Wooldridge from Winchester and Thomas and James Orgill from Jamaica. Wooldridge's father and brother were solicitors but Henry became a surgeon. The Orgills were planters (elite landowners). Thomas became a cleric and James a doctor. A classical education provided a firm foundation for their future careers.

Only the wealthy could afford to send sons to Hyde Abbey School. In 1779 the cost for admission was £3 13s. 6d.. Annual expenses amounted to £31, broken down into £24 14s. for board, £4 4s. for teaching of classics and other inferior branches of literature, and £2 2s. for writing and accounts.[26] A surviving account book gives details of the pupils and fees for each boy during 1824-6.[27] The costs for Frederick Arney for half the year were:

	£	s.	d.
Half year's board to mid-summer	17	0	0
Latin & Greek	2	2	0
Reading, writing & geography	2	2	0
Servants		10	6
School library		5	0
Weekly allowance		19	0
School fire & candle		2	6
Journey		13	
Sundries		8	6
	£24	2s.	6d.

The early 1800s were years of prosperity and rising prices. In 1824 the annual costs had risen to £48 5s. - boarding costs had increased to £34 p.a. and teaching costs had doubled with the widening curriculum. There were other expenses not included in the board, for example, heating and light and the library. The journey to and from the school had to be paid and boys received a weekly allowance of about 9d. as well as the benefit of servants. The boarding income for, say, 90 pupils would have amounted to £3,060 p.a. and tuition costs raised £756. The school would have employed daily help and provided local tradesmen with a guaranteed outlet for their produce. Tradesmen provided consumables, clothing and services. The largest outlay in 1824 was £334 to Jacob and Johnson, who were book binders and stationers. Food was provided by Cully (a grocer and general dealer), and Edwards (a baker). The boys' clothes were provided by Bayspool (the hatter), Burt (a boot and shoe maker), Flight (a tailor) and Silver (a breeches maker). Wools were the linen drapers, Cave was employed as the house painter, and Rogers ran coaches to Southampton. Lyford, who was the surgeon at the Bridewell, provided medical care (Table 5.2).[28]

Table 5.2: Tradesmen's bills for Hyde Abbey School 1824

	£	s.	d.
Bayspool (hatter)	9	16	9
Burt (boot and shoe maker)	50	0	10
Cave (decorator)	17	18	0
Cully (grocer & general dealer)	2	10	6
Edwards (baker)	32	10	10
Jacob (book binder & stationer)	334	16	6
Lord	91	14	4 ½
Lyford (doctor)	13	15	0
Montraillant	25	4	0
Pourchier	28	7	0
Rogers (coaches)	31	14	6
Silver (breech maker)	26	11	10
Wigg	29	4	6
Wools (linen draper)	6	12	4
	£700	16s	11 ½d

Source: HRO:11M70/C3/2

In 1828 Rev. Richards (senior) retired from the school, although he still retained the living at St Bartholomew's until his death in 1833. His son Charles, who was rector of several parishes in the county, succeeded his father as headmaster. However he died at the age of 51, only two years after his father, in 1835. The school was closed and the premises were auctioned by the executors.[29] Over 75 years Hyde Abbey School had provided a first class education to future leaders in Parliament and the Church – Prime Ministers of the UK (George Canning) and New Zealand, the Deans of Winchester and Christchurch (Oxford) and several Bishops.

Reform

Later travellers were shocked by the desecration of the Abbey's remains when the prison was built. The political journalist - William Cobbett - writing on Oct 30th 1825 exclaimed:

> How, then, am I to describe what I felt, when I yesterday saw in HYDE MEADOW, a COUNTY BRIDEWELL, standing on the very spot, where stood the Abbey which was founded and endowed by Alfred, which contained the bones of that maker of the English name, and also those of the learned monk, ST GRIMBALD, whom ALFRED brought to England to begin the teaching at Oxford![30]

The County had two buildings for the detention of prisoners - the County Gaol and the Bridewell. The Bridewell held prisoners mainly sentenced to less than one year in prison, although there were a few serving sentences of 18 months or 2 years. There were also prisoners on remand awaiting trial at the County Court held in the Castle.

The County decided to build the Bridewell in 1785 and suitable land on the site of Hyde Abbey was purchased from Thomas Knight. As a distant landowner, who had recently inherited this estate, he had no sentimental attachments to the sacred site. He would have been keen to maximise Abbots Barton's financial yield and saw the offer as an opportunity to sell unproductive land.

A detailed bill of quantities provided a basis for bids for the construction of the Bridewell. These detailed the foundations, brickwork and internal fittings to be used. The Keeper's House consisted of a parlour, kitchen, brewhouse, cellar, pantry and attic. The work for a carpenter, plasterer, painter, plumber, glazier, mason and provision of ironmongery were described precisely in terms of type and measurement of materials.[31] Rooms were to be given two or three coats of plaster on the ceilings and walls. Windows were to be glazed with second Newcastle or Bristol Crown glass in the lead lights and square glass. Purbeck stone, used for door cills, steps and paving, was to be laid throughout the ground floor, with the exception of the parlour. Portland stone was used for the window cills, kitchen sink, in the brewhouse and in the chimneys and hearths.[32]

The felons' building was secured against escape. A smith was required to provide five iron bars and a cross bar, measuring 3½ by ½ inches, at the windows and cell door gratings. The bars were of iron and the quality was specified by value at 14s. per cwt.. Gratings were also needed in the chimneys. Water was supplied by wells under each washhouse, which were 3 feet in diameter and sunk 3½ feet below the water level. Sanitation consisted of six privies measuring 4 feet by 5 feet.

The building was to be completed by Christmas 1787, with the money advanced in tranches as follows: £500 on the completion of the ground floor; £500 for the next floor; £1,000 when the building was roofed; £500 when the Infirmary was finished; £1,000 when the Keeper's house and Felon Cells were finished; and the final £500 when the boundary walls around the courts were complete. Payment by instalments was a common method and ensured tradesmen completed to the specifications laid down and on time. The balance was to be paid within two months of completion.

Tenders were received in January 1786 but few actually met all the specifications. Half the bidders appeared not to want to commit to the foundation work, either through lack of experienced or competence. For example, the bid from Hayes and Lucas for £4,958 did not include planking or piling. The lowest bid of £3,795, from Kent and Collins, met all the specifications. Mr Gover's bid of £5,543 included a paved path to the Governor's house and to the Infirmary. Who was awarded the contract is not known, but on price alone it should have been Kent and Collins. The workmen set about the job with little regard for the archaeological remains. Milner describes how 'at almost every stroke the mattock and spade some ancient sepulchre or other was violated, the venerable contents of which were treated with marked indignity.' Stone coffins were damaged or turned into water troughs and bones tossed about. Artefacts found included marble column fragments and monastic paraphernalia such as a chalice and rings. Most importantly was the discovery of three coffins which were thought to contain the royal bones of Alfred, Ealhswith, and their son Edward the Elder. The lead of the main coffin was sold for two guineas.[33]

In April 1788, not long after the opening, there were nineteen prisoners; 14 had committed a felony, three were vagrants, one was a cheat and disorderly person, and one was remanded to give evidence against another prisoner. Most were serving sentences of three or six months close confinement or imprisonment, although some received a sentence of hard labour. Even women like Sophie Meads, could be sentenced to one year's imprisonment with hard labour. Her crime is not known as few details of offences were recorded. Charles Talmage and George Trowbridge were given three months under the Game Laws for destroying fish and game respectively. Charles Tuffin's duplicity in military service got him into trouble. He received six months imprisonment for 'enlisting into his Majesty's 61st Regiment of Foot, he being a subst. in Wilts Militia.' Thomas Cousins must have committed a heinous crime. He received six months imprisonment to hard labour and was then to be whipped from East Gate to West Gate.

Those lucky enough to be employed by the County were paid well. The keeper of the Bridewell received a salary of £200 p.a., but could not receive any further fee, gratuity or emolument, except a proportion of the earnings of prisoners and the produce of the garden and plot of ground attached to the prison. The first and second turnkeys received £45 p.a. and £40 p.a. respectively, and the chaplain £120 p.a.. The surgeon received £100 p.a., and he (or his assistant) were required to visit three times a week. There was a matron or female attendant on a salary £20 p.a., and this role was often taken by the wife of the Bridewell keeper.

Even in those unenlightened years, there was a concern for prisoners' welfare and measures to prevent disease spreading. Every prisoner was to be seen weekly and given directions for the preservation of health and cleanliness, and their person, clothing, bedding and cell examined. Each day the prisoners were required to wash, comb their hair and attend prayers.

Men shaved twice a week, washed feet as directed, and were given clean linen on Sundays. Prisoners received 1½ ounces of soap on entry and every Saturday afternoon. The sick were seen once a day by the surgeon or his assistant. Incoming prisoners were bathed, their hair cut short, and then examined by the surgeon. Those with a contagious disease were isolated. Clothes were taken away, fumigated and purified, and kept until a trial or discharge. Prison uniform was made from coarse material.

Incarceration was not an easy life. Prisoners rose at 6 a.m. in the summer and 7.30 a.m. in winter. Their beds had a straw mattress, two coarse sheets, two blankets and coverlet. The County provided one loaf of good household bread, one day old weighing 1½ pounds.[34] Those with hard labour or profitable work received an additional allowance. Coal was available to preserve health and protect from extreme cold. Disorderly prisoners forfeited earnings. Visitors were allowed between the hours of 9a.m. to 11a.m. and 1p.m. to 3p.m. for half an hour.

There were strict and detailed rules running to 65 pages issued in 1818 by the County of Southampton for the running of the County Gaol and Bridewell (or House of Correction), which covered the duties of the justices of peace, governor and deputy governor of gaol, keeper and turnkeys of the Bridewell, the chaplain, and the surgeon, and the treatment, employment and classification of convicts, felons and other criminals.[35] Although paid well, the Bridewell keeper's job was onerous and his role multifaceted. Administration was important. The keeper was required to keep detailed records of prisoners, convicts and felons, which included names, ages, descriptions, trades or professions, and details of the crimes and sentences. Financial accounts of the inventory, donations, subscriptions, bequests and expenses were to be up to date.

Discipline was of prime concern. Complaints were heard, occurrences of misbehaviour recorded and punishment given. There was zero tolerance for those who broke the strict rules. Prisoners could be put in solitary confinement on a bread and water diet for up to three days for the following offences: assaults on another when no dangerous wound or bruise was inflicted, profane cursing or swearing, gaming, indecent or contumacious behaviour, irreverent behaviour towards the chaplain, and idleness or negligence in work. If prisoners behaved in a turbulent or refractory manner or showed any disposition to escape then they were put in handcuffs or fetters. Each prisoner was seen twice every day in their cells to check if there was any indication that an escape was planned.

The employment of prisoners was deemed important for control and to discourage those who preferred a bed with food to sleeping rough. Adding to the administrative tasks, the keeper was required to keep a workbook which gave a weekly account of employment. This detailed if the prisoner was required to undertake hard labour, the nature of employment and remuneration. There were several stakeholders for any income from the work – the County, the governor, and the prisoner. Prisoners could be employed in the garden but not outside the walls. As well as growing food, the garden may have been used for animal husbandry, but it was a regulation that no officer was to keep poultry, pigeons, rabbits, pigs or domestic animals, except security dogs, within the walls.

The keeper was not allowed to show any favour, partiality or personal resentment to prisoners. He had to ensure that subordinate officers showed the same compassion and good temper towards prisoners. Staff were only allowed to hit a prisoner in self-defence. A humane and caring approach was clearly embedded in the regulations and the foundations of modern day practices set.

Control of the prison system was carefully monitored by the county. Two JPs were appointed to inspect the Bridewell three times a quarter to prevent abuses and grievances and to correct irregularities. JPs' duties were to: examine the state of the building, the conduct of officers, the condition and treatment, classification and behaviour of prisoners, to recommend gaolers, and appoint the chaplain, surgeon and instructors. They regulated expenses of the gaol and the earnings of prisoners. They were empowered to spend up to £200 p.a. on repairs, the purchase of implements, materials and books for employment and instruction of prisoners, and purchase bedding and clothing.

In 1819 the Bridewell contained 141 men, 16 women and 6 children. Thomas Baring's report, in his role as JP, classified the offences of the 163 prisoners (Table 5.3). [36] A large percentage of the inmates were awaiting trial – 40 per cent of men and 44 per cent of women. Of the 85 men serving a sentence, 37 had committed a felony and 21 had flouted the Game Laws, usually by poaching or receiving dead meat. In most respects, females were treated the same as males, but women with babies could receive extra food from friends.

Table 5.3: Offences of Bridewell prisoners in 1819

	Male	Female
Felon sentence over 1 year	26	1
Felon sentence under 1 year	11	2
Game laws	21	0
Uttering base coins	1	2
Disobeying order of filiation	3	0
Bastards	0	2
Assault	9	0
Misdemeanours	14	2
Prisoners for trial	56	7
Total	141	16

Source: HRO: 92M95/F2/1/19

The Courts were not lenient and most of the prisoners received hard labour. Rev. Hon. G. Herbert committed three men and two women to one month's imprisonment with hard labour for wandering and sleeping in the open air. Rev. A. G. Legge and Rev. R. Wright gave 30-year old Sarah Watmore a year with hard labour for being a lewd woman. Michael Foster was given one year for 'having unlawfully wilfully and knowingly in his possession part of a deer which had been unlawfully killed and not having produced the party of whom he received the same'. In comparison, George Hayter was only given six months for having 'unlawfully and wilfully killed a certain fallow deer' in the New Forest.

By 1828, the numbers of prisoners were increasing and more cells were needed. The keeper, in a letter to Baring, described the alterations carried out for the provision of more yards. Progress was as follows: two yards completed, two more nearly finished, three yards for separation of females covered in, and one more to be started in the Spring which gave nine yards in total, exclusive of the infirmary yard. [37]

At the forefront of the move to establish prisoners' employment, the Bridewell plans for employment and arrangement for classing prisoners was adopted nationally. Prisoners were required to be gainfully employed but this was difficult to achieve. Two corn mills kept prisoners in active employment and there were handicrafts for those unable to do hard labour. There was demand in Winchester to send wheat to the Bridewell to be ground and managers of two local charities (not named) wanted to purchase bread from the prison. Income from baking amounted to over £100 p.a.. To extend the work, plans were drawn up and submitted to Mr Gover who approved them. In what capacity Gover was involved is not known but he was one of the bidders for the original building. The plans proposed that all grinding was to be done at the north end of the prison yard and the south side was to be converted to a second bakehouse. Two ovens were necessary if the County was to make bread for the hospital and the letter states:

> Here I beg most respectively to submit that the magistrates must not forget that a commission is paid upon the wheat purchased for the Gaol and Bridewell which added to the price of the wheat ought to be a reason why the County should not undertake to make breads for the hospital under the baker's price.

It was impossible to supply both prison and hospital as the full capacity of the current bakehouse was reached by the consumption of eight or nine bushels per day plus the sale of flour. There were strong reasons not to enter into a contract with the hospital below baker's price as both improvements and running costs, such as the frequently dressing of the stones, were expensive.[38]

Female prisoners had no regular employment except washing, knitting, carding and spinning. Full employment for prisoners may have had the effect of reducing the number of farm servants and vagrants entering the prison; there was no quiet life here. In 1828 there were 175 prisoners in custody as follows: 40 men at the two treads, 48 at the capstans leaving 97 prisoners unemployed. The keeper commented to Baring 'which I no doubt you will consider a fearful number particularly when you take into account the offences with which very many of those have been charged.' [39]

The keeper also had strong views on the demon drink and hoped for the state of society that beer shops would be closed. Public houses open to midnight were a source of vice:

> Government is not aware of half the mischief that results from the trade. Men who go to these shops not radical reformers but radical rascals who set the authority of the King and every man as a magistrate at defiance and were taught to hate and despise everyone in a higher station in life than themselves. Government I know are slow to hear and not easily persuaded but as I love my country with all its faults I do most earnestly hope the day is not far distant for the sake of Society that the beer-shops will be soon closed for ever.[40]

In 1848, the County decided to build a new prison on West Hill, to replace the prison in Jewry Street and the Bridewell in Hyde. The Bridewell suffered the same fate of the Abbey before it. The buildings were quickly knocked down and stones recycled where possible.

Figure 5.9: Hyde in the late 1790s

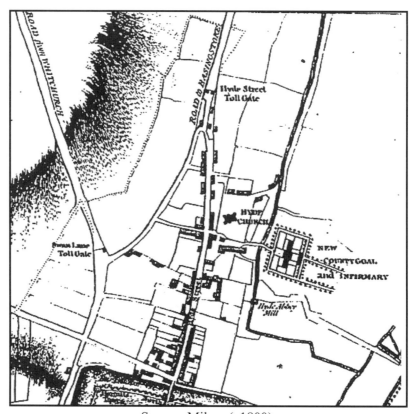

Source: Milner (c1800)
The Bridewell complex dominates the meadows behind the church. The Swan Lane and
Hyde Street toll gates are located close to the village

Industry

Since monastic times the Abbey and the Abbots Barton farms, along with other local agricultural holdings, provided the essential ingredients - barley and, later hops - for malting and brewing. The process changed little since the Dissolution, though increasing mechanisation reduced labour intensity. In Hyde, all stages of the supply chain were in close proximity: the barley grown on the uplands; the hop-fields close to the City to receive all the manure it could supply; and the malthouses and breweries in Hyde Street and Swan Lane.

Hops were planted in the autumn and poles strung up in February in preparation for plant growth. From April, agricultural workers trained the vines to climb clockwise up the string. The choice of hop variety determined the flavour of the beer. After harvesting in late August, the hop cones were left to dry before transportation to the brewery. Malting consisted of several stages. The grain was soaked in a steeping pit or cistern for a few days to start germination. It was then drained and transferred to wooden boards and then laid on the growing floor, where the grain was allowed to sprout over a two-week period. Once the husks split, the grain was dried or heated to prevent further growth. Keeping the process under control required careful supervision by experienced maltsters. As the process was affected by high temperatures, maltings mainly operated over the winter months when the agricultural workers were in abundance to provide the seasonal labour needed in the maltings.

During the nineteenth century, many small maltings and breweries went into decline when mechanisation improved techniques, allowing maltings to operate throughout the year. Breweries took on more roles in the production line on-site and shortened the supply chain rather than buying ingredients in from independent maltsters. The railways allowed the transport of grain across the country and, more important economically, the transport of cheaper, imported crops. The brewing process was governed by regulations, for example, the construction of the cistern to allow inspection of the grain by the excise officer. Regulations covered the environmental effects of the process, and satisfactory adherence was recorded in a ledger of the operations. The maltster was required to give notice of 24 hours (or 48 hours if outside the town) before wetting the grain which then had to be kept covered for two days, except for one hour when the water was changed. The grain could only be transferred to the cistern between 8a.m. and 2p.m. and taken out between 7a.m. and 4p.m..[41]

Like today, the brewery industry was a lucrative source of government income. Malt was taxed between 1697 and 1880. The volume of the grain was carefully measured, noting length, width and height, and the duty assessed. In 1697 the tax on malted barley was 6d. per bushel but was increased fivefold by 1834. This duty contributed 11½ per cent of tax revenues, which increased rapidly to finance the Napoleonic Wars of 1793 to 1815. The cost of the main ingredients, malt and hops, fluctuated according to the harvests.[42] The 1872 accounts for Simonds of Reading (who were related to William Simonds) gave these costs as 50 per cent of turnover. Expenses such as wages, transport and cask makings took 35 per cent and the other 15 per cent was accounted for by fixed liabilities, such as interest payments, and profits.[43]

Brewing was a necessary requirement to provide safe drinking in the age of polluted water supplies. The oldest malthouse belonged to the Abbey and over time had been demolished and replacements built. The earliest surviving records, which relate to several malthouses and breweries along Hyde Street and Swan Lane, date from the 1770s. The now called Barton Farm's malthouse lay behind the remaining wing of Hyde Abbey House. There was a malthouse (referred to as Malthouse No. 2) in the northern part of Hyde of which Hyde Tavern is today's only reminder (Figure 5.10). Malthouse No. 1 lay on the west side of Hyde Street and Malthouse No. 3 dominated Swan Lane. The key events in ownership of these properties are given in Table 5.4.

Table 5.4: Key events in the history of Hyde Brewery 1770 – 1807

1770	Samuel Waldron purchased two messuages and a garden in the north part of Hyde
1785	Robert Page, maltster raised a £550 mortgage on a messuage, orchard and garden. He built Malthouse No. 2 on the land.
1791	Two messuages and the White Swan formed part of the marriage settlement between Samuel Maunders and Ann Mason.
1795	Robert Page is declared bankrupt.
1798	Thomas Knight, landowner, sold part of Hyde Garden to Thomas Deane.
1801	Thomas Deane sold part of Hyde garden to Nicholas Pyle, brewer.
1804-6	Nicholas Pyle purchased 24 acres of land including 14 houses and gardens, and two malthouses.
1807	Thomas Deane (wine merchant) sold two messuages, which had been built over a cellar or vault, to Nicholas Pyle.

Source: HRO:206M85W

As today many businesses did not flourish and owners experienced financial difficulties and often ruin. In the earliest record relating to Malthouse No. 2, dated 1770, Samuel Waldron obtained two messuages and garden through a lease and release on which he paid 5s. poor rate charges. In 1796 Waldron raised a mortgage by demise from Edward Smith. However, Waldron experienced financial problems and in 1804 the two messuages and gardens were sold by Waldron's creditors to Nicholas Pyle, a Hyde Street brewer.[44]

In 1786 Robert Page, a Hyde maltster, raised a mortgage of £500 on a messuage with orchard and garden. The property was described as 'adjacent to St Bartholomew on the east and the King's highway leading from the City to Worthy Mortimer and bounded by the vicarage land and partly with the churchyard on the east formerly in the possession of Thomas Godwin afterwards Robert Moule (or Mould).' [45] In 1795, Page was declared bankrupt in the Court of Chancery and the recently erected malthouse, storehouse and outbuildings were sold. His occupation and fate was described as follows:

> Nine years past in the trade and business of maltster, mealman, dealer and chapman by buying of seeds, barley and oats and working and converting such barley and oats into malt and oatmeal and selling the same and sought and endeavoured to get his living thereby as others of the same trade and business usually do and that in the course of his trading and dealing he became indebted to John Moody for £100 or more.[46]

After Thomas Knight's death, his widow Catherine and Edward Austen instructed Thomas' executors, Deedes and Cage, to sell part of Hyde Garden to the brewer Thomas Deane who already held the tenancy. The plot, which extended to just over one acre, was conveyed in 1799 for £316 15s.. The land was enclosed with walls on the west and south and a fence in the north. Another part of Hyde Garden was purchased by Rev. Charles Richards.[47] Plaques were placed on either side of the adjoining wall indicating which land belonged to Richards and which to Deane.[48]

Documents often provide details of surrounding properties, owners and occupiers. The house belonging to Mr William Meaden lay close to the centre of the partition wall and was occupied by Mrs Hernott, a widow. The adjacent meadow (belonging to Abbots Barton), which was formerly rented to Thomas Pink, was then occupied by Deane and Abraham Knight. On the west side, the garden or yards and outbuildings of houses in Hyde Street were occupied by Mrs Hernott, Deane, Samuel Waldron and John Harris. Deane rented the City ditch and the Town Ponds in the south. Deane did not retain his part of Hyde Garden for long and in 1801 sold it to Nicholas Pyle for £400, giving him a profit of 26 per cent over two years.[49]

Figure 5.10: Malthouse No. 2 in the north of Hyde Street

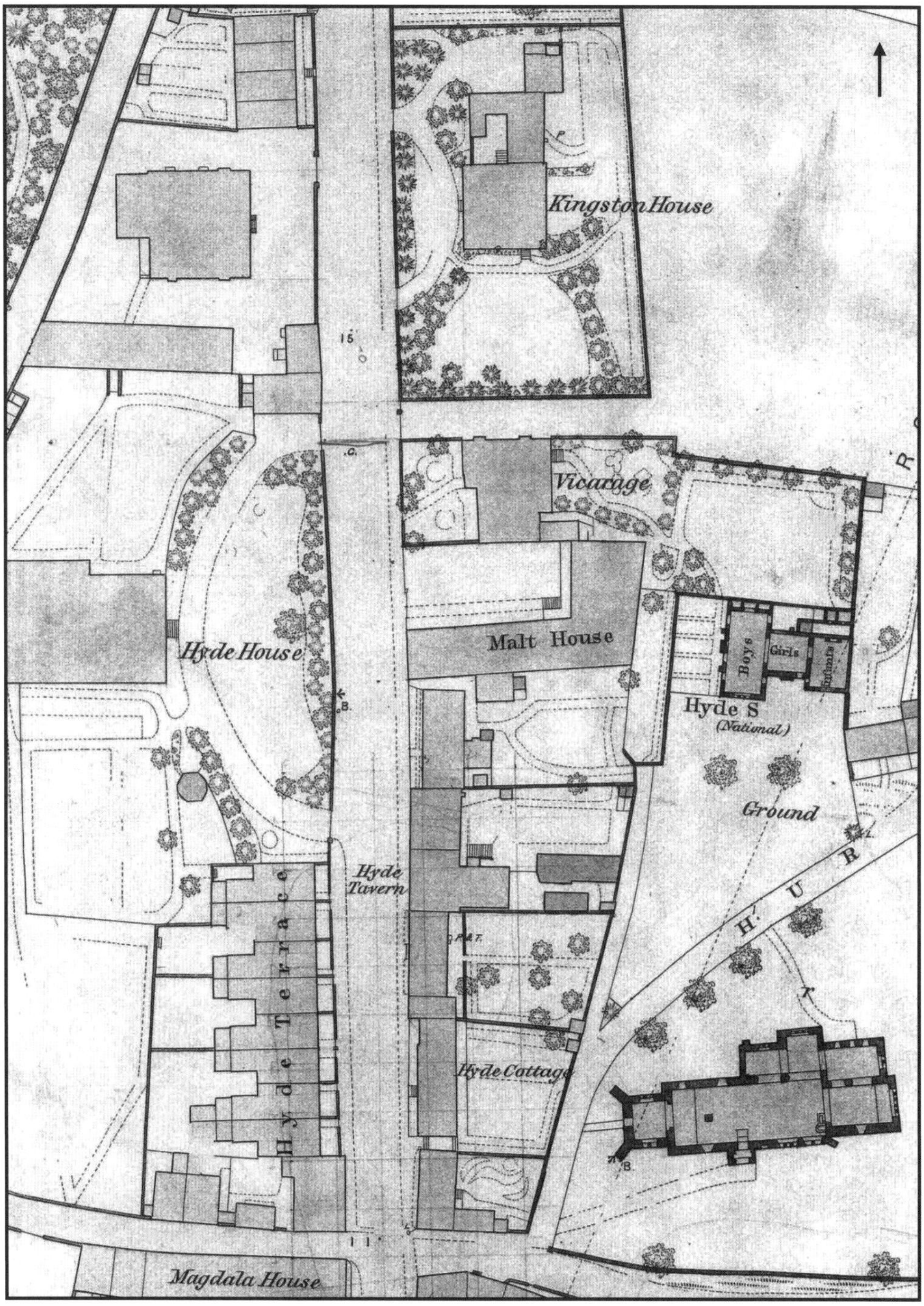

Source: O.S. Map 1st Edition 1873

In 1873 the malthouse was surrounded by residential properties. The most exclusive were Kingston House to the north and Hyde House opposite.

Nathaniel and Mary Fletcher owned considerable real estate in the parishes of St Bartholomew, St Maurice (within the City) and St John. Details of land sales (given below) suggest the estate formed part of the holdings of a brewery and its public houses. In 1791 Thomas Hall leased six messuages, two malthouses and a brewhouse from the Fletchers.[50] In 1804, they sold the freehold and leasehold estates with 24 acres of land in these parishes to Nicholas Pyle. Other freehold estates had already been sold to Daniel Kingsgate and Richard Page. Pyle's acquisition included 14 houses and gardens, a brewhouse, two malthouses, storehouse, cart house, two stables and a yard. The marriage settlement of the Fletchers gives a more detailed description of the Hyde properties:

> Messuage and malthouse with outhouses and garden plot in Hyde Street; close or parcel of ground containing two acres planted with hops; a messuage garden and backside on Hyde Street; property lying on the east side of Hyde Street described as between the tenement in occupation of Robert Phillips on the north, west by the street, the wall of orchard of late Abbey on the east and the tenement occupied by Collis Grant, then George Barber on the south; part of orchard containing 'twenty-two lugs, one quarter and eleven feet' occupied by Harry Colpes followed by John Doswell. [51]

Colpes may have been related to Henry Colpes who had inherited from Edmund Clerke.

Pyle's brewing business in Hyde was expanding throughout Winchester with ownership of the Rodney's Head in St John's Street, the Britannia in Lower Brook Street and a messuage with two tenements, a shop and piece of ground by the poorhouse of St Maurice.[52]

The history of the White Swan can be traced back to 1767 with a lease & release between Edward Gray (a wine cooper), his daughters - Ann Maunder and Mary Gray - and John Beadburne and John Doswell.[53] The tenement, vault, malthouse, hereditaments and premises were occupied by John Tompkins and William Thomas, tenants of Samuel Maunder. The 1791 marriage settlement between Samuel Maunder (a miller) and Ann Mason featured several freehold messuages, their backsides and two leasehold garden plots belonging to the Corporation.[54] Such settlements were not only used by the gentry to secure rights. The use of the property resided with Mason until her marriage, then to Samuel Maunder for life, then back to Ann for her life, before passing to their children. [55]

In 1806 and 1807 Pyle extended his holdings, raising finance by way of a mortgage from Mr Dowling, Sarah Dix (widow) and James Drover, a cooper of Lymington.[56] The White Swan site, which included a stable and shop (adjoining the malthouse) and a tenement (adjoining the Inn) with vault and malthouse, was acquired from Maunder (a printer and bookseller residing in Bromley). It is not known what Maunder's relationship was to Ann. Two freehold messuages, which were built over a cellar or vault, and gardens were acquired from Thomas Deane, by then described as a wine merchant.

Pyle paid £650 for Malthouse No. 2. A fuller description of the site and adjacent properties retold the history:

Messuage, orchard and garden bounded by Vicarage Lane on north, land formerly of John Sheppard, late of John Doswell and now Mrs Earle on the south and partly by Vicarage land and partly by churchyard there on east. The premises were formerly in the possession of Thomas Godwin, then Robert Moule (or Mould), then Robert Page, and late of Thomas Deane and Digory Mill. The malthouse, storehouse and outbuilding had been recently erected and built by Robert Page on part of the orchard and garden. A part of the land was reserved to Thomas Deane.[57]

The separate brewery sites fell under one owner.

Figure 5.11: Swan Lane c.1875

Source: WINCM:3793

Malthouse No. 3 lies behind the cottages. Part of the brewery tower and chimney can be seen in the background. At the end of the street is the White Swan.

Figure 5.12: Malthouses No. 1 (Hyde Street) & No. 3 (Swan Lane)

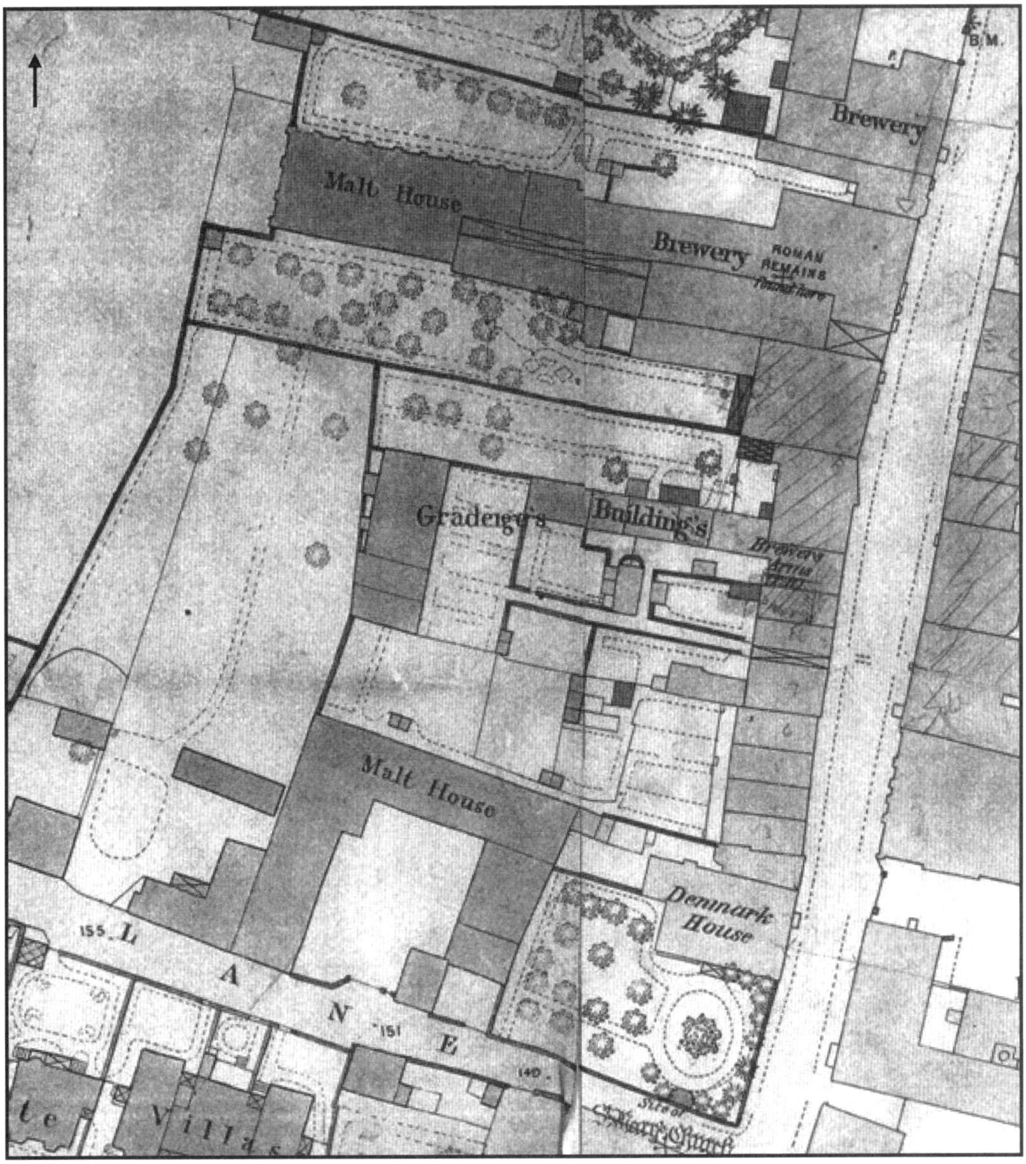

Source: O.S. Map 1ˢᵗ Edition 1873

Malthouse No. 1 lay behind one of the two brewery buildings on the west side of Hyde Street. Malthouse No. 3 dominated Swan Lane. Note also Gradeige's Buildings and Denmark House standing in extensive gardens. The house was built on Purdew's freehold plot.

Conclusion

During the eighteenth and nineteenth centuries, spurred on by the new network of toll roads, Hyde Street grew from a village community to an industrial hub. Brewing was an important industry and the community benefited from three malthouses. However this was a period of change and for some financial difficulties. Ownership of the malthouses passed through several hands until all were acquired by Nicholas Pyle, under whom the Brewery expanded its outlets into neighbouring parishes.

The church, schools and reforming institution were important contributors to Hyde's history and development. The famous Hyde Abbey School ensured that Hyde was well known throughout the country for providing a classical education. Rev. Charles Richards, headmaster and vicar of St Bartholomew's, was immortalised in the tales of Rood Priory. The school and grounds were well maintained during the school's existence and Richards' passions ensured the survival of many interesting architectural features and artefacts.

The construction of the Bridewell destroyed any surviving traces of the Abbey and desecrated the supposed resting place of Alfred, his wife Ealhswith, and son Edward the Elder. Like the monks in the Abbey, the inmates in the cells were well-cared for and provided service to the community. Although the building of the Bridewell was controversial to those who revered the Abbey's remains, its practices became a model for the nation to adopt.

Figure 5.13: The White Swan and Northfield House in Hyde Street

Part 3: The Making of the Modern Suburb

William Simonds, a farmer who was not afraid of progress, facilitated the path of the railway through his land, even though it cut through his 50-acre fields. His death coincided with a decline in agriculture and his son, William Barrow Simonds, stayed financially solvent through diversification into urban development.

During the late nineteenth century the population of Hyde grew substantially. Hyde Street increasingly became industrialised and dominated by breweries. Employment in agriculture declined as the acreage of farmland waned and a greater level of mechanisation was adopted.

The land lost to housing during William Simonds' custodianship of the former Abbey's farms was limited. However, over 54 years William Barrow Simonds changed Hyde from a village, which had expanded little over the 300 years since the Abbey was destroyed, to a suburb with desirable homes set in leafy countryside for the eminent citizens of Winchester.

Compact streets were built for the upwardly mobile middle and lower classes. The first of these followed the closure of the Bridewell in 1850 when, once again, the site of Hyde Abbey was desecrated. Simonds was responsible for only one of these new estates; an established Hyde family and a lord also made their mark.

Chapter 6 begins with the law suit which challenged William Simonds' ownership of Abbots Barton (brought by distant members of the Knight family). Like characters out of a Jane Austen novel, they claimed to be the rightful owners of the land by the entail set up in Elizabeth Knight's will. The greatest impact on the farm and Winchester was the coming of the railway. Farmland was transformed and small parcels of land were released for development. In Hyde Street, the brewing business expanded managed by one of Simonds' relatives.

Chapter 7 records the continuous eroding of the farmland as Barrow Simonds satisfied the needs of the expanding professional classes and details how the green fields were replaced by leafy suburbs.

Chapter 8 describes the processes by which urban sprawl finally destroyed any remnants of the former Abbey and farmland, although Hyde escaped the 'row upon row' seen in other cities.

In Chapter 9, Hyde is seen through the eyes of a time traveller who maps the changes in Winchester's northern portal over the past 100 years.

Nine hundred years of changing ownership gives a fleeting overview of the key events and the men and women that have shaped the modern suburb of Hyde and those determined to keep its history.

Figure 6.1: Georgian terraced houses in Hyde Street

Chapter 6: William Simonds, the farmer

The law suit

During the 1760s, the Winchester branch of the Simonds family moved to Priors Barton in St Cross where they leased extensive farm lands from the Dean and Chapter. The lease was based on three lives rather than a number of years. One of the lives was George III and, as John Barrow Simonds remarked in 1968, the family 'did well out of that'.[1] William Simonds never lived in Hyde, but preferred to stay in the house where he was born, even though he became the owner of Abbots Barton Farm in 1811.

Landowners were frequently embroiled in litigation over both land and family issues. Litigation had potentially serious consequences for the future of their estates and decisions as to which members of the extended family could inherit were central to preserving the estates intact. Land concerns ranged (in descending importance): validity of the title of a property, extent of manorial rights, lease conditions and boundaries, and non-payment of rents and breaches of covenants. In recent years, compulsory land registration displaced the common law position that the owner of land was the person who had the best claim. In the past, occupiers could be displaced at any time if a superior claimant emerged. There were plenty of lawyers willing to assist those who saw themselves in this advantageous position, irrespective of the merits of the case. Family matters were centred on inheritance issues associated with entails, marriage settlements and wills.

Simonds purchased the title of Abbots Barton in good faith. Seven years later, in 1818, he was horrified to find this was challenged by Jane Baverstock and her half-brother John Knight Hinton, neither of whom had been a party to the original sale. Jane was the daughter of Rev. John Hinton by his first marriage to his cousin Martha Hinton (a distant relative of the Knights of Chawton). John Knight Hinton was one of four children by John Hinton's second marriage to Jane Harrison. Until the death of Catherine Knight in 1812 the inheritance could not be questioned since her possession was in accordance with the entail. Edward Austen, on inheritance, had changed his name to Knight, which inflamed the Hinton-Baverstock family, and they seized the opportunity to claim the fortune that they saw as rightly theirs by virtue of their lineage. Whereas Edward, as an adopted heir, failed to satisfy the conditions in the entail, they were the descendants of Thomas Knight's nearest male relative.

The challenge to William Simonds was linked to a law-suit brought against Edward Knight by the Hinton-Baverstock family in October 1814 when they laid claim to the Chawton Estate as heirs-in-law to Elizabeth Knight. Jane's son, James Hinton Baverstock, described as a 'clever and rather scampish brewer of Alton,' was the chief claimant along with his sister Mary Dusautoy.[2] The challenge is well known to Jane Austen aficionados as she mentioned the case in several of her letters. The Chawton claim was not settled until 1818 (after Jane

Austen's death), when Edward agreed to pay £15,000 in settlement to the Hintons. Vast tracts of timber were felled on the estate to raise the money.

The claim to the legal title of Abbots Barton centred on Edward Knight having sold something he did not possess, not being the true heir. Since Catherine Knight was still alive at the time of the sale, which was undertaken by Thomas Knight's trustees, the claim may not have been upheld. However legal bills were likely to be high, could continue for many years, and therefore best avoided.

The deed of confirmation brought by John Knight Hinton of Chawton and Jane Baverstock (now a widow who had moved from Chawton to Windsor), was dated 5 June 1818, claimed that Jane was entitled to the premises, formerly part of Elizabeth Knight's estate. The detailed recitals refer to the will of Elizabeth Knight and explained how Hinton and Baverstock had legal title to the premises. The entail had been broken as Edward was not an heir of the body. The claim traced the family lineage in detail as evidence of the legal title:

Table 6.1: The Hinton and Baverstock claim to legal title of Abbots Barton

Whereas the said Thomas Knight the older, William Lloyd and John Hinton tenant for life of the said manors and hereditaments under the will of Elizabeth Knight have severally departed this life and there has been a failure of the entail male of Thomas Knight the older and William Lloyd respectively and John Knight Hinton is the only surviving son of John Hinton, the only other son having died an infant and before marriage. And Jane Baverstock is the only surviving child and heir of law of Martha Hinton only daughter and heir of Rev Edward Hinton late son and heir of Joan Martin afterwards wife of John Hinton which Joan Hinton was daughter and heir of Edward Martin the brother of Richard Martin who was grandfather of Elizabeth Knight formerly Elizabeth Martin daughter of Michael Martin and Elizabeth Knight had not any sister and her only brothers Richard Knight formerly called Richard Martin and Christopher Knight formerly called Christopher Martin respectively died in her lifetime without output and Elizabeth Knight formerly Elizabeth Martin afterwards intermarried with William Woodward afterwards called William Knight and said Jane Baverstock is the cousin and heir at law of Elizabeth Knight and John Knight Hinton and Jane Baverstock alleges that the recovery suffered by Thomas Knight the elder and Thomas Knight the younger was defective.

Source: HRO:13M85W/41&42

The claim would have broken the chain of conveyance on which William Simonds' title depended. Simonds had not, at that point, been in possession of the land for sufficient time to claim ownership through adverse possession. William Simonds and his lawyers were satisfied that the purchase had a good title and that the claim was not valid. However to avoid further litigation they agreed to purchase:

a release of all the right whatever it may be of and were formerly the estate of Elizabeth Knight for the price of £650, one third to be paid to John Hinton Knight and two-thirds to Jane Baverstock, for absolute purchase of their respective rights, tithes and interests.[3]

In effect Hinton and Baverstock provided a bill of sale that extinguished any rights they may have had in the land. The matter was resolved legally in November 1818 by a process of Common Recovery whereby William Simonds was shown to have absolute title and the contenders were paid off. If he had been unwilling to pay Hinton and Baverstock or they had won the case, the future of Hyde could have been very different.

Figure 6.2: Barton Farm and the remnants of Hyde Garden

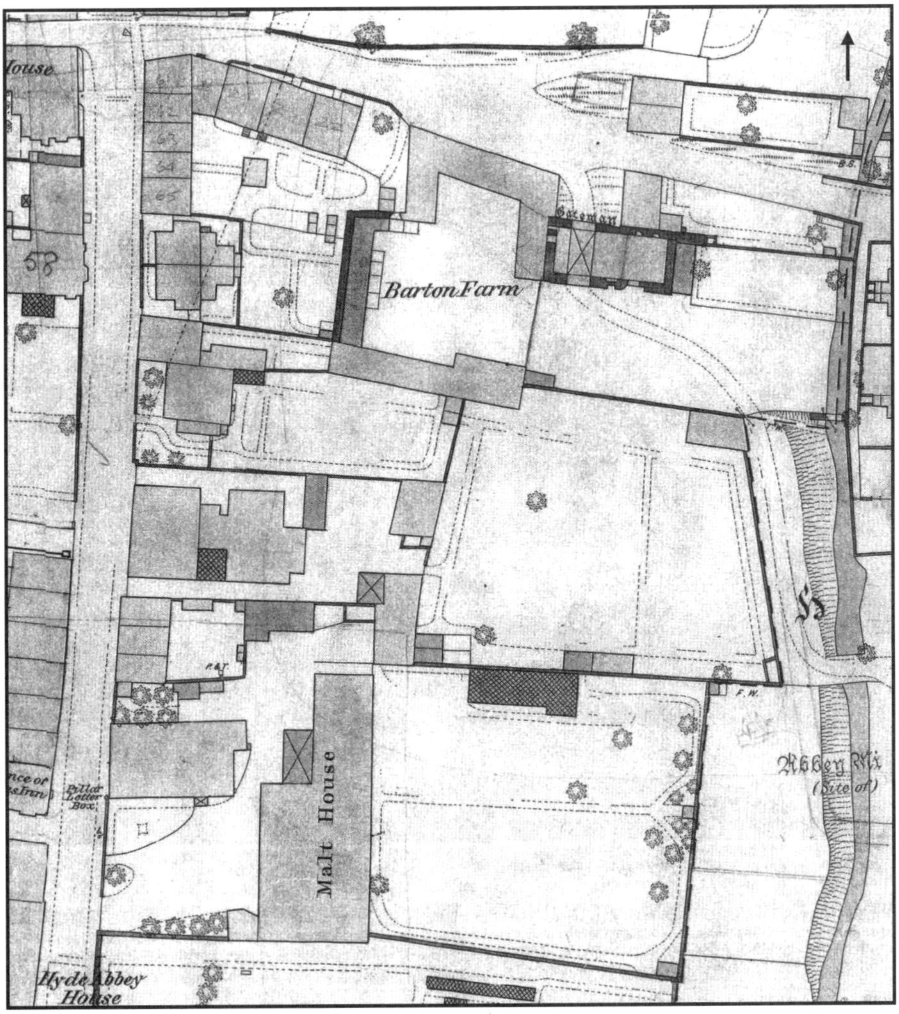

Source: O.S. Map 1st Edition 1873
The garden plots to the east and north-east of the malthouse have not changed since the 1560s (Figure 2.2).

The coming of the railway

The coming of the railway had a profound effect on Winchester's economy, increasing the flow of produce and people in and out of the City. Abbots Barton Farm was divided into two as the line cut through the arable fields. Proposals for Winchester's first rail link from London and on to Southampton gathered momentum in the 1830s. The potential benefits were promoted in the London & Southampton Railway pamphlet of 1832:

> Although the advantage to be derived from a railway to those parts of the country through which it may pass; to the places which may be brought into intimate connexion by its means; and to the trade, commerce and agriculture of the nation, are now generally admitted, it is deemed proper, briefly to show on what grounds the projected railway between London and Southampton, may lay claim to consider and support; for which purpose the following pages have been compiled. [4]

The coming of the railway provided an important link for the whole of Hampshire. Francis Giles, the civil engineer, discussed the capability of the port of Southampton to meet increasing demand from commercial trade. Expansion of the port had been hindered by the lack of inland infrastructure for the distribution of imported goods. The construction of the line needed the support of the landowners along its proposed route as well as that of the towns through which it went. The railway was seen as beneficial to both landowners and the local economy with a boost in employment both during construction and afterwards for maintenance. The pamphlet was signed by many Hampshire landowners, who consented to take shares in the project in payment for the amount of land required for the railway.[5]

Although Winchester, as a county town, had a cattle market and farmers had a ready local outlet for their produce, the railway would reach a larger customer base. The report estimated that the line could increase the value of a farming estate by 30 per cent. The railway provided an essential service that changed the system of farming to provide an efficient method of reaching the London markets. For farmers doing business in Smithfield market, there was a long and expensive journey by coach taking several days for the round trip. The railway allowed dairy farms to send fresh milk and butter to more distant markets. Cattle driven on foot to market were often injured, lost condition, suffered sore feet, and many were sold on the road at a low price. The cost of driving cattle over 40 miles by road and the subsequent selling expenses was 10s., 70 per cent of which was the journey. Many cattle were lost and farmers were willing to pay a premium of around 20 per cent for safe transit. Lambs and calves could not easily be sent to London by road. Sheep driving cost 1s. a head and those driven 80 miles had a weight loss of half a stone, valued at 4s. 6d. a stone. The transporting of dead meat in hot weather was undesirable, whereas the railway allowed live animals to arrive in good health.

The railway was beneficial to a range of businesses and services, for example, the transportation of goods such as bullion to the banks, or the correspondence between landowners and lawyers in London. Although local troops could march to their barracks when there was no urgency, the railway provided faster conveyance with a typical speed of 20 miles per hour. [6]

Railway companies paid landowners a 'great sum for gravel, timber, stone taken from estate, for making bricks etc., they have paid very large sums.' Simonds received full compensation for any damage to his land and inconvenience from restricted access. Evidence suggested that turnpikes were in a better state of repair due to less traffic. Financially the parishes benefitted as the railways were assessed for local rates on net income, with landowners and tenants experiencing corresponding reduction in rates. Furthermore property rents rose by about one-fifth. [7]

In September 1833 a call for capital of £1m was made. [8] The importance of the proposed link was highlighted. From Southampton, the steam packets sailed to Guernsey, Jersey, the Isle of Wight, and the ports of Cherbourg and Le Havre. To encourage investment, the prospectus claimed that the proposed line had the consent and co-operation of nearly all the landed proprietors. The soil and levels on the route were described as 'well adapted to its formation and to its permanent maintenance at a moderate expense.' The management and maintenance charges were estimated at less than £56,000 p.a. with a moderate traffic level. [9]

Shares were priced at £50 each fully paid, and only a £2 deposit was needed until an act of Parliament was obtained. Further payments were by instalment, with no call of greater than £5 per share afterwards, and three months' notice between calls. With the support of the landowners, the intention was to initiate the act of Parliament in the next session and the prediction was that within two years the railway would have reached 20 miles out of London. Work was begun by the end of 1834 with the contractor, Thomas Brassey, being responsible for the section from Basingstoke to Winchester.

The route was first surveyed in 1831, but the plan was opposed by Sir Thomas Baring M.P.. The proposed route passed east of West Gate and necessitated the demolition of lower class housing. After the third survey in 1834, an acceptable proposal was made. The final route passed through St Bartholomew's, across part of the sparsely populated parish of Weeke, and south through St Faith's. This necessitated buying 23 plots of land in Weeke and 14 in St Thomas belonging to the main institutional landowners, some of whom assented (Churchwardens of St Bartholomew), others were neutral (Winchester College and St John's Charity) but the Dean and Chapter did not reply. [10] New bridges were built and turnpikes re-routed.

Prior to purchasing Abbots Barton, William Simonds farmed a substantial acreage in St Faith's around the village of St Cross. A few acres were freehold, but most were on long lease from the Dean and Chapter. In 1835, the London and Southampton Railway Company paid Simonds £7,150 for land required for the railway. This was broken down into £5,160 for 11 acres of freehold land in Hyde and £1,990 for Simonds' interest in the leasehold premises in St Cross. The railway's route cut through Abbots Barton Uplands between the Andover and Worthy Roads, splitting the six 50-acre arable fields.

The route map showed four fields around the northern boundary, a field stretching across the middle of the area and a field at the southern end. Simonds had opened up the fields for arable and the boundaries no longer coincided with those shown on the Knight's estate map (Figure 4.7). The Downs, Long Field, the Upper, Middle and Lower Bottom closes, the Hangar, Round Field, Gallows Field, Old Hop Garden and Limekilns were no longer distinct areas. The rail track restricted access for Simonds by dividing the Uplands into two. This would have significantly increased his working expenses and lowered the value of the whole farm.

The railway company covenanted to erect several bridges and arches at their expense. One bridge or archway was to be sited at the fence dividing the southern two fields with the roadway (now Park Road) and was constructed eighteen feet above the level of the top of the rails. The other bridge or archway was to be placed about one-third of the way along the northern boundary at a point on the railway line where the embankment was between 18 and 20 feet high (the farm track from Andover Road to Worthy Road). Two other archways in St Faith's, one in St Faith's Field (now one of the main accesses to the University of Winchester via Ranelagh and Airlie Road) and the other at Barnes Close (which provides pedestrian access from St Cross to Stanmore - which was then fields), were built. The railway company were not allowed to erect any building or establish on any part of Simonds' freehold or leasehold land any station, wharf, toll or turnpike gate or other building or make any branch road or footpath without his consent.[11]

Mogg's 1841 guide to the London and Southampton Railway details the whole line. The approach to Winchester station through Hyde is described as follows:

> Here occurs a short cutting crossed by an occupation bridge, a little beyond which the 63 milestone is attained. The last remaining 1½ miles to Winchester is divided into nearly equal proportions, viz. The Hyde embankment and excavation, so named from the village they approach in the vicinity of Winchester; from the former the traveller gets a distant view on left of the beautiful valley through which runs the river Itchen, and here the City of Winchester with its venerable Cathedral first rises into view; near the latter the turnpike-road to Andover is carried over the Railway which here reaches the Winchester station.[12]

The arrival of the railway significantly impacted on Hyde, changing Abbots Barton's agricultural practices and leading to the growth of manufacturing industries like brewing. The railway facilitated immigration and increased the demand for housing. Opportunities to travel for pleasure and business increased with London now easily accessible. Servants and horses could be taken by train at a price. Manufacturers, tradesmen and builders from Southampton, Portsmouth and Reading were attracted to the developing suburbs. Mixed class trains ran from Winchester to Southampton four times daily; first class trains twice; goods trains in the early morning and evening; and the mail train, which also took passengers, left at 11:11p.m.. The time from London to Winchester varied between two and a half hours and just under three hours. The first class trains were a little faster and were non-stop between London and Woking. The afternoon goods train took five hours. The fares from London to Winchester, a distance of 64 miles, varied according to class and train. Seats on the first-class faster trains cost 18s. 6d., with servants charged 13s.. There were stipulations for the wealthy. The number of servants carried was limited and they had to be in livery. The mixed-class trains seats were priced at 17s. 6d. for first class and 12s. for second class. Third class passengers had a reduced fare of 6s. 6d., but had to travel on the day goods train. The fare from Winchester to Southampton is missing from the document. However, the fares for the 77 miles from London to Southampton were 21s. for first class with servants charged 15s. on the fast train, 20s. for first class and 14s. for second class on the mixed trains. Third class passengers paid 8s..[13] The railway company misjudged demand and further services were added. Local shareholders who had invested £8,450 (including £1,000 from Baring) must have been very satisfied.

Passengers were allowed to carry on personal luggage but not merchandise. Like air transport today, there was a weight limit dependent on class – 112 lbs. (a cwt. or 50.8 kg) for first class, 56 lbs. for second class and 28 lbs. for third class, with an excess charge of 1s. 6d. per cwt.. Passengers with a large quantity of luggage had to arrive at least 15 minutes before departure. The train also took carriages and horses - providing a day's notice was given and they arrived at the station 20 minutes before departure. Transportation of one horse cost 36s. from London to Winchester and 42s. between London and Southampton. Two horses were discounted at approximately one-third and three horses were charged on the same basis pro-rata. Travel overseas became easier. From Southampton boats left daily for Le Havre, four times a week to the Channel Islands, the Peninsular and Orient Company (P&O) sailed weekly to Spain and Portugal, and the Indian mail was sent monthly via Malta and Alexandria. There were regular departures to the seaside resorts along the south-west coast and on to Dublin.

The impact of the railway on farmers and producers like the Simonds family cannot be overstated. It gave them access to wider markets but also generated competition from domestic sources and imported goods. One of the factors behind the Great Depression which affected farmers in the late nineteenth century was cheap foodstuffs from abroad. The railway promoted business links with London. Locally born professionals, like solicitors and architects, who went to London for training were able to maintain strong links with their home town. New design ideas infiltrated into the suburban developments in Hyde that took place in the latter part of the century.

Early land releases

At the start of Victoria's reign, the medieval village of Hyde had changed little over the centuries. With the exception of Hyde Street and a few surrounding lanes, the parish was completely rural with Abbots Barton Farm dominating the landscape. In the early 1800s there was little population growth. In 1841 the total population was only 776, an increase of less than 10 per cent from 1801. The male population was mostly employed in agriculture and related industries. There were few large houses needing female servants or other sources of employment for women.[14]

The purchase of the Abbots Barton estate in 1811 put the Simonds family in an influential position in Hyde. The farmland stretched from North Walls in the south to the parish of Headbourne Worthy in the north, and from the Andover Road in the west, across Worthy Road to the water meadows in the east.

During the nineteenth century, economic difficulties led to a decline in farming with the subsequent sale of land. This national phenomenon began after the riots of the 1830s and gathered speed throughout the rest of the century. City growth was an important source of income when agricultural estates suffered financial difficulties.[15] The 16 acres sold for the railway, was the beginning of the process. Over 70 years, father and son, William and William Barrow Simonds, released farming land for building development, both for housing and other uses. They maintained an interest in the fields released for estate development either by issuing a long lease or through restrictive covenants that constrained future development.

The only record of any release of land by William Simonds for development was Highfield Lodge, which was situated in four acres of grounds at the junction of Worthy Lane and Andover Road. The lease and release dated May 1838 involved three parties - William Gover and his wife - May Ann, William Theolophilus Graeme, and William Henry Cotterill (probably Graeme's lawyer). Simonds issued a building lease to Gover. When the house was completed in August, the land and house was conveyed to Graeme. In December 1838, Graeme raised a mortgage from Henry Boders, George Smith Thornton and George Robert Marten with the property being re-conveyed by them in 1851 when the loan was repaid.[16] Even in late Victorian Winchester, building societies were still a limited source of borrowing so money was raised privately.[17] In 1861 Graeme was described as a County Magistrate and Distributor of Stamps.[18] Ten years later, at the age 88, he still lived at Highfield. In March 1875 Graeme raised another mortgage for £2,000 plus interest from James Crowden and Robert Hill Crowden, brush manufacturers in the City of London, and from Robert Hill, from Sutton in Surrey. At the same time Graeme gifted the property to Alice Rideout (a spinster), whose relationship to Graeme is not known. He died two years later in 1877 and his estate passed to Rideout, who sold the property for £4,750 to Giles Henry Pointer, a Winchester brewer. The property was described as:

All freehold messuage of tenement called Highfield Lodge with the lodge stable, coach house, gardens, pleasure grounds and paddock comprising of four acres in the parish of St Bartholomew.

For reasons only known to him, Pointer declared his widow was not to be entitled to dower.[19]

Hyde Lodge and grounds stood just north of Highfield Lodge at the junction of Worthy Lane and Hyde Street and this plot was released for development by Simonds at approximately the same time (Figure 6.3)

Figure 6.3: Hyde Lodge

Details about house ownership and property descriptions give an insight into the stability of the population of Hyde and the social standing and aspirations of the owners and tenants. Both Hyde Lodge and Highfield Lodge had a similar design suggesting that Gover built both properties. By 1841, George Rashleigh, a clergyman attached to Winchester College, his wife and two young children - Laura aged five and Lydia aged two - had moved in to Hyde Lodge. However, in 1861, the property was rented out to Sophia Watson, a fundholder, who was rich enough to employ five servants. The property remained in the Rashleigh family until June 1883 when George's two children - Laura Anne Arundel Rashleigh and Lydia Cumming Rashleigh – sold it to Beverley Robinson. In 1891 Robinson, who lived on his own means, purchased additional land from Frederick Bowker (the younger), the owner of Lankhills (which lay to the north). This increased the property to five acres. Robinson (aged 62) was recently widowed - his wife probably died in childbirth - and he employed five servants to look after his children aged nine, seven and one.

The layout of the property was unlikely to have changed much when it was sold in 1912. The estate agent describes the house as occupying a:

> Beautiful position within easy walking distance of the railway station, Cathedral and college, golf links and tennis and croquets grounds. Three excellent rooms, large conservatory, extensive offices, eleven bedrooms and dressing rooms, fitted bathroom and usual convenience... these combine to make Hyde Lodge a perfect country home with all the advantage of a town residence.[20]

The house reflected the standing and accommodation expected in a gentleman's residence of the age. There was an impressive entrance and three reception rooms - the drawing room, a morning room and a dining room - along with a conservatory. The offices where the servants carried on the running of the household were typically separate from the family area. Principal and secondary stairs ensured that the household and servants were able to access all parts of the house independently of each other. Along with the usual kitchen, scullery and pantry, there was a dairy and a fruit and vegetable store. A butler needed his own space including a pantry, cupboards for the precious china and glass and a large wine cellar. Older properties such as Hyde Lodge were still built with a basement or downstairs mimicking the grander London houses. This provided a large servants' hall and housekeeper's (or man's) room. The property was extensive; it not only had five bedrooms in the main house but a further four rooms in the wing. These were described as secondary bedrooms and so may have been used by higher ranking staff, whereas the maids were accommodated on the second floor.

The grounds of Hyde Lodge were as an important feature when sold in 1912, as they would have been to the original owner. The five acres was described enthusiastically as having excellent modern stabling, a walled kitchen garden, pleasure grounds and timbered pasture. The lodge entrance was approached by an 'avenued carriage drive with a picturesque thatched cottage at the entrance and residence stands on elevation facing and overlooking its charming grounds.'[21] This was a country mansion and the size of the grounds and its ambience allowed for a rural existence. There were fruit and vegetable plots, glasshouses for tomatoes and cucumbers, and a poultry run and piggeries. However by 1912, modern conveniences had arrived. The house was connected to main drainage and electric lights were installed, albeit on hire. Although provision was made for horses and coaches, a bicycle shed had taken over one of the coach houses and there was a motor house with the necessary washing pitch needed to keep up appearances.

Hyde Street

Perhaps the most important event in Hyde during William and William Barrow Simonds' tenure was the building works carried out on the historic and beautiful church of St Bartholomew. The church had served the Abbey's fraternity well but had been allowed to fall in to disrepair under subsequent custodians of the Abbey's lands. However the church was transformed between 1836 and 1879 when £3,000 was spent on restoration. In 1838, Rev. William Williams (who was vicar between 1833 and 1869) provided funds for the rebuilding of the chancel on its original foundations. Further monies were offered by Charles Deane, who had the 'right to feed' in the church yard, – a generous £12 towards building the wall on the south side and £1 10s. p.a. to rent the churchyard.[22] In 1853 Dr Moritz Behr, who ran the boys' school, proposed that the Chancel should be rebuilt and enlarged. Renovation took place in 1859, when William Barrow Simonds financed the building of a north aisle in memory of his parents William Simonds and Ellen Barrow. This provided extra accommodation in church services for the Simonds family and their farm servants. During the 1860s and 1870s, the nave was restored, the transept rebuilt and the roof repaired.[23]

The main source of finance over this 40-year period was the steady sale of church land. In 1837 Weeke field, which lay north of Swan Lane, was sold to the Railway Company. The sale of two tenements and gardens in Hyde Street in 1859 raised £150.[24] In 1873 the churchwardens received offers for 2¼ acres called Sheep Fair Field from Rev. George Rashleigh (who owned Hyde Lodge) of £1,000 and Frederick Bowker (who owned Lankhills) of £1,100.[25] Shrewdly the churchwardens divided the field into lots for sale by auction and obtained permission from the Charity Commissioners for its sale. The money raised benefited both the church and the poor of the parish. Three years later, in 1876, freehold land on the east side of Wales Street in Winnall was sold. Income from all these sales was wisely invested in Consols (Government stock).

The vicarage lay to the north west of the church, now on the south side of Egbert Road. The buildings between Egbert Road and King Alfred Place were built on medieval foundations. Two years after taking the position, Rev. William Williams replaced the old brick and timber parsonage with a new vicarage at the north end of the plot (Figure 5.10 and 6.4). This cost £550 but was not sufficient for Williams needs, and was enlarged in 1847.[26] The vicarage had five bays, the end ones had high gables decorated with bargeboards. There was a panelled choir room at the south end.

By 1824 Hyde Abbey School was not alone in attracting children to Hyde to be educated; Miss Street's boarding school was open. There was no parochial educational provision for the children whose families lived and worked in Hyde. From 1835 these children were educated with those in the adjoining parish of St Thomas. Finance was raised and a parish school was built in 1845 on vacant ground behind the vicarage. An infant school was added in 1854.[27]

Figure 6.4: The northern part of Hyde Vicarage

The first building was designed by Owen Browne Carter, who built many of the grand terraces on West Hill and whose designs mimicked those in Bath.[28] The school building housing girls and infants was designed by local builders Henry and Martin Macklin. As Hyde grew, a larger building was needed. By 1884 the attendance had doubled in size and the building was again enlarged in 1894. The original buildings were typical of church schools in Hampshire and built in the vernacular style of flint with brick dressings. The later building was built of brick. [29]

Further provision for those who could pay came in 1854 with the establishment of a large gentleman's academy – Hyde House - at the north end of the street. It was run by Rev. Edward Firmstone and Dr Moritz Behr, who was of German descent. By 1861 the school had 7 tutors and 87 boarders aged between 9 and 19. Boarders came from all over England, Scotland and Ireland, with 27 from Hampshire. The number of Winchester boys is not known (only one boarder was local). Many were sons of families in the army or colonial service, with 19 from India and two from the West Indies. With the railway connected to the seaport of Southampton, Winchester was now easier to reach from the colonies. There was also a small school (probably at No. 2 Hyde Street) which in 1861 was run by James Withers.[30]

From 1841 Hyde started to become a modern suburb. William Simonds, then aged 50, preferred to live in St Cross with his wife Helen (40) and children - William (20), Helen (12), Mary (6), Tom (4) and Jane (1).[31] The 1841 census recorded 57 properties in Hyde Street with 248 residents and a further 14 houses with 75 people in Hyde Churchyard. The census listed two large houses – Highfield Lodge and William Young's house. Charles Moody, his family and servants (totalling 13 people) lived at Abbots Barton farmhouse and a further 15 people lived in farm cottages. The Bridewell swelled the numbers in the parish. The governor, his wife, their three children and eight employees lived alongside the 83 inmates. Another 22 people lived at Bridewell House. Farming and brewing were the largest employers. James Arrowsmith and Thomas Cover ran the inns. Widgwood Gillum, Isaac Benham, James Dear, Richard Barnes and John Gradeige were brewers or maltsters. The industry was well supported by craftsmen - coopers, blacksmiths, whitesmiths and wheelwrights. The developing building industry needed bricklayers, carpenters and plasterers. There were plenty of labourers to work on the farms or in the malting and brewing industries. The everyday needs of the community were met by bakers, the butcher, the tailor and shoemaker, and, of course, the clergy.

Details of property owners and occupiers are given in the rate books.[32] It should be remembered that the owners cited in the rate books were not necessarily freeholders, but may have held long leases. Within the parish bounds, William Simonds' property included Barton Farm, the dairy, gardens and four houses in Hyde Street and Little Denmark, which he leased from St John's Charity. Thomas Deane owned two meads in Hyde Churchyard and 16 houses. His son, Charles March Deane, also owned a mead. The properties in Hyde Street were in a number of hands; most owners had just one property.[33] However Gradeige owned ten cottages and the brewhouse on the west side of the street. There were few owner-occupiers – only the affluent magistrate James Theobald and brewer James Wyeth could afford properties and desired to buy. Mr Cleverly owned six properties in Swan Lane. Mr Gover and Mr Burnett both owned meads that were 'ripe for development'.

By 1851[34] the Hyde brewery was run by James Simonds, who lived on the premises with his wife Cicely, and his children Laura, William and Henry Aldolphus.[35] Mary Arrowsmith, now widowed, ran the Swan Inn. Apart from George Durant, a bank manager and James Withers, a schoolmaster, most of the heads of households living between the brewery and Bridewell Lane (now King Alfred Place) were employed in farming.

Residents in Hyde Churchyard included George Smith (a surveyor who later ran a letting agency) and several labourers who worked either for the brewery, in the building industry or on the railway. Isaac Hammond, the gun maker lived on the north corner of Bridewell Lane. His neighbours - Francis Knight and John May - were employed in the brewery. Several widows - Sarah Wincap, Elizabeth Switzer and Mary Gradeige - who were financially reliant on investments and house ownership, lived at the north end of the street. The houses in Hyde Terrace (just north of Hyde Church Lane) were homes suitable for a solicitor's clerk, a surveyor of taxes and a building surveyor. William Young, a proprietor of houses, lived at No. 26 (later renumbered No. 34). The blacksmith's forge marked the northern limit of the small properties on the west side of the street, which were homes to brewery labourers and railway porters.

There were several large properties which provided accommodation suitable for those of the middle classes who did not want to live in the City. These included James Theobald and Isaac Warner. Theobald described himself as a fundholder, magistrate and landed proprietor. He had nine children and five servants. Warner, a solicitor, was already widowed at 36. He had three servants to help look after his four sons, whose ages ranged from one to 11 years. The eldest, Frederick, became a solicitor like his father. The street was a popular abode for investors in real estate. Henry Barnes found his investments lucrative enough to support his ten children, whose ages ranged from new-born to 19 years, and to pay his four servants.

The residents did not have to travel far for their daily needs. Provisions were supplied by butchers - John Castell and John Gradeige - and James Wyeth's bakery was one of three shops selling groceries. The walk to the fruiterer and greengrocer was a little further on to North Walls. William Joyce made boots and shoes; linen could be purchased from Charles Gaiger; and for those who needed their sporting trophies mounted, there were two taxidermists.[36]

One important resident was Henry Frampton who had four children, including Henry Swift, then four years old. Father and son were to play an important part in Hyde's Victorian and Edwardian developments, as will be explored in later chapters. Henry was a builder's merchant but in 1851 described himself as an oil and colour merchant. Secondary to this he cited his occupation as a builder employing 26 men. If he was not involved in building the new houses on the Bridewell site, he was selling materials to the builders.

Figure 6.5: Nos. 31 and 32 Hyde Street

The brewery and the Simonds

In the 1800s, the brewing industry started to dominate the suburb and became the second largest employer after Simonds' farm. The brewery had several owners in the first 50 years of the nineteenth century. Nicholas Pyle had purchased 24 acres of land, tenements and malt houses in 1804-6. As the Dean and Chapter was not, at this stage, selling land but renting it on long leases, the land must have formerly belonged to the Abbey.

Pyle retained the properties until February 1815 when they were sold in four lots to John Eames Waight, brewer, and his partner Thomas Godwin, an upholsterer.[37] Mortgages were raised from Widgwood Gillum of Bishops Sutton and Sarah Earle.[38] At this date, the brewery holdings, which included two freehold messuages, was described as:

> A messuage with garden, an adjoining parcel of land used as a yard and a piece of garden ground containing 1 acre and 21 perches (this was described as part of Hyde Garden and formerly two messuages); a messuage and orchard with the Malthouse No. 3, a storehouse and outbuildings lately erected on the orchard; and the brewery, dwelling house and garden, malthouse and stable on Swan Lane.

The brewery had started to expand and the business owned several public houses and other property in the City, including the Angel (Middle Brook Street), the Britannia (Lower Brook Street), and the Rodney's Head (St John's Street). Waight's partnership with Thomas Godwin ended in 1821. It is likely that Godwin was a 'sleeping partner' who provided some of the finance. When the loans were paid off the ownership of the properties passed to John Eames Waight.[39] He died in 1830, and his trustees, John Dunn and Benjamin Whitear sold the brewery to Charles Marett (from Southampton) in order to pay inheritance dues.[40]

In 1843 Charles Marett commissioned an inventory as a prelude to the sale of the business. The inventory provides a valuable record of all the premises in Hyde and provides an overview of the business's expansion with a list of the tied houses throughout Winchester.[41] The properties in Hyde were listed as: the brewery, the counting house, Mr Gillum's dwelling and garden, Mr Corderey's house south of brewery gates, the White Swan with a bowling green and garden, No. 1 Malthouse on the west side of Hyde Street, No. 2 Malthouse on the east side of Hyde Street, Mr Findon's House adjoining, Knight's Cottage adjacent, May's House (The Coopers Arms), and No. 3 Malthouse in Swan Lane with two brick tiled tenements adjacent. Brewery employees like the cooper - John May - and the maltster - James Knight - were housed on the premises. The location of these properties can be found in Figures 5.10 and 5.12.

Figure 6.6: The Counting House next to the Swan Inn

The main freehold premises were described as:

> An excellent brick tiled building with entrance yard and gates. Coal room in front. Malt and hop chambers, brewer's room, mill room with mill rack under, cask washing place, tun rooms and capital arched vaults extending under adjacent premises to a road leading to the north wall of the City. Counting house and other offices on the south side of the yard. And a meadow or orchard adjacent (called Hyde Garden). [42]

The inventory contains details of each building and its rooms, listing plant, utensils, casks, horses, dray wagons, malthouse, fixtures and effects. The beermakers' works consisted of a tanning room, two beer tun rooms, a racking cellar, long vault and vat cellar. The brick cellars, which provided cool storage facilities, were extensive. [43] There was a mill room containing hoisting tackle for the malt mills, sack hoisting tackle and mashing gear. Apart from the brewhouse there was also a hop loft, mash tun and lumber room. In the yard behind the buildings was the mill, horse stable, copperage, carpenter's shop and spirit store, and most importantly the counting house, and not to be forgotten - a dog kennel. Every little detail was included including the colours and names of the prized horses: the dark brown 'Champion', 9 years old, the black 8-year old 'Colonel', and a brown mill horse 'Punch', who were all kept in the dray-horse stable in Swan Lane. Horse transport was a necessary part of the supply chain and both the care and feeding of the horses and the maintenance of the carts by the wheelwrights were important jobs. Beer was stored and transported in six different sized casks. There are no records of the turnover of the brewery but some estimation of the size of the brewery trade at this time can be drawn from the inventory of casks (Table 6.2). The total capacity was nearly 33,000 gallons, of which 47% was in trade and 53% on the premises. This suggests an efficient business where the supply was kept at a good margin above demand. The furthest distance beer could be transported was limited to a day's journey for the dray horses.

Table 6.2: Inventory of casks at the Hyde Street brewery 1843

	Hogshead 54 galls	Barrel 36 galls	Half hogshead 27 galls	Kilderkin 18 galls	Firkin 9 galls	Pin 4.5 galls
In trade	235	44	17	24	18	44
On premises	280	51	9	11	1	6
Total	515	95	26	35	19	50

Source: HRO 206M85W/17.

There were several properties for senior employees. Mr Gillum's dwelling, on the north side of the brewhouse, had a large garden measuring just over one acre. The house was described as having a parlour and drawing room separated by a passage at the front, and a small sitting room at the back. There was a large paved kitchen, store room, scullery, pantry, dairy, good cellars and coal hole with rooms over, a yard and small garden with a spring. Upstairs were two pairs of bedrooms, a further bedroom and two more in the attic. The house had a brick front but was faced with tiles at the rear. The surveyor reported that the back rooms with the offices were 'much out of repair'.[44]

Mr Corderey, a farmer, rented the house south of the brewhouse gate for £28 p.a.. It was built of red brick with a central doorway. Downstairs were a parlour and anteroom on the right and a drawing room, with a Sienna marble chimney piece, on the left. At the rear was a stone paved kitchen, a detached washhouse with pump and sky-lights, and a pantry. There were four bedrooms - the ones at the back were under a sloping roof and in need of painting. In the roof were two interconnecting garrets with three roof sashes. These were 'decaying for want of paint, sills rotten and floors bad.' There were cellars under the whole house, a yard with privy and a small garden.[45]

The current Swan building dates from the seventeenth century but was extended and altered in the eighteenth, nineteenth and twentieth century. The Inn had a tap room and a smoking room. There was a maze of other rooms for eating, entertaining or sleeping. A good-sized stable yard with two stables accommodated 30 horses, and a further open stable housed another six. Housing was also needed for the carriages. Linen was dealt with in the on-site laundry whilst several privies and a dung pit coped with human and horse detritus.

The Swan's customers had the benefit of a garden with bowling green, refreshment room and skittle alley. The garden, on the site of the City ditch, was held under a 40-year lease from the Corporation. The lease was renewable every 14 years at a cost of £15 15s. and chicken money of 4s. 8d., whereby the mayor received a chicken or equivalent annually.[46] In addition, James Arrowsmith paid rent of £50 p.a. in 1843.

Marett owned all three malthouses in Hyde, which were not part of Barton Farm. Malthouse No. 3 in Swan Lane was described as an eleven-quarter steep granary with capacity for 20 quarters of barley and 300 quarters of malt. There was a brick stable for seven horses with four stalls, a loft and another brick stable with timber lofts with three stalls. Also on the site was a poultry house, privy, lock up coach house, a two-bay wagon house and loft, and a large yard. These were described as 'all in a bad state'. Adjoining were two brick tiled tenements containing four rooms each with a cellar underneath, a loft and a large garden. These were occupied by Primmer and Marman, workmen in the Brewery who paid 2s. a week rent each. Malthouse No. 1 on the west side of Hyde Street had a difficult entrance through a narrow passage at the back of the pork butcher's shop. There was a ten-quarter cistern, and capacity of 100 quarters of barley and 200 quarters of malt. There was a barley loft but this was above the washhouse belonging to the pork butcher. Like other parts of the real estate, the brick and tiled building was in a bad state.[47]

Malthouse No. 2, the oldest property, was located 'in a recess on the east side of Hyde Street near the top', had a twelve-quarter cistern and capacity of 100 quarters of barley and 200 quarters of malt. The very old brick, tiles and floors were deemed 'indifferent.' There were three adjacent properties which had substantial frontage onto the street but little depth. Figure 5.10 shows the area at the time of the 1873 Ordnance survey map. The malthouse still existed along with the old cottages south of the Vicarage and the tap (bar area). Mr Findon's house had two parlours in the front. There was a kitchen, cellar and basement pantry, three front bedrooms and small room in the back. The back area contained a wash house and a privy and led to a good garden. The back door gave access to St Bartholomew's churchyard. Although dilapidated, the freehold property was let at £29 p.a.. Knight's Cottage had only a small room at the front and a large room in the back; there were two rooms in the roof, a washhouse, a further small room and good garden with a well that supplied the next door property. The state of the building was mixed. Although the floors were good, the tiling was bad and the pump wanting. As a consequence, the rent was only 2s. per week (equivalent to £5 4s. p.a.).[48]

Mr May's house was known as the Cooper's Arms. The front room was used as the tap which May had enclosed and provided furnishing and fixings. The bar had access to a spacious cellar under both houses. There was a washhouse, a pantry, garden with spring and a workshop built by May. The survey provided sales data for the tap in 1841 and 1842. The average sales for three (unspecified) products were 62, 26 and 35 barrels. [49] The 1841 Census indicated that Mr Findon's house lay south of the Vicarage. Knight's Cottage and May's house lay between it and the three large houses north of the current King Alfred Place. The surviving buildings are shown in Figures 6.7 and 6.8.

In 1843 the number of public houses owned or leased by the Brewery had increased considerably within the City and included: the Dolphin (High Street), the Bell and Crown (St George's Street), the Crown and Anchor (High Street), the Spread Eagle (renamed Cross Keys in Middle Brook Street), the Britannia (Lower Brook Street), the Cart and Horses (Middle Brook Street), the Rodney's Head (St Johns Street), the Lamb (The Square), the King's Head (St Thomas Street) and the Crown and Cushion (corner of North Walls and Jewry Street).[50]

The brewery holdings dominated Hyde and the rest of Winchester and the business must have employed a large percentage of local male workers. However, the survey indicated that the buildings had been neglected and either Marett, prior to selling, or the new owner would be faced with considerable expenses to ensure the investment maintained its value.

In 1850 Charles Marett sold the Hyde Street Brewery to a member of the experienced Simonds family brewers of Reading. William Simonds of Abbots Barton was related to the Simonds dynasty of brewers in Reading through his great-grandfather Thomas. His sister Charlotte Emma had married James Simonds, the fourth and youngest son of William Blackall Simonds and Elizabeth, daughter of Basingstoke brewer Thomas May.

Figure 6.7: Knight's Cottage and Mr May's house (later Hyde Tavern)

Figure 6.8: Hyde Tavern and adjacent Georgian houses

As youngest son, there were few opportunities for James in the family brewery at Reading, so it is not surprising that he sought employment in Winchester where his distant relative and future brother-in-law owned a large estate. When he moved to Hyde is not certain. In the rate book of 1846, James Simonds is named as liable to tax as the owner and occupier of the brewhouse, the three malthouses, the vault, several houses and bowling green.[51] Other sources cite that James leased the site of the Swan in 1847. In the next year, he took on the leases from St John's Charity of the Dolphin, Angel and Britannia.

James was not the only member of the Reading Simonds family to move to Winchester. After Blackall Simonds retired from the Reading Brewery, he moved to Winchester with his wife, Emma. The 1851 census gives Blackall Simonds' occupation as retired brewer with income from land, houses and investments. Blackall and Emma Simonds lived in Tower House (close to Hyde). Mary Muller, the sister of James and Blackall Simonds, had married a merchant and their son was born in Calcutta. By 1851, Muller and her son had moved to Abbey House in the High Street; however no mention is made of her husband. James Simonds and his family lived opposite the brewery at Nos. 2 and 3 Hyde Street.

The description of the brewery premises gave details of the owners of the surrounding properties and adds further to the knowledge of Hyde at this time.[52] The main property was the Swan Inn with stables, vaults and yard. On the north was Waldron's premises and part of Hyde Garden which extended down the east boundary. To the south was the City Ditch owned by the Corporation. There were also several cottages, a malthouse, garden and orchard which lay between the street and land belonging to Isaac Warner (which had previously been owned by Rev. Richards' widow). There was also a house occupied by James Wyeth.

In the north part of Hyde Street was the Coopers Inn with gardens occupied by John May and James Knight, and Francis Findon's property. These properties were described as situated between the Basingstoke Turnpike Road and the churchyard. There was also a house, orchard and garden between the vicarage and Findon's house with the malthouse, storehouse and outbuilding built by Robert Page.

For the purchase of the Brewery, James borrowed £2,292 from his brother-in-law, William Simonds, and his eldest brother, Blackall Simonds, who was owner of the Reading brewery. Other members of the family also had a financial interest in the business. The part of Hyde garden, formerly belonging to Deane, was not sold by Marett until 1852. James Simonds raised money for this purchase from Robert Withington Simonds, Barrow Simonds' brother.[53]

The death of William Simonds

William Simonds died on 7 November 1858 and was buried in St Cross next to his wife Helen Barrow. He had owned Abbots Barton for 47 years, but had preferred to live at Priors Barton Farm in the parish of St Faith and left the daily running of the estate to a farm manager. In 1851, after his wife had died, five children - William Barrow, Edward, Elizabeth, Mary Saunders and Thomas - were still living with him. His total estates were valued at £38,700 and produced an income of £1,578. Most of his wealth was in Hyde. Properties included Abbots Barton, with a sale value of £30,000; the malthouse, with the remaining wing of Bethell's Hyde house (occupied by James Dear) valued at £1,800; and Durngate Mills valued at £1,600. The annual rental values for these properties were estimated at £1,145 14s. 7d., £120 and £100 respectively. The family had lived in St Cross for several generations and the value of the leasehold estates in St Faiths were given as £7,703. Simonds was one of the largest farmers in the Winchester area. Running an estate was an expensive business and there were not only taxes to pay but repairs needed to prolong the life of the buildings. The assessment for death duties made allowance for various costs including land tax, rents and repairs. The main costs off-set against inheritance tax were land tax of over £50 and repairs of £80 to Abbots Barton. Repairs needed to the malthouse and Durngate Mills amounted to a further £38.[54]

The Inland Revenue account for probate gives a fuller picture of the wealth and liabilities of an established farmer in the mid-1850s. The fixed assets (not converted into money) were valued at £99,750 and current assets were estimated at £1,887, mostly cash at the bank. Equipment used on the farm, such as horses, carriages, stock and implements of husbandry were valued at £3,536. Investments formed the greatest part of the liquid assets. He had £66,666 invested in three per cent consuls and a further £2,000 in an East India Bond. He was an avid investor in local utilities and other businesses with £1,335 worth of shares in the Corn Exchange, Cemetery, Waterworks and Gas Light and Coke companies. The leasehold properties in St Cross were assessed at £7,703, the value of the profit rent he enjoyed. The profit rent was the difference between the market rent and that paid to the Dean and Chapter. The cost of probate was high – nearly £1,607 compared to the funeral cost of £146. After allowing for various payments and deductions, tax was assessed at one per cent on £33,114. This was the amount payable by the estate; beneficiaries for named assets had to meet their own share of the inheritance tax.

 William Barrow inherited the land, which included the residues of the leases in St Cross held from the Dean and Chapter. The youngest son, Thomas, received £10,000 but with payment postponed until he reached the age of 25. Taxes charged on inheritance varied according to the relationship between the deceased and receiver. His daughters, Elizabeth and Mary, paid tax of £1 3s. on the silver plated articles and agricultural prize cups worth £115 13s. that he left them. His other executor, Robert Guy Barrow, a merchant from Bristol, being a 'stranger in blood', was charged duty an exorbitant £10 on his legacy of £100.

Conclusion

William Simonds' family were long-time residents in St Cross. Although he had custodianship of Abbots Barton for 47 years, he chose to remain living in the house in which he was born rather than move to Hyde. He thought he had legally purchased the Hyde estate, but his title was challenged by two distant relatives of the Knight family, who argued that the entail set up by Elizabeth Knight was still operational. Fortunately, they did not pursue their claim and accepted payment in recompense.

The railway transformed the landscape of Abbots Barton cutting through the six 50-acre fields. However the benefits of easier access to London markets compensated for this. The profits from sheep and cattle were assured as fewer died on the journey to market. The railway, which was connected to the port of Southampton, brought links to the colonies. However whilst schools in Hyde benefitted from the railway, increasing competition from imported crops threatened the livelihood of Simonds. In 1841, agriculture was the major occupation in Hyde, but by 1851 its dominance had declined. The change could be partially attributed to the adoption of new farming methods rather than solely seen as the result of changing economic circumstances. However, possibly in response to falling agricultural returns, William took the first steps of releasing farmland for development. Two large houses with extensive gardens were built on the south-west edge of Abbots Barton estate. Hyde's breweries continued to flourish and provided a demand for Simonds' hops. This outlet was assured when his distant cousin, a member of the Reading brewing dynasty, settled in Winchester and married his sister, Charlotte. Simonds, along with his brother, seized the opportunity to invest in the purchase and expansion of the Simonds' Hyde brewery.

Figure 6.9: Nos. 61 to 65 Hyde Street

Source: HRO: W/C5/10/23/71/1

In 1861, the properties on the corner of Hyde Street and Bridewell Lane were home to several farm workers. The dairy, built of recycled stones, can be seen in the background.

Chapter 7: William Barrow Simonds, the developer

The Simonds' family

The Simonds family were the longest owners of the Abbey and Abbots Barton Farms after the Dissolution. However the family caused the final demise of the Abbey's farms by opening up the land for development. The family's longevity protected those areas that still survive in agricultural use today but parts of these are now threatened by development. William Simonds' son, William Barrow was born in 1820 - Barrow was his mother's maiden name. William Barrow was still single when he inherited Abbots Barton at the age of 38. By 1861, he had married Ellen Lampard Bowker. Ellen, the daughter of Winchester solicitor Frederick Bowker, was 19 years younger than William. The census records the couple and five-month old daughter, Ellen, living at the newly-built Abbotts Barton House. William was not quick to give up Prior's Barton Farm in St Cross which stayed in the family until 1868. In 1881, William (then aged 60) and his wife Ellen (41) had four daughters living at home. Barrow Simonds had considerable standing in the community and had the lifestyle to match. He employed eight servants, including a governess, gardener, lady's maid, parlour maid, house maid and school-room maid. He was a justice of the peace, alderman, deputy lieutenant of the county and served as an MP between 1865 and 1880.[1] Even though the estate was shrinking, the farm still employed a considerable numbers of workers. The bailiff, Dennis Barnes, and his wife (who was employed as a dairy woman) lived at the farm cottage with four young farm servants aged between 13 and 18. The gardener, Esrom Astridge, and his family lived at Barton Lodge. There were several cottages for agricultural labourers. Henry Judd served as coachman and Thomas Noyce was the resident shepherd. Altogether 49 workers and their dependants lived on the farm.[2]

Two of Barrow Simonds' brothers, Henry T. and Robert Withington, were solicitors with a practice in St Thomas Street. In 1861, Henry lived at No. 19 St James Terrace on West Hill, and Robert at nearby Westbourne Lodge. James Simonds, part of the Reading side of the family and owner of the Hyde Brewery, had died in 1858, in the same year as Barrow's father. Barrow Simonds' aunt, Charlotte (James's widow), was described as a fundholder in the 1861 census. She lived in Southgate Street with her children William, who was employed in life assurance (43), Laura (41), and Georgina (24). Ten years later they had all moved up the hill to No. 23 West End Terrace.

Barrow Simonds had seven children: Ellen (born 1861), Alice (1863), Marian (1864), William (1865), Lucy (1868), Constance (1870) and Olive (1884). Figure 7.2 gives the family tree. The brewing interests of the family grew when Constance married James Allen Young of the family that controlled Young's Brewery of Wandsworth. In 1901, James Young (34), Constance (31) and their four children Ellen (5), William Allen (4), Constance (2) and James Allen (1 month) lived in Wandsworth with eight servants. In later life, Constance returned to Winchester and lived at No. 13 St Thomas Street for over 15 years. The house had been purchased by William Simonds for Constance's sister, and on her death had been left to Constance's son. Locals remember Constance as an eccentric old lady who kept a horse in St Swithun's Street.[3]

Barrow Simonds' son William became a barrister and married Cicely Broughton. In 1901 they were living at Waterside, just north of Abbots Barton in Headbourne Worthy, with Mary (6), twins John and Joan (4), and Ivy (1). Their other son Robert was born in 1905. Joan married her cousin William Allen Young, who was at Winchester College with her twin John. One of their four sons, John Allen, who was born in Winchester in 1921, played a prominent role as chairman of Young's Brewery until his death in 2006. Apart from charity work, he is best remembered as an initiator of the return to the traditional draft beer that his forefathers produced in Hyde.

Figure 7.1: Abbotts Barton House 1858

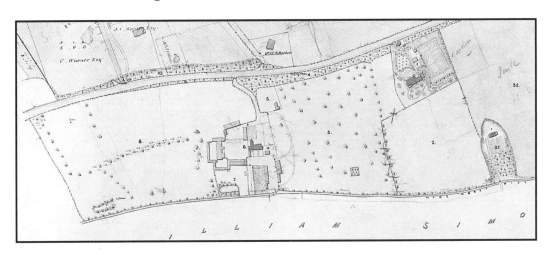

Source: HRO:13M85W/48

Built by Barrow Simonds for his family when he inherited Abbots Barton.

Figure 7.2: The Barrow Simonds Family Tree

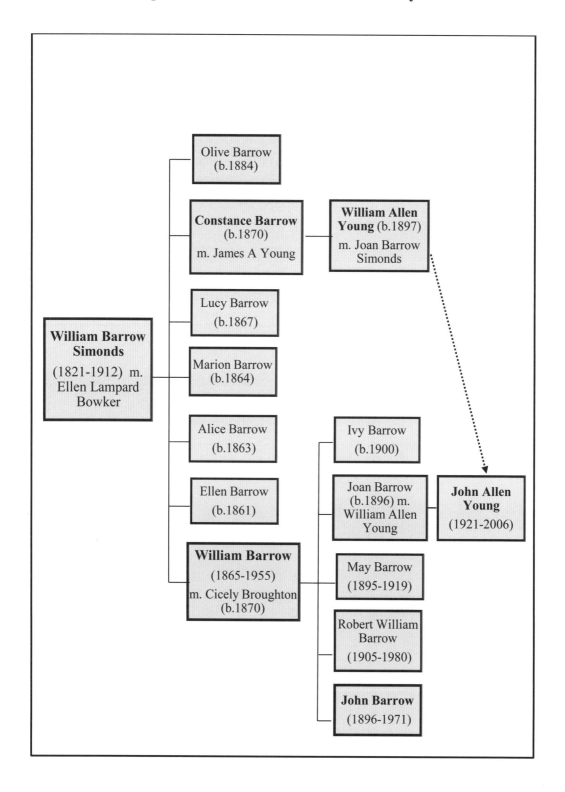

The decline in agriculture and the fragmentation of Abbots Barton Farm

When Barrow Simonds took over the farm in 1858, Winchester's population of 13,704 had two MPs for 842 electors, who were then known as £10 householders. There were 2,077 inhabited houses and the annual value of local property taxes stood at £43,357.[4] In the first 20 years of Barrow Simonds' ownership farming continued to be a financially sound occupation. However the boom eventually came to an end in the 1870s when wheat and, to a lesser extent, meat prices fell. Agriculture, as a percentage of national product, fell dramatically from 33 per cent in 1801, to 20 per cent in 1851, then to a paltry 7 per cent in 1901. Agricultural output rose from £88m in 1800 to £195m in the early 1870s, and then dropped by 20 per cent to £155m in the early 1900s. By this time over 50 per cent of British food was imported. This had a significant effect on farmers like Barrow Simonds, who maintained an intensive arable-livestock mix, which accounted for 86 per cent of the land under arable.

Figure 7.3 emphasises how agricultural rents fell in the last quarter of the nineteenth century as British farmers came under pressure from imported grain and livestock products from North and South America, Australia and New Zealand. The first refrigerated cargo of New Zealand lamb arrived in the 1870s. The expensive water meadows system made British lamb uncompetitive in comparison. This economic downturn, known as the Great Depression in agriculture, was to have a significant effect on the future of Abbots Barton Farm.[5] Wheat production in England fell from 20 per cent of the arable land in 1874 to 8½ per cent in 1895. Malting required a high quality of barley. This was cheaper to import and the local grown crop, which accounted for only 8 per cent of arable, was fed to livestock.

Figure 7.3: Index of agricultural rents 1850 to 1914

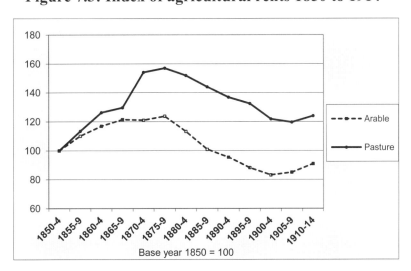

Base year 1850 = 100

Source: Turner (2004)

The once important sheep walks were used only for exercising the breeding ewes. Their diet was supplemented by other feedstuffs which had become much cheaper. The cost of farm labour rose steeply by 18 per cent (10s. 9d. to 12s. 8d. per week) between 1871 and 1898. However increasing productivity ensured that such increases were easily absorbed. The adoption of more efficient farming practices allowed a reduction from nine to five men on an average farm. Grass (used as part of rotation) output rose from 24 per cent of arable in 1874 to 36 per cent in 1895. There was also an increase in catch crops like rye grass, trefoil and mustard. These provided extra crops within the rotation schedule and had a positive effect on efficiency, as well as providing additional animal feed.

Over the same period the average proportion of a farm in permanent pasture increased from 14 to 25 per cent.[6] As artificial fertilisers became more readily available in the late nineteenth century, the reliance on sheep for manure declined. New strains of early grasses were developed and little benefit could be derived from managing the water meadows to force grass growth during the breeding season. Most financially challenging for Barrow Simonds was the importation of lamb from New Zealand and the use of the railway for the transportation of milk to towns. The effect on many farms was the replacement of a sheep and corn mix with dairy farming.

There was a high level of financial uncertainty. Rents fell from a peak in the mid to late 1870s and the capital value of land fell. Interest rates decreased and the price of Consols, which were inversely related to the interest rate, increased. The rate of capitalisation for agricultural land, that is the number of years purchase, also fell typically to between 20 and 25 years compared with 30 to 40 years before the agricultural depression.[7] As a result, the expected yield on agricultural land increased from between 2.5 and 3.3 per cent to 4 or 5 per cent. This represented a massive change in the risk premium being attached by investors to agricultural land. Many landowners would have experienced a fall in the value of their land to less than half its pre-depression worth. Strategically, farmers had few options unless the farm was close to an expanding town. Then falling returns could only be offset by seeking opportunities for urban development.

A second railway line - the Didcot, Newbury and Southampton Railway (DNSR) – was built in the mid-1880s and cut through the eastern boundary of Abbots Barton. There were 50 local shareholders including Rt. Hon. Thomas Northbrook (who owned property in Hyde) and Lt. Colonel Philip Campbell (who had purchased Lankhills). However there was no financial reward accruing to William Barrow as the first railway had to his father. The DNSR was more controversial but, as it served the eastern side of the City, had little impact on the Hyde residents. The negotiations were more difficult as the proposed line ran below the eastern escarpment and passed alongside the water meadows in Winnall over land then owned by William Barrow, Dr Hitchcock (whose family were landowners in Weeke), the Dean and Chapter, St John's Hospital, and other small owners. Small strips of land were exchanged or purchased. Barrow Simonds employed A. C. Gale, a land agent, to act on his behalf. No landowner wanted to accept an offer less than the railway company was offering to the others. The project required irrigation works, so that the meadows were left in proper order and a footpath had to be diverted.[8] In an interview with Constance, Barrow Simonds' daughter in 1969 when she was 100 years old, she reflected:

> Of course my father was very upset about it because he said it spoiled all the fishing and he said it will never pay and they said 'oh yes it will' and they gave him a sum of money and a certain amount of shares and he never got anything from it at all...no, it never did pay, I don't think. [9]

Winchester's second railway line was not a great success and the line was closed to passengers in 1960 and freight six years after.

To what extent Barrow Simonds' decision to release land for housing development was financially driven is not known. Abbots Barton Estate produced the first substantial release of land for large villas outside the City. As soon as Barrow Simonds inherited the land from his father a survey was commissioned. The farm extended to nearly 400 acres.[10] The greatest proportion of land, 83.3 per cent (342 acres), was given over to arable, pasture accounted for only 8.8 per cent (36 acres), and plantations (which were mainly small coppices) just 2.3 per cent (9½ acres extending to 16 sites). The railway took up 3.7 per cent and farmhouses and other buildings 1.8 per cent. Many of the former field names had disappeared (details are given in Table 7.1).

There was considerable demand for country houses from professionals who wanted to move away from the unhealthy City, with its poor drainage and lack of adequate sewage system. The release of land at Abbots Barton provided building opportunities within a short carriage ride from the City. The 1858 map was annotated to show the development of three building estates which lay between the Andover and Worthy Roads on the former fields known as Limekilns, the Old Hop Garden and Gallows Hill (Figure 7.4). These areas are shown in the south-west corner of the Upland survey map - Figure 4.7. The nature of the development on the three was similar. Over the next 50 years land on these estates were leased, or occasionally sold, for superior housing. Residents included some of Winchester's wealthiest families who formed a tight social circle.

An owner could sell land outright which gave no control over what development subsequently took place. With a small acreage, owners could exert little influence over an area and the value of their property would be substantially influenced by the neighbourhood.[11] However, most landowners wanted some control over what happened, especially if they had continuing interests in the locality or were releasing land in tranches, and hence sought to protect both present and future developments.[12] Landowners, releasing parts of extensive estates, sought to control the development and future use through covenants. This was certainly true of Barrow Simonds when selling off parts of Abbots Barton. Most of the development land was offered as leasehold. Freehold was available but the cost was 32 times the annual rent.[13] For the middle classes, renting was both acceptable and desirable:

Table 7.1: Abbots Barton Farm 1858

	Area	Use	a.	r.	p.
1	House, buildings, yards, gardens & Lodge	House	2	2	32
2	Dell Close	Pasture	6	3	8
3	Broad Close	Pasture	10	3	15
4	Plantation	Plantation	1	0	32
5	Rick, yard & buildings	House	0	1	24
6	Farm house, barns, buildings & road	House	2	3	21
7	The Orchard	Pasture	0	3	12
8	Coney Garden	Pasture	15	2	18
9	Plantation	Plantation	0	1	4
10	Plantation	Plantation	1	1	20
11	Old Hop Garden	Arable	24	0	28
11a	Private road	Road	0	1	25
12	Three Cornered Piece	Arable	10	2	27
13	Plantation	Plantation	0	3	21
14	Plantation	Plantation	1	3	23
15	Gallows Hill	Arable	13	2	5
16	Barton Mark	Arable	48	1	11
17	Barton Mark	Arable	47	2	15
18	Plantation	Plantation	0	3	16
19	Plantation	Plantation	0	2	11
20	Round Field	Arable	37	2	19
21	Plantation & road	Plantation	0	1	13
22	Yew Tree Field	Arable	19	0	32
23	Yew Tree Plantation	Plantation	0	0	20
24	Yew Tree Field	Arable	23	2	34
25	Plantation	Plantation	0	0	17
26	Basingstoke Road field	Arable	54	1	35
27	Plantation & road	Plantation	0	2	3
28	Plantation	Plantation	0	0	12
29	Plantation	Plantation	0	1	13
30	Plantation	Plantation	0	1	17
31	Waterside field	Arable	14	3	37
32	Waterside field	Arable	11	2	24
33	Waterside field	Arable	22	3	12
34	Plantation	Plantation	0	1	8
35	Chalk Dell field	Arable	13	2	0
36	Plantation	Plantation	0	1	28
37	Two tenements & gardens & Chalk Pit	House	1	1	7
38	Bunting Mead	Pasture	1	3	38
	LSW Railway		15	0	5
	Total		410a.	2r.	22p.

Source: HRO:13M85W/48

Land could be rented for leisure and status without the fixed cost of ownership, while alternative sources of gentrification offered a substitute for land ownership. [14]

House ownership was not an important measure of status, and flexibility in residence was advantageous. Hence, such control strategies did not conflict with the desires of the Victorian middle classes. Barrow Simonds offered building leases, which allowed the builder a short length of time, say twelve to eighteen months, to construct the property. Barrow Simonds demanded that the building plans were agreed by him or his representative.

Once completed, the building lease was converted to an ordinary lease. [15] Restrictive covenants prevented future development or a change of use without permission. An example was the lease of land in Hyde between Hyde Abbey Road and Upper Brook in 1891 to Rev. Canon Luke Gunning to build an elementary school. The covenant stated that 'if no longer used as a school...can alter, convert or extend same units and build not more than eight tenements or cottages, each not to have a value less than £13 p.a. rental.' [16] After completion, the developer was free to sell the leasehold property. In a small number of cases, Barrow Simonds retained the ownership. The property was offered for rent, with conditions imposed on the tenant to ensure the investment did not depreciate. There were no formal roads so rights of access had to be clearly laid out. In 1909 the tenant of Bonville in Park Road, Ursula Nisbett, was given the:

> Right of way for herself friends and servants and others requiring access to premises for all purposes with or without horses, carts, carriages, motor and other vehicles over the private road. [17]

Bonville could only be used as a dwelling house; no activity was allowed that detracted from the exclusiveness of the neighbourhood. Barrow Simonds sought to reduce the costs of leasing and the amount of churn in the neighbourhood by limiting when the tenant could give up the lease - three or five years with six months' notice. However, the premises could be let furnished for periods up to six months; longer only with Barrow Simonds' permission and if the sub-tenant was respectable and responsible. This was a full repairing and insuring lease. For the annual rent of £105, the tenant had to keep the interior and the outside of the property decorated and in good repair. This included cleaning the kitchen boiler and clearing the gutters and pipes of leaves.

Appearances were important and the garden had to be kept immaculate and unchanged. Lawns were to be mown and all trees and shrubs were to be preserved and replaced if they died. Insurance was required to protect against fire and weather damage, along with the risk of explosion from coal gas. The new risk of fire from a motorcar or petrol kept on the premises was noted. After regular inspections, the tenant was given three months to rectify any fault. There are no details of what happened if they did not, but eviction was a likely outcome. Perhaps these middle class tenants were carefully screened. [18]

Figure 7.4: Barrow Simonds' Plan for Park Road

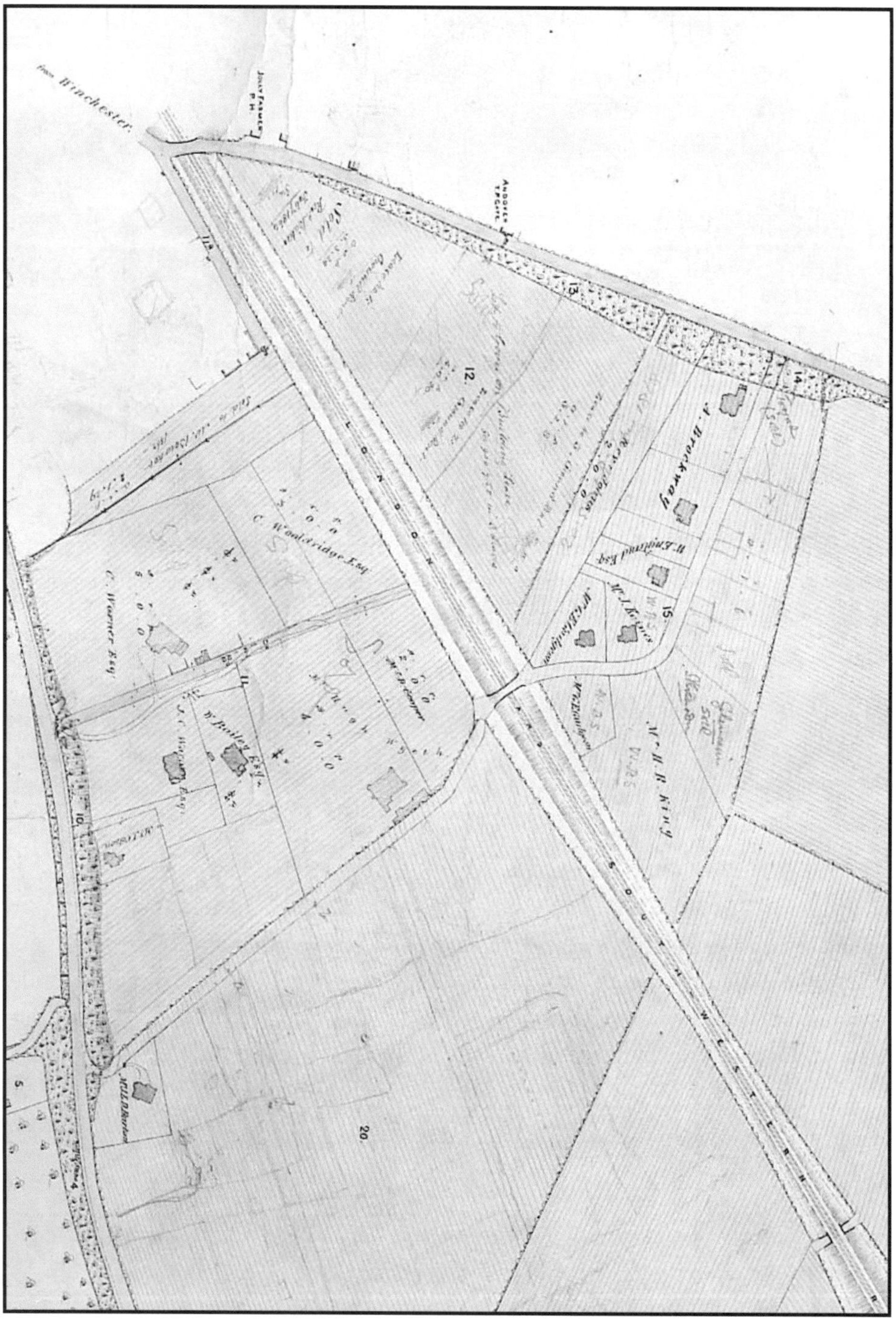

Source: HRO:13M85W/48

The Old Hop Garden Development

The Old Hop Garden extended to 24 acres and lay between the railway and Worthy Road (Figure 7.5). The sale of this land provided influential townspeople with desirable properties. Many owners or occupants were solicitors like Charles Warner, who was also a JP, city auditor and became Mayor of Winchester, and Walter Bailey, town clerk and clerk of the peace. Other professionals included John Barton, a retired naval officer, John Colson, an architect, and Hugh Wyeth, a maltster and brewer.

The earliest development at the southern end of the Old Hop Garden followed the sale of 2¼ acres to Frederick Bowker for £525 (equivalent to £233 per acre). Barrow Simonds was not keen to sell his land but preferred to lease. However since Bowker was Barrow Simonds' father-in-law, an exception was made. The house and its lodge, known as Lankhills, were built by 1861, and lay on the east side of the railway with access by a strip of land adjacent to the railway leading from the Andover Road. The house had a rateable value of £152 in 1909 and, after the purchase of further land, stood in 5½ acres of grounds.[19] The lease forbade the building of any other house with the exception of a lodge, gardener's cottage or stables; unless it could be let at a rack rent or value of not less than £60 p.a.[20]

Frederick Bowker was a Winchester solicitor who lived with his wife Eleanor and their daughter Alice. He was well known as the solicitor for the Tichbourne family in the case against the Tichbourne claimant.[21] Their son Frederick, who was to follow in his father's profession, was away at Marlborough College for the 1861 census. By 1871 Bowker's wife had died and he married Julia, by whom he had three more children: William James, Alfred and Edith, who were looked after by six servants and two nurses. By 1881, the younger Frederick was married with two daughters and lived at No. 50 Hyde Street.[22]

South of Lankhills stood Osborne House. In 1871, Henry Hetley an 83-year old widower and magistrate for Wiltshire lived there with four servants. Ten years later the house had been sold to Lt. Col. Philip Campbell. Osborne House was renamed the Beeches, and, although still owned by Mrs Campbell, was rented out in 1891.[23]

North of Lankhills, Abbey Road gave access to large houses in extensive grounds built prior to 1881: Northlands (5¼ acres), Abbey Lodge (2¾ acres), Salcot (1½ acres) and Caer Gwent (1 acre). The desirability and respective size of these properties can be appreciated from their rent and rateable values. The most expensive property was Northlands, with a rateable value of £180 p.a., Abbey Lodge - £168 p.a., Salcot - £140 p.a., and the cheapest, Caer Gwent, at £112 p.a. Appendix 1 gives details of acreage, ownership, and rent and rateable values.

Charles Warner, a JP and District Auditor, lived at Northlands with his wife, three daughters and three servants. His gardener, Thomas Munt, and his wife and seven children lived at the Lodge. In 1883, Charles Warner died and left the lease to family members - James Charles Warner, Edmund Brooks Warner (of Copthall Court, London) and Frederick Isaac Warner.

Figure 7.5: The Old Hop Garden and Park Road East

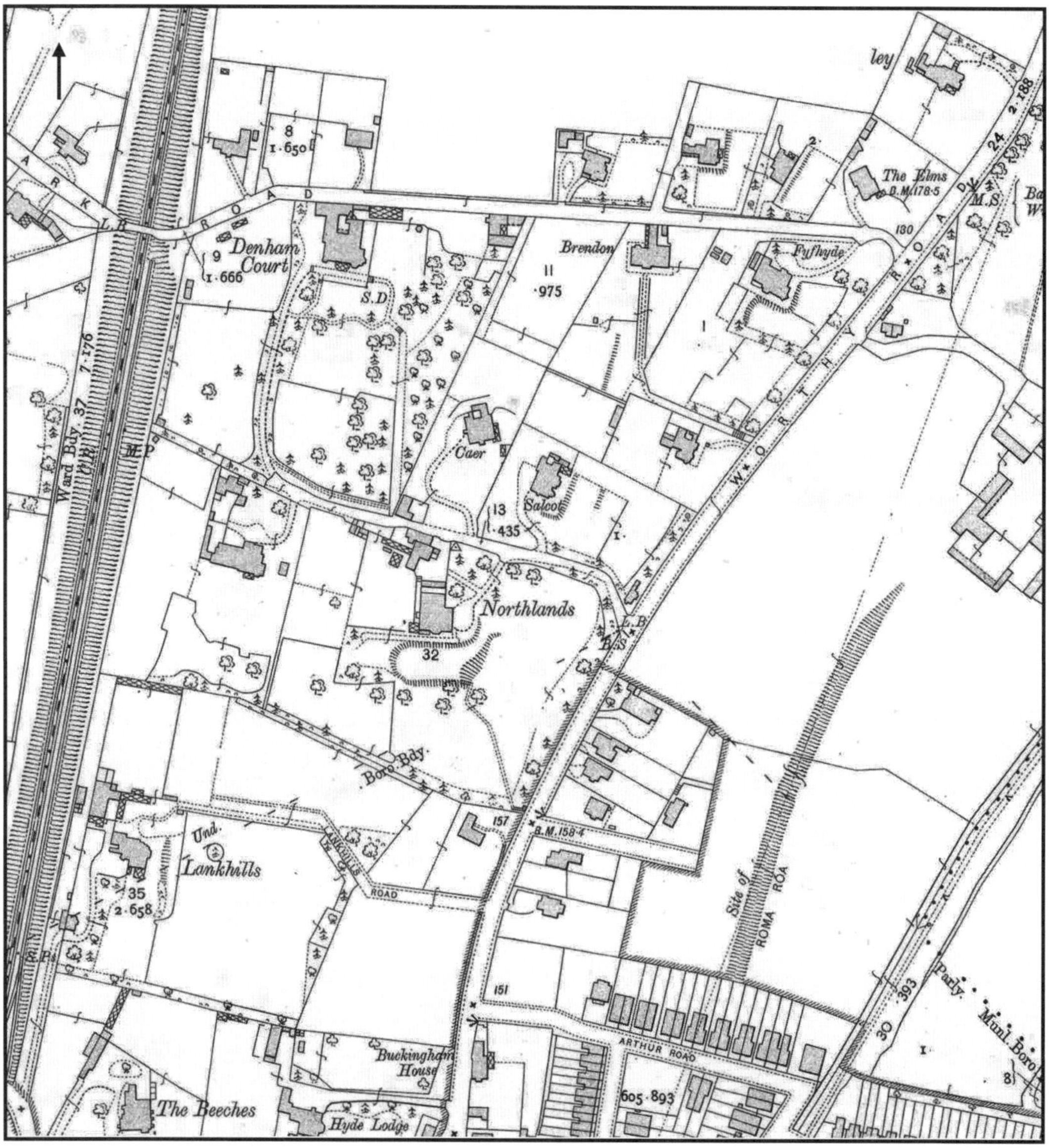

Source: O.S. Map 3rd edition 1909

The map shows development between Worthy Road and the railway. In the south, either side of the junction of Worthy Lane and Hyde Street, are the established Hyde Lodge and the new Conygary estate. Note the site of the Roman Road which originally passed close by the church.

Figure 7.6: Northlands, Worthy Road

Source: HRO:76A03W/7

The site for Northlands was released in 1870 and a long lease issued in 1876, earning Barrow Simonds £55 p.a in ground rent.[24] Access to the property was by a shared road used by Hugh Wyeth and Charles Wooldridge. Charles Warner was also a lessee of an adjoining piece of land on the north side. The freehold was purchased in 1893 for £1,815 by Mrs L. M. Johnston. She was described as living on her own means and she still owned Lankhills in 1912.

Walter Bailey leased a one-acre plot, with a ground rent of £14 p.a., on which he built Caer Gwent.[25] He and his wife had two young daughters and four servants. The lease, dated 1874, allowed for the erection of a house and offices at Bailey's expense. The design was approved by Barrow Simonds and the property was completed by December 1880. A covenant restricted any alterations or extra buildings without permission. Responsibility for insurance and painting the exterior every seven years fell on the lessee.[26] In 1894 there was a family conveyance between Barrow Simonds (senior and younger), Cicely Delves Broughton and Robert Henville Simonds (and others), followed by a Deed of Exchange in 1896 of Caer Gwent with Brendon (which lay to the north of Caer Gwent) whereby Barrow Simonds conveyed Brendon to Robert Henville Simonds and others in return for Caer Gwent. Presumably this was for the freehold.[27]

To the east of Northlands lay Abbey Lodge, the home of John Tysen, a retired naval captain, his family and five servants in 1881. Nothing is known about this property.

In 1891, Salcot was owned by James Charles Warner (son of Charles) who after being educated at Winchester College also became a solicitor. The house was named after the last Abbot of Hyde Abbey. James resided in Beaufort Road, in St Faith's and Salcot was rented out.[28] A later sale describes the property as being on rising ground, in a well timbered and unfrequented district.[29] The house, built on three floors, had a drawing room, dining room, study, offices, principal and secondary staircases, four principal bedrooms and a dressing room. On the top floor were two secondary bedrooms and two servants' bedrooms. The Lodge on Worthy Road, which still stands, was built of brick and flint and had a living room, a sitting room, a scullery and two bedrooms. The Lodge has undergone some changes including a large extension on the back.

Figure 7.7: Salcot Lodge, Worthy Road

Beechwood on Worthy Road lay north of Salcot and had a rateable value of £64 p.a.. It was the home of John Colson, his wife, three unmarried daughters and two servants. A prominent Winchester architect, his eminence is reflected in his membership of Royal Institute of British Architects from 1858, the same year as he was appointed as Cathedral architect. Membership of RIBA was not mandatory for architects and fewer than 10 per cent of those calling themselves architects belonged. He is best remembered for his ecclesiastical work, including some 120 churches built or restored. His greatest work was the restoration of the Cathedral, which continued for half of his 40 years in his position as Cathedral architect.[30] His early work included vicarages built in Jacobean style and church schools in Tudor style. However his architectural plans demonstrate versatility with churches in Early English and Norman styles. Gothic Revival, the major style prescribed by Pugin and others, was favoured by Colson in several projects.

Colson's house, set in 1½ acres of land, had three reception rooms and six bedrooms, with the principal room overlooking the lawn to the south. In 1912 Beechwood was owned and occupied by Miss Barrow Simonds. Either the house was sold back to the Simonds family or the lease had come to an end. The latter was more likely. The property was still described as leasehold when sold in 1944. [31] It would seem that William Barrow's descendants had a similar view to him.

The Limekilns Development

Limekilns was a triangular field which formed part of the western boundary of Abbots Barton. The plot lay between Andover Road, the railway and the northern boundary of Winton House (Figure 7.8). Access would have been difficult from the main farm, and the area was totally isolated from the rest of Abbots Barton, until the construction of Park Road. Barrow Simonds was less restrictive about Limekilns' development and split the area into three sections. He issued three building leases to Mr Gover. Lease No. 1, the four-acre southernmost plot, was sold to Rev. Baker in Feb 1864 and became the site of North Hill House. Lease No. 2, the site of Ashbourne Lodge, which covered two acres, was released for building at an earlier date. Lease No. 3, the future site of Winton House, covered three and a half acres.[32] A further strip to the north, part of the Old Hop Garden, was sold to Rev. Johns in 1868 which increased his site to six acres.

The three properties on the Andover Road site were all run as schools. Whether this was the intention at the development stage or whether schoolmasters saw these sites as an opportunity to run their businesses is not known.[33] In 1912 Winton House had a rateable value of £380 p.a., North Hill House was valued at £120 p.a., and the smaller Ashbourne Lodge was valued at £104 p.a.. The properties had further buildings attached: the headmaster of Winton House had his own small residence valued at £20, and North Hill House had several cottages valued at £23 10s.. In 1871 Winton House was occupied by E. Johns, his wife Ellen, their two children and nine servants. His son Charles was described as a schoolmaster. No pupils are recorded but the boys may have been on vacation as the census took place around Easter. A photograph dated about 1870 shows the boys playing croquet on the lawn beside the large Victorian premises.[34] In 1881 Willingham Rawnsley, his wife Julia and his brother (also a schoolmaster) were in residence with 33 boarders aged from 8 to 13, looked after by eight servants. In 1891 Julia Johns, by then widowed, was still living at Winton House. In 1912 it was still run as a school and owned and occupied by Edward Johns, who was then 50 years old.

George Beckwith (age 36) was a minor canon of Winchester Cathedral and chaplain of Winchester College). He lived at Ashbourne Lodge with his wife Emily, two young children, five servants and twelve pupils aged between 7 and 14. Ten years later, the house was no longer run as a school but was occupied by Major General Francis Carey, his wife, four daughters and four servants. Emily Beckwith, by now a widow at only 34, had moved to Christchurch Road, on the south side of the City. At North Hill House there was another school run by Rev. James Baker (a chaplain at Winchester Cathedral). By the age of 45 he was widowed and his sister-in-law helped look after his five children. There were 14 boarders aged between 9 and 13, looked after by nine servants. By 1881 Baker had married again and the school was a similar size to 1871 - 13 scholars and eight servants. North Hill House built with three reception rooms, ten bedrooms on the first floor and a further four servant bedrooms in the attic, and set in extensive grounds must have been well-suited for school use.

Figure 7.8: Limekilns, Gallows Hill and Park Road West

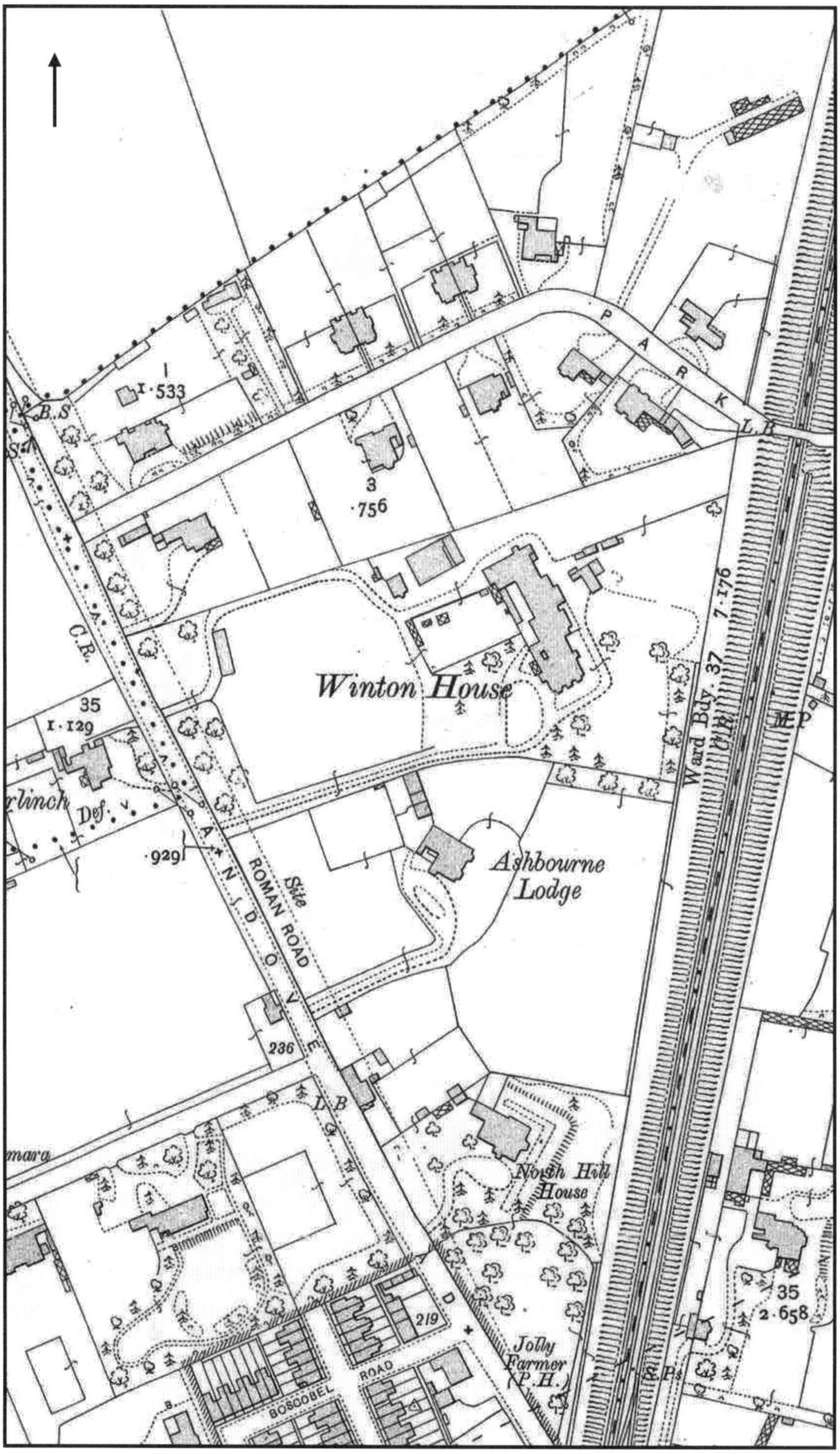

Source: O.S. Map 3rd Edition 1909
The Andover Road formed the western boundary of Abbots Barton

The Gallows Hill Development: Park Road West

The Gallows Hill site, lying on the western side of the railway and north of Winton House consisted of 13½ acres (Figure 7.8). It was not developed until the area was opened up by the construction of Park Road, which linked Worthy Road and Andover Road (Figure 7.8). Building leases were first advertised in 1884, but the development at the remoter western end of Park Road was slow.[35] Access was limited; the narrow railway bridge was built at a time when the only traffic was horses and carts. The road has not changed; only one car can pass and pedestrians must cling to the parapet.

Travelling eastwards from Andover Road, the first two plots on the south side were leased to Alfred & Aaron Brockway, who were building houses on Barrow Simonds' Hyde Abbey Road estate (see Chapter 8). Plot 1, leased in 1885, was the site of Beaconsfield and had a 323½-foot frontage and ground rent of £18 8s. p.a.. Beaconsfield had three reception rooms and ten bedrooms or dressing rooms. The wooded grounds extended to 1¼ acres and it commanded a rateable value of £96. Plot 2, leased in 1884, was the site of Winton Lodge, which had a frontage of about 160 feet and a ground rent of £11 5s. p.a..[36] Winton Lodge had a sweeping driveway and, like Beechwood, the principal room faced southwards. There was no study, but there were three reception rooms - a morning room, a drawing room and a dining room. The house was very large with eight bedrooms and a dressing room on the first floor and a further four bedrooms above for the servants. The grounds extended to just ¾ acre and the rateable value was the same as Beechwood.[37] Both Beaconsfield and Winton Lodge were owned by Frederick Bowker but rented out.[38] The Bowkers continued to benefit from the family relationship and were able to build up a considerable portfolio of properties on the former Abbots Barton Uplands.

Two adjacent plots were originally taken by the Brockways, but were passed on to William England, a doctor practising in Southgate Street. Whether he purchased the completed property or employed the Brockways to build to his design is not known. Only the east plot, Norton, was developed by 1912. The house had three reception rooms and ten bedrooms. In 1912 Norton was owned and occupied by Admiral Dickens.[39]

The final two plots on the south side of the road, the Cedars and Rosslyn (originally called St Agnes), were developed in about 1882. Although the Cedars is now painted white, the two houses have identical facades, suggesting both were built of red bricks with yellow brick features. See Figure 7.9 for a picture of Rosslyn. The Cedars had three reception rooms, four bedrooms on the first floor and a further bedroom in the roof. The servants' quarters were modest and, like many houses of the era, had a tradesman's entrance.[40] The accommodation was similar to all the other houses built for the middle classes, but had an east wing and featured an L-shaped living room. At this time, horse transport was a necessity, so The Cedars was well-equipped with stables, with two stalls, harness room and a room above which could be used as living accommodation.[41] In 1912 the properties were occupied by John Kaines, the pork butcher, and Col. Peyton respectively. Whilst ownership of the Cedars had passed to William Barrow Simonds (junior), Rosslyn was sold to George E. Gudgeon of the family firm of auctioneers.

The north side of Park Road West was developed as Queen Victoria's reign was coming to the end and styles in architecture were changing. Although the plots were smaller than the south side of the road and the houses a mix of detached and semi-detached, this was still a desirable location. The rumble of trains and smoke pollution were not attractive for those seeking a country life. H. R. M. King leased 2½ acres of land extending along the railway for a nursery. Barrow Simonds still held the land in 1912, but at some later stage, it was sold and a market garden with a small property, outbuildings and greenhouse flourished.[42] Part of the road frontage, opposite to Rosslyn, was sold to Gudgeon. The detached Glencairn, which stood adjacent to the nursery, had typical Edwardian features. These included a timbered gable, small panes of glass in the upper part of the windows, and a porch which stretched across the door and bay window. Glencairn had a 100-foot frontage and the 1½ acre plot was large enough to support orchards and fruit bushes, as well as two large brick and timber greenhouses.[43] Barrow Simonds still owned the property in 1901 but, by 1912, it had been sold to Lewis Carter, one of the extended family, who built many of Winchester's suburban houses.[44]

In 1895, Thomas Micklam, an architect and the developer of Hyde Abbey Road purchased the land stretching from Glencairn to Andover Road.[45] Woodside, which extended to 1½ acres, and Nos. 1, 3, 5 and 7 Park Road were built prior to 1901 (Figure 7.10).[46] Woodside's grounds were screened by trees and it had orchards and stabling. The location still remained desirable some 30 years later. In the 1929 sale particulars for Woodside, estate agents emphasised 'surroundings all that could be desired and free from nuisances' and 'the outlook to the north being over undulating country.'[47] In 1912 Woodside was owned and occupied by Colonel Seymour Toogood, who lived at Denham Court until 1900. Woodside is now split into two properties.

Micklam's semi-detached houses, built in Arts and Craft style, were very impressive with three-storey gabled timbered bays at the front and side of the property. They offered extensive accommodation, including a large hall, drawing and dining rooms and offices, which were described as well shut off. There were bedrooms on the two upper floors and the benefit of a good wine cellar.[48] As common in many Winchester suburbs, developers opted to retain the ownership of many of the properties. Ownership provided a sound investment and guaranteed income in retirement. After death, the rents or sale of property ensured a comfortable stand of living for the widow and children. By 1912, Mrs Micklam had become the owner of Nos. 1, 3, 5 and 7 along with other properties throughout Winchester which had been built by her late husband.

Figure 7.9: Rosslyn, Park Road

The right wing is a later addition.

Figure 7.10: Arts and Crafts design in Micklam's houses, Park Road

The Gallows Hill Development: Park Road East

Plots along Worthy Road were easily accessible and consequently were developed before those in Park Road (Figure 7.5). John Barton, a retired naval instructor, his wife and six children along with two boarders - an elderly member of the clergy and a young scholar - lived at the Elms on the northern corner of Park Road. [49] The older children had been born at Dartmouth and the family had moved to Winchester within the previous five or six years. The house was built in the vernacular style - mostly flint with brick dressings - and was accessed by a carriage drive from Park Road. The one-acre grounds were described as shaded and picturesque. Like Rosslyn, it had stables for two horses as well as a coach house. [50] On the north side was the larger Donnithorne, built in about 1893. [51] The one-acre plot was accessed from Worthy Road. Both the Elms and Donnithorne had ample bedrooms over two floors. These houses were attractive as residences and as investments to high ranking officers including, in 1912, Col. A. Hill at The Elms and Admiral R. P. Hampage at Donnithorne. The 1912 rental values were £120 p.a. and £150 p.a. respectively.

Byrmelmscote was one of the first houses to be built at this end of Park Road in 1899. It was designed for Mrs Atkinson by Ernest Shearman, a qualified architect with a practice in London. Ernest was the son of Henry Shearman, a painter, and was possibly the brother of William, the builder. The house was built by Carter & Son. The house faced east and had drawing and dining rooms, a library, offices on the west side and five bedrooms.

The houses were also attractive to successful business men. Hugh Wyeth, a maltster and brewer, with premises in Hyde Street employing eight men, lived at Hyde Park House (later known simply as Park House) with his wife, three adult children and three servants. His son was described as 'learning brewing'. Park House was one of the larger houses with 1¼ acres of land and a rateable value of £112 p.a.. In 1912 Park House was owned by Lewis Carter. With south and west aspects, the house had three reception rooms, ten bedrooms, a dressing room and a conservatory. [52]

Fyfhyde lay on high ground at the entrance to Park Road and the grounds extended to 2¼ acres. There was a winding carriage drive, well-timbered and secluded grounds and views over the Itchen Valley. The house was built for Frederick Bowker's own occupation and befitted his standing in the community. There were three reception rooms, eight principal bedrooms, and a further four bedrooms for servants on the top floor. [53]

Even in the 1900s, Barrow Simonds had not changed his modus operandi. He commissioned houses and leased them rather than sell to a builder. Most of the other houses in Park Road (east) were built between 1905 and 1907. The architect practice Colson, [54] Farrow and Nisbett designed Lynton, St Waleric and Brendon (Figures 7.11, 7.12 and 7.13). St Waleric was built for Barrow Simonds by Carter & Son and was rated at £80 p.a.. The house had an outer and inner hall, verandah, drawing and dining room, the usual offices served by back stairs, five bedrooms, a boudoir, two WCs and a bathroom. Brendon was also designed for Barrow

Simonds but he later sold the property, unlike St Waleric, which in 1912 was rented out to one of the Bowkers. The size of Brendon was reflected in the rateable value of £120 p.a.. The house had dining, drawing and morning rooms, four bedrooms on the first floor and a further three bedrooms and a box room on the second floor. Offices were uniquely placed in a wing which extended forward to the road.

Figure 7.11: Lynton, Park Road

Figure 7.12: St Waleric, Park Road

Now used by the Health Service

Figure 7.13: Brendon, Park Road

The unimposing tradesmen's entrance
Now used for health and social care

The wealth of the residents can be measured by the 1914 valuation for insurance made by Gudgeons, the auctioneers, for Capt. Radford of Park House, in Park Road. The house had two reception rooms, the usual offices, three bedrooms, day and night nurseries and three servant bedrooms. The total contents valuation came to £3,450 16s.. The breakdown for each room or type of item is given in Table 7.2 and selected details are given on Table 7.3. The most expensive furnishings were in the hall (£278) and drawing room (£241) followed by the dining room (£107) where visitors might be entertained. The dining room table was lavishly laid with the best china, cutlery and serving dishes valued at £90. The silver worth £320 included an Irish teapot, sugar bowl and sauce tureen. Ornaments decorated the furniture (£80) and walls were brightened up with pictures (£69). The furniture in the three bedrooms totalled nearly £175 whereas the servants' bedrooms were frugally furnished.

An officer and his family needed to dress in the latest fashions purchased from exclusive tailors. The wearing apparel was valued at £728 and jewellery at £564. Mrs Radford owned several diamond rings, and a sealskin coat, stole and muff. These values can be compared to the costs of staff. Scullery and kitchen maids, aged 19 or 20, earned £13 p.a.. Housemaids earned £16 p.a. whilst the more experienced parlour maids and cooks earned £20 p.a.. A lady's maid was paid £24 p.a.. She reported to the mistress, rather than the housekeeper, and the position was reached after five or ten years in service. The housekeeper reached the position at the age of 40 and earned about £53 p.a..[55]

Musical entertainment was important to the Edwardian family and the Radfords owned two pianos, kept in the hall and drawing room. Furniture included Chippendale and Sèvres pieces. Capt. Radford had a full drinks cellar of Taylor's Port, claret, whisky, champagne and liqueurs worth nearly £100. He was interested in hunting, fishing, and golf. All these pursuits were well catered for in the area. The River Itchen was home to fly-fishing, a pursuit enjoyed by Barrow Simonds.[56] The Westley Richards gun and a Webley revolver may have been from Redford's army service. The family entertained friends with croquet and bowls.

Following the death of Frederick Bowker in 1907, Lankhills was put up for sale with permission for the development of the land. Barrow Simonds no longer had any control over the future of the property as he had sold it to his father-in-law 46 years before. The sale included a house valued at over £500 on the former Sheep Fair Field (purchased from St Bartholomew's Church in 1873) which lay adjacent to Worthy Road, a house with a rateable value at over £60 p.a. on the north side of the site, and a house with a rateable value of over £70 p.a. in the south. The land was purchased by Ashton Sawyer, an architect, who in 1908 submitted plans for the Lankhills Building Estate. Lankhills remained in the Bowker family as the sale of part of the grounds was sufficient to meet the inheritance conditions of the will and other calls on the estate.[57] In 1912 Sawyer owned Rooks Acre, Fayre Acre and the Lawn Tennis Club, but had sold Dane's Acre and The Garth. Sawyer purchased and developed several plots around Park Road including Valentio, Short Acre and Abbot's Acre (Figures 7.14 & 7.15). Short Acre was built in 1909, had three reception rooms, six bedrooms and extensive views.

Table 7.2: Inventory of Park House for Capt. Radford, 1914

	£	s.	d.
Servants 1	8	5	6
Servants 2	4	14	6
Servants 3	5	14	6
Back landing	4	2	0
Night nursery	12	3	0
Dressing room adjacent	7	19	0
Day nursery	11	13	6
Principal bedroom 1	58	13	6
Principal bedroom 2	80	3	6
Principal bedroom 3	34	9	6
Dressing room adjacent	41	9	6
Bathroom	3	4	0
Housemaids & linen cupboard	5	5	0
Landing and stairs	43	17	6
Smoking room	78	3	0
Prints –framed and glass	53	11	0
Hall	278	1	0
Drawing room	241	9	0
Ornaments	80	8	0
Silver on table	30	4	6
Various ornaments	39	12	6
Pictures	69	1	6
In curio table	15	2	0
Dining room	107	10	0
Cutlery	12	9	0
Offices	74	1	0
Glass	26	12	6
China	21	13	6
Passage	1	14	0
Plate articles	104	0	6
Silver plate	321	9	0
Jewellery	564	5	0
Children's silver and jewellery	23	8	6
Linen	75	0	0
Wearing apparel	728	0	0
Various effects	97	0	0
Wine	96	6	0
Total valuation	£3,460	16s.	0d.

Source: HRO:106M86W/1

Table 7.3: Details in Inventory of Park House for Capt. Radford 1914

Wine:		
6 doz. Taylor's Port 1896 Vintage 70 shillings	£21	
12 doz. Taylor's Port 1900 Vintage 50 shillings	£30	
6 doz. Taylor's Port 1900 Vintage 40 shillings	£12	
4 doz. Smith Woodhouse 1900 Vintage 34 shillings	£6	16s
2 doz. Claret 40 shillings	£4	
1 doz. Whisky	£2	14s
2 doz. Pol Roger Champagne 90 shillings	£9	
2 doz. Desbordes Champagne 78 shillings	£7	16s
Liqueurs brandy various	£3	
	£96	6s
Hall:		
Upright grand pianoforte in walnut case by Brinsmead	£40	
Pianola & records with stained stand	£30	
5 large carved oak armchairs with high backs, coronets and velvet seats	£30	
Grandfather clock in plain mahogany case with brass dial - 8 day	£15	
Four-foot carved Chippendale hall table with marble top and shaped legs with festoon of flowers	£21	
Drawing room:		
Boudoir grand piano in burr walnut case by Keps	£60	
20 inch Sèvres and ebonised work table on three leg porcelain stand with figure and tulip wood fittings, old mirror and ormolu mounts	£28	
Six-foot Dutch Marquette china cabinet enclosed by a pair of glass doors over and panelled doors under lined red cloth	£25	
Silver plate:		
Oval engraved teapot Irish 1807 24ozs.	£24	
Oval sugar basin with double handles and a cream jug. Irish 21ozs.	£26	5s
Oval sauce tureen with gadrooned border, square base and slender handles 1797 by Paul Storr 21ozs.	£25	5s
Fluted and gadrooned tea service-teapot, sugar basin and cream jug 47ozs.	£23	10s
Jewellery:		
Diamond pendant with large turquoise	£75	
9 stone diamond ring	£50	
9 stone diamond ring flat shaped	£40	
Wearing apparel:		
Sealskin coat	£60	
Sealskin stole and muff	£15	
Sable stole	£25	
Various effects:		
Hammerless ejector gun by Westley Richards and case rook rifle, Webley revolver, Hardly fishing rod, Golf clubs, Croquet set, Bowls.	£50	

Source: HRO:106M86W/1

Figure 7.14: Valentio

Valentio was built in Arts and Crafts style with a typical steep pitch tile roof and wide oriel windows on the upper storey.

Figure 7.15: Abbots Acre

A design harking back to earlier days.

Worthy Road Development

The Old Hop Garden, Limekilns and Gallows Hill developments met the demands of the professionals – armed forces, solicitors and successful businessmen. They sought modern palatial accommodation, on wooded gentle slopes, which was only a short horse and carriage journey into Winchester. After these areas were developed, Barrow Simonds started developing the smaller fields between his farmhouse and Hyde Street. These properties were smaller than those in Park Road and reflected the economic downturn and market saturation for larger properties.

In 1898 Barrow Simonds released meadow and pasture land along Worthy Road. The plans for the Abbots Barton Building Estate of 'two storey houses with or without attics' of 'good class villa residences' were submitted by H. J. Weston, an architect and surveyor from Southampton.[58] The planned estate stretched from the Worthy Road down to Nuns Walk. There were to be 27 plots of which 12 on the south side of Edington Road had a depth of 100 feet and a width of 25 feet. On the north side of the road there were four plots (Nos. 19 to 23) with a further four plots (Nos. 24 to 27), in Sandall Road, which was to be built perpendicular to Edington Road. The roads were named after Bishops of Winchester. Another 5 plots (Nos. 14 to 18), with a width of 80 feet and depth of nearly 200 feet, were set out in Worthy Road. Only seven houses were built between 1898 and 1902 and the intended layout was abandoned to give only six properties on Worthy Road and one in Edington Road (Figure 7.5). The first two building plans in 1898-9 did not come to fruition. There appears to have been issues with the drainage.[59] In 1912 the undeveloped land, which extended to 4½ acres was used as allotments, which still remain today.

The plots on Worthy Road allowed the building of one house of not less than £500 in value. The most southerly property, Donnington, was designed by G. A. Barnard for J. Holder in 1901. The large house contained drawing, morning and dining rooms, kitchen and scullery at the side, four bedrooms, a further bedroom or dressing room, bathroom and WC, and two further box rooms in the roof. There was only one set of stairs; live-in-servants were not so prominent in the smaller Edwardian house. Next door, the original design for a pair of semi-detached houses was not realised, and only Woodlands was built. Designed by Barnard for T. Bidden, the house featured a full height six-sided turret. It had similar accommodation to Donnington but with the addition of a conservatory in the tower, two staircases and a cellar. Both houses had a rateable value of £48 p.a.. Lancing Cottage was smaller with a rateable value of £36 p.a.. There was no morning room and only one staircase, although there were five bedrooms, and a servant's bedroom in the attic. Modern conveniences had arrived - each house had a bathroom and WC on the first floor and a servant's WC at the back of the house.

Eldon Lodge was designed and built by George Weeks. The house had three reception rooms, a cellar, four bedrooms and attic rooms. Weeks built Selborne Lodge next door in the Arts and Crafts style similar to Micklam's houses in Park Road (Figure 7.15). Selborne Lodge had a dining and drawing room, kitchen, scullery, conservatory, a small basement, four bedrooms, and, in the attic, a further two bedrooms and box room. Weeks, who could be described as a small developer, built property throughout the suburbs and retained some for rental. These included No. 32 Cranworth Road, Nos. 26 to 28 Greenhill Road, Nos. 32 to 37 and Nos. 50 to 53 Parchment Street. The last house was described as having a builder's workshop.[60]

Thomas Stopher designed Fernbank for Miss Gowan in 1899. In 1901, Mrs Gowan, a widow, lived at Highfield with three daughters and four servants. The daughters' ages ranged from 32 to 38 but which one owned Fernbank is not known. This was a spacious property and even featured a 'carriage sweep'. The house had dining, drawing and morning rooms, five bedrooms and a dressing room, and may have been one of the first houses in Winchester to be designed with a motor car house. The last property built on the estate, Walzell, was designed and owned by Nisbett, an architect. The house was built in brick with the latest look – half-height roughcast and was valued at £68 p.a,. It had a drawing and dining room, a nursery at the front of the house, study and isolated servant offices at the back with staff stairs. Off the galleried landing there were only three bedrooms and a dressing room, although one bedroom had a night nursery attached.[61]

Barrow Simonds' last proposed speculative development in 1910 was for four new streets at the junction of Worthy and Park Roads.[62] Easton and Burnett of Southampton were the civil engineers. Denewulf and Courtenay Roads ran parallel to Worthy Road and Waynflete and Abbot's Roads ran parallel to Park Road. The tradition of using Bishop's names continued. Abbots and Courtenay Roads were to be developed first with 'good class houses standing on nothing much less than ¼ acre per plot.' By 1912, there was little evidence of progress and only two houses - Roundfield and Abbot's Acre – had been built.[63]

Figure 7.16: Selborne Lodge, Worthy Road.

Conclusion

After the Dissolution, the Abbey's farms remained largely unchanged under the ownership of a succession of families until sold to William Simonds in 1811. William Barrow Simonds was the prime mover in the development of desirable villas for the aspiring middle classes. The former Abbey's fields were eaten away and transformed into leafy suburbs.

The earlier developments on the Old Hop Garden, Limekilns and Gallows Hill areas were of houses with extensive grounds. The land was offered as leasehold with the exception of Lankhills, which Barrow Simonds sold to Frederick Bowker, his father-in-law. Bowker built up a portfolio of properties throughout the developments. Barrow Simonds did not relax his strategy of keeping control over the former Abbey's lands. However, the short leases seen in earlier developments were replaced by long leases which gave similar security to freehold. Developers like Gover and the Brockway brothers took over large plots and built the houses in Park Road which were then sold. However, Micklam was affluent and could retain his development. Smaller plots were, in the main, purchased by prospective investors, but some houses were designed as family homes for Winchester's elite.

From the first release of part of Abbots Barton Uplands in the early 1860s, the area became a magnet for Winchester's professionals and successful business men. Occupancy of these large properties reflected wealth and social position. Of the 16 sole or family-run solicitors named in the 1871 Census, four had moved from their business premises to Hyde.[64] The growing importance of building professionals, such as architects and surveyors, like Colson, Gover and Micklam, is apparent. In addition 'new money' gained in production was also creating demand. For example, Kaines, a pork butcher, and Wyeth, the Hyde maltster and brewer, both sought country abodes.[65]

Without conveyance details there is no incontrovertible proof that the owners recorded in the rate books and the 1912 Valuation survey did hold the freehold. These documents give the owners and occupiers who were responsible for paying the rates. However it is likely that these owners had only acquired a long-term lease rather than the freehold of the property. The Simonds family continued to retain considerable control of the former Abbey's land by means of long leases and covenants, and by so doing, ensured a continuous income from ground rents.

The historian - Harold James Dyos - commented that:

> Architectural tastes, like manners, travel downwards and it must have seemed unthinkable that one's house should not bear some resemblance, however remote, to the façade and the layout of more exclusive properties.[66]

The properties built on Abbots Barton were designed to mimic many of the features that gentry families like the Knights experienced in their county seats. However, modern conveniences like bathrooms had arrived. As the new century progressed, the stabling and ancillary accommodation for the coachman was replaced by a shed for the 20 horsepower car.

By 1912, Barrow Simonds had released some 80 acres for urban development, albeit for housing Winchester's most affluent citizens and for educational purposes. In doing so, £4,457 was added to the rateable value of the City's real estate. Many of the original owners, occupiers, or their families still had a presence. Although the rental market was buoyant, 49 per cent of owners (freehold or long leaseholders) lived in their property. The Appendix gives details of these properties – location, owner, occupier, acreage, and rental and rateable values.

Figure 7.17: William Barrow Simonds

Source: Jenkinson (1994) *The History of Peter Symonds*

Barrow Simonds was active in all parts of local politics. As well as standing as Winchester's Mayor in 1852 and MP from 1865 to 1880, he was a Gubernator of Peter Symonds Hospital from the late 1850s until his death. He was instrumental in negotiations with the Charity Commissioners to increase the educational provision for poor boys. Peter Symonds School was founded in 1896 and a site found on land belonging to Winchester College.

Chapter 8: Suburban Estates for the Mass Market

The house building process

Several small estates were built on the former Abbey's and Dean and Chapter's lands between 1850 and 1910. King Alfred Place was built on the site of the Bridewell in the 1850s. In the 1880s, Barrow Simonds released land for Hyde Abbey Road and Lord Northbrook purchased land and developed Eagles Field. At the turn of the century Arthur Elliot Deane developed the Conygary and Oxlease Estates on the former meadows behind St Bartholomew's church.

Housing development was a complicated process which could only come to fruition under the right conditions: the acquiescence of a landowner who desired to maintain his lifestyle in the difficult economic climate affecting farming; the availability of risk takers to undertake the development; and financiers to provide the capital needed by the builders and mortgages for the investor. Development would not be sustainable without demand by the end-users who sought to escape crowded and unsanitary accommodation in a city or who were attracted to a new life in a desirable city.

The strategies of Barrow Simonds and the Dean and Chapter were different. Barrow Simonds sought to determine how the land was to be developed. He employed a developer to lay out the estate. Building plots were usually offered as leasehold. He had to invest considerable sums in laying out roads to make the estates attractive. Even so, estate development was more valuable than agricultural use. The Dean and Chapter went for a low risk and low involvement development strategy. Land was sold to the highest bidder and they had no interest, beyond restrictive covenants, in future development. The Dean and Chapter's income was certain at the point of sale but they did not share in the development profits.

Ideally, the cost of laying out the estate was shared between the developer and builders. Where the plots were sold as freehold, profit was received up front. Where land was offered leasehold, the owner retained control of the process and received an income from the ground rents for the length of the lease. At the end of the lease, the property reverted to the ground landlord, who could retain it as an investment or grant a new lease. The lessee bore the risk of voids and the costs of maintenance and management. In a long lease, returns were spread out throughout the term. Initially a premium was received for the lease followed by the half-yearly ground rent. As there were no rent reviews, the ground landlord did not share in any capital growth until the lease was renewed. Today any lease would be subject to frequent rent reviews allowing the landlord's interest to increase with inflation and economic growth.

The integrity of the development, both immediately and in the future, was guaranteed by the use of restrictive covenants. Covenants required the approval of building plans by the landowner's architect, controlled the type of property built, and set minimum specifications in terms of costs of work. A building lease at a peppercorn rent was issued giving the builder 12 or 18 months to complete the building. On completion, a longer lease was issued. When the lease was short, say 40 or 60 years, the building and land reverted to the landowner at the end of the period. Many landowners offered the freehold during the first few years of the lease at some multiple of the ground rent. The period of grace varied considerably: Barrow Simonds allowed a seven-year window in Park Road, Lord Northbrook gave six years in the Eagles Field Estate, and on the Conygary Estate, Deane offered only three years. The cost of the freehold offered by Barrow Simonds and Northbrook was 32 times the ground rent, which was consistent with agricultural returns.[1]

The risks and associated profits varied according to the landowner's approach to development. When the landowner developed the land, built the houses and sold the completed product, greater risk was involved but, when demand was high, so were the profits. The landowner took the developer's profit and doubled his returns. Some landowners developed the land, built the houses and retained them in their investment portfolio, offering the properties for rental.

When the site developer built and then let, he took the developer's and the landlord's profit. But he risked voids (or empties) when tenants left and rent failed to materialise, rent arrears, and the possibility of falling rents, either through an economic downturn or by the need to remain competitive in an over-supplied market. Cheaper houses were let by the week or quarter so voids and arrears were a problem. Moonlight flits were common as Marie Lloyd famously sang.[2] Better quality and, thus more expensive houses, had seven-year leases, which gave stable returns, but rent was fixed for the duration. When leases were short, there would be frequent reversions to the market rent - a benefit in a buoyant economy. The developer could sell the freehold or lease to an investor, who then became the landlord, or the property could be retained and used as security to finance new projects. In the latter case, profits came from the improved rents, not merely from house building.

Builders often erected properties quickly and cheaply. Speculative building in late Victorian times was governed by new byelaws, which stipulated minimum road and house specifications typifying respectable middle-class housing. Carriage roads were set at 36 feet wide and others at least 18 feet with a full width entrance, although the width could be reduced if there was open space on one side. Houses could not be taller than the distance from houses on the opposite side of the road. A house must be set in 150 square feet of open space and the distance between buildings started as a minimum requirement of 10 feet for two storeys with 5 feet added per extra storey. Low ceilings and poorly ventilated spaces were no longer allowed. Habitable rooms in basements and ground floors tended to have a height of 8½ feet; other rooms, except in the roof, a height of 8 feet, and in the attic, at least half the area of the room should have a height of 8 feet. Habitable rooms should have at least one window, of area greater than one-tenth of the area of the room. Drains must be glazed stoneware or fire clay pipes connected to the sewer and no cesspools were allowed unless unavoidable. In large cities, terraced houses were built at about 40 to the acre, usually in long straight roads. The plot width was a minimum of 15 feet, but houses could be three times deeper.

In 1880 a local byelaw extended the building requirements and gave clear criteria for development. Streets over 100 feet long must be wide enough to take carriages. There was a ban of the use of faecal matter, animal or vegetable matter under foundations which had to be asphalted or have a layer of good cement, concrete or rammed solid at six inches thick. Building walls were to be constructed with quality brick, stone or other hard and incombustible materials, with suitable mortar and lime, and clear sharp sand or cement. The ground floor was to have boarded floors with nine inches space above surface of earth, asphalt or concrete to allow for air circulation and prevent dampness. Houses were now built with a back access as the main access was not to be used for removing contents from privy, ash-pit or cesspool. Covenants prevented any house from being used for manufacturing, trade or business.

The new estates laid down in Hyde were less densely packed, with a mix of semi-detached houses and short terraces. Builder is an umbrella term for developers and craftsmen. The smaller builders and tradesmen, took on a building lease, raised the finance, and made their profit by selling on the houses as they were built. However, several developers, including Albert Evans, William Shearman and two building families - the Carters and the Fielders - built and retained the houses as investments, earning an income from the rents generated. Other substantial owners of real estate were successful businessmen like Henry Frampton, a builder's merchant, who acted as a developer. A property portfolio provided a regular income for a widow and children. Trustees or executors often took control whilst the children were young. Later the property passed to the children or was sold and the proceeds shared.

Both estate developers and builders of individual houses needed finance and Winchester was not short of moneylenders and investors. As Winchester was small, a direct approach to financiers was possible, but usually finance was raised through a solicitor representing several lenders. Builders borrowed money by way of advances and solicitors were employed to check their progress. These short-term investments, if not repaid, could be converted to a mortgage on completion of the building. The importance of local people in providing mortgages is apparent. Respectability 'mores' saw widows and spinsters lending money at five per cent, a mostly safe and guaranteed return. Properties were conveyed to the lender, a gentleman, widow or spinster, until the mortgage was paid off. There was an equitable right to re-conveyance when the loan was paid off.

Some developers experienced problems with cash flow, over-stretching with extensive interests, or misjudging the market and finding difficulty in selling the completed properties. Pressures from investors and other creditors resulted in the scaling down of businesses or even bankruptcy, although most creditors preferred to see some returns rather than none, and often gave the builders an opportunity to complete their developments.

The closure of the Bridewell

The land south of Bridewell Lane was part of Barton Farm. On the corner with Hyde Street was an L-shaped block of eight small farm cottages which had a rateable value of £5 p.a.. They are shown on Milner's map (Figure 5.9) and so date back to the ownership of Thomas Knight, or possibly to the Duke of Bedford. The cottages were roughly rendered, had paired doorways, and one window up and down. They were occupied by employees of Barrow Simonds - shepherd, farm servant or labourer and gardener. King Alfred Place was the northern limit of Barton Farm and this part of the Abbey's former estate was still intact. With the exception of Nos. 66 and 67, Barrow Simonds owned all the land and properties south to Hyde House. Henry Collis was a dairyman who farmed at Headbourne Worthy and rented a stone house and shop (No. 68 Hyde Street). *Ye Olde Hyde Dairy* was most probably established soon after William Simonds took over the farm. A 1907 photograph of the employees, their horses and two-wheeled milk floats proclaimed 'Established nearly a century ago'. Dressed in Sunday best with flowers in their button holes, the men stood proudly beside the shoulder high horses, clutching milk churns and two silver cups won in a parade.[3]

Figure 8.1: No. 68 Hyde Street

Development east of Hyde Street began in 1850 with the sale of the Bridewell site following an act to allow the disposal of prisons. The site consisted of 3¼ acres, described as 'valuable productive land with most substantial residence,' which was 'part of Hyde Abbey and lately used as the County Bridewell.' It appears that the Bridewell had been pulled down, but the Governor's house remained. The advert proposed a range of potential uses; either as a sole residence or for development or cultivation:

> This property is most advantageous situate close to the rapidly increasing City of Winchester, and within a very short distance of the Railway Station, and is capable of being rendered, at moderate expense, one of the most desirable private residences in the vicinity. It also offers an eligible opportunity to parties requiring extensive premises for business purposes, while the land, from its desirable position, and highly productive quality, is available as building ground, or for potential cultivation.[4]

The property included a chapel, coach house and stables. On the ground floor was a dining room, kitchen, washhouse, pantry, offices and servants rooms. There were cellars and wine vaults below. On the first floor was a dining room, best bedroom and WC and on the second floor, three bedrooms and attic or store room over. The property was bordered by Deane's land on the north and north-west and Barrow Simonds' land on all other sides.

Charles Witham Benny, an alderman, purchased the property and land for £1,350, equivalent to £415 per acre. Land was conveyed to Jesse Carter in 1857 and 1860.[5] Carter was an important Winchester builder who employed 49 men and 5 boys in 1861, and also stood as a town councillor. By 1871 Carter had built 19 properties in King Alfred Place. Two terraces (Nos. 4 to 8 and Nos. 15 to 20) rated at £10 10s. p.a. were built with long front gardens and a back yard (Figure 8.1). The Carters owned the shorter terrace and the rate books cited Henry White as the owner of the longer terrace which backed on to one of the numerous streams in the area. White may have provided financial help – there was a Henry White, a nurseryman who lived in a large house in Christchurch Road. The three pairs of semi-detached houses (Nos. 9 to 14) were larger with a value of £12 p.a.. Four were owned by Northbrook and two by Blake.[6] The layout of the development is unusual with long gardens on the south (Nos. 4 to 8) and east (Nos. 9 to 20). The Victorian builders may have been avoiding difficult building terrain. The former Bridewell had been recently demolished and foundations and rubble may have not been completely removed. Abbey remains were also best avoided.

Four of Simonds' cottages were re-designated Nos. 22 to 25 King Alfred Place. Two small cottages on the edge of the Bridewell site which belonged to Charles March Deane became Nos. 1 and 2 King Alfred Place. The Deanes were long-time residents of Hyde and Thomas Deane had acquired the glebe land either side of the Mill Ditch Stream. The history of No. 3 King Alfred Place, a detached house with garden, and the large plot lying to the north which consisted of a cottage with stabling and stores, is not known. Both belonged to Mr A Smith in 1912. All these properties are clearly marked in Figure 8.1.

Figure 8.2: King Alfred Place 1873

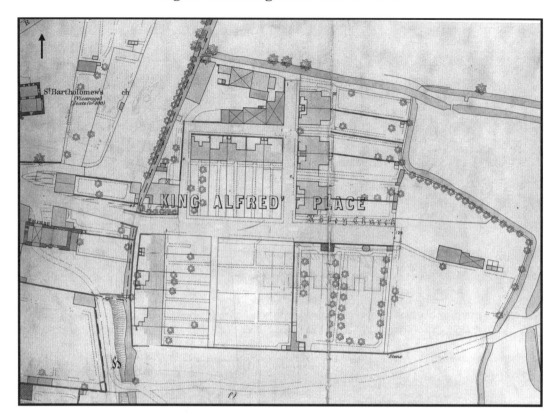

Source: O.S. Map 1st Edition 1873

An interesting layout – perhaps avoiding sacred ground

Initially the Hayles family had the legal ownership of the majority of the new houses in King Alfred Place as a result of the need for security for loans. Edward, a retired grocer who lived comfortably in Edgar Road, owned Nos. 3 to 8, Charles owned Nos. 9 to 14, and James owned Nos. 15 to 21. In 1881 Blake (a carpenter who built houses in Greenhill and Western Roads on West Hill) had repaid the Hayles the loan needed to build his two houses. Carter took a longer period to repay his loan, but five houses were in his name by 1912. They were designed for the better-off working classes and this is reflected by rateable values of between £10 10s. p.a. and £13 p.a.. In 1881, the houses were tenanted by shopmen, cabinet makers, a hotel porter, labourers, a police constable, a grocer's clerk and a parish clerk.

Figure 8.3: King Alfred Place

The terraced and semi-detached properties have long front gardens and a small backyard.

Some backed on to the Mill Stream. The Abbey's stone walls and bridge can be seen in the top right picture.

North Walls and the Refuge

North Walls formed the southern boundary of the former Abbey Farm. This land formed part of the City ditch and was owned by the Corporation who leased it out between 1665 and 1821. In 1821 the Mayor & Bailiffs and Commonalty of Winchester sold land adjacent to the brewery for £126 to Richard Hall Tombs of Winchester. After he died in 1828 it passed through various relatives. In 1850 Frederick Tombs Edwards, a coal merchant of Chelsea, used the property as collateral to raise mortgages totalling £1,100. These mortgages were later assigned to William Courtney of Woodmancote.

Development along North Walls began in 1856 with a building lease given to Henry Smith (a carpenter). The plot, measuring 70 feet in length and 90 feet in depth, allowed him to build three houses over a six month period. They were later known as St Peter's Terrace (Nos. 15 to 17) North Walls, and had net aggregate rent of £50 p.a.. A small strip of land was also sold to John Peaty, a tobacconist.[7]

St Peter's Villa consisted of a tenement, outhouses and other buildings with a 438-foot frontage on to North Walls. The property was rented first by Rev. Anthony Crowdy, who ran a school for 13 scholars, then by John Tammedge Twyham, and finally by Mrs Sargent. In 1861 the house was unoccupied and the land adjacent to the house, once a ropewalk, was used as a garden.[8] This plot's former use is remembered in the name of the present housing development that stands on the site. In 1861 Courtney sold St Peter's Villa to Isaac Warner, a Winchester solicitor, for £1,025.

Immediately, Warner sold some of the surplus land attached to the villa for building. James Cole received the most westerly parcel, which had a 17-foot frontage and 114-foot depth, and was subject to a ground rent of £3 p.a..[9] Elias Evans received three parcels. The first had a 60-foot frontage and average depth of 93 feet. It had a ground rent of £10 p.a.. The second had a 30-foot frontage and 97-foot depth with ground rent of £5 p.a.. The third had 60-foot frontage and 101-foot depth with a ground rent of £9 p.a.. In 1862 William Smith owned a plot with a frontage of 42-foot and depth of 112-foot, which lay between Evans's land on the east and Cole's land on the west.

The Victorians were great philanthropists and the wives of important citizens sought to do charitable works. One of the organisations supported by Anthony Edmond's Charity was the Winchester Refuge for Fallen or Penitent Women.[10] The Refuge was registered as a charity in 1847 and had the objective of reclaiming fallen women by teaching them to work in the laundry. They were given life skills - plain cooking, household and needlework - in order to qualify them for service. The Refuge was managed by a committee, a house committee and lady visitors. The Committee consisted of important representatives from the religious and educational institutions of the City. These included the Venerable Archdeacon of Winchester (President), Rev. H. E. Moberley, the headmaster of Winchester College (Secretary), T.

Waters (Treasurer), the Very Rev. Dean of Winchester, the Warden of the College, canons of the Cathedral and Winchester parochial clergy. The chaplains of the forces, prison, Winchester Union and hospital, and the mayor were ex-officio members.

In 1861, the Refuge, originally sited in Little Minster Street near the Cathedral, was run by a matron, widowed with a three-year old child, and had six inmates. The opportunity to grow came in 1862 with the relocation to No. 1 North Walls, formerly called St Peter's Villa.[11] When the Refuge moved to St Peter's Villa in North Walls, the property had three buildings at the front of the plot, a garden and appurtenances, a frontage of 165 feet and depth of 90 feet which was enclosed by a wall (Figure 8.4). In 1862 a contract for sale was drawn up between Issac Warner and Rev. George Augustine Seymour and Rev. Henry Edward Moberley on behalf of the Managing Committee. Of the sale price of £1,100, £400 was paid immediately to Warner and the rest was due in instalments with the second payment of £200 before the end of September 1863. The Refuge was given three years to pay the remainder. Any outstanding debt was subject to interest at 5 per cent p.a.. If the Refuge defaulted, Warner could sell and dispose of the dwelling house and premises by public auction or private contract.

In a report to the trustees in October 1867, Rev. Seymour spoke of the inmates:

> It is found by experience that many of these poor persons are lamentably ignorant and incapable of earning their own livelihood by honest means – and all of them need proper training before they can be engaged in the ordinary business of life.[12]

The home was run by a matron and sub-matron, who received very low salaries (according to Seymour). Subscribers to the Refuge paid a 5s. subscription. The income received from laundry work increased rapidly in the early 1860s from £35 in 1861 to over £100 in 1864 and 1865. The institution was supported by voluntary subscriptions amounting annually to about £100 and income was increased by some large donations. In 1871 the Refuge had 13 inmates (aged between 15 and 22) looked after by two matrons. In 1881 the 12 inmates were described as laundresses and the Refuge was run by two matrons and a laundress.

Isaac Warner died in 1872 leaving the property to his brother Charles Warner to dispose of as he thought fit. Only £700 of the loan to the Refuge had been paid leaving £450 outstanding. Once the sum was paid the freehold passed to the Committee of the Refuge.[13] The finances of the Refuge continued to be problematic. Demand was increasing and accommodation was not adequate to meets the needs. However an opportunity soon arose.

Hyde Abbey Road

A substantial part of the former Abbey Farm was low lying water meadows and not suitable for development. Drier areas could not be developed as they were not accessible from any road. However in 1880 Barrow Simonds seized the opportunity to purchase a strip of land from the Refuge giving him access from North Walls. This allowed the start of development on the southern tip of Abbots Barton Farm. The Refuge was in need of the cash injection and raised £180 from the sale. The Trustees of the Refuge sought to secure their privacy. Barrow Simonds was required to build a brick and flint wall eight feet above the roadway which became the property of the Trustees. In addition a restrictive covenant required that occupiers were 'Not to open or permit to be opened any window in south side of any building that is erected on his property bounding the remaining properties of the vendors on the north side.' The Trustees thus ensured that occupiers of any new houses could not shout at or talk to the girls in the Refuge. This restricted any future building plans - non-opening windows would alienate future purchasers or occupants. Today it would violate building regulations. In 1881 Barrow Simonds negotiated for the release of the covenant and, on payment of £300 to do this, the development of the Hyde Abbey Road estate began.[14]

Figure 8.4: The Refuge and its extensive grounds

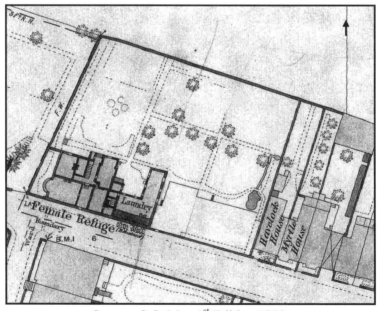

Source: O.S. Map 1st Edition 1873

The estate plan is now too fragile to be viewed. Thomas Micklam, a Portsmouth-born architect, designed the layout and acted as a contractor. Micklam's work was well known to Barrow Simonds as he had developed part of Park Road.[15] He subsequently lived at Ivanhoe and retained ownership of many of the houses. The site was compact and space was limited. 55 terraced houses were built, 5 on the access road and the rest on roads forming an inverted

'T'. Micklam as the estate developer and architect had immense influence over the final designs, although all plans were approved by Barrow Simonds (Figure 8.5).

Building land was sometimes offered freehold by landowners, requiring substantial capital investment at the start to buy the land. Only established developers, with a track record that gave access to finance, could take advantage. Commonly houses were built by small craftsmen who obtained building leases and financed work by short term borrowing. Unless there was an option to buy the freehold, the property was subject to an annual ground rent payable to the landowner. Whether it was Barrow Simonds' preference or the unwillingness of owners to pay the cost of the freehold, leasehold tenure dominated the late Victorian estate. Building plans survive for 39 houses although some of these are fragile and cannot be inspected (Table 8.2). Micklam designed 37 houses and a further 11 can be attributable to him. Garfield Terrace was designed by Gover, who had been involved in developing other land in Hyde.

Figure 8.5: Hyde Abbey Road

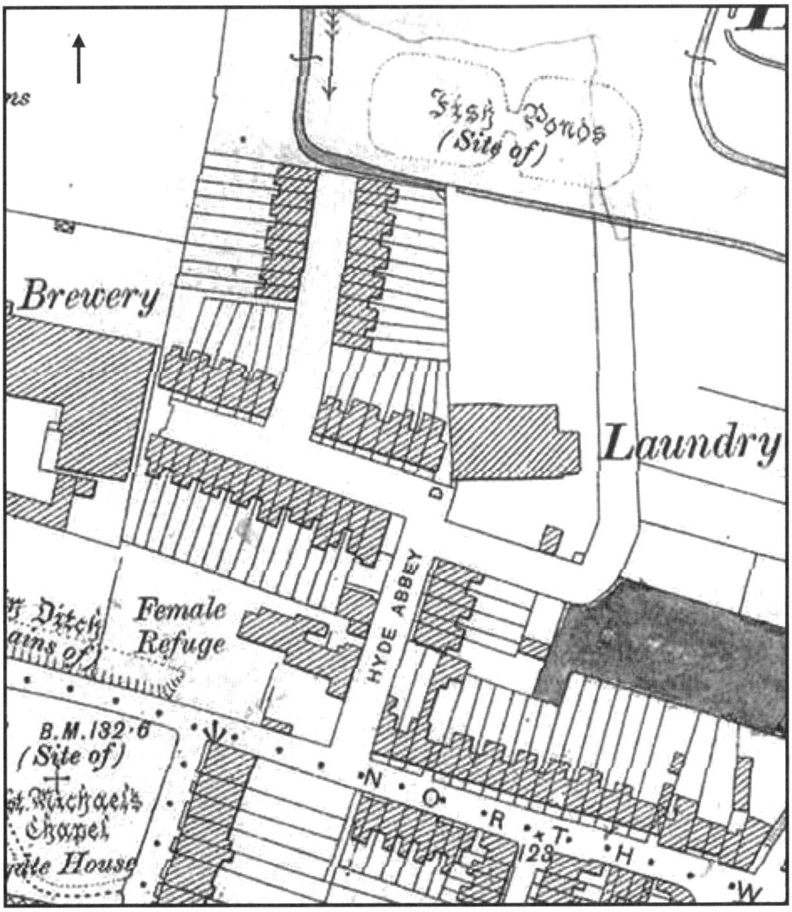

Source: O.S. Map 3rd Edition 1909
The Refuge has been rebuilt.

Twenty-five of the properties were built by two building partnerships - Aaron and Alfred Brockway and Penny, Read and Lumsden. The Brockways also built houses on Barrow Simonds' Park Road development. Stephen Penny was a bricklayer as was his younger brother George. Walter Read was a wheelwright. William Lumsden was a bricklayer and Berry, who built five cottages, was a carpenter. When Micklam acted as a developer, he dealt with all stages of the process and kept many of the properties for his own portfolio. Penny, Read and Lumsden also retained their houses. The Brockways always sold on completion; some of these Micklam added to his portfolio.

Table 8.1: Hyde Abbey Road development 1881 to 1888[16]

Place	Date	Type	Architect	Clients
Avon Terrace?	1881		Micklam	Barrow Simonds
Cavendish Terrace	1881	5 houses	Micklam	Penny, Read & Lumsden
Cavendish Terrace	1881	1 shop	Micklam	Penny, Read & Lumsden
Hamilton Terrace	1881	11 cottages	Micklam	Brockway
Waverley Terrace	1881	5 cottages	Micklam	Berry
Cavendish Terrace	1882	3 cottages	Micklam	Lumsden
Garfield Terrace	1882	1 house	Micklam	Johnson
Ivanhoe	1882	1 house	Micklam	Micklam T.
Garfield Terrace	1884	8 houses	Gover A	Brockway A. & A.
Abbotsford Terrace	1888	5 houses	Micklam	

No. 3 Hyde Abbey Road was one of the few houses under owner-occupation. Henry Jewell, an engineer, raised a mortgage of £250 in 1883. He resided in the property until 1897 when it was sold to Allen and O'Neill, confectioners for £287. Many of those involved in the construction of the properties, for example Read, Brockway and Lumsden, retained ownership personally or within the family at least until 1891. Micklam's widow still owned six properties in 1912.[17] Long term owners of several properties included Henry David Johnson (4) and Shenton (5). In 1881 Johnson was described as a grocer's assistant but had been promoted to manager by 1891. Harriet Jackson seems to have provided a mortgage and is named as joint owner in the rate books of 1891 and 1901.[18]

The terraced development took place in blocks of between 5 and 11 houses. Cavendish (8 houses), Hamilton (11 houses), Waverley (9 houses) and Avon (7 houses) terraces were fully occupied in 1884.[19] The small properties were mainly two-storey. The majority were flat-fronted but their plainness was reduced by the use of yellow bricks. House designs were fairly basic and, except for Ivanhoe which was built for Micklam's own occupation, had only one WC and, as usual for this time, no bathroom. Nos. 6 to 8 were larger and deeper with four rooms downstairs - a parlour, living room, kitchen and scullery, a WC at the rear - and three bedrooms upstairs. No. 13 was a shop. Nos. 14 to 24 and 29 to 33 were smaller and had a parlour, living room, washhouse, but only two bedrooms and what was described as a lumber room. Rateable values for houses ranged from £10 10s. p.a. to £14 p.a., with the shop at No. 13 commanding a premium at £19 10s. p.a.. Typical occupiers in 1891 included those involved in the building trade, cabinet makers, a carman, grocers, a police sergeant, a railway porter, tailors and watchmakers.

Garfield Terrace seems to have been built in two stages, with seven houses occupied in 1884 and the other eight in 1885. Amos Johnson a builder and contractor, who employed 21 men and three boys in 1881, had a building lease for Nos. 1 to 4 Garfield Terrace. It is likely he built all the seven houses which had a similar design. The Brockways borrowed £335 from Adams (solicitors) to build the other eight houses and, after construction, raised a mortgage for £400 on four of the leasehold houses from Harriett Jackson. As a well-off spinster she would have seen investment in real estate as a safe option with guaranteed returns.[20]

The three storey houses in Garfield Terrace were considerably larger, had a frontage of 15 feet and depth of 102 feet, and a rateable value of £16 p.a.. No. 55 had a parlour, living room, kitchen, scullery, conservatory and an internal WC at the bottom of the stairs, which were placed centrally. There were three bedrooms on the first floor and a further one in the roof. No. 52, which backed onto the Refuge, was purchased from the Simonds family in 1920 by its successor, the Diocesan Maternity Home.[21]

Abbotsford Terrace was the last to be built in 1889. The names of the terraces were drawn from the writings of Walter Scott. Abbotsford was his estate. Waverley and Ivanhoe (Micklam's residence) were books and the other houses had names (for example Garfield) or properties (for example Hamilton) taken from Scott's novels. Gordon Terrace opened up another part of Barrow Simonds' meadows and the three properties here were built by Micklam.

Hyde Abbey Road properties were affordable by the lower middle classes and were larger than the older housing in King Alfred Place or Hyde Churchyard. Some of the original investors' families, like Micklam and Shenton, still owned the properties over 30 years later. Shenton owned seven of the newly built houses, which had passed to his widow by 1912. Shenton, a solicitor, usually acted as a financier. The duration of family ownership indicated that this was not an outstanding mortgage but was either originally an investment, or the builder had experienced financial difficulties and failed to repay the loan. Smaller investors held just two or three properties. These houses were sold infrequently, usually on the death of the owner. The property could pass to the widow, trustees or directly to children; a married daughter would have a different surname so the family connection may not be obvious. If the properties were sold, they were offered as a block and little fragmentation of ownership occurred.

Figure 8.6: Houses in Hyde Abbey Road

In many houses the yellow brick decorations around the windows, the string courses and quoins have been painted. Bricks were used for relief patterns such as dentil and billet courses. Terraces were individualised by the use of different colour bricks. Florentine arches are decorated with grey bricks. Parapets are an unusual feature of the 1880s. Micklam used terracotta bricks with sunflowers and tendrils on Ivanhoe.

Eagles Field Estate

Changes in land law were important catalysts to suburban growth. Development only took place if selling of land was feasible and the landowner desired to do so. The major landowner in Hyde, Barrow Simonds, regularly released parts of his land from 1858. His prudence prevented the market from being flooded and depressing prices. However, land owned by institutions rarely came onto the market and the law often prevented such sales. For example, the Bridewell site could only be sold after new legislation.

The first Copyhold Act of 1841, later consolidated by a further Copyhold Act in 1894, allowed the enfranchisement or conversion of land held under copyhold tenure into freehold.[22] The 1841 Act provided a statutory method of enfranchisement where both the lord and copyholder were in agreement. Further reform was necessary because the power to enfranchise the tenure was inconsistently applied, largely due to a lack of understanding or a desire to preserve traditional privileges and authority.[23] A further act in 1852 introduced the principle of compulsory enfranchisement by one party, but this was really only practical when there was agreement.

The Select Committee on the Enfranchisement of Copyhold Bill (No. 2) recommended the extension of the 'Acts for the Commutation of Manorial Rights, and for the Gradual Enfranchisement of Lands of Copyhold and Customary Tenure.'[24] As a result the Dean and Chapter were required to sell copyhold land. If it failed to do so by 1860, the Ecclesiastical Commissioners were empowered to take over ownership.[25] In 1878 the Commissioners advertised 13 lots of land lying in the parishes of St Faith's, Weeke and Chilcomb. The land, which formerly belonged to the Cathedral Priory, had passed to the Dean and Chapter at the Dissolution. This sale took place at the same time as Barrow Simonds was seeking to develop his land adjacent to North Walls.

Thomas Baring, the first Earl of Northbrook resided at Stratton Park. He served as an MP, held several Government posts, including Viceroy of India and First Lord of the Admiralty. In 1890 he held the post of Lord Lieutenant of Hampshire. Former holders of the position included many generations of the Paulet family and two Wriothesleys. When the Dean and Chapter's Eagles Field was advertised, Lord Northbrook seized the opportunity to develop the whole area.[26] He already claimed the frontage on Hyde Close where he owned property on the north side (Figure 8.9). The plot was conveyed in December 1878. Although the land was originally in the parish of Weeke, it was isolated by Andover Road and later became subsumed into St Bartholomew's.[27]

The land was described as a valuable plot of freehold building land consisting of approximately 2¾ acres of meadows with a 380-foot frontage on to Andover Road. The plot had the attraction of being adjacent to the railway station and suitable for houses and shops. The Eagles Field Estate, named after the Eagle Hotel on the corner of the City and Andover Roads, extended along Worthy Road. The estate consisted of new development on the south side of Hyde Close, the new Victoria Road, and houses on the Andover Road and Thurloe Place on Worthy Road.

Figure 8.7: Eagles Fields

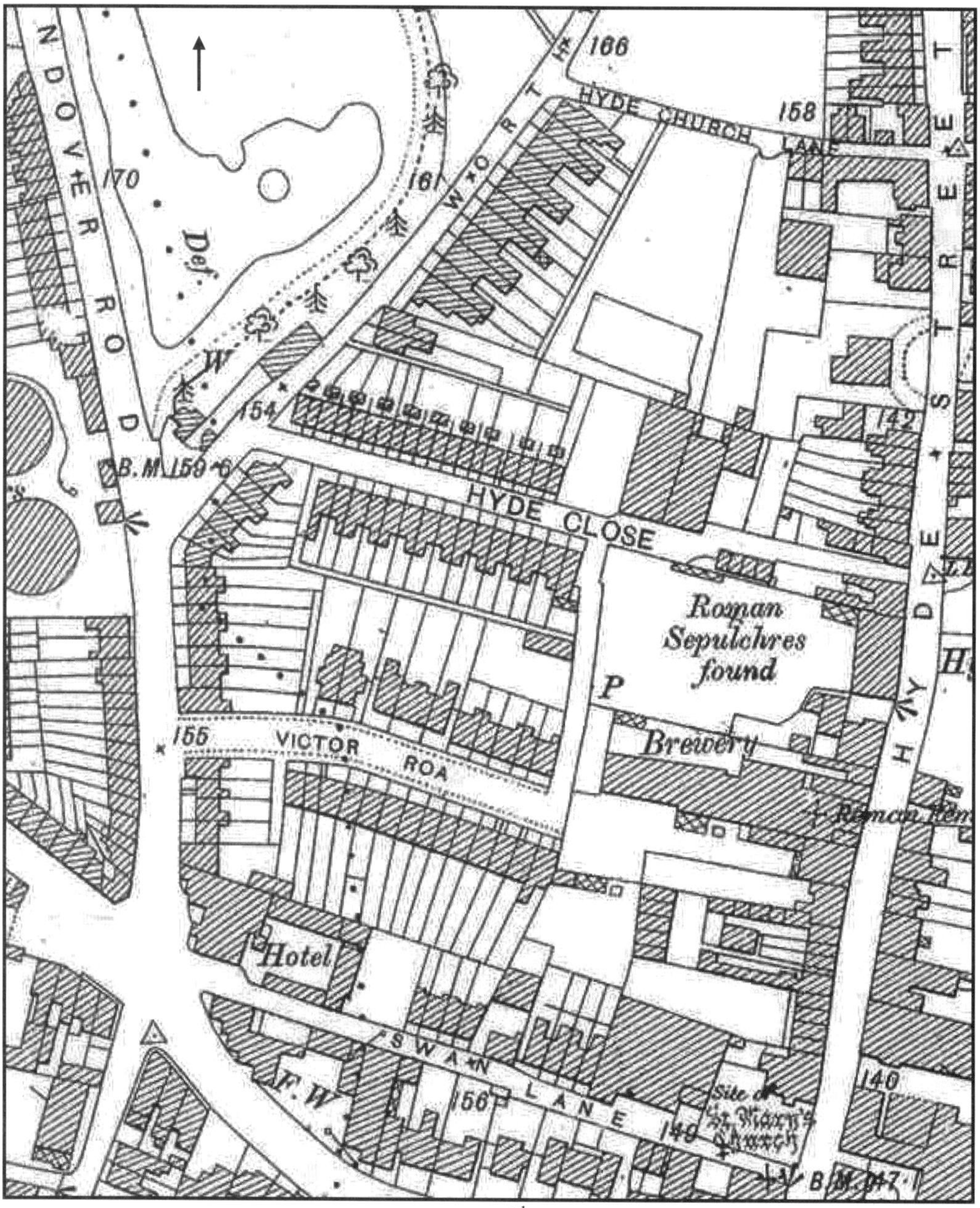

Source: O.S. Map 3rd Edition 1909

The estate was named after the Eagle Hotel standing at the west end of Swan Lane. The north side of Hyde Close was already developed. The Roman Sepulchres were in the garden of No. 23 Hyde Street.

Jesse Carter was cited in the 1875 rate books as the owner of the small flint cottages on the north side of Hyde Close and probably built them. The exact nature of his tenure is not known but, by 1881, Lord Northbrook was named as the owner.[28] There are two possibilities: either Carter was the developer and sold the houses to Northbrook, or Northbrook had the land rights, and issued a building lease. There is no evidence to suggest the Carter family had any desires to take on long leases at this time. To do so would mean tying up considerable sums of money in real estate and extending the building business into the rental market.

The earliest building plan for Eagles Field, dated 1879, was for a new street (Victoria Road) adjoining the Eagle Hotel.[29] Lord Northbrook employed Thomas Stopher who was a prominent architect, alderman and antiquarian. His papers include a wealth of material including notes on Winchester buildings, council records, personal diaries, and photographs. He came to Winchester in 1840, aged three, when his father (also Thomas) was appointed County Surveyor. He trained as an architect and surveyor in his father's office. Thomas (junior) succeeded his father as surveyor to Winchester College and St John's Hospital. He was prominent in Winchester life, including being elected mayor on three occasions, serving as a magistrate and being involved in the governance of both Christ's Hospital and St Cross Hospital. He was commissioned to draw up plans for a plethora of houses both within the City and the suburbs, ranging from small working class cottages to speculative houses for the middle classes on the new estates, where he was also involved in designing new roads.[30]

Northbrook took a close interest in the development process, offering long leases once the building leases had expired. The exception was the south side of Hyde Close (Nos. 27 to 44), which was opposite his earlier development. These houses were built for Northbrook in 1880 by Henry Sanders (a Southampton builder).[31] The main estate architects were Thomas Stopher and E. J. Grimwood. Edward Carter and Son designed, built and retained houses in Thurloe Place. John Frederick Goodwin was a carpenter who lived in Tower Street. He later built part of St John's Road on Morn Hill. The other builders involved were Alfred Edward Evans (a Southampton builder), Henry Frampton, Samuel Newman and the Brockways (Table 8.2). All but the Brockways retained ownership after building. Frampton was a builder's merchant and later important in further suburban development in Hyde. Samuel Newman was a mason and sculptor employing twelve men and three apprentices in 1881. He had a stonemason's yard in Victoria Road.

There are two ways of controlling future development: granting a lease which contains restrictions or the sale of the freehold with restrictive covenants. A lease contains conditions designed to protect the value of the reversionary interest. Although the Dean and Chapter was not overly concerned with the future, developers like Northbrook and smaller landowners sought to protect their future interests in the estates and surrounding land. These conditions specified the extent and type of building, value, and future use. There were limits on the number of houses to be built on a particular plot with the value given either as a building cost (materials plus labour) or in terms of a rental value or rack rent (market value).[32]

Figure 8.8: Eagles Field Estate

In Victoria Road there is a small terrace with high level of detailing which include stone brackets under roof and cills. Note the use of the terracotta feature above the door and the frieze, which extends the length of the terrace. It is said all motifs are different.

Andover Terrace and Thurloe Place (below) offered larger properties.

Table 8.2: Eagles Field development 1879 to 1883[33]

Place	Date	Architect	Client
Victoria Road (street)	1879	Stopher T.	Lord Northbrook
1 & 2 Victoria Rd	1881	Godwin J. F.	Godwin J. F.
11 to 24 Victoria Rd	1881	Grimwood E. J.	Grimwood E. J.
6 to 10 Victoria Rd	1881	Edmeades A.	Edmeades A.
35 to 38 Andover Rd (includes 2 shops)	1881	Grimwood E. J.	
Thurloe Place	1882	Carter E. & Son	Carter E. & Son
41 to 47 Andover Rd	1882	Stopher T.	Evans A. E.
3 to 5 Victoria Rd	1883	Stopher T.	Newman S.

Northbrook controlled what was built. Building leases specified:

> No erection shall be commenced on the said piece of land or any part thereof until plans of the same have been submitted to and approved of by the said lessor or his surveyor or agent.[34]

Density and standards were ensured by the requirement that:

> No more than one house shall be erected on the said piece of land and that such houses shall at the time of completion be of the value of £50 at the least and that no such house should be erected in front of the building line as shown on the said plan.

Northbrook minimised his expenses by specifying that 'all costs and expenses of the lessor's solicitors in connection with the purchase shall be borne and paid by the lessee.' The estate was a residential neighbourhood and protected from non-conforming or undesirable usage. Restricted covenants forbade the property from being used as an 'alehouse or beershop or for the sale thereon or there from of ale, porter, wine or spirituous liquors' and as a 'slaughter house, manufacture of soap or candles' or creating a nuisance in the neighbourhood.[35]

Property sizes varied, with the most expensive properties being on the main road. In the 1880s, a mixed class estate was acceptable as an investment and occupiers' choices were still limited. There were clear stipulations on the value of properties to be built, both in term of the cost of construction and the rental value, which varied according to the plots. Those plots fronting the Andover and Worthy Roads were more valuable, whilst those behind were less so; a common feature of Victorian developments. In 1882 Alfred Edward Evans took a lease on plots along the Andover Road (Nos. 41 to 47 Andover Terrace). Ground rents varied slightly according to plot size. Typically plots were 17½ feet wide, with a depth of about 100 to 120 feet. The properties had a yearly ground rent of between £4 and £4 17s. 6d. 'clear of all rates, taxes, tithe rent charges and other deductions and abatements whatsoever except property tax.' Only one house could be built on each plot and its annual rental value was to exceed £25. Evans was given twelve months to build on the land. During the first six years, the lessee could purchase the fee simple (freehold) of the land and any buildings to be erected on it for £100, equivalent to 25 times the ground rent. [36]

In 1882/83 the Brockways leased six plots (Nos. 35 to 40 Andover Road). Houses were to have rental value of between £20 and £25 and freeholds cost between £100 and £112.[37] Evans raised £600 from siblings William Shenton, a solicitor, Edward Knight Shenton, local wine and spirit merchant, and Mary Evans Shenton. The Brockways raised sums of £450 and £350 from George Shenton (resident in Australia) and £700 from Joseph Tanner (a retired draper living in City Road).

The 1891 rate books record Evans owning Nos. 41 to 47 Andover Road. [38] Documents show that Evans had put the newly built Andover Terrace up for sale in July 1883.[39] The sale was aimed at small capitalists and investors. The properties had moderate ground rents and the whole terrace had an estimated annual rental value of £175. Each property was vacant with the exception of Nos. 1 and 2, tenanted by Mr Nobbs and G. A. Easton, which had yearly rents of £25. Each was well finished and fit for immediate occupation and were very spacious. The accommodation consisted of a basement, with kitchen and sitting room, two sitting rooms and a lobby with WC on the ground floor, two bedrooms on the first floor, and a further two large rooms in the attic. No sale took place. It may be that Evans did not receive the price he wanted or he decided the property was a good investment. Alternatively he found that money was reasonably available for a mortgage and he could release equity for future building projects. The houses were used as collateral for a loan and in 1891 and 1901, William Shenton and then his executors were named as owners. At this time a mortgage involved the conveyance of the property to the lender until the loan was paid off. In 1912, Evans had also mortgaged Nos. 1 and 2 Victoria Road and Nos. 41 to 47 Andover Road.

In 1891 Thomas Carter owned Nos. 6 to 8 and Eliza Newman owned Nos. 9, 10 and 24 Victoria Road. Although there is lack of direct evidence that Henry Frampton was the developer of Nos. 11 to 24 Victoria Road, his ownership in 1891 suggests this may have been so. By 1901, these houses had been sold to Charles Payne (or Pain), a successful fancy stationer, who lived on St Giles's Hill. The family still owned the houses in 1912. Ten of the eleven houses in Thurloe Place, built by Carter & Son, had passed to Lewis Carter by 1891.

There were a few exceptions to the dominance of the developers where pockets of owner-occupation existed. Ben Holden, a grocer, lived at and owned No. 40 Andover Road in 1891. Carrying out a business was often an incentive to own the property. Alfred Macklin (a carpenter) lived at No. 39 in a house owned by William Macklin. By 1901 George Robertson (a tailor) had purchased No. 37 where he had lived in 1891, but which was mortgaged to John Tanner. William Hoad (a waiter) owned No. 24 Victoria Road in 1891 and 1901. No. 3 Thurloe Place was owned and occupied by Edwin Moody (a printer's manager). By 1912, Moody had added to his portfolio and purchased the adjacent houses. The new middle classes were moving into house ownership, not only for occupation, but also as an investment.

The properties in Eagles Field varied considerably in size. The terrace of houses (Nos. 6 to 10) on the north side of Victoria Road commanded a rateable value of £14 to £16 p.a., whereas Nos. 11 to 24 were only valued at £12 p.a.. Although providing a large floor space, Nos. 6 to 10 had a small footprint. The basement contained the living room, kitchen and pantry. On the ground floor were a sitting room, parlour and WC, with just two bedrooms upstairs. Nos. 1 and 2 were large houses with a cellar, parlour, kitchen, scullery and WC on the ground floor, three bedrooms, a second WC and an attic valued at £20 p.a.. Nos. 3 to 5 commanded £16 p.a. for the end properties and £19 10s. for the larger middle house. The 15 new properties in Hyde Close had a comparable rateable value to Victoria Road at £15 p.a.. The houses had two parlours, a kitchen and washhouse, basement and three bedrooms. The most expensive and largest houses were on the Worthy Road rather than the back streets. The superior properties in Thurloe Place commanded a rateable value of £21 to £24 p.a., with No. 11, a large corner property, valued at £33 10s. p.a.. Nos. 41 to 47 Andover Road had a value of £18 p.a. and Nos. 48 to 52 a value of £26 p.a..

Even in a small estate as Eagles Field, there was social stratification. In 1891, the occupants of the smaller houses in Victoria Road and Hyde Close had varied occupations, including farmer, fly proprietor, grocer's assistant, tailor, upholsterer, retired army sergeant major, dressmaker and laundress. Andover Terrace had a corn dealer, lodging housekeeper and two general labourers. The residents of the more expensive Thurloe Place included an accountant, a banker's clerk, a draper, a printer's manager, and three spinsters living on their own means.

Figure 8.9: Old and new houses in Hyde Close

Conygary Estate

The Conygary and Oxlease Estates were built on former glebe land owned by the Deane family, who were long-time residents of Hyde. It is not known when the Deanes came into possession of the land. The St Bartholomew's Tithe Apportionment of 1850 was annotated 'Thomas Deane.' in two areas lying east and west of Nuns Walk. [40] The Conygary Estate consisted of Egbert, Saxon and Arthur Roads. The name Conygary probably derived from the former Conyger or Coney Garden – there was a rabbit or coney warren here. The Oxlease Estate was named after the fields Great and Little Ox lease adjacent to the water meadows, and consisted of Nuns and Monks Roads, Nuns Walk and Birinus Road.

Charles March Deane, a banker, lived at Nos. 9 and 10 St Thomas Street in the City during the 1860s to 1880s. His son, Arthur Elliot, was also a banker. Charles March took no interest in development, but on his father's death, Arthur, was free to enter the property market. Deane developed the Conygary estate in 1896 and the Oxlease estate in 1900 along with Henry Frampton. Alfred Frampton, Henry's son, was employed as the architect. The Framptons were another important family in the area. In 1861 Henry Frampton lived in Hyde Street and was described as a paper, glass and colour merchant. By 1871 he had moved to No. 39 Jewry Street and traded as an oil merchant. Beside the involvement of Alfred, who lived at No. 14 Jewry Street, another son, Henry Swift, was a foreman in the business. By 1881 the family business was well established as a builder's merchant, with premises at Nos. 42 and 43 Jewry Street.

The Conygary Estate has a mix of terraced, semi-detached and detached properties whereas the Oxlease Estate consists of more densely packed semi-detached houses with a narrow access between them. Frampton appears to have closely controlled the development. Most of the houses were built by Frederick William Macklin or the firm of Hughes and Green from Eastleigh. The successful Macklins were a large family of bricklayers and some rose in the building trade. There were at least three brothers born in Winchester. In the 1861 census, Martin, a bricklayer aged 37, had three sons - Alfred (then aged 13), Frederick (8) and Arthur (4). In 1881 Martin was well established as a builder employing three men. In 1871 Henry Macklin (51) was described as a contractor. Charles Macklin, a bricklayer (60), had four sons - Alfred (32), Walter (25), Frederick (21) and Arthur (18). In 1881 the family business had expanded - Henry Macklin (aged 40) had six sons, the eldest of whom followed in the family trade. Which Macklin was involved in a particular development is unclear. With so many bricklayers they must have been involved in constructing a large percentage of the houses in Winchester. The most staggering contribution to Hyde's development was made by Frederick William Macklin from 1897 to 1905 during which time he developed 150 properties on the Conygary and Oxlease estates. Many houses on the Fulflood Estate (Cranworth, Fairfield and Hatherley Roads) were also built by him. There may have been a loose partnership within the family, with Frederick taking some form of overall control.

Figure 8.10: Conygary and Oxlease Estates

Source: O.S. Map 3rd Edition 1909.
Conygary lies to the west of the Mill Stream which runs besides Saxon Road. Oxlease lies to the east of the Mill Stream and north of King Alfred Place. King Alfred Terrace was built later south of King Alfred Place.

Alfred Frampton, described as an architect with offices in London, submitted the plans for the Egbert Road Building Estate in 1896.[41] The next year he submitted plans for the widening of King Alfred Place.[42] The plan consisted of four streets, Ethelbald Road (later to be called Egbert Road), Ethelbert Road (Arthur Road), Ethelred Road (Danes Road) and Ethelwulf Road (Saxon Road). The roads were initially named after Saxon kings. Egbert Road had 53 plots and Saxon Road 32 plots. However, the development did not adhere that closely to the plan. On Saxon Road, 12 semi-detached properties were built, rather than the 17 terraced houses planned. Seven plots adjacent to the King Alfred Public House (originally described as a hotel to allay local opposition) were not built on. Confusingly, some of the older properties in Hyde Churchyard were renumbered as Saxon Road. In Egbert Road 19 terraced houses were built instead of the six terraced and eight semis planned. Finally in Arthur Road, the 32 plots proposed were replaced by larger semis and two nursing homes. A block of seven houses south of Danes Road were not built. The surviving building plans are fairly comprehensive. In 1897 plans for groups of eight, six and five houses were submitted followed by plans for groups of two to four houses. Frampton was involved with the house design for all but one house designed by Thomas Stopher. Altogether Frampton submitted 30 plans for over 300 houses on the Conygary and Oxlease Estates.

There were two main local builders and also the involvement of an outside firm (Table 8.3). The houses on the western side of Egbert Road were owned and built by Frederick William Macklin, who also developed just over half of the houses in Arthur Road. On the eastern side of Egbert Road and in Saxon Road, Hughes and Green were cited as the owners in the building plans but since Henry Swift Frampton owned these properties in 1901, it seems likely that they had a building lease. Between 1897 and 1905, Alfred Frampton worked with Macklin and Green & Hughes to design 175 houses on the Conygary and Oxlease Estates. Of the 56 plans agreed and executed, Macklin undertook 61 per cent and Hughes and Green 27 per cent. Frampton was adept at morphing the standard semi-detached house to create considerable variations and ensuring the drab uniformity that characterised London suburbs did not occur in Hyde. This was less of a problem in Winchester as the developments were small compared to London's suburbia. Differentiation was achieved by changing the shape of the bays, roofs and gables. Brick patterning, rubble panels and finials further added interest (Figure 8.9).

As the century progressed building lease conditions became more prescriptive, although they all had the common feature of not allowing noxious or alcoholic businesses. The lease conditions between Deane and Hughes and Green were very precise and protected the land owner's interests.[43] The quality of the property was guaranteed by the restriction that pairs of houses were to have a value of over £650 exclusive of land value and the external design was to be approved by Deane, his architect or surveyor. Like most astute developers, Deane pushed a proportion of the costs of the upkeep of Saxon Road on to the builders. The ambience of the neighbourhood and the value of the property were protected by several requirements. Every third year the outside woodwork and ironwork was to be painted with two coats of proper oil colours. Every seventh year the internal rooms were to be painted and

Table 8.3: Architects of the Conygary & Oxlease Estate 1896 to 1911

Road (total number of properties)	Architect	No. of houses designed
Egbert Road (48)	Frampton	40
	Unknown	8
Saxon Road (20)	Frampton	16
	Stopher	2
	Unknown	2
Arthur Road (22)	Frampton	18
	F. W. Macklin	3
	Unknown	1
Nuns Road (53)	Frampton	41
	Likely Frampton*	11
	F. W. Macklin	1
Monks Road (48)	Frampton	42
	Stopher	6
Nuns Walk (3) & Birinus Ave (4)	Frampton	7
Total		198

* Plans not found but 1912 ownership suggests this.

papered and the inside wood varnished. The lessor, or his representative, visited twice a year to determine what repairs needed to be done. No manufacturing, slaughtering, making of bricks, or production and sale of alcohol was wanted here. The lease conditions required the lessee to maintain and insure the property and protect the value of the reversionary interest. This minimised the lessor's costs and ensured the rent was purely profit. Alterations and repairs could amount to about 20 per cent of the annual rent. Deane gave the builders the option to purchase the freehold within three years of construction, but few did.

Saxon and Egbert Road had three terraces of smaller houses designed by Alfred Frampton for Macklin and built between 1897 and 1900.[44] Of the total of 27 houses, Macklin still owned six houses (Nos. 32 to 42) in 1912. They had sitting and living rooms, a kitchen or scullery, outside WC and three bedrooms. Bathrooms were still not the norm for the standard three up, three down houses and the rateable value of £11 p.a. to £12 p.a. reflected this. Frampton's designs for larger semi-detached properties, with a rateable value of £20 p.a., were built by Hughes and Green.[45] The rectangular footprint allowed for a drawing room, kitchen and back dining room, with the scullery accessed from the kitchen. The upstairs had two front bedrooms, a middle bedroom and a back bedroom. The bathroom and WC was above the scullery. The utility area, with larder, coals, storage and WC was not built above. Like many of these estates, Egbert Road had a shop rated at £28 p.a.. Nos. 12 and 13 Saxon Road were designed by Thomas Stopher for Arthur Joyce (a carpenter) who lived at No. 12. His house had drawing and dining rooms, a conservatory, kitchen and WC, and four bedrooms, bathroom and second WC upstairs.

Frampton was the architect and William Shearman the owner and builder of three pairs of semi-detached houses in Arthur Road built after 1898.[46] These houses, known by name, had the same design as those built by Hughes and Green. The other houses in Arthur Road had a more traditional four block design, where the extension contained the kitchen and beyond it was the scullery. Upstairs the bathroom was positioned at the beginning of the extension and the third bedroom stretched across giving access through to bedroom four.

In the majority of cases the original building plans were realised. However the potential flexibility of the plans is demonstrated at the end of Arthur Road, next to the Mill Stream. Originally plans for two pairs of semi-detached houses were submitted. An amendment converted the last pair into one property, giving several extra rooms by the removal of a second kitchen, scullery, stairs and bath. In 1904, Deane and Alfred Frampton submitted plans for the extension of Arthur Road to meet Worthy Road. [47]

The first residents on the Conygary Estate had varied occupations. Craftsmen involved in the building trade lived in the smaller properties in Egbert Road. There was a stonemason, bricklayer, carpenter, plumber and housepainter, and a blacksmith whose skills would have been used in the production of the iron railings in the new houses in Nuns and Monks Roads. Young men were often clerks in solicitor practices or in life insurance. Two of the larger houses in Saxon Road were multi-occupied, each by two families, and another was used as a lodging house. In Arthur Road, there was a solicitor, a bank clerk and an Inland Revenue Officer. The Aged Pilgrims Home and a nursing home catered for the elderly and infirm and Mrs Downes and her daughter offered apartments to single ladies.[48]

By 1912, the majority of houses on the estate belonged to Henry W Frampton (25) or Macklin (6). Frampton owned 20 out of the 25 houses built by Hughes and Green, the rest being owned by Vokes. The 20 per cent built by Hughes and Green, but not owned by Frampton, represented their fee. As elsewhere, those involved in the development did not sell. Other substantial owners were Hiram Spencer (5), Vokes (6), Charles Hayles (or Hale) (16), William Tanner (4) and James Burfitt (4). Often only surnames were given making identification difficult but Vokes may have been James, a stonemason. [49] Whether these were investors or mortgagees are unknown, since a mortgage still involved conveyance of the property to the financier.

Figure 8.11: Conygary Estate

Large semi-detached with set-back side extension and turret, deep square bay with triple window. On the first floor is a paired window with small gable.

Smaller terraced houses with classical arch doorway, single storey bay and paired sash windows.

Semi-detached houses and small terraces are given an individual look by changes in the bay's shape and roof or gable design. These photographs show semi-hexagonal, square and round bays. Roofs and gables vary from polygonal to circular and triangular to Dutch.

The Oxlease Estate

Evoking memories of Hyde Abbey, the aptly named Nuns and Monks Road were laid out by Alfred Frampton. Forming the other sides of a rectangle were three houses in Nuns Walk and four houses in Birinus Road. Deane commissioned Frampton to lay out the estate. Whether the plots were offered openly as building leases or freehold is not known.[50] These two roads provided a further 100 houses to those migrating from the City or older suburbs or into Winchester. Estates developed after 1900 were aimed at the lower end of the suburban rental market.[51] Characteristically properties were compact and high-density, mostly without bathrooms.

The first plans for houses in Nuns Road were submitted in 1900, and ones for Monks Road a year later. The site was not easy to develop. The land was low lying next to the water meadows and building regulations were becoming more stringent. Correspondence over several months in 1900 detailed the crux of the difficulty as being slow or inadequate run off from the sewers.[52] The City engineer was proposing iron not stoneware pipes stating that the former, as proposed by Frampton, would 'not give a self-cleansing velocity and should not be approved'. The engineer's comments were scathing:

> It is clear to me that Mr Frampton knows very little about iron pipes in drainage works. He has probably never heard of Dr Angus Smith's process of coating.

The problem was the level land:

> Mr Frampton is naturally anxious to keep down the levels in order to save filling, but the effect in so doing is to spoil the gradients of the sewers.

The engineer's advice was to reject the plan due to the possible future costs of rectifying the problems, which would accrue to the Corporation on adoption. Poor foundations and in-filling caused problems much later on. In the 1960s the end properties in Nuns Road suffered subsidence and had to be pulled down.

Anecdotal evidence of the problems is given by Reginald Best who was born in 1897:

> Where Monks Road and Nuns Road are, there was a sloping bit of water meadow and they filled it up with garbage from all the dustcarts and so on. They put houses on top of the old garbage and tins and everything. Within a few years some of the ground there sank six foot. Eventually they had to pull one of the end houses down, but for over 20 years the sewage used to come over the top of the pan in four of the houses and run over into the river where the animals used to drink. The sewage from the big houses at Abbots Barton ran straight into the river there too.[53]

Building regulations seem to have been flouted here.

Figure 8.12: Exterior Design on the Oxlease Estate

HRO:W/C11/2/563. Reproduced with permission of
Winchester City Council.

Figure 8.13: Interior Design on the Oxlease Estate

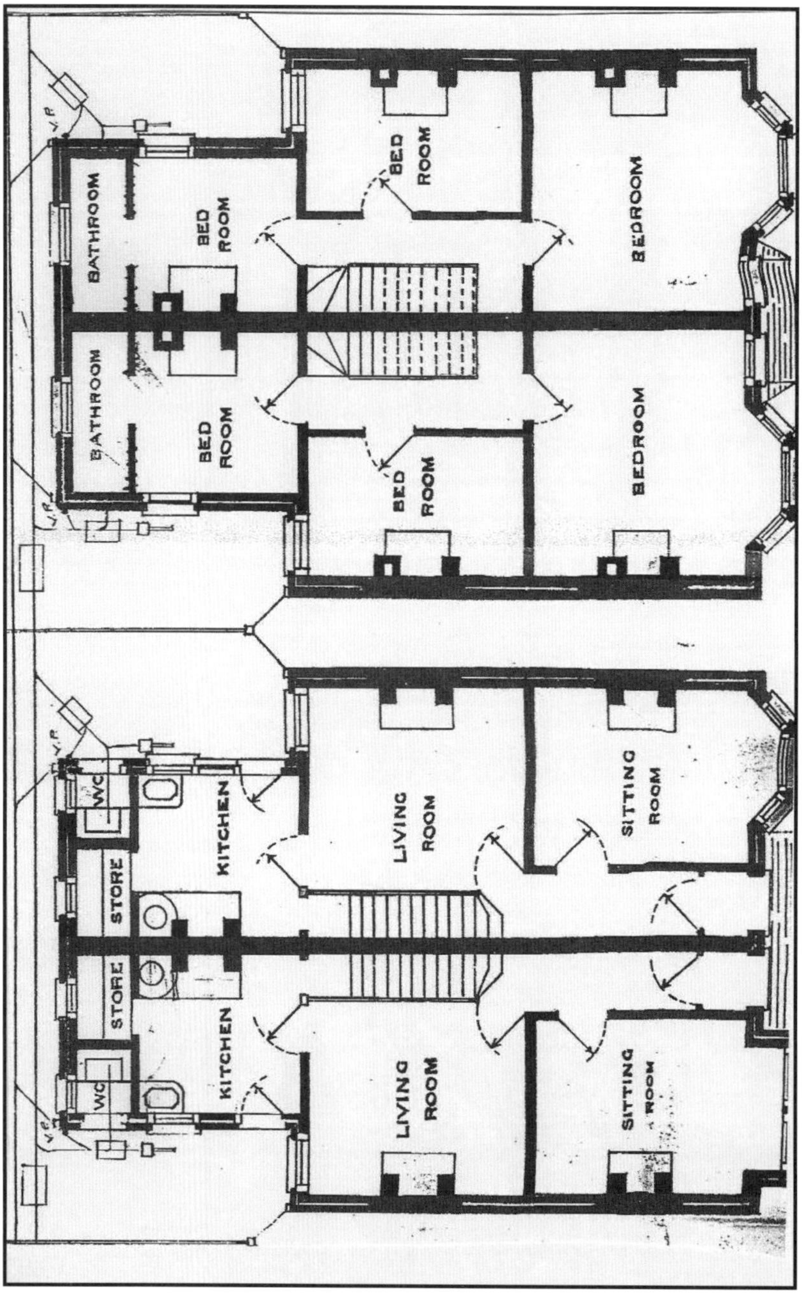

HRO:W/C11/2/563. Reproduced with permission of Winchester City Council.
The bathroom situated off the back bedroom has been removed from the plan. The position of the bathroom was common in house designs of this era, although inconvenient to those sleeping in the bedroom. Luckily there was a WC out the back.

Alfred Frampton designed all the houses except six (Nos. 21, 23, 45, 47, 48 and 50 Monks Road), which were designed by Stopher. However, the designs were consistent with those of Frampton (Figure 8.11). The plans gave Macklin as builder and owner, except for the houses in Nuns Walk. These three properties, built in 1908 as a symmetrical terrace with four doors, were owned by Henry Swift Frampton. Evidence suggests that houses built for the speculative market with a rateable value of about £13 were deemed not to need bathrooms or internal WC even in the twentieth century. In Frampton's design the bathroom, placed at the back of the upstairs extension off the third bedroom, was deleted from the plans and the partition wall removed (Fig 8.13).[54]

Head of households were employed in a wide range of occupations: manufacturing, building, retail and the army. Clerks and bookkeepers were needed at the post office and in insurance offices and were also employed by local businessmen – the butcher, miller and surveyor. Engineers had much wanted skills for cycles, motor cars and for submarines. Less common were the traveller in cattle oils and condiments and a registered money lender.

In 1912, the 'Hyde Estate' owned 47 houses, Henry William Frampton owned 43 and Henry Swift Frampton owned seven. No details are known about the Hyde Estate. However, the properties in Nuns Walk, commissioned by Henry Swift Frampton, were owned by the Hyde Estate four years later. It seems likely that the Hyde Estate was a business enterprise owned by Deane. If so, like Barrow Simonds, he had no desire to lose control of the former Abbey's meadows, which his family had owned for many years. It may have involved a partnership with Henry Swift Frampton. The properties were small and cheaper than those of the adjacent Conygary Estate. The semi-detached properties commanded a rateable value of only £12 to £13 and the few detached properties £16 to £17.

Figure 8.14: No house the same

Other developments

There were several small developments - often just a terrace - in the south part of Hyde. In 1896 Richards submitted a plan for four houses (Rossdale, Cartery, St Clements and Glencoe) on part of the former Hyde Garden, purchased from Thomas Knight. These were sizeable properties with a rateable value of £24 p.a.. The end properties were dominated by a wide gable and all the houses had flat roofed bays on the ground floor. In 1912 the family business still owned them.

King Alfred Place was widened in 1898 enabling the development of Alswitha Terrace, consisting of 14 properties, including a shop, built by Hardman, Mansbridge and White (Figure 8.16). These cottages consisted of two sitting rooms, a kitchen, three bedrooms and, unusually, an upstairs WC. Some had a second WC downstairs. In 1912 Henry Mansbridge still owned two houses. Ten houses, including a shop, were owned by Mrs Baker and Collis (a local shopkeeper) owned two. It is not possible to tell if these were real estate or financial investments.

A further 20 houses were built in 1905. King Alfred Terrace was designed by Thomas Stopher and built by Shearman as an investment. These properties had a sitting and a living room, scullery and four bedrooms, and commanded a rateable value of £11.50 p.a. or £14 p.a.. Residents included the head teacher of St Clement's School, a deaconess and a river keeper of trout.

Figure 8.15: King Alfred Terrace

Figure 8.16: Alswitha Terrace

Corner shops were a feature of Victorian estates. The baker's shop is no longer.

Conclusion

In the 1850s, after the closure of the Bridewell, and between 1880 and 1910, new housing estates sprang up in Hyde to satisfy demand from the lower middle classes and those flourishing in the new economic environment of the late Victorian city. Estate development was initiated by the landowners of the urban fringe and undertaken by local builders and tradesmen, who became successful developers and whose families remained investors in real estate.

A new exodus from the City to Hyde had taken place. Barrow Simonds' developments catered for all needs. Barrow Simonds continued releasing land until his death. However his later plans for the Abbots Barton Building Estate did not come to fruition. Developments over one-mile from the City centre were aimed at the affluent townspeople, whereas land released closer to the City in King Alfred Place and Hyde Abbey Road was destined for the lower middle classes. The gap in the market and in the urban continuity was filled by the Deane family, long term residents of Hyde.

The Edwardian years saw a slowing down of Hyde's urban growth as economic circumstances changed. Estates that were set out at the start of the century took a decade to complete. Supply may have exceeded demand or, in the case of Barrow Simonds' developments, tenurial conditions were no longer attractive to investors. Any new developments, for example Richard's four houses in Hyde Street and Shearman's King Alfred Terrace, were built by the developers as an investment for their own portfolios.

Some of the last land releases before Barrow Simonds' death in 1912 were close to the junction of North Walls with Hyde Abbey Road. The housing market had reached saturation point and many of the former water meadows were not suited for housing. However, Barrow Simonds could help satisfy the modern Edwardian's desires for home creature comforts and a place to spend increasing leisure time. Barrow Simonds made available the remaining drier meadow lands which were easily accessible to the City, as much needed sites for the Steam Laundry and the Electric Light Company. The lower lying lands, with their network of channels to facilitate flooding the meadows to promote the fresh green shoots for ewes and lambs, were sold in 1902 to the Corporation for a recreation park. The price raised from the utility companies is not known but the land for the recreation ground was sold for £5,350 – a considerable amount of money for land in the Itchen's flood plain.

Over 60 years Winchester's urban fringe had moved northwards by one mile to swallow up many of the fields belonging to the Abbey's historic grange farm. The meadows, once owned by the Knights and the Duke, were replaced by the red bricks of suburbia. The possible views of those who hankered after the old Hyde and remembered the time when the great Abbey was the resting place of the King Alfred, can be summed up by this verse from a poem.

Written by Arundell Esdaile and published in 1912 it was called 'On the so-called Tomb of King Alfred, by the Church of St Bartholomew, Hyde Winchester'

Nothing royal here: rough turf alone
Clothes the slope – and, past the straggling hedge,
Raw red streets of brick and slate are grown;
Only at our feet this doubtful stone,
Nameless, at the town's mean edge,
Marked his half remembered dust...[55]

Figure 8.17: Victorians at leisure

Source: Warrens & Sons (1905)

The water meadows are now a public park.

Chapter 9: Barrow Simonds' Hyde – then and now

Hyde Street

Edwardian Hyde Street was an exciting bustling place, a mixture of a few large Georgian houses, some with sweeping drives, adjoining small dwellings. Interspersed were shops, inns and brewery taps, and blacksmiths. On a weekday, the street would have been busy with fully laden brewery drays slowly climbing the hill to take the beer to the public houses in Winchester and beyond and returning empty at a trot to get back to the stables in Swan Lane. There was the strong smell of malt and manure and, on a wet day the road would have been slippery for those using the new-fangled bicycles. These were increasingly popular as a mode of transport for young and old. Only the large houses still used horse transport. The two-wheeled dog-carts, with their smart coachmen, transported a doctor or lady around the town. The advent of the motor car and inexperienced drivers would have added to the melee. Dr Thomas Richard was one of the first people in Winchester to own a motor car. He lived in St Thomas Street and, as he was married to William Barrow's daughter Lucy, the car would have been a regular sight in Hyde. Others, like Barrow Simonds, preferred to use a horse. [1]

A traveller standing with his back to the Crown and Cushion, which stood on the corner of North Walls and Jewry Street, would have seen no evidence of the City's former North Gate. This was demolished, along with East Gate and South Gate, in 1770, under an act for paving and improving the City. The Crown and Cushion, which belonged to the Winchester Brewery Company, was a large hotel, with an impressive facade of stone quoins, patterned terracotta tiles, gables and decorative glass windows. Hyde Street, which sloped downhill, was narrow and dominated by the tall red brewery buildings. The Winchester Brewery had accumulated extensive properties in the street. The Welsh Brewery Co. owned the Hyde Abbey Brewery and the Hyde Abbey Hotel, formerly the site of Malthouse No. 1.

The traveller walking down the west side of Hyde Street would have passed buildings of various designs, some recently built or renovated, whilst others had stood there for over a hundred years. After the Dissolution, Bethell owned the northern part of this side of Hyde Street and the Dean and Chapter owned much of the southern part. In 1912 Bethell's land was under three owners – Henry Hall, Rev. Edward Firmstone and Mrs Ford.

No. 1 Hyde Street stood on the south corner of Swan Lane. It was a tall two-storey building with further rooms in the roof. The property consisted of a house, shop, yard and stable. H. Collis had run a shop and bakery there in 1908 but, by 1912, the Fisher family had taken it over.[2] The family still ran the business in the 1930s – a photograph from that time shows the building covered with advertisements for Cadbury's chocolate and cocoa, Fry's chocolate and Player's cigarettes. On the north corner of Swan Lane was Denmark House with its large garden which was owned or leased by Major G. Faunce. The brick house had three storeys, was rather plain, and had a rateable value of £36 p.a.. Adjoining was a terrace of four small brick cottages (Nos. 3 to 6). Three of these were owned by the Winchester Brewery Company, which also owned No. 18. This old squat property, used as a shop and accommodation, was dwarfed by adjacent buildings.[3]

Just north of Swan Lane George Phineas Osmond, the pork butcher, carried out his trade. His employees dressed in blue and white baize aprons and straw hats were a common sight pushing carts loaded with meat boxes.[4] Osmond's business occupied compact parcels of land which were formerly owned by the Dean and Chapter or the City. These included an L-shaped plot of land consisting of Nos. 7 to 17 Hyde Street and Nos. 1 to 4 Swan Lane. No. 7 Hyde Street was both a house and shop. Behind it, and accessed by a narrow path (known as Gradeige's Passage), was a slaughterhouse, smoking house for curing bacon and a stable. There were two clusters of five and three cottages which were very old and basic, and rated at only £6 10s. p.a.. Nos. 16 to 18 had a frontage on the street. Joseph Osmond ran the confectioners at No. 17 and next door was a greengrocer. The Dean and Chapter owned the Hyde Street properties until 1866 when, following change in land law, it was conveyed by the Ecclesiastical Commissioners to the cattle dealer John Gradeige. In what was known as 'Gradeige's buildings', two of the tenements dated back to 1836 and three further tenements were built in 1858. An 1866 conveyance described a public house called the Blue Posts (later called the Brewers Arms), several cottages and other buildings, a bakery and two cottages.[5]

Mrs Gifford owned Nos. 19 and 20 Hyde Street. No. 20, where she lived, was a three-storey brick property set in a ¼ acre garden which extended to Victoria Road. The size is reflected by the rateable value of £56 p.a.. Past occupants included the miller and baker Samuel Maunder in 1775 and his son Joseph, who raised a mortgage from Thomas Deane in 1799.[6] In 1800, the properties passed to Rev. Charles Richards, who also leased pasture land behind the properties (part of Eagles Fields) from the Dean and Chapter. Frederick Warner, a solicitor, purchased the land in 1880 and it remained in his family until 1897. The Gifford family, who were corn merchants, purchased the properties in 1900 and sold them for £1,500 in 1932.

Nos. 25 and 26 were symmetrical houses, built in the late eighteenth century or early nineteenth century, which stood either side of Hyde Close. They were three storeys high and had eight bedrooms.[7] By the 1860s, No. 26 had become a public house, known as the Prince of Wales. Eldridge Pope & Co owned the premises in 1912. The property continued as a public house until 2003 when it reverted to a residence. Next to the public house was a terrace of six brick and flint cottages (Nos. 27 to 30b) built c.1871 by Barrow Simonds which replaced earlier tenements. Pairs of doorways stood side by side under a brick archway and individual ogee curve hood (back cover). The Clarke family (possibly related to the Clerkes) owned several tenements on the plot which were first mentioned in 1728 in the will of William Clarke, yeoman of Hyde.[8] Rev. Charles Richards' son purchased the cottages in 1812 and then sold them to James Theobald in 1834. In 1871 William Barrow Simonds purchased the dwellings from James Theobald's widow and promptly demolished the old buildings. The last property had a blacksmith's forge attached where, in 1908, John Best worked as a farrier.[9] The new houses stayed in the Simonds' family until 1922, when Reginald Best, a blacksmith, purchased them.

With the exception of the terrace of cottages, the surrounding land stretching between Hyde Close in the south, Hyde Church Lane in the north and the gardens of Thurloe Terrace in Worthy Lane to the west, belonged to Henry Hall. Hall farmed 200 acres of land and employed seven men. The New County School for Girls (headmistress Miss E. M. Cunningham) was located at Exeter House. The property, built as a private residence probably between 1873 and 1878, had grounds of a ¼ acre and was rated at £48 p.a.. Nos. 31 to 33 Hyde Street were also sizeable brick and stucco Georgian houses rated between £28 p.a. and £36 p.a.. No. 31 had a square hall, drawing and dining room, three bedrooms and a servant's bedroom.[10] No. 33 had a return frontage of 87 feet on to Hyde Church Lane and benefited from three bedrooms on the first floor, a further three attic rooms and a large cellar. The rear stone building was used as paint shop and oil and colour store.[11] In Hyde Church Lane, Hall owned two old cottages, a corn store, yard, stable and gardens sited on one acre of land. In Hyde Close was a house, a large hall and another building, which formerly comprised the Soldiers' Home School, on a plot measuring nearly ½ acre.

Rev. Edward Firmstone, who was ordained as Rector of Weeke in 1877, owned the area north of Hyde Church Lane - No. 34, the terrace Nos. 35 to 42 Hyde Street, and Nos. 1 and 2 Hyde Church Lane. No. 34, older than the adjoining houses, was built of red brick on a stone plinth. As the house was opposite the former entrance to Hyde Abbey, the stone was, possibly, the remnants of an older building. The houses had a small front garden, two rooms and a kitchen downstairs, and three bedrooms upstairs.[12] Firmstone died in 1900 and his estate was still in the hands of executors in 1910. William Gradeige had built Nos. 37 to 40 Hyde Street in 1827. He had demolished a previous property whose providence is traceable back to the late 1770s.[13] William's brother, John, was a butcher.

North of the Red House was a terrace of four small properties rated at £8 p.a.. These had a small front garden, two reception rooms and a kitchen, but only two bedrooms. The back garden gave access to Worthy Road.[14] The north-facing Beaufort House stood at the junction of Hyde Street with Worthy Road. Mrs Ford owned all these properties.

Frederick Bowker (junior) owned three properties south of Arthur Road. Buckingham House (now split into two properties) with its ½ acre grounds was rated at £64 p.a.. No. 51, a small brick property which was rated at £9 p.a., may have been a mews. The larger Rozel rated at £40 p.a., was the residence of son Alfred. Frederick had a considerable property portfolio as he had inherited Lankhills and owned Beaconsfield, Winton Lodge and Fyfhyde in Park Road. Between Rozel and Egbert Road was another large property on a ¼ acre plot. Although occupied by Edwin Hillier, Miss A. E. Hillier owned Kingston House (No. 53). It had two storeys and was built of grey brick with wide eaves. The house had a large conservatory and a large greenhouse in the garden. Edwin Hillier owned a flower and seed shop in the High Street and the business of Hillier and Sons operated a 15-acre nursery in Romsey Road, which is still in business today. Hillier's business flourished during the twentieth century. In

1950 land was purchased at Ampfield, south of Winchester. In 1977 Sir Harold Hillier presented the estate to Hampshire County Council. The gardens and arboretum, now open to the public, bear his name and Hilliers continues to win gold medals at the Chelsea Flower Show.[15]

With the exception of Nos. 58 to 60 Hyde Street, the parcel of land lying south of Egbert Road was held by St Bartholomew's and its vicar, Rev. H. G. W. Living, was responsible for taxes. The church's ownership was at that time more extensive than at any period since the Dissolution. There were five vicars during Barrow Simonds' time at Abbots Barton: William Williams (until 1869), Charles Slogett (1869-1878), Lewis Humbert (1878-1895), George Athill (1895-1898) and Henry George Downing Liveing (1898-1912). During the Rev. Charles Sloggett's incumbency, the vicarage was enlarged at a cost of £550.[16] Next door was the Parish Hall and club, which was added during Rev. Lewis Humbert's time. In 1875 the parishioners purchased the old malthouse at the rear, which dated from 1770, from Richard Moss of Hyde Brewery.[17] The hall was renovated in 1899 and 1903. The north wall was built of stone and rubble but the core of the building was much older. William Simonds had added a new facade in memory of his wife who had died by 1851. At this time, he was clearly involved in the community at Hyde while living at Priors Barton Farm with the unmarried 30-year old Barrow Simonds and his other children. The facing consisted of bricks on the ground level and roughcast above. The porch with its bowed pediment projected to the building line and the arched windows were embedded in a stone casing clustered together in groups of fives and fours (Figure 9.1).

The land to the north and north-east of the church had been part of the Abbey's home farm. At some stage the plot came under the ownership of John Doswell (a butcher) who, in his will dated 1792, left a house and eight acres of land to his son, also called John. In 1804 part of the land passed to Richard Page, the keeper of the Bridewell, who held the land until his death in 1815.[18] Another plot passed to William Wigg (a dairyman), then to John Dench (a publican).[19] In 1838 this was sold to Stephen Deaker (a carpenter), who built a row of cottages, in the path known as Hyde Churchyard. The picturesque two-storey stone and flint cottages with their red brick dressings had a rateable value of £6 10s.. S. R. Shaw and the builder John Newman owned them in 1912. Newman had premises in nearby City Road.

Land south of King Alfred Place stretching to No. 75 Hyde Street (with the exception of Nos. 66 and 67) was part of Barton Farm. Although many of Barrow Simonds' farm servants lived here, some of the larger properties were rented out. Henry G. Hall, who owned extensive property on the west of Hyde Street, lived at Barton Cottage (No. 69) which had a yard and stables attached. As well as being a coal merchant, Albert Faithfull ran the Mineral Water Works at No. 71. The business was based in Tower Street when it started in 1885 but then relocated to Hyde in the early 1890s. Albert's sons, Edgar and Archibald Thomas, joined the thriving business in 1905.[20] Henry Herbert Holloway (a coal merchant) and later James Alexandra Gray (who made ginger beer) previously occupied the premises.[21] Nos. 72 to 74 was a terrace of small brick cottages, decorated with flint dressings, valued at £7 10s. p.a.. Nothing remained of the sixteenth century Hyde House built by Richard Bethell and demolished when Thomas Knight purchased the property from the Duke of Bedford in 1767. The service extension survived as did the malthouse built on the site of the mansion. Chaplin & Co, general carriers, rented the property from about 1900, when they set up a furniture depository in the old barn and malthouse buildings.

Land that had been in the ownership of Rev. Charles Richards, remained in his family. Richards & Sons, who were cab and carriage proprietors, owned part of Hyde House's garden, along with four small cottages in Hyde Close adjoining the former Hyde Abbey School. The major change in this part of Hyde Street was four new houses built in 1896, one of which – Glencoe - was home to Joseph William Richards, a saddler and lay clerk at Winchester College. Even though there was access to the street, the land behind these houses, formerly the site of orchards and subsequently hop fields, went undeveloped. John Castell had used a ½ acre plot hidden behind commercial premises as a market garden between 1833 and 1895. Hayward and Slade ran a motor cycle works and the garage and repair shops. Next door, A. J. Gurney, a coachbuilder, had a yard, stable, workshop and stores. There were a few properties under private ownership - Thomas Wareham (a market gardener) and William Fennell who had offices here.

Figure 9.1: Hyde Parish Hall

The breweries

James Simonds died in 1858, the same year as his brother-in-law William Simonds. In 1859 Hyde brewery was conveyed to James's widow Charlotte Emma Simonds and his sister Mary Muller. Some limited expansion had taken place under James's ownership. The estate consisted of the Hyde Brewery, a messuage and outhouses, a brewhouse, a malthouse and stables, the Britannia, two tenements adjoining the Angel, the Spread Eagle and the Cart and Horses The properties were heavily mortgaged and Mary Muller paid sums of £3,000, £1,000 and £500 to the creditors to take full control of the business.[22]

William Barrow Simonds invested £4,000 in the business in 1862 which enabled Mary Muller to purchase land forming part of the garden of the White Swan Hotel. The plot measured 107 feet along North Walls and was 80 feet deep. The brewery already held the land under a lease from the Mayor, Aldermen and Citizens of Winchester.[23] The Corporation were not at liberty to sell the land without the necessary procedures governed by the 1835 Municipal Corporations Act. The Mayor, Alderman and Citizens were required to apply for permission to the Lord Commissioners of H.M. Treasury to sell and alienate the garden plot.[24]

A new stage in the history of the brewing, malting and spirits business in Hyde began with the establishment in 1864 of the Simonds & Co partnership between Mary Muller and Richard Moss, which was to run for 42 years.[25] Moss was born in London but became a prominent figure in Winchester. He worked as a brewery valuer for a London firm and married Mary Snow, his employer's daughter, in 1858. After he visited Winchester in 1860 in a professional capacity, he set up home with his family in the City. By 1884 Moss had moved elsewhere in Hampshire, first to Southampton and then to Farnborough. He was active in local politics at ward and national level, serving as MP for Winchester from 1865 to 1880.

Since her brother's death, Mary Muller had not only been the owner of the freehold, copyholds and leaseholds of pubic houses, beer houses, and hereditaments connected to the business, but took an active part in the operations. The Hyde premises included the main brewery along with the counting house, stabling, vaults, residence and large garden. The White Swan Hotel had stabling, garden and a bowling green. There was the malthouse and premises in Swan Lane and, in Hyde Street, another malthouse and premises, and the Coopers Arms public house with cottage adjacent. The brewery had a sound foothold in Winchester and beyond. Business was growing and the brewery owned several freehold properties - 17 in Winchester and 6 elsewhere in Hampshire. In addition, there were 17 leasehold public houses.

The partnership agreement barred Mary Muller from having an interest in any other business, but Moss could carry on a business other than that of brewer, maltster or spirit merchant within 40 miles of Winchester. Moss had exclusive rights over the management of the business, including the contraction or expansion of the business, purchases of real estate, and taking on of leases. He could also hire or dismiss staff, such as travellers, clerks, assistants and servants. Moss had no special allowance or remuneration, apart from travelling and personal expenses, for his management role to which he agreed to give all requisite personal attention.[26] Joseph Parker Mew managed the business on a salary of £275 with a share of the profits. At the start of the partnership, Muller owned a two-thirds share and Moss a one-third share, for which he paid £3,000. Within two years, Moss invested a further £3,000 thus equalising partnership rights.[27] The two branches of the Simonds families still owned most of the shares in 1865: Robert Withington (£3,880), William Blackall (£5,200), Mrs James Simonds (£2,292) and Henry T. (£1,200). Further investments by Moss and others in 1868 raised the share capital to £20,722.

As expected in a manufacturing and retail business, real estate, valued at £22,278 in 1865, accounted for the majority of the company's value.[28] By comparison, the equipment and fittings were valued at £2,733. The stock, consisting of raw materials and finished goods, had a similar value of £2,111. Little money was tied up in the horses and related equipment. The company was growing and three years later its worth had increased by 26 per cent to £28,079.

Mary Muller, now living in Norwich, conveyed the properties to Moss when the partnership was dissolved in 1871. The portfolio had expanded and included two tenements near St Cross Hospital, three tenements near Fishers Pond and two parcels of land on Owslebury Down (both near Winchester), along with public houses and other lands in Southampton. The reason Muller sold the business is unknown, but it may have been to release assets to set up her son, John, in his new career as a clergyman. Although the business was valued at £26,635, outstanding mortgages of £13,172 reduced the net worth to £13,664, leaving Muller only £7,157 once Moss's investment and interest had been deducted.[29] Even though the partnership was dissolved, Blackall Simonds (William Blackall's son who lived in Ryde on the Isle of Wight) and Muller still had shares in the business. After Muller died in 1890, Moss paid off the Simonds family's remaining interests in the Hyde brewery.[30]

Expansion required new brewery buildings. Figures 9.2 and 9.3 show the growth between 1873 and 1897. In the 1880s three new maltings and kilns and a brewery tower were added. The four-storey tower, crowned by a water tank, measured about 20 by 28 feet and was 60 feet high. Between 1889 and 1903 various works were carried out, including a new malting, the rebuilding of a cartshed and additional stabling. The construction of a new brewery building in 1905, with similar architectural features to the 1821 building, added symmetry to the facade. Measuring 18 by 35 feet, it lay perpendicular to the road and had no external access except through the old building. With expansion came the urgent need for more office space, which was added in 1907.[31]

Figure 9.2: Hyde Brewery 1873 & 1897

Source: O.S. Map 1st Edition 1873

Source: O.S. Map 2nd Edition 1897

The Winchester Brewery Company Ltd was registered as a joint stock company in 1893, with nominal capital of £150,000 in 500 six per cent preference shares of £100 each and 5,000 ordinary shares of £20 each. Of these 500 six per cent preference and 4,000 ordinary shares were issued and fully paid, giving a total capital of £130,000. The company assets were valued at £32,250 at registration. Like the Simonds' brewery business, investors were predominantly family members. These included Richard Moss, his sons John Snow Moss and Arthur E. Moss, and Alfred Edmeades who were all employed in brewing. Other investors were Arthur E. Deane, a banker and developer, Capt. E. C. Trollope, a retired officer Royal Artillery of Isleworth, and Moss' daughter, Ada Mary, who lived in London.[32]

In 1894 Moss conveyed the assets of the business to a new company as a means of raising further capital. The buildings, machinery, plant, implements, tools, stock in trade, materials and utensils, business and undertakings of the company, money and credits were valued at £22,407. The brewery continued to have a strong presence in southern Hampshire with 36 premises, including seven in Winchester and eleven in the Southampton area.[33] In 1895 the Winchester Brewery Co. Trust secured more capital to feed expansion by issuing £250,000 of debenture stock and raised a further sum of £270,000 in 1908. In 1897 the company purchased the King Alfred pub in Saxon Road from Arthur Elliot Deane, by which time the company accounts valued the business at £137,675.[34] However the valuers, Collins, Tootell & Co, estimated the assets to be worth far in excess of this at £200,000. Premises in Winchester included the Hyde Brewery properties and ten public houses: the Bell and Crown, the Forester's Arms, the Dolphin Inn and properties, the Crown and Cushion Hotel, the Fox Inn, the Robin Hood, the Battery Inn, the Wagon and Horses, the Fulflood Arms, and the Railway Refreshment Rooms. The brewery owned 38 public houses throughout the south of Hampshire chiefly in Southampton and its suburbs. The location of public houses on the west side of Portsmouth suggests that a local brewery was absorbed.[35]

There were several established breweries in Winchester and each dominated different areas of the City, including the Cheesehill and Lion Breweries in the east and the St James Brewery on the corner of St James Lane and Southgate Street. Change occurred in 1898 when George William and Mary Pointer, having sold their Cheesehill brewery to B. B. Colson, sold their pubs to Moss. These included the Bell Inn in St Cross, the Eagle Hotel, the Heart in Hand and the Phoenix Inn in Twyford.[36] Further expansion saw a presence across the south east of England. In 1904, the company, whose Head Office was in Hyde, had offices in Portsmouth, Southampton, London and Croydon. The accumulation of premises and other legal work kept local solicitor practices, like Scotney & Shenton, Warner, and Wooldridge, in business.[37] Moss died in 1905, ending years of stability in the business. The business continued to flourish under the directorships of John Snow Moss, Alfred Edmund Moss (who lived in Gloucester), Arthur Elliot Deane and Edward Charles Trollope.[38]

Figure 9.3: West side of Hyde Street looking north

Source: T W Warren (ed.) (1903)

At the turn of the century, Hyde was an industrial suburb. On the right hand side of the street is the Winchester Brewery. Its tall brick façade dwarfs pedestrians. The Welsh Brewery's tower and chimney dominates the other side. In the foreground are older houses and shops belonging to Osmond, the pork butcher. The Dutch gable of Hyde House can just be discerned in the background.

The Winchester Brewery Company was not the only brewery operating in Hyde Street in 1912. In 1860 Charles Currry Kilham, acting as Muller's agent, sold the malthouse on the west side of Hyde Street to James Wyeth for £300. [39] The title for the property dated back to 1830, although there was a lease and release of the land dated 1801. Wyeth ran the business for 37 years, extending the property in 1887 and constructing a new malthouse in 1895, before selling to Welsh & Co in 1897.[40] The ¼ acre site, which stretched back to the bottom of Victoria Road, had a rateable value of £192 p.a.. The buildings consisted of a brewery, cellars and offices. The Brewery's four-storey tower and chimney was visible throughout Hyde and stood as a statement of business success (Figure 9.3). Thomas Stopher, the successful Winchester architect, designed the Gothic building in 1869.[41] The site had a 36-foot frontage on Hyde Street, a depth of nearly 250 feet, and a rear frontage of 75 feet on Victoria Road. Access to the covered yard was by means of double doors. The ground floor had a racking shed and setting room. The first floor had fermenting and malt rooms and offices. The second floor had stores and cooling and mess rooms. The third floor provided more storage.[42] The Brewery also owned the adjacent Hyde Abbey Hotel and coach house. Welsh Brewery took over the Cheesehill Street Brewery in the east of Winchester but, since there was a malthouse there, the one in Hyde became surplus to requirements.

Figure 9.4: The King Alfred

Originally built as the Saxon Hotel to avoid opposition to a public house on the estate.

House ownership in 1912

Property ownership in 1912 related the story of housing development. Victorian developers often retained houses on their estates. If not, they were quickly sold to shrewd Victorian investors – predominantly successful tradesmen or widows. In the age before pensions, a portfolio of properties provided for a widow or children. Houses were often mortgaged to release capital for the family to live on. When properties were sold, usually on the death of the owner, preference was given to selling the portfolio intact, as fragmentation increased management costs. As time elapsed from the date of construction, ownership of a block of houses was likely to become more diverse.

Those in the building profession owned most of the new houses in King Alfred Place. Lord Northbrook owned the others. In Hyde Abbey Road, Micklam's widow still owned nine properties, but investors like H. D. Johnson and Chiddy owned the majority of the rest. The Shentons were moneylenders, but Mrs Shenton's seven properties in the road were probably an investment. The Winchester Brewery owned three houses in the road, one of which was the shop and off-licence. This was formerly run by Thomas Wareham, a grocer and baker. The Edwardians may have objected to industrial premises next to residential but the Winchester Steam Laundry owned the three houses adjacent to the site. These may have been purchased to house key workers who were expected to be on call all hours.

In Eagles Field, Evans had mortgaged nine properties to finance further developments. Lewis Carter had inherited eight of the houses in Thurloe Place and Lord Northbrook firmly held on to his properties in Hyde Close. On the Conygary Estate, where some of the houses had been built by Hughes and Green, Henry W. Frampton owned 25 properties, Macklin owned six houses and a further 16 houses were mortgaged. On the newly built Oxlease Estate, the Hyde Estate owned 45 per cent, Henry W. Frampton 40 per cent and Henry Swift Frampton just seven per cent of the total 107 houses. Whether this overwhelming control by the developers was intended, or whether economic circumstances stifled any interest in a long lease or buying the freehold is not known.

In the exclusive and secluded developments on the Abbots Barton Uplands, the Simonds family still owned many of the houses. The owner and occupier of Beechwood was Alice Simonds and William Barrow (junior) owned the Cedars, where John Kaines lived. St Waleric, where Miss Bowker lived, and the Park Road Nursery were held by executors after Barrow Simonds' death. The Johns and Baker families still owned the two schools - Winton House School and Asbourne Lodge. The developer Sawyer Ashton owned Short Acre where he lived, Abbots Acre, Rooks Acre, Fayre Acre and further undeveloped land. In retrospect, these seem inappropriately named, no doubt with an eye to marketing. Short Acre, the largest site was only ½ acre in size, whilst the others extended to little more than a ¼ acre. The Bowker family, related by marriage to the Simonds, had a considerable portfolio throughout the City. Most properties were small with the exception of those in Hyde. Frederick Bowker owned Fyfhyde where he lived, Winton Lodge, Beaconsfield, Buckingham House, Rozel and

No. 51 Hyde Street. His son owned Lankhills. The widow of Thomas Micklam, Barrow Simonds' Hyde Abbey Road developer, owned considerable properties throughout the suburbs which her husband had built, including four houses in Park Road.

Apart from the farm, the Simonds family owned Durngate Mill, the housing for the farm workers in King Alfred Place and Nos. 61 to 75 Hyde Street. On the west side of the street they still owned the terrace built by Barrow Simonds – Nos. 27 to 30b. The Halls owned properties in Hyde Church Lane and those adjoining Hyde Street. Firmstone's executors still had control of the former school estate. The vicar was proprietor of the church premises at the north end of the street.

Other properties in Hyde Street, once belonging to the Cathedral Priory and then to their successors the Dean and Chapter, were owned or leased in what were essentially medieval clusters. Many old tenements fell down or were demolished and new houses were built on old foundations. The Winchester and Welsh breweries owned most of the west side of Hyde Street up to Hyde Abbey House with the exception of the butcher George Osmond's premises - Nos. 7 to 17 - and the contiguous properties in Swan Lane.

Although older properties failed to survive intact, new houses or just new facades were built to satisfy society's changing tastes. The old boundaries varied little as the plots were transferred through multiple tenants and owners during the reigns of the Tudors, Stuarts, Hanoverians down to Victoria and Edward VII.

Figure 9.5: No. 26 Hyde Street

Whereas the Swan, later called the White Swan, stayed in business, other public houses did not. In 1871 this property was an inn (name unknown) but by 1881 it was called the Prince of Wales. The property has now been converted to flats.

Hyde 2012

A time traveller from a century ago would be shocked by the disappearance of many of the well-known landmarks in Hyde Street and overwhelmed by the buildings that have replaced them. The tall red brewery buildings no longer hem in the top of the Hyde Street, although sustenance can still be obtained at the pub. However, with little regard to history, the business has just been sold and the Swan is now a Mucky Duck – the local nickname.

In the first half of the twentieth century portfolios of houses were sold en-bloc. This created a glass ceiling for property ownership for the small investor and prevented an increase in owner-occupation. Nos. 34 to 39 Hyde Abbey Road, Nos. 41 to 46 Andover Road and No. 1 Victoria Road were sold as one portfolio in 1934. Even as late as 1965, nine houses in Hyde Close (Nos. 5 to 7, 9, 16, 17, 19, 29 and 30) were offered for sale together.

Many of the small properties built before 1850 have not survived. Neglect, war damage and the desire to increase standards of living led to the decision to demolish some groups of properties. No1 Hyde Street was pulled down in 1951, Nos. 8 to15 in 1955 and Nos. 7, 16, 17 and 18 in the 1960s. New planning initiatives saw further changes. In 1972 Danemark House and Nos. 3 to 6 Hyde Street were demolished and replaced by Homerise House which provides 51 flats for the elderly. Nos. 11-24 Victoria Road were replaced by modern housing. Small parcels of land allowed intensive development. In about 1980 a strip of glebe land, which provided access to the former school site, was sold for housing.

The survival of the villas and town houses in Hyde was dependent on change of use and particularly purchase by the public and voluntary sectors for education and health. Hyde House needed considerable repairs when acquired by Winchester City Council in 1974. The Historic Resources Centre was established following building improvements. In 2009 the centre moved to the Guildhall and the building was let. After undertaking renovations, an architectural practice has recently moved in. The historical site is in good hands; the practice specialises in Victorian and traditional design, and employs the writer and broadcaster Professor Dan Cruikshank as a consultant. Many large houses were converted for educational purposes and their grounds intensively used for new buildings. Plans for Lankhills and The Beeches as a school for children with special educational needs date back to 1919.[43] In 2002 Lankhills was renamed Osborne School, the old premises were demolished and a new school built, partially financed by the sale of two acres of surplus land for housing. Hyde Abbey House remained in educational use as a boarding house for St Swithun's School from 1885 until 1948. North Hill House was an early casualty when sold for development in 1935. Abbotts Barton House, built by Barrow Simonds for his family, Brendon and Park House in Park Road became nursing or residential homes. St Waleric, owned by the NHS, is used as a day hospital and Beaconsfield provides office space for several community action groups. This property is now on the market as offices with residential development potential.

Other large houses, including the former vicarage, were converted into flats. Those with large gardens, for example Hyde Lodge, were ripe for intensification of use. In 1977 the Georgian-built Hyde House was divided and the extensive grounds provided space for four terraced town houses and two further buildings – now known as Hyde House Gardens. Exeter House was pulled down to make way for Rosewarne Court, which provides 21 homes. In Worthy Road, Donnington and Woodlands were replaced by blocks of flats, named after the former houses.

The time traveller would see that many of the large villas built on the old fields have gone and been replaced by new closes packed with houses. With the exception of Brendon and Beechwood, the large houses east of the railway between Lankhills and Park Road have all gone. These include Northlands, Salcot, Abbey Lodge and Denham Court. In Park Road Winton Lodge and Nortons have met a similar fate and, in a trend seen all over Winchester, part of the garden at Woodside was sold for development. The Council rented nearly ten acres for an allotment from the 1920s, until it was purchased in 1951. On the west side of the railway, Hampshire County Council owned Winton House and Ashbourne Lodge. In 2007 an application was approved for 77 dwellings on the 6½ acre combined site. There was already some intrusion by Winton Close, but the plans were for the demolition of the old properties and the construction of properties sympathetic to the designs of the 1860s houses. The plans allowed for 11 three- or four-bedroom houses on the Ashbourne Lodge site and, on the Winton House site, 66 houses and flats, of which 31 were to be affordable and 35 offered in the open market.

The Refuge continued to grow on the reduced one-third acre site. It was rebuilt in 1886 and additions added in 1889 and 1913, giving a floor area of 5,800 square feet with a detached chapel building. In 1915 the Winchester Diocesan Union took over the Refuge for preventative and rescue work. No. 52 Hyde Abbey Road (4 Garfield Terrace) was purchased in 1920 providing an additional five double bedrooms for the girls at the Diocesan Home. The house was sold in 1960 for £1,150. In 1928, the former Refuge was renamed the Diocesan Maternity Rescue Home. The home mainly served the Winchester Diocese but did accept girls from elsewhere in Hampshire and neighbouring counties. The role had not changed much from its early days; unmarried mothers were the main concern. The girls remained in the home at least four months, but preferably six months, after the baby's birth. The entrance fee was one guinea, Diocesan referrals were charged 10s. per week and other referrals 12s. 6d. per week. Only those expecting for the first time were eligible; serial offenders were not wanted.[44] The Superintendent's Reports published every year up to 1972 give details of the inmates. From May to November 1928, for example, seven girls were discharged; one was married, four found situations but, of these, one kept her baby and two went to other Refuges. Six girls were admitted, but one of these refused to stay the twelve months required and was removed to another house. In the six months, seven babies were born bringing the total residents to 14 girls and 9 babies. Many girls returned to their families and some to foster parents, but few kept their babies.[45]

By the 1960s, social attitudes were changing. The stigma of having a baby out of wedlock was disappearing and the difficulties of an unsupported mother bringing up her child had lessened. The Home was closed in 1967 and sold for £13,000 at auction. The main reason cited for closure was the difficulty in appointing midwives for the requisite number of hours. They found plenty of employment in the NHS. The large property must have been expensive and difficult to maintain. In 1964, a surveyor reported that the old flint wall, part of the City's defences, was six inches out of plumb for quite a considerable length.

Businesses came and went. Durngate Mill had ceased milling in 1946 but was not demolished until 1966, when the road was widened. The centuries-old link with the owners of Abbots Barton was ended. The brewery buildings on the west side of Hyde Street were used as a chemical factory by Richardson, a chemist, and Starling, a petroleum engineer, who had perfected a treatment for the extermination of death-watch beetle. The remains of the buildings were demolished in 1985, but the name of the former brewer – Wyeth – is remembered in the new building. The Hyde Abbey Hotel ceased to trade in about 1966. The site of Barton Farm was still linked to agricultural output in the 1970s. South Coast Dairies, owned by Unigate, had a depot between King Alfred Place and Hyde Street, and used No. 68 and Barton Cottage as offices. This is now the site of St Bede's Court, built in 1999. During the construction, excavations found further remains of the Abbey's Inner Court. The thriving Hyde Abbey Motors, built on the former Hyde Garden, was extended in the 1960s. The four late Victorian houses built by Richards were removed to make way for petrol pumps and a showroom. In 2000 its successor - the Evans Halshaw garage - was demolished. The land parcels on the east side of Hyde Street had considerable depth which allowed for the construction of new housing and a business centre.

In 1923 the Winchester Brewery Company took over the Edward's Brewery of Bishops Waltham, near Winchester. However, in the same year, the enlarged Winchester Brewery with 108 licensed premises succumbed to a takeover by Marston, Thompson and Evershed of Burton-on-Trent. After 150 years, the Hyde brewery, which had grown from small beginnings on a site behind St Bartholomew's Church, and subsequently extended to other parts of Hyde Abbey's former lands, was no longer a locally controlled enterprise. The new owners stopped production in 1927, although the business continued as a bottling plant until 1969.

An archaeological survey carried out by students of King Alfred's College (now the University of Winchester) in 1980 prior to the demolition of part of the brewery, gave an insight into earlier buildings.[46] The oldest surviving block had two storeys and was built of brick. A stone inscribed 'Hyde Brewery Rebuilt 1821' attests to the age. The building had five bays, the middle three contained in pilaster strips, which formed part of three archways rising to a gable. The building was still used as offices and stores in the 1980s. Today the only remaining buildings on the site are the counting house, now a private residence; the White Swan, still doing a good trade; and the adjoining property, now a house with a sunken garden lying to the south below the City wall.

In 1998, over two hundred years of brewing history came to an end when an application by Banner Homes was approved to build 53 dwellings and associated garages or parking on the former Marston Brewery Depot. The plans for social housing provided for shared ownership and assured tenancies, with the council retaining the right to nominate 75 per cent of the tenants. The site of the former Winchester Brewery was extensive. A new access road on Hyde Street was constructed, but the old Marston gateposts on Hyde Street and North Walls were preserved. As normal for developments in a historical area, archaeologists were given access after the old buildings were destroyed.[47]

Land east of Hyde Abbey Road was developed for a multitude of purposes. In 1912 there was an electric power station and, in the mid-twentieth century, a saw mill and timber yard. Most industrial traces have been removed with the exception of Winchester Steam Laundry in Hyde Abbey Road. The laundry was built in the late nineteenth century and remained in business as an industrial cleaning company until 2007, when it moved out of the residential area to a new site. The building, with its many twentieth century additions is still standing and awaiting re-development at the time of writing. New buildings include Arlington Place which was built on the site of the former medieval fishponds.

In 1911, the 90-year old Barrow Simonds lived with three unmarried daughters - Ellen (50), Alice (40) and Olive (26) - and five servants His daughter Marian was married to a bank manager. His son, William Barrow lived at Waterside, north of Abbots Barton, with his young family.[48] When Barrow Simonds senior died in 1912, the estate passed to his son who lived at Abbots Barton until his death in 1954. William Barrow (junior) was an army reservist, barrister and JP. He married Cecily Broughton and they had five children: twins John and Joan, Robert William, Mary and Ivy. John became a City councillor but died a bachelor in Guernsey in 1971. Joan married into the Young brewing family and her son John Allen Young was born in 1920 in Winchester. He was to become prominent in the brewing trade until he died in 2006 aged 86.

Many of the Simonds family still lived at Abbots Barton in the mid-twentieth century, for example, John Barrow at the Dairy Cottage and Olive Barrow next door. In 1957, 55 acres of land north of Abbotts Barton House and 219 acres of water meadows were offered at auction, but the reserved price was not reached. In 1964 the council purchased Abbots Barton Farm, ending the long duration of Simonds' ownership. The farmhouse was initially rented to a college lecturer and then archaeology students. The dilapidated outhouses had to be demolished.[49] The remaining fields were further eroded in 1968 when a housing estate was built on Coney Garden.

During the Simonds family's and then the Council's ownership the former Abbey lands, that for centuries survived in agricultural production, succumbed to development. However, the names of many of the developments echo the centuries of history attached to the land since the founding of Hyde Abbey in 1110: Abbotts Road, Abbey Hill Road, Austen Close, Chaundler Road, Coney Green, Corham Close, Danemark Court, Hussey Close, Knight Close and Simonds Court. Although many houses and other buildings in Hyde Street survived until the later part of the twentieth century, they were swept away to be replaced by intensification of land use and 'cells' in the sky.

The Victorians who carried out several excavations of the Abbey site during the latter part of the nineteenth century sought the truth of what happened to the bones of King Alfred, his wife Ealhswith and son Edward the Elder. Professional archaeologists and amateur historians today are trying to determine the exact extent of the Abbey precincts. The redevelopment of Hyde Street has allowed many opportunities for the discovery of what lies below the surface. The great Abbey of Hyde is not forgotten. In 2007 Hyde Abbey Gardens was established on the site of the Abbey's church (Figure 9.6). Unfortunately, the beautiful engraving of Hyde Abbey by local artist Tracey Sheppard suffered the same fate as the Abbey when vandals destroyed the glass in July 2010. The photo on the front cover was taken before it happened. Celebrations in 2010 commemorated the relocation of the Benedictine community to Hyde 900 years ago with a procession of 'monks' and three coffins from the site of New Minster to Hyde Abbey Gardens.

It should not be assumed that Abbots Barton Farm is unknown to the present inhabitants of Hyde or the rest of Winchester. Since the 1990s there has been continual pressure to satisfy the demand for housing in an attractive and expensive city. The last remaining green-field wedge of land in the suburban ring lying between Andover Road, the railway and to the north of Park Road West is a prime building site. The first development plan for 450 houses on the 87 hectares at Barton Farm in 1997 was rejected and a public enquiry followed. A recent application for 2,000 houses, which included employment, retail, community and education facilities along with the re-routing of the busy Andover Road, was also rejected. The plan, although offering 800 affordable homes, was not seen as a solution to short term needs.

Local opposition expressed concern at the risk of environmental damage to the Itchen by run-off and sewage when present needs are only just met and where areas of Barton Farm and the City were liable to flooding. Concerns were raised whether the medieval City could sustain the increase in motor transport the development would bring. Following a public enquiry and a court case, the City council and residents await the outcome of the most recent appeal made by the developers to the courts. Perhaps the residents of Victorian and Edwardian Hyde also criticised the developments that the owner of Abbots Barton and other landowners undertook. The destruction of the Abbey and the later desecration of its ruins when the Bridewell was built shocked those generations. Certainly the increased traffic from the expansion of the brewery and the fouling of the river from the large houses on the Uplands would not have been welcome.

Nine hundred years of changing ownership

Hyde: From Dissolution to Victorian Suburb tells the story of the northern portal of Winchester, Alfred's great capital and an important religious centre. Hyde changed from being a small village, serving the great monastery of Hyde Abbey into a major agricultural hub and, as the agricultural importance waned, an industrial and service centre. The economy of the village prospered as renowned schools and breweries provided work and business opportunities for the occupants. The site of the Abbey became the location of new cells for the undesirable and criminal elements of the county, whilst the land of the former Abbey's grange farm was transformed into a garden suburb for the rich citizens of the growing Victorian city. The expanding middle classes and upwardly mobile working classes moved out of the insanitary city attracted by the pleasant environment. They found homes on what had been pastures and water meadows worked by those that benefitted from the Dissolution. Ownership had passed from the purchasers of Thomas Wriothesley's ill-gotten gains, to the Knights and the Duke, and finally to the descendants of a member of a brewing dynasty who decided he wanted to be a farmer.

The Abbey, built in 1100, dominated the northern suburb of Winchester for nearly 450 years before it closed in 1538 on the orders of Henry VIII. The Abbey owned vast tracts of land in Hampshire and throughout neighbouring counties. Under the brief tenure of Thomas Wriothesley, the Abbey site and home farm was separated from its grange - Abbots Barton.

Ownership of the farms and nearby lands passed through the hands of only a few families between 1538 and the twentieth century. Ownership of the great Abbey of Hyde's site and farms in the first centuries after the Dissolution determined the form of the modern day suburb. The Bethells purchased the Abbey site and the family held the ruins and the Abbey Farm until about 1592, when they were obliged to sell to the Clerkes. On his death in 1693, Edmund Clerke left the farm to three relatives. The land was heavily mortgaged to release capital and the last survivor sold it to the Duke of Bedford in 1733.

The Chaundler family held Abbots Barton until 1650 when Thomas Chaundler, heavily in debt, was forced to sell to Anne Mynne, the first of the Knight dynasty. Abbots Barton passed through the hands of generations of the Knight family who somehow managed to keep the lands within their extended family in spite of the absence of direct heirs. The Knights were better known as the owners of the extensive estates of Chawton in Hampshire and Godmersham in Kent. In 1767, the Duke of Bedford, whose London estates were in need of a financial injection, sold the Abbey Farm and meadows to Thomas Knight. Born in Godmersham as Thomas Broadnax, he changed his surname first to May and then to Knight. This was required as a condition of inheritance from distant relatives - Sir Thomas May of Rawmere, Sussex and Elizabeth Knight of Chawton. The Abbey site and its two farms were once again reunited. However, some 20 years later, Thomas Knight's son, also called Thomas, sold the Abbey site to the County for a Bridewell.

When Thomas died his estates were left to his widow Catherine for her lifetime and then to his adopted son and heir - Jane Austen's brother Edward. There were legal wrangles over the title due to Elizabeth Knight's entail. The new owner of Abbots Barton, William Simonds only discovered this in 1818, seven years after he purchased the farm and only at considerable cost did he obtain unchallenged title to the land. William Simonds was related to the Simonds brewing dynasty of Reading who also ran the brewery in Hyde. The Simonds family retained ownership of Abbots Barton until 1966, when the vastly reduced holding was sold to the Hampshire County Council.

The Abbey was not the only landowner in Hyde. The Corporation owned land close to the City walls and ditch. Land belonging to the Dean and Chapter, established at the Dissolution and headed by the Minster's prior, encircled much of the City. This land was not made available for development until changes in copyhold law in the nineteenth century enabled building plots to come on to the open market. This was the opportunity for Lord Northbrook, to develop the Eagles Field Estate off Worthy Lane.[50]

Before 1538, Hyde Street was a thriving suburb which served the Abbey and pilgrims travelling between the tombs of St Swithun in Winchester and St Thomas à Becket in Canterbury. Over one hundred and fifty years, the population declined and the old tenements fell down. However, from about 1750, Winchester's elite saw Hyde as a convenient place to build new mansions a little distant from the City's squalor. Hyde might be described as an industrial suburb with only one processing industry – brewing. Brewing was an important part of the economy in Hyde and, besides Abbots Barton and Abbey Farms, one of the major employers in the area. Brewing provided a market for the agricultural products and, in return, the farms created a demand for the manure from the horses that delivered the beer to the tied houses in Winchester and beyond.

From 1800 the brewing sites scattered around Hyde came under the control of Nicholas Pyle, who also purchased part of Hyde Garden - sold to Thomas Deane by Thomas Knight. The brewery continued to grow as it passed from Pyle to James Eames Waight, then to Charles Marett, and finally into the hands of James Simonds in 1850. James Simonds was married to Charlotte Emma, the sister of William Simonds. Both James and William died in 1858. The brewery was left to Charlotte and James's sister Mary Muller, who paid off the mortgages and took control of the business.

During the second half of the nineteenth century, the brewery premises were extended and a large number of public houses were acquired. There was some rationalisation with the sale of premises on the west side of Hyde Street to James Wyeth. The Simonds' family control of the brewery began to diminish when Muller took on Richard Moss as a partner and eventually, with increasing age and other interests, she retained only a small investment. The Moss family's interest continued until 1923, when the Winchester Brewery Company was taken over, and any local connection terminated.

The Dissolution caused the Abbey's former ecclesiastical lands to come into private ownership. However, the rural landscape hardly changed until William Simonds, already an established Winchester farmer, purchased the reunited Barton and Abbey Farms from Edward Austen in 1811. The site of the Abbey was lost and further desecrated with the building of the Bridewell. Simonds' custodianship of Abbots Barton saw the first significant encroachment into the agricultural landscape with the coming of the railway. Simonds also released small pockets of land for development close to the City.

When the Great Depression struck agriculture at the end of the nineteenth century, the owner of Abbots Barton grubbed up the fields and moved into estate development. William's son, William Barrow Simonds, was the major mover and shaper of the urban development in Hyde. He released fields on the Uplands for the development of country villas and the meadows for housing estates for the lower middle classes. He was not the only developer; Lord Northbrook and local residents - Arthur Elliot Deane and the Frampton family - also made their mark.

The Liberal Government's Finance Act (1909-10) was a response to the deepening economic crisis and the desire for social legislation. In his 1909 budget speech, Lloyd George planned swingeing taxes on the landed aristocracy and gentry, who he saw as social parasites reaping what they had not sown. He pointed out that, whereas the value of agricultural land had been stable for 20 to 30 years, there had been an enormous increase in urban values. The owners of the landed estates had greatly benefitted but contributed little.[51] Plans were drawn up for a land and property tax, which taxed unearned wealth from increasing land values around developing towns. The Act required that a valuation be carried out on all the land in the UK, giving an estimated value for 30th April 1909. September 1912 saw the publication of a professional real estate valuation carried out by Hall, Pain and Goldsmith who had offices in Portsmouth, Fareham and Petersfield.[52] Along with details of ownership, occupancy and extent, this survey provided a professional valuation for all properties, including residential, industrial, and rights such as advertising hoardings and fishing. Since each hereditament was numbered and shown on an Ordnance Survey map, the valuation provides an accurate picture of Hyde 800 years after the foundation of the Abbey and 370 years after its demise.[53]

William Barrow Simonds death in 1912 marked the culmination of housing developments initiated in the Victorian and Edwardian eras. Most of the suburban development of Hyde was the legacy of Barrow Simonds' efforts to maintain his family's wealth, to provide for his seven children, and protect the future of farming at Abbots Barton. His sales of development land were usually of a leasehold interest so that his family retained the freehold. The cost of the freehold was high and developers may have been unhappy with this additional cost. Properties were offered as collateral by developers to raise money for new ventures.

Major changes have occurred in Hyde since the 1950s as houses, which had been neglected by landlords and failed to meet modern living standards, were demolished. The large, once desirable villas were too expensive to maintain. Either they were sub-divided, put to new uses, or were knocked down and replaced by flats or closes of modern dwellings. Many local businesses have been taken over or forced to close.

Over 900 years of Hyde's history was swept away under new development. Today, planning applications for changes of use in Hyde Street, now a conservation area, are carefully considered by the City of Winchester Trust. Their mission is to 'preserve the distinctive and evolving character of the City, by seeking to influence the decisions of both City and County Councils and the proposals of developers.' The future of Hyde House is now assured. The restoration and refurbishment includes a new link between the sixteenth-century house and eighteenth-century Hyde Barn (the malthouse). The vestiges of Barrow Simonds' country houses are also being protected. A planning application to demolish Park House, recently used as a nursing home, and replace with six two-bedroom flats and four five-bedroom houses was rejected in January 2012.

Modern Hyde would have been very different if the Abbey had survived the machinations of Thomas Wriothesley. The meadows and fields would have been frozen in time, mirroring those that Keats enjoyed in his walks beyond Winchester's southern gates. Here Winchester College's ownership has retained much of the medieval land and townscape.

Figure 9.6: Hyde Abbey Remembered

Hyde Abbey garden with the engraving by Tracey Sheppard before it was vandalised.

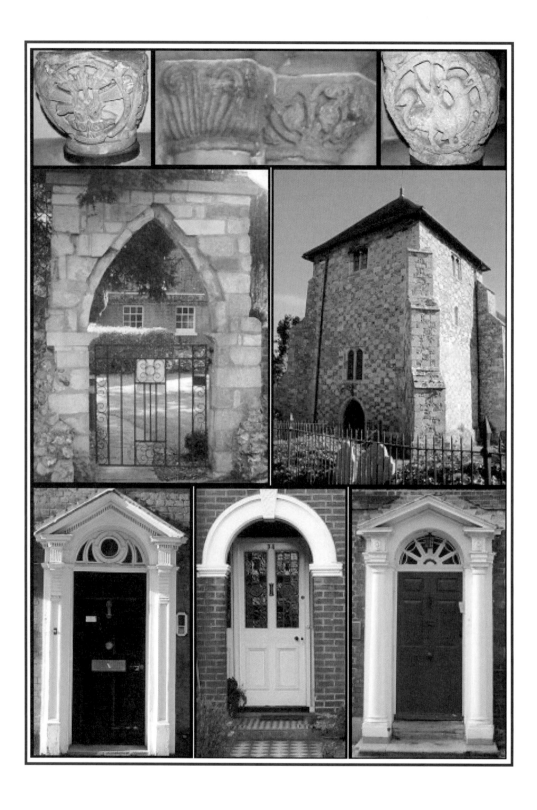

Appendix

Table A1: Details of property ownership on the former Uplands 1912

House	a	r	p	Owner	O/O	Rent £ p.a.	RV £ p.a.
Abbey Road							
Caer Gwent	1	0	22	Hughes Capt	√	140	112
Northlands	6	1	20	Johnston Mrs	√	231	180
Abbey Lodge	2	3	27	Lidner G. M.	√	210	168
Salcot	1	2	6	Warner J. C.	√	175	140
Andover Road							
Ashbourne Lodge	2	0	37	Baker Mrs		130	104
North Hill Cottages				Baker Mrs		42	23.5
North Hill House	1	3	36	Baker Mrs		150	120
Beaconsfield	1	0	37	Bowker Frederick		120	96
Lankhills	5	2	30	Bowker L.		190	152
Highfield	3	3	26	Byron Major R.	√	250	200
The Beeches	3	1	29	Campbell Long Mrs		225	180
Winton House School	6	0	7	Johns E. J.	√	475	380
Master's house	6	0	7	Johns E. J.	√	25	20
Rooks Acre		1	25	Sawyer J Ashton		85	68
The Garth		3	20	Scott Col.	√	100	80

O/O = owner occupation

Table A1 continued

House	a	r	p	Owner	O/O	Rent £p.a.	RV £p.a.
Park Road							
Winton Lodge		3	2	Bowker Frederick		120	96
Bouville		2	36	Brooker Miss A.		108	86.5
Lynton		2	18	Carter Lewis		85	68
Park House	1	1	10	Carter Lewis J.		140	112
Glencairn	1	2	37	Carter Lewis J.		110	88
Nortons		3	27	Dickens Admiral	√	130	104
St Waleric		2	7	Barrow Simonds Execs.		100	80
Park Rd Nursery	2	2	0	Barrow Simonds Execs.		40	12
Rosslyn		1	39	Gudgeon G. E.		110	88
Brandon	1	0	34	Lethridge Mrs	√	150	120
adjoining		3	36	Lethridge Mrs	√	5	0
Roundfield		1	18	Merriman Miss	√	56	45.75
No. 9		1	25	Micklam Mrs		63	50.25
No. 7		1	25	Micklam Mrs		61.5	59
No. 5		1	25	Micklam Mrs		61.5	59
Valentio	1	0	26	Morris W.		85	68
Short acre		2	6	Sawyer J. Ashton	√	65	52
Denham Court	6	0	20	Toogood Col. S. H.		300	240
Woodside	1	2	5	Toogood Col. S. H.	√	140	112
The Cedars		1	25	W Barrow Simonds		60	48
Worthy Road							
Danes Acre		1	28	Alexander Miss	√	85	68
Beechwood	1	0	20	Barrow Simonds Miss	√	80	64
Fyfhyde	2	1	6	Bowker Frederick	√	160	128
Donnithorne	1	0	2	Hampage Adam R. P.	√	150	120
The Elms		3	9	Hill Col. A.	√	120	96
Hyde Lodge	5	0	3	Little Col. Hunter	√	200	160
Abbot's Acre		1	16	Sawyer J Ashton		95	76
Byrnelmscote		2	38	Sherman C. C.	√	95	76
adjoining		2	22	Sherman C. C.	√	13.25	12.5
Fayre Acre		1	29	Sawyer J. Ashton		55	44

Source: HRO: PL3/19/34.

Table A2: Main Property Owners in Hyde in 1912

Owner	Road	Properties
Mrs Baker (widow of Rev Baker)	Alswitha Terrace	1 to 12
	Andover Road	Ashbourne Lodge Northhill House & cottages Land & market garden
Bowker family (solicitors)	Andover Road	Beaconsfield House, Lankhills
	Hyde Street	51, Rozel
	Park Road	Winton Lodge
	Worthy Road	Buckingham House, Fyfhyde
Carter family (builders)	Hyde Street	Hyde Abbey
	King Alfred Place	4 to 8
	Park Road	Park House, Lynton, Glencairn
	Thurloe Place	4 to 11
	Victoria Road	6 to 8
Evans (mortgages) (builder)	Andover Road	41 to 47
	Victoria Road	1 & 2
Firmstone (Executors)	Hyde Church Lane	1 & 2
	Hyde Street	34 to 42
Ford Mrs	Hyde Street	45 to 48
Frampton family (developers)	Arthur Road	5 to 12
	Egbert Road	18 to 30 (even)
	Monks Road	5,7, 8 to 32 (even), 38, 40, 17 to 43 (odd)
	Nuns Road	1 to 10, 12 to 22 (even), 32 to 38 (even)
	Saxon Road	14 to 23
Hayle (or Hale) (financiers)	Egbert Road	6 to 14 (even), 25 to 45 (odd)
Hall	Hyde Church Lane	3 & 4
	Hyde Street	31 to 33, Exeter House
	Hyde Close	Former Soldier's Home
Hyde Estate	Birinus Road	1 to 4
	Monks Road	6, 25, 45 to 48, 50, 52
	Nuns Road	11 to 23 (odd), 24 to 30, 31 to 39 (odd), 40 to 53
	Nuns Walk	1 to 3

Table A2 continued:

Living Rev H. G. W. Vicar St Bartholomew	Hyde Street	Vicarage, 55, 56, Parish Hall, Parish Club
Macklin (builder)	Egbert Road	32 to 42 (even)
Micklam Mrs (widow of Thomas)	Gordon Terrace	1 to 3
	Hyde Abbey Road	29 to 33 & 56
	Park Road	5 to 9 (odd)
Newman family (builders)	Hyde Churchyard	15 to 20
	Victoria Road	Stonemason's yard
Northbrook, Earl of (landowner)	Hyde Close	1 to 19, 28 to 39
	King Alfred Place	9 to 12
Osmond George (butcher)	Hyde Street	1 to 4, 7 to 17,
	Swan Lane	Slaughterhouse, smokehouse, stable
Pain C E (inc. Executors)	Andover Road	48 to 52
	Victoria Road	11 & 12
Richards family (inc family business)	Hyde Close	22 to 25
	Hyde Street	54, 55, 76, 76a, Glencoe, Ross, Rossdale & St Clements, Motor garage, work and repair shops, stable and pub
	Worthy Lane	1 & 2
Shearman (builder)	Arthur Road	Benhilton & Northmead
	King Alfred Terrace	1 to 20
Mrs Shenton (widow of solicitor / financier)	Hyde Abbey Road	34 to 40
White H (builder)	King Alfred Place	15 to 21
Winchester Brewery Co.	Hyde Abbey Road	11 to 13
	Hyde Street	3 to 5, 18, 82, Hyde Tavern, Northfield, White Swan,
	Saxon Road	The King Alfred Pub
Winchester Steam Laundry	Hyde Abbey Road	6 to 8. Laundry

Source: HRO:PL3/19/34

Endnotes

Chapter 1: The Dissolution of Hyde Abbey

[1] Kjølbye-Biddle, Birthe (n.d) *The 7th century minster at Winchester interpreted.* Found at http://ads.ahds.ac.uk/catalogue/adsdata/cbaresrep/pdf/060/06017001.pdf.

[2] Miller Sean (2001) *Charter of the New Minster, Winchester. Anglo-Saxon Charters IX.* Oxford: Oxford University Press (Published for the British Academy) p.xxv-xxvi.

[3] Biddle Martin (1985) *Winchester in the early Middle Ages.* Winchester Studies; Vol.1. Oxford: Clarendon p.317.

[4] A full discussion of these grants and their provenance is given in Miller Sean (2001) pp.xxxvi-lxii.

[5] See Bailey Keith 'The Hidation of Buckinghamshire', in *Records of Buckinghamshire*, Vol.32, 1990 pp.1-22.

[6] The details of each charter can be found in Miller Sean (2001) pp lxiii-lxiv. A further list is found in Edwards Edward (ed.) (1866) *Liber Monasterii de Hyda; Chronicle of the Affairs of England, from the settlement of the Saxons to the reign of King Cnut and a Chartulary of the Abbey of Hyde, in Hampshire A.D. 455-1023.* London: Longmans, Green, Reader and Dyer pp xxix-xxx. He lists the Hampshire lands as Abbot's Worthy, Slackstead, Abbots Barton, Woodmancote, Laverstoke, Alton with Benstead and Kingsley, Presshaw with Lomer, Alton-Eastbrook, Bighton, Brown Candover, Monkmead, Worting, Leckford, Foughlerton (Fullerton) and Abbot's Ann. Within the Micheldever Hundred were Northbrook, Southbrook, Popham, Chilton-Candover, North Stoneham, East Stratton and Dottersley.

[7] Miller Sean (2001) pp.lxi-lxii.

[8] Biddle Martin (1985) p.318.

[9] The plot measured from north to south – 5 furlongs and 5 rods (1,127 ½ yards) on the western edge, 5 furlongs and 26 rods (1,243 yards) in the middle and 5 furlongs (1,110 yards) on the eastern side. The east to west measurements were 3 furlongs and 1 rod (665 ½ yards on the northern edge, 3 furlongs and 27 rods (808½ yards) in the middle and 3 furlongs and 11 rods (720½ yards) on the southern edge. A yard is equivalent to 0.9144 metres. Miller Sean (2001) p.133.

[10] In Biddle's map the northern boundary ends at Chalk Mead and the south extent is marked by the Mill Stream as it changes direction eastwards. See the map of the water meadows in Chapter 5. However there seems to be uncertainty whether the abbey site was part of the Moors and if the boundary lay to the east of Great and Little Ox Lease. See Biddle Martin (1985) opposite pp.266, 258.

[11] A copy of Speed's Map can be found in many historical books on Winchester including Kitchen G. W. (1890) *Winchester.* Historic Towns series. London: Longmans, Green & Co and James Thomas Beaumont (2007) *Winchester from prehistory to the Present.* Stroud: Tempus p.15.

[12] Winchester Discovery Centre March-May 2010. The likely extent and configuration of the Abbey is based on a series of archaeological digs undertaken by the Winchester Museum Services.

[13] The name Abbots Barton or Abbotts Barton is used inconsistently between different sources. For example, the OS 1:50,000 map (1986) describes the historical area as Abbott's Barton yet refers to Abbots Worthy. By contrast the OS 1:25,000 (1988) describes the civil parish as Abbotts Barton and the historical site as Abbots Barton. Victorian sources used Abbots Barton and this form is adopted here.

[14] Biddle Martin (1985) pp.166-169, 266-267.

[15] There were twenty shillings to a £ and twelve pence to the shilling.

[16] At this time a tenement was rented accommodation.

[17] There are difficulties in converting sums to present prices, however £10 in 1300 is estimated as worth £5,900 using the Retail Price Index and £127,000 using average earnings in 2009. See Lawrence H. Officer and Samuel H. Williamson (2011) Purchasing Power of Money in the United States from 1774 to 2010. (www.measuringworth.com/ppowerus/) which provides a converter for the purchasing power of the pound from 1245 to (currently) 2009. An article by Phelps Brown & Hopkins (1956) provides an index for the price of consumables and builders' wages in southern England from 1264 to 1954 using 1451-1475 as the base. The unit of consumables had risen from 83 to 3,825 over this period.

[18] Biddle Martin (1985) p.369.

[19] Although grammatically there should be an apostrophe the Victorian Ordnance Survey maps and present road names refer to Nuns and Monks Road, and King Alfred Place.

[20] Grover R. and Ng'ombe A. (2012) 'Land Owners'. In: Susan J. Smith, Marja Elsinga, Lorna Fox O'Mahony, Ong Seow Eng, Susan Wachter, Sasha Tsenkova, editors. *International Encyclopedia of Housing and Home*, Vol 4. Oxford: Elsevier. pp.152–156.

[21] For example, in 1729 Mary Wayte held 55 acres on a copyhold for three lives from the manor of Abbots Worthy paying a reserved rent of £1 16s. 3d. p.a. but with an improved value was £34 3s. 9d.. Even when allowance is made of a renewal fine of £130 and a heriot of the three best beasts, this left a substantial profit rent for the copyholder. HRO 77M95/2.

[22] In Abbots Worthy Manor in 1729, Richard Winnall held 33 acres on a lease of three lives with a reserved rent of £1 2s. 2d. but an estimated improved rent of £18 17s. 10d. This left a substantial profit rent even allowing for a surrender fine of £28 and a heriot of £2 10s. Hampshire Record Office - HRO :77M95/2.

[23] Keene Derek (1985) *Survey of medieval Winchester. Winchester Studies*; Vol. 2 Oxford: Clarendon. The City's Tarrage Rolls recorded the annual ground rent paid to the King as Lord of the City. Surveys were undertaken at regular periods, including 1410 and 1590, giving a record of land ownership both before and after the Dissolution of the monasteries.

[24] A coloured map of Hyde Abbey's land in the northern suburb in 1417 can be found in James Thomas Beaumont (2007) *Winchester from prehistory to the Present*. Stroud: Tempus Colour plate 11.

[25] Pennell R. F. (1909) *Account of the Parish of Hyde*. Winchester: Gilbert p.17.

[26] Woodward G. W. O. (1966) *Dissolution of the Monasteries*. London: Blandford Press Ltd p.2.

[27] Knowles M. D. & Hadcock R. N. (1971) *Medieval Religious Houses: England and Wales* p. 494.

[28] Hare John (1999) *The Dissolution of the Monasteries in Hampshire*. Hampshire Papers No. 16. Winchester: Hampshire County Council p.1.

[29] Hare John (1999) p.2.

[30] Woodward G. W. O. (1966) p.13.

[31] Traditionally, demesne land was retained by the lord of a manor for his own use.

[32] Jack Sybil (1965) 'Monastic lands in Leicestershire and their administration on the eve of dissolution'. *Leicestershire Archaeological and Historical Society Transactions 41,* pp.9-40.

[33] Bernard G. W. (2011) The Dissolution of the Monasteries. *Journal of the Historical Association.* Vol. 96. No. 324 pp.390-409.

[34] Edwards Edward (ed.) (1866) p.lxvi.

[35] Gardiner James (ed.) (1888) *Letters and Papers, Foreign and Domestic of Henry VIII* Vol.11. Found at www.british-history.ac.uk/source.aspx?pubid=852.

Text found at www.bbc.co.uk/radio4/history/sceptred_isle/page/48.shtml?question=48

[36] Woodward G. W. O. (1966) pp.50-52.

[37] Edwards Edward (ed.) (1866) p.lxxx.

[38] Bernard G. W. (2011).

[39] The abbot Richard Whiting, even though old and in poor health, was sent to the Tower on the charge of stealing from his abbey and hence hung, drawn and quartered. Foster R. E. (2008). The nursery rhyme *Little Jack Horner* is said to be inspired by the story of events leading up to the closure. In order to protect the Abbey's future, the Abbey's steward, Horner, was sent to bribe the King with the deeds of 12 manors which were hidden in a pie for safe travel. Horner, realising that the bribe would be unsuccessful, extracted one of the title deeds from the pie – that of the manor of Mells which contained lead (plumbum) mines. Hence the words 'He pulled out a plum'.

[40] Youings Joyce (1971) *The Dissolution of the Monasteries*. London: George Allen & Unwin p.5.

[41] Woodward G. W. O. (1966) pp.134-138.

[42] Bernard G.W. (2011).

[43] Edwards Edward (1866) p.lxxi.

[44] Oxford Dictionary of National Biography. Available online.

[45] HRO:5M53/988.

[46] See Kitchen G. W. (1890) *Winchester*. Historic Towns series. London: Longmans, Green & Co. p.69 for a full list.

[47] Rowse A. L. (1965) 'Thomas Wriothesley. First Earl of Southampton' *The Huntington Library Quarterly.* Vol. 28 No 2. pp.105-129. California: University of California Press.

[48] Sir William Sandys also benefitted by his friendship in the royal court, although unlike Paulet his roles were minor. He became a Knight of the Garter in 1518, Lord Sandys in 1523 and Lord Chamberlain in 1530. At the Dissolution he received Mottisfont Priory from the King in exchange for land in Chelsea and Paddington. Mottisfont suffered much the same fate as Titchfield under Wriothesley's hand. The cloisters survived as the main court of the

house but other parts of the priory were demolished. Sandys died in 1540 and the former monastic properties passed to his heir. The Vyne, near Basingstoke, where little of Sandys' original building has survived, and Mottisfont are now owned by the National Trust. There were few changes of ownership between the Dissolution and the present day. The Chute family purchased the Vyne in 1659 when, as a result of the Civil War, the Sandys needed to release capital. After 300 years of ownership the Chute family passed the estate to the National Trust in 1956. Mottisfont remained in the Sandys family until 1934 when it was sold to Gilbert Russell. Russell was a descendent of the priory's founder and also a relative of the Dukes of Bedford. Russell's wife gave the estate to the National Trust in 1957.

[49] Hare John (1999) *The Dissolution of the Monasteries in Hampshire* Hampshire Papers No. 16. Winchester: Hampshire County Council. pp.13-14.

[50] Rosen Adrienne (1975) *Economic and social aspects of the history of Winchester 1520-1670*. Unpublished D.Phil, University of Oxford.p.67.

[51] Woodward G. W. O. (1966).

[52] Pennell R. F. (1909) p.20.

[53] Doubleday Arthur H & Page William (eds.) (1973) 'Houses of Benedictine monks: New Minster, or the Abbey of Hyde.' *A History of the County of Hampshire: Vol. 2* pp.116-122.

[54] A fuller description is given in Page William (ed.) (1912) *A History of the County of Hampshire*. Victoria County History Vol. 5 p.20.

[55] Jack Sybil (1965).

[56] The location of these meadows is not specified. Connyngar (later spelt Conyger) is probably the plot of ground to the south of Abbots Barton farmhouse later called Coney Green Close. Coney was a rabbit warren. See William Godden's map of Winchester, 1750. HRO:3M46/1.

[57] The Soke was the land outside the City's north and east walls and belonged to the Bishop.

[58] Pennell R. F. (1909) *Account of the Parish of Hyde*. Winchester: Gilbert p.20.

[59] Page William (1908) 'The parish of Micheldever', *A History of the County of Hampshire:* Volume 3. pp. 390-394. Page William (1909) 'Parishes: Kings Worthy', *A History of the County of Hampshire:* Volume 4, pp. 430-433. Page William (1912) 'Winchester: Hyde Abbey', *A History of the County of Hampshire:* Volume 5, pp.20-21.

[60] Details of the Wriothesley's machinations within Parliament can be found in Rowse A. L. (1965) pp.123-4.

[61] www.baringarchive.org.uk/barings_people/biographies/sir_francis_baring.

[62] Lineage and dates for the family trees were extracted from a number of sources and triangulated to ensure accuracy.

[63] Grover Christine (2008) *The Suburban development of Winchester from c1850 to 1912*. Unpublished Ph.D. thesis, University of Southampton.

Chapter 2: Papacy and Plots

[1] James (2007).

[2] Rosen Adrienne (1981) 'Winchester in transition 1580-1700' in Clark Peter (ed.) *Country towns in pre-industrial England* pp.144-185. Leicester: Leicester University Press p.147.

[3] Bird W. H. B. (1925) *Black Book of Winchester* Winchester: Wykeham Press. Atkinson Tom (1963) *Elizabethan Winchester* London: Faber and Faber pp.31-33.

[4] Atkinson Tom (1963) *Elizabethan Winchester* London: Faber and Faber p.29.

[5] During the sixteenth to eighteenth centuries a series of maps were produced; some with pictographic presentations of buildings and others professionally surveyed. These give some indication of the changes within Hyde over the centuries. Although Speed's map of 1611 is criticised as being inaccurate in its proportions and lacking in detail it does give an indication of the extent of development at this date.

[6] Rosen Adrienne (1975).

[7] Rosen Adrienne (1975) p.212.

[8] Hampshire Observer and Winchester News (1846) *Hampshire Notes and Queries Vol. III* p.95. Winchester: Hampshire Observer Office. Rosen Adrienne (1975) p.213.

[9] James (2007) p.118.

[10] Rosen Adrienne (1975) p.75.

[11] Keene, Derek (1985) p.1162. Rosen Adrienne (1975) p.70.

[12] Rosen Adrienne (1975) p.70.

[13] Rosen Adrienne (1975) p.75.

[14] Rosen Adrienne (1975).

[15] HRO:W/A2/10.

[16] Pennell R. F. (1909) pp.30-31.

[17] A rod is 40 perches. Four rods makes an acre.

[18] Pennell R. F. (1909).

[19] Turner Alex Paul (1993) *Socio-economic aspects of non-local stone buildings in Winchester 1500-1800*. M.Phil, University of Southampton.

[20] Such lengthy and expensive procedures were immortalised in Charles Dickens's *Bleak House* and the case of Jarndyce v Jarndyce.

[21] Pennell R. F. (1909) pp.33-35.

[22] www.historyofparliamentonline.org/volume/1558-1603/member/bethell-zachariah

[23] The stone was worth 6s. 8d. per load, the burrs and flint 7s. per load, the sand 4d. per load and the chalk 16d. per load. Pennell R. F. (1909) p.35.

[24] Atkinson Tom (1963).

[25] Pennell R. F. (1909) p.43.

[26] Pennell R. F. (1909) p.90.

[27] A quit rent was payable to the King or owner of the freehold whereby the price is paid up-front and a nominal rent is reserved to acknowledge tenure. The name derives from a manorial system whereby the payer was no longer liable to provide a service to the lord.

[28] HRO:W/D6/7 and Pennell R. F. (1909).

[29] Pennell R. F. (1909) p.44. HRO: W/F1/31/1.

[30] Page William (1911) 'Parishes: Headbourne Worthy', *A History of the County of Hampshire:* Volume 4, pp. 426-430.

[31] The tradesmen were a powerful and opinionated body within the City. In 1664, four years after Charles II started his reign, Captain Edmund Clerke, probably the same Edmund owner of Hyde Abbey Farm, threw the Mayor and some aldermen into the prison at the Castle. The charge was not made clear and the King's Council intervened and ordered Clerke to give a full account and apology to them. He failed to do so and was sent to prison himself.

[32] HRO:13M85W/1-2.

[33] HRO:13M85W/1-2. A messuage refers to the property which could include a house, outbuildings, a yard, gardens or orchard. A capital messuage is the main residence on an estate.

[34] Legal terminology was often derived from French. Bargain and sold was similar to feoffment (or gift usually of the freehold) which was the predominant method of land transfer until 1536, although it was still recognised until the land tenure reforms of 1925. 'Feoffment by livery of seizin' was the ceremony of delivery of possession. Documents used the past tense recording what had taken place and were used in the eighteenth and nineteenth centuries to add validity to the legal process.

[35] Land on the east side of Worthy Road, south of Abbots Barton farmhouse.

[36] HRO:13M85W/1-2.

[37] HRO:13M85W/3.

[38] Kemble, J. V. H. & Kirby, W. S. (1995) *The History and Development of the Abbotts Barton Estate.* Winchester Private publication pp.9-10.

[39] Gardiner James (ed.) (1883) *Letters and Papers, Foreign and Domestic. Henry VIII* Vol. 7. HRO:1521B/29.

[40] Kemble, J. V. H. & Kirby, W. S. (1995) p.35.

[41] HRO:5M53/313, 319.

[42] Rosen Adrienne (1975) p.69.

[43] See Parker Karen (2009) *A comparison of Winchester and Southampton house interiors and furnishings from probate inventories, 1447-1575.* Unpublished Ph.D. Thesis, University of Southampton.

[44] Otterbourne is a village just south of Winchester and Selborne, home of Gilbert White the naturalist, is 16 miles away.

[45] Pennell R. F. (1909) p.25.

[46] Pennell R. F. (1909) p.25.

[47] Kemble, J. V. H. & Kirby, W. S. (1995) p.11.

[48] Pennell R. F. (1909) p.27. The location of Penynton is not known.

[49] HRO:5M53/338.

[50] 1559 Act of Supremacy. The Monarch was the supreme governor of Church of England. Clergy were required to take an oath of supremacy on pain of deprivation.

1559 Act of Uniformity. This imposed the Book of Common Prayer. Those failing to attend church on a Sunday were fined one shilling.

1563   Forbidden to defend papal supremacy. Those that did were subject to forfeiture of property (Praemunire).

1571   Treason to call monarch heretic or to introduce papal bulls.

1581   Treason to convert or to be converted to Catholicism. Recusants were fined £20 per month.

1585   Treason for Jesuits or seminary priests to enter the country.

1587   Suspected recusants who failed to appear for trial incurred guilt.

1593   Recusants restricted to within five miles of their homes.

1605   Convicted recusants were to receive Anglican Communion once each year. Failure to do so resulted in a fine and eventual forfeiture of property.

1605   Recusants barred from office and professions.

1678   Recusants barred from Parliament.

1692   Recusants incur double Land Tax.

1699   Recusants barred from purchasing or inheriting land.

1778   Relief Act. Catholics were permitted to own land.

1791   Relief Act. Catholic clergy were permitted to exercise ministry.

1829   Emancipation Act: Catholics permitted to hold office and to sit in Parliament.

Source : www.catholic-history.org.uk/nwchs/recushandbook.htm#Penal_next

[51] Rosen Adrienne (1975) *Economic and social aspects of the history of Winchester 1520-1670.* D.Phil. Oxford: University of Oxford pp.80-88.

[52] Rosen Adrienne (1975).

[53] Pennell R. F. (1909) p.41.

[54] HRO:W/H3/22.

[55] Pennell R. F. (1909) pp.37-42, 47.

[56] Page William (ed.) (1911) 'Parishes: Brown Candover', *A History of the County of Hampshire:* Vol. 4 pp.183-184.

[57] Warner Richard (1795) *Collections for the History of Hampshire and the Bishopric of Winchester.* Vol. 1. London: Warner (self-published). Quoted in Pennell R. F. (1909) *Account of the Parish of Hyde.* Winchester: Gilbert p.42.

[58] Turner Alex Paul (1993).

[59] HRO:5M53/638.

[60] Kemble, J. V. H. & Kirby, W. S. (1995) *The History and Development of the Abbotts Barton Estate.* Winchester. Private publication p.14.

[61] See Figure 1.9 and above.

[62] More detailed maps are found in Keene Derek (1985).

[63] Keene Derek (1985) p.948.

[64] Keene Derek (1985) p.960.

[65] www.hants.gov.uk/hampshiretreasures/vol04/. The cornice was a decorative band crowning a building. The dentil pattern features a tooth effect.

[66] Keene Derek (1985) p.964.

[67] Keene Derek (1985) pp.1039-1040.

[68] Keene Derek (1985) pp.965-966.

[69] Keene Derek (1985) pp.968-70.

Chapter 3: The custodians of Abbots Barton

[1] www.epsomandewellhistoryexplorer.org.uk/MynneG.html.
Malden H. E. (1911) 'Parishes: Epsom', *A History of the County of Surrey:* Vol. 3 (1911), pp.271-278. www.british-history.ac.uk/report.aspx?.

[2] Page William (ed.) (1911) 'Parishes: Steventon' *A History of the County of Hampshire:* Volume 4, pp.171-174.

[3] HRO:39M89/E/B614/8, 39M89/E/B605.

[4] Page William (ed.) (1911) pp.171-174.
www.epsomandewellhistoryexplorer.org.uk/MynneG.html.

[5] Burke John (1835) *History of the Commoners of Great Britain and Ireland.* Vol. 1. London. Leigh William Austen and Knight Montague George (1911) *Chawton Manor and its owners.* London. Smith, Elder & Co.

[6] HRO:39M89/E/B615.

[7] HRO:39M89/E/T/17.

[8] Leigh William Austen and Knight Montague George (1911).

[9] HRO:39M89/E/B614/8,9.

[10] Cited in 39M89/E/B132. This is a revised copy where Thomas May is later referred to as Knight.

[11] Coss Peter (2003) *The Origins of the English Gentry.* Cambridge: Cambridge University Press pp 2-11. The author and reviewer of this book disagree whether the terms lesser aristocracy or lesser nobility who existed from late Anglo-Saxon until Victorian times are synonymous with gentry (www.history.ac.uk/reviews/review/402).

[12] This contrasted with the later phenomena of the 'pseudo' gentry, who received income from urban property and various investments in trade, transport and stocks and shares.

[13] HRO:39M89/E/B611/9-11.

[14] Nokes Davis (1997) *Jane Austen. A life.* London: Fourth Estate Ltd p34.

[15] HRO:39M89/E/B132.

[16] HRO :39M89/E/B132.

[17] HRO:13M85W/3,5,6.

[18] HRO:13M85W/4.

[19] HRO:13M85W/7-8.

[20] HRO:13M85W/9-12.

[21] HRO:13M85W/13-15,17.

[22] HRO:13M85W/18-26.

[23] HRO:13M85W/27.

[24] Habakkuk John (1994) *Marriage, debt and the estate system: English Ownership 1650-1950.* Oxford: Clarendon Press p.372.

[25] Hasted Edward (1798) 'Parishes: Godmersham', *The History and Topographical Survey of the County of Kent:* Volume 7, pp.319-332.

[26] Nokes Davis (1997) pp.72-3.

[27] It is recorded that they had ten children but none survived. See Plantagenet Roll of the Blood Royal available at www.ancestry.co.uk.

[28] Nokes Davis (1997) p395. Letter 52.

[29] Both Lewis Cage and William Deedes were brothers-in-law to Edward Austen by their marriages to Sir Brook Bridges' eldest two daughters Fanny and Sophia respectively. Mary Deedes and Fanny Cage are mentioned in Jane Austen's letters. Le Faye (1995 3rd edition) *Jane Austen's Letters*. Oxford: OUP

[30] HRO:13M85W/38.

[31] Le Faye Deirdre (1995, 3rd ed.) p.34.

[32] The history of the bookshop is given in Bolton Clare (1991) *A Winchester Bookshop and Bindery 1729-1994.* Winchester: P & G Wells. Le Faye Deirdre (1995, 3rd ed.) p.22 (footnote 10 p.362).

[33] Le Faye Deirdre (1995, 3rd ed.) p.23. 'Mr May' was likely to be have been Thomas May, whose daughter married Blackall Simonds, a Reading brewer in 1783. William Simonds, who purchased Abbots Barton from Edward Knight in 1811, was a relative of Blackall Simonds. See Chapter 6 for the history of this family and their connection to Hyde.

[34] HRO:13M85W/39-40.

[35] HRO:13M85W/36-37.

Chapter 4: Abbots Barton and Hyde Abbey Farms

[1] HRO:39M89/E/B616/1-14.

[2] HRO:39M89/E/B616/1-14.

[3] HRO:39M89/E/B616/1-14.

[4] HRO:39M89/E/B616/1-14.

[5] HRO:39M89/E/B616/1-14.

[6] HRO:39M89/E/B616/1-14.

[7] Vancouver Charles (1810) *General view of the agriculture of Hampshire including the Isle of Wight.* London: Richard Phillips p.105. This is available as a Google digitalised book.

[8] HRO:AV12/11/51.

[9] Vancouver Charles (1810) pp.55-58.

[10] Vancouver Charles (1810) p.79.

[11] No date given. Vancouver Charles (1810) p.218.

[12] Vancouver Charles (1810) pp.218-251. Note the computational errors in the printed text have been corrected. One square yards equals 0.836 square metres.

[13] Vancouver Charles (1810) p.80.

[14] The River Itchen and its streams, meander southwards through Martyr Worthy and Abbots Worthy, entering the City in the north east at Durngate, close to Winnall Moors. Passing through the City by means of its main channel and Upper, Middle and Lower Brooks, the Itchen emerges on the south side and continues on its path past St Catherine's Hill, through Otterbourne and eventually out to the sea at Southampton.

[15] HRO:18M61 Box F, Bundle 1. 18M54, C of 6, Box H, Pkt F, No. 27.

[16] Vancouver Charles (1810) p.461.

[17] Vancouver Charles (1810) p.462.

[18] Vancouver Charles (1810) pp.201-204.

[19] For a review see Bettey Joseph (1999) 'The development of water meadows in the southern counties' in Cook Hadrian and Williamson Tom *Water management in the English landscape*. Edinburgh: Edinburgh University Press.

[20] Bettey Joseph (1999) p.179.

[21] Bowie, G. G. S. (1978) 'Watermeadows in Wessex: a re-evaluation for the period 1640-1850'. *Agricultural History Review*, 35. p.155.

[22] Bowie G. G. S. (1978) p.156.

[23] Bettey Joseph (1999) p.182.

[24] Bettey Joseph (1999) p.181. One foot is equal to 0.305 metres.

[25] Jones.L (1960) 'Eighteenth-century changes in Hampshire chalkland farming'. *Agricultural History Review* 8 pp.5-19. Afton Bethanie (1996) 'The great agricultural depression on the English chalklands: the Hampshire experience'. *Agricultural History Review*. 44 pp.191-205. Bowie, G. G. S. (1978) pp.151-158. Bettey Joseph (1999) pp.179-195.

[26] Vancouver Charles (1810) pp.276-277.

[27] HRO: 18M54, C of 6, Box H, Pkt 1.

[28] HRO:149M89/R4/6032.

[29] HRO:149M89/R4/6032.

[30] Reynolds J., Burrell C. and Dignell D. (1967) 'Durngate Mill, Winchester' *Proceedings of the Hampshire Field Club and Archaeological Society.* Vol. 24. pp.103-12.

[31] Oxford Dictionary of National Biography. Available online.

[32] Oxford Dictionary of National Biography. Available online.

[33] HRO:149M89/R4/6032.

[34] HRO:149M89/R4/6032.

[35] HRO:W/F5/1/10.

[36] Roberts Edward (2003) *Hampshire houses 1250-1700: their dating and development.* Winchester: Hampshire County Council p.249.

[37] HRO:39M89/E/B561/7.

[38] The writing is sometimes difficult to interpret and there may be errors in this transcript.

[39] HRO:39M89/E/B560/1-11.

[40] HRO:13M85W/22-23. This document refers to the two undivided one-third parts and this has been removed from the description given.

[41] The total from the table has an error of one rod.

[42] *Oxford Dictionary of National Biography*. Available online.

[43] HRO:W/K4/1/15/1.

[44] See Chapter 2.

[45] HRO:5M53/210.

[46] HRO:13M85W/30-31.

[47] Kemble, J. V. & Kirby, W. S. (1994) 'Abbots Barton Estate, Winchester. Land Use in the 16th to 20th Centuries.' *Hants Field Club 21* pp.17-20.

[48] HRO:13M85W/32.

[49] The area became the site of Highfield Lodge and Hyde Lodge in the late 1830s.

[50] The map has been divided to aid clarity.

[51] Kemble, J. V. & Kirby, W. S. (1994).

[52] Hornsey Ian Spencer (2003) *A history of beer and brewing*. Cambridge: Royal Society of Chemistry p.324.

[53] There was a mill at Durngate for over 700 years and it was first named in a lease in 1213. It was demolished in 1966, unlike the City Mill further south which survived and is now owned by the National Trust.

[54] Reynolds J, Burrell C and Dignell D. (1967) 'Durngate Mill, Winchester' *Proceedings of the Hampshire Field Club and Archaeological Society*. Vol. 24 pp.103-12. HRO:13M85W/95.

[55] HRO:13M85W/34.

[56] HRO:13M85W/34.

[57] HRO:13M85W/36-38.

[58] HRO:13M85W/36-37.

[59] HRO:13M85W/99,100.

[60] HRO:13M85W/95,100

Chapter 5 : Hyde Street and its community in the eighteenth and nineteenth centuries

[1] HRO:39M89/E/B614/8,9 1717-24 Computation of the annual revenue of Winchester Turnpike.

[2] HRO:39M89/E/B614/8,9.

[3] Details of ownership are given below. *Oxford Dictionary of National Biography*. Available online.

[4] HRO:44M69/G1/129.

[5] Allen Mark (1999). *A Railway Revolution? A census-based analysis of the economic, social and topological effects of the coming of the railway upon the city of Winchester c1830-c1890*. Unpublished Ph.D. thesis, University of Southampton.

[6] Allen Mark (1999).

[7] Pennell R. F. (1909) *Account of the Parish of Hyde*. Winchester: Gilbert pp.50-55.

[8] The Bridewell and Hyde Abbey School are discussed later in the chapter.

[9] Smith Mark (ed.) (2004) *Doing the duty of the Parish: Survey of the Church*. Hampshire Record Series Vol. XV11. Winchester: Hampshire County Council.

[10] HRO:W/F5/1/10.

[11] See Chapter 6 for a history of the Swan.

[12] See Chapter 2 for a history of Hyde House and garden.

[13] www.hants.gov.uk/hampshiretreasures/vol04/.

[14] Gapper Claire, Parker Karen and Robert Edward (2002) 'Elizabethan and Jacobean Decorative features at Hyde, Winchester' in *Hampshire Studies. Proceedings Hampshire Field Club Archaeological Society*. Vol. 57. pp.59-80. See pp.76-79

[15] Winchester Museums PWCM 15996.

[16] Keene Derek (1985) *Survey of medieval Winchester*. Winchester Studies; Vols. 1 &. 2 Oxford: Clarendon.

[17] HRO: 157M89W/5/2422.

[18] Winchester City Museum: PWCM 16559. www.hants.gov.uk/hampshiretreasures/vol04/.

[19] Milner John (1798) *The history and survey of the antiquities of Winchester Vols. 1 & 2*. Winchester: Robbins.

[20] HRO:55M81W PO3 and HRO:Q22/1/271.

[21] The parish included properties in North Walls.

[22] HRO:55M81W PO3.

[23] Dickens Charles (1850) *Household Words* Vol.1 No. 8. London: Bradbury & Evans. Found at http://www.djo.org.uk/household-words/volume-i/page-187.html.

[24] HRO:11M70/C3/1&2.

[25] HRO:13M85W/161.

[26] Pennell R. F. (1909) pp.68-71.

[27] HRO:11M70/C3/2.

[28] He also looked after Jane Austen prior to her death in 1817. Hawkridge Audrey (1995) *Jane Austen and Hampshire*. Hampshire Papers No. 6. Winchester: Hampshire County Council. p.27.

[29] The schoolroom had several different uses including a Dissenters' Chapel, Hampshire Museum (1847-1851) and, from 1877 the Soldier's Home ran by the Misses Perks.

[30] Cobbett William (1967) *Rural Rides*. Aylesbury: Penguin p.254. Cobbett's book was first published in 1830.

[31] For example, the kitchen was to have one course of oak plugs 9 in. by 2¼ in. all round for the skirting board, 9in. high, a discharging piece over the chimney arches 8½ in. by 4½ in. of fir; an inch deal shelf, 9in. wide over the chimney; doors of 6ft 6in. high by 2ft 10in., with four panel doors, with plain mouldings on both sides of the doorway; windows frame to be 5in square of oak and the inside of the windows to be lined all round with inch deal with a bead in the edge rabbeted to receive plastering.

[32] HRO:44M69/E18/1/94.

[33] Edwards Edward (ed.) (1866) *Liber Monasterii de Hyda; Chronicle of the Affairs of England, from the settlement of the Saxons to the reign of King Cnut and a Chartulary of the Abbey of Hyde, in Hampshire A.D. 455-1023*. London: Longmans, Green, Reader and Dyer p.lxxvi.

[34] The frequency is not given.

[35] HRO:44M69/K1/16, HRO: 44M69/E18/1/94.

[36] HRO:92M95/F2/1/19.

[37] HRO:92M95/F2/1/44-46.

[38] HRO:92M95/F2/1/44-46.

[39] HRO:92M95/F2/1/44-46.

[40] HRO:92M95/F2/1/46.

[41] *HMSO (1835)* Commissioners of Inquiry into the excise establishment, and into the management and collection of the excise revenue throughout the United Kingdom. Malt. London: His Majesty's Stationery Office. pp.1-69.

[42] *HMSO (1835)* pp. 1-69.

[43] Corley T. A. B. (1975) 'Simonds' Brewery at Reading 1760-1960' in *Berks Archaeological Journal* Vol. 68 pp.77-88.

[44] HRO:206M85W/19-21,23-25.

[45] HRO:206M85W/34.

[46] HRO:206M85W/35.

[47] HRO:206M85W/88,89.

[48] Photographs of these plaques are held by Winchester Museum Services. The name Deane has been severely eroded.

[49] HRO:206M85W/90,91.

[50] Little is known about Nathaniel Fletcher, however he may have been the person made deacon in 1788 and priest in 1809 in the Winchester diocese.

[51] HRO:206M85W/36,37.

[52] HRO:206M85W/38. The Rodney's Head, The Britannia and similar named public houses are written more simply using 'the'.

[53] HRO:206M85W/60,61.

[54] HRO:206M85W/52.

[55] HRO:206M85W/52.

[56] HRO:206M85W/54-59.

[57] HRO:206M85W/66,67.

Chapter 6: William Simonds, the farmer

[1] HRO:AV12/11/51.

[2] Le Faye Deirdre (1995 3rd ed.) *Jane Austen's Letters*. Oxford: OUP p.495.

[3] HRO:13M85W/41,42.

[4] HRO:13M85W119.

[5] HRO:13M85W119.

[6] HRO:13M85W119.

[7] HRO:13M85W119.

[8] HRO:13M85W 120-121.

[9] HRO:13M85W120-121.

[10] See Allen Mark (1999) for a map.

[11] HRO: 13M85W122-123.

[12] Mogg Edward (1841) *Southampton Railway and Isle of Wight guide*. London: Mogg p22.

[13] Mogg Edward (1841).

[14] The National Archives - TNA:1841 Census Winchester.

[15] See Massey Doreen B & Catalano Alejandrina (1978) *Capital and land: landownership by capital in Great Britain*. London: Edward Arnold p 81.

[16] TNA:1851 Census Winchester.

[17] Grover (2008).

[18] TNA:1861 Census Winchester.

[19] HRO:67M92W/8/7.

[20] HRO:67M92W/26/3.

[21] HRO:67M92W/26/3.

[22] Pennell R. F. (1909) pp.78-80.

[23] Wells C. W. and Charles (1961) *The Story of St Bartholomew's Hyde*. Ramsgate: Graham Cumming.

[24] Pennell R. F. (1909) p.97.

[25] HRO:55M8/W/PW2 Book 38B. The 1907 sales catalogue for Lankhills, built by Bowker, includes Sheep Fair Field, next to the Worthy Road.

[26] Pennell R. F. (1909) p.85.

[27] Pennell R. F. (1909) pp.85-6.

[28] Freeman Robin (1991) *The art and architecture of Owen Browne Carter (1806-1859)*. Winchester: Hampshire County Council.

[29] For a photograph see Winchester Museums Services: 16304-16305.

[30] *Sadler's Directory of Hampshire 1784, Pigot's Directory of Hampshire 1828,* and *Gilmour's Directory of Winchester 1854.*

[31] TNA:1841 Census of England and Wales.

[32] HRO:55M81/W.

[33] Mrs Gradeige (1), Mrs Batt (4), Mr Curtis (4), Exors of James Young (2 plus a store), Mr Barnes (1), Mr Duke (2), Mrs Theobald (6), Mr Burnett (1), James Theobald (1 plus two meads), Charles Shutin(?) (1), Theobald (brew house, stable and house), James Wyeth (1), Mr C Richards (1), Mr Fry (1), Mr Gradeige (10 and a brewhouse), Mr Gover (3), Mr Banner (1), Mr Pragnel (1).

[34] TNA:1851 Census Winchester. In the 1851 census, the houses were numbered consecutively from the Swan Inn northwards.

[35] See Chapter 6 for the history of the Brewery and the Simonds family of Reading.

[36] *Gilmour's Winchester Directory 1854.*

[37] HRO:206M85W/26,27,43,44,62,63,66,67.

[38] HRO:206M85W/45,46.

[39] HRO:206M85W/68-73.

[40] HRO:206M85W/78.

[41] HRO:206M85W/17.

[42] HRO:206M85W/17.

[43] In the 1980s, the surviving cellars stretched along the northern boundary of the site with a perpendicular passage at the far eastern end and another L-shaped extension closer to the street. Doughty Martin (1989) 'The history and archaeology of the Hyde brewery,

Winchester. Part one: The archaeological survey' in *Proceedings of Hampshire Field Club Archaeology* 45 pp.191-212. Part two was never written.

[44] HRO:206M85W/17.

[45] HRO:206M85W/17.

[46] HRO:206M85W/17.

[47] HRO:206M85W/17.

[48] HRO:206M85W/17.

[49] HRO:206M85W/17.

[50] HRO:206M85W/17.

[51] HRO:55M81/W.

[52] HRO:206M85W/81

[53] HRO:206M85W/81,82,96.

[54] HRO:13M85W/136,137.

Chapter 7: William Barrow Simonds, the developer

[1] *Oxford Dictionary of National Biography.*

[2] TNA: RG11/1231-1233 1881 Census Winchester.

[3] HRO:AV/12/19/51. Professor Tom Beaumont James, private communication.

[4] Edward James (1858) Statistical Table of the population, taxation, number of electors, inhabited houses, £10 householders and MPs in the United Kingdom of Great Britain and Ireland. London: Houlston and Wright.

[5] Turner Michael (2004) 'Agriculture, 1860-1914' in Floud Roderick & Johnson Paul (eds) (2004) *Cambridge Economic History of Modern Britain Vol.2 1860-1939*. Cambridge University Press. Turner cites the 1850 to 1854 annual rents for arable at approximately 22s. and for pasture at 18s. per acre.

[6] Afton Bethanie (1996) 'The great agricultural depression on the English chalklands : the Hampshire experience'. *Agricultural History Review*, 44. pp.191-205.

[7] Habakkuk John (1994) *Marriage, debt and the estate system: English Ownership 1650-1950*. Oxford: Clarendon Press p.649.

[8] HRO:13M85W124i.

[9] HRO: AV/12/19/51.

[10] HR26O: 13M85W/48.

[11] For example, Eagles Field was a compact plot just outside the walls, surrounded by older housing and commercial developments in Hyde.

[12] Dennis states that the ground landlord's preference for tenure depended on whether his interests were short or long term (although influenced by the political, sociological and economic conditions pervading at the time). See Dennis Richard (1984) *English industrial cities of the nineteenth century: a social geography*. Cambridge: Cambridge University Press. Aristocratic landlords sought a regular income with capital gains realised when the leases fell in. As discussed previously, new leases resulted in increased ground rent and the potential of a managed rack rent. Small-scale landowners might seek to have immediate returns by selling

the freehold especially on fragmented holdings. Some cities had a preponderance of one type of tenure or the other. However, Winchester was mixed. The Dean and Chapter went for freehold and Simonds favoured leasehold.

[13] This was consistent with the multiple for agricultural land. See discussion in Nicholas Tom (1999) 'Business and land ownership in the late nineteenth century' *Economic History Review, New Series* Vol.52 No. 1 pp.27-44.

[14] Nicholas Tom (1999) p.43.

[15] Massey states that the landed aristocracy was not allowed to sub-let its estates without an Act of Parliament, hence development proceeded only by assigning building leases. Massey Doreen B. & Catalano Alejandrina (1978) *Capital and land: landownership by capital in Great Britain*. London: Edward Arnold.

[16] HRO: 13M85W/56. St Bede's School, still in existence today, has recently suffered flooding following wet winters and the resultant increasing height of the water table. This has necessitated the raising of the floor to prevent further ingress of water and illustrates the continuing problems of drainage within the low lying meadows. Even the Cathedral's crypt is often under water in winter months.

[17] HRO:13M85W/63.

[18] HRO:13M85W/48.

[19] HRO: PL3/19/34&63c.

[20] HRO:13M85W/49.

[21] The story was made into a film in 1998.

[22] Information referenced 1861 and 1871 are found in the respective censuses. THA: RG9/691-693 1861 Census (Winchester). TNA:RG10/ 1209-1212,1871 Census (Winchester).

[23] Information reference as 1891 is found in the 1891 census. TNA: RG12/936-938 1891 Census (Winchester).

[24] HRO:13M85W/57.

[25] The Celtic name for Winchester.

[26] HRO:13M85W/53.

[27] HRO:W/E10/1/23. HRO:13M85W/59.

[28] HRO:W/E10/1/8,13,23.

[29] HRO:157M89W/2 p.865.

[30] For a full account of Colson's life and works see Poole Brenda (2000) *John Colson: a Hampshire architect of the Victorian age*. Hampshire Papers No 20. Winchester: Hampshire County Council.

[31] HRO: 157M89W/1 p.120.

[32] HRO:13M85W/48.

[33] Schoolmasters, even those employed in the church or Winchester College, commonly set up their own schools. Many of Winchester College's houses, for example in Edgar Road and Compton Road, were built to house Commoners. See Grover (2008).

[34] Roberts Edward (1977) *In and around Winchester*. Alresford: Laurence Oxley plate 69.

[35] HRO:38M48/229.

[36] HRO:13M85W/48.

[37] HRO:157M89W/1 p.144.

[38] In c1910 Frederick Bowker also owned No. 24 to 29 Wales Street, Nos. 20-22 St Thomas Street and No. 3 Southgate Street as well as his own residence Fyfhyde.

[39] HRO:13M85W/48.

[40] HRO:157M89W/2 p.806. When the house was sold by Mrs Kaines (date unknown), one of the reception rooms was described as a 'smoking room'.

[41] HRO:157M89W/1 p.148.

[42] HRO:157M89W/3 p.68.

[43] HRO:51M76/P/6/44.

[44] HRO:W/E10/1/43,44 St Bartholomew's rate books.

[45] There is some discrepancy between the estate map which clearly states the land was sold to Micklam and later sales details which talk of a 1,000 year lease.

[46] HRO:W/E10/1/43.

[47] HRO:157M89W/3 p.348.

[48] HRO:157M89W/1 p.56.

[49] Financially-strapped families and widows often took on lodgers. Those described as boarders may have been relatives or had some other social connection.

[50] HRO:157M89W/1 p.192.

[51] HRO:98A02/6.

[52] HRO:157M89W/4 p.1487.

[53] HRO:157M89W/4 p.1421.

[54] John Barnes Colson had followed his father's footsteps as Cathedral architect.

[55] Survey by Board of Trade in 1890s using 2,000 households. www.nationalarchives.gov.uk/education/victorianbritain/divided/source6.htm

[56] The Abbots Barton stretch of the Itchen is regarded as the home of fly-fishing. George Edward Mackenzie Skues, a London solicitor, developed the technique in 1910 and published the results in *Minor Tactics of the Chalk Stream* in 1910. www.flyfishinghistory.com/skues.htm.

[57] HRO:4M94/2, W/C11/2/1130, 117M85W/3-6.

[58] HRO:W/C11/2/347.

[59] HRO:W/C11/2/323,341,352,358,432,450, 503, 519,542,554.

[60] Building Control Plans HRO: W/C11/1/n (1878-95) and W/C11/2/n (1895-1963).

[61] HRO:157M89W/1 p.142.

[62] HRO:W/C11/2/1361 and HRO:38M48/223.

[63] HRO: W/C11/2/1361.

[64] The 1871 census for Winchester is available on CD. Allen Mark & James Tom Beaumont (2006) *The 1871 Census of Winchester* (CD). Winchester: Wessex Historical Databases.

[65] See James T. B. (1993) *Winchester: a pictorial history,* for a picture of Kaines's shop.

[66] Dyos H. J. (1961) *Victorian Suburb*. London: Leicester University Press p.83.

Chapter 8: The suburban estates for the mass market

[1] Details of these estates are given later in the chapter.

[2] The first verse of the music hall song 'My old man said follow the van' began:

> We had to move away
>
> 'Cos the rent we couldn't pay.
>
> The moving van came round just after dark...

[3] James, T. B. (1993) *Winchester: a pictorial history*. Chichester: Phillimore.

[4] HRO:13M85W/46.

[5] HRO:13M85W/44. The first plot bounded by the river, measured 11 feet 6 inches in the north, 48 feet in the south and 116 feet north to south. The second plot, a corner piece, is described as being 'near Mr Simonds hatch, 109 feet 3 inches siding the river.'

[6] HRO:W/E10/1/8. TNA:1871 Census of Winchester. Northbrook's contribution to the development of Hyde is discussed later in the chapter. Blake was a developer.

[7] H/CS2/2/75-76.

[8] Ropewalks were common on the edges of towns in the late eighteenth and early nineteenth centuries, especially in ports like Liverpool. A description of the craft can be found in Sharples Joseph (2004) *Liverpool*. Pevsner Architectural Guides. London: Yale p.196.

[9] These are average measurements, the exact measurements were: Cole (17ft. broad, west 114 ft. 6in. and east 113 ft.); Evans (south 60 ft., north 59 ft. 6 in., east 90 ft., and west 96 ft.); Evans (south 30ft. 4in., north 29ft. 6in. depth, east 96 ft., and west 98 ft. 6in.); Evans (south 60 ft. 4in., north 59ft. 6 in. east 98ft. 6in., and west 103 ft.); and Smith (south 42 ft., north 41 ft .9in., west 113 ft., and east 110 ft.).

[10] 34M91W/771.

[11] 283M87W, W/F3/30,32.

[12] HRO:34M91W/771.

[13] HRO:13M85W/51.

[14] HRO:13M85W52.

[15] Micklam was also involved in limited development and ownership on the Highcliffe estate, in the eastern part of the city. Building plans which were required to be submitted from 1878 give an indication of an architect's importance in the City. Between this date and 1911 Micklam submitted 31 plans (8.3 per cent of the total) for 123 houses (7.4 per cent of the total).

[16] W/C11/1/138a, 149a, 157, 205, 318a & 518.

[17] HRO:W/E10/1/23 and PLS/19/33-37.

[18] HRO:W/E10/1/8,13,23.

[19] There are no directories for 1882 and 1883.

[20] HRO:305M87W. HRO: 67M92W/5/12.

[21] HRO:44M68/F2/461.

[22] For a full discussion of land law see: Simpson, Alfred William Brian (1961) *An Introduction to the History of the Land Law*. London: Oxford University Press especially pages 53, 133 and Chapter VIII. Best Geoffrey Francis Andrew (1964) *Temporal Pillars.*

Queen Anne's Bounty, the Ecclesiastical Commissioners, and the Church of England. Cambridge: Cambridge University Press. pp.348-380.

[23]See British Official Publications Collaborative Reader Information Service. www.bopcris.ac.uk/bop1833/ref3681.html.

[24] www.bopris.ac.uk/bop1833/ref3686.html.

[25] Massey (1978) *Capital and land.* p.83.

[26]Northbrook was involved in the development of several parcels of land in Winchester as well as being a philanthropist. He financed the building of Westfields School in 1877 lending £10,000 at 4% p.a. and later helped financially when the premises were re-opened as West Downs School. The school closed in the 1980s and after being vacant for several years, the building and the Master's Lodge were rescued and renovated by the University of Winchester and is now known as the West Downs Campus. See *Old West Downs Society - Memories of the Herbert/Brymer Era 1897-1922.* Found at www.westdowns.com/cornhist.htm.

[27] HRO:130M89W/1, HRO:67M92W/25/4.

[28] HRO:67W92.

[29] HRO:W/C111/1/89.

[30] He submitted 107 plans (28.9 per cent of the total lodged within the City) between 1878 and 1911 which accounted for 364 houses (22 per cent of the total planned).

[31] HRO: 67M92W/12/4.

[32] HRO:67M92W/6/4.

[33] W/C11/1/89, 140, 173, 202, 256, 260, and 296.

[34] HRO:67M92W/6/4 Eagles Field.

[35] HRO:67M92W/6/4.

[36]HRO:67M92W/18/30, HRO:67M92W/10/7 & 67M92W/5/9.

[37] HRO:67M92W/6/4. HRO:67M92W/25/4.

[38] *Monty* Evans could not be traced in the 1881 census, but could be the nickname of or be related to Albert Evans.

[39] HRO:67M92W/12/24/2.

[40] HRO:21M65/57/259/1,2.

[41] HRO:W/C11/2/145.

[42] HRO:W/C11/2/145, 184.

[43] HRO:67M92W/8/24.

[44] HRO:W/C11/2/188, 232, and 289.

[45] HRO:W/C11/2/189, ,219, 252, 304, 361, 427, and 458.

[46] HRO:W/C11/2/188 and 189, 214, 219, 252, 273, 276, 289, 293, 304, 329, 361, 382, 427, 456, 458, and 470.

[47] HRO:W/C11/2/763.

[48] The Aged Pilgrims' Friend Society was set up in 1807 to provide grants and pensions to elderly Christians.

[49] Vokes and Beck the stonemasons in Stockbridge Road only ceased business in 2006.

[50] HRO:49M95/605.

[51] Oxlease in Hyde, Queensland in Weeke and Barton Close in St. Cross.

[52] HRO:W/C1/5/273.

[53] Sanitation was a continuing issue in Winchester well into the twentieth century as Best adds "And you'll hardly credit that until after the (second) war too they still had bucket sanitation at St John's – right close to the Guildhall." Bussey Sarah (2002) *Winchester voices*. Tempus Oral History Series. Stroud : Tempus.

[54] See HRO:W/C11/2/539,563,821,853,850,904,1057.

[55] Locke A. Audrey (1912) *In praise of Winchester* London: Constable & Co Ltd.

Chapter 9: Barrow Simonds' Hyde – then and now

[1] HRO:AV/12/11/51. Memories of John Barrow Simonds. HRO:AV/19/51 Memoirs of Constance Young (nee Barrow Simonds).

[2] There is a photo of the extended Fisher family taken in the early 1900s. Winchester Museum Collection. PWCM27489.

[3] Numbering was continuous along the west side of the street. At the north end of Hyde Street, the numbers continued on the east side, in a southerly direction. Photographs of these properties can be seen in the Winchester's Museum Collection. PWCM27499, PWCM6233 and PWCM16960.

[4] HRO:AV12/11/51 Memories of John Barrow Simonds.

[5] HRO:W/F1/18.

[6] HRO:157M85W/1-53.

[7] HRO:157M89W/4/1317.

[8] It is unclear whether he was related to the Clerkes who owned Hyde Abbey up to 1693.

[9] HRO:101M91W/1.

[10] HRO:157M89W/2/940. In 1925 it was sold for £1,050.

[11] HRO:157M89W/4/1461. Not dated.

[12] HRO:157M89W/2/528.

[13] HRO:18M68W/248-263.

[14] HRO:157M89W/2/681,890.

[15] A full account of the history of the Hillier family can be found at www.weekehistory.co.uk/weeke/other/hillier.htm.

[16] Pennell R. F. (1909) p.85.

[17] HRO:114M97W/8. See Chapter 6 for a further history of the site.

[18] Previous to this, in 1786, a Richard Page built a malthouse in the area. However he was declared bankrupt in 1795 and the buildings sold. See Chapter 6.

[19] HRO:117M89W/1-19.

[20] Alton Bottle Club. http://webspace.webring.com/people/wa/altonbcc/winchester.html

[21] Roberts Edward (1977) *In and around Winchester*. Alresford: Laurence Oxley Plate 82.

[22] HRO:206M85W/97.

[23] HRO:206M85W/80.

[24] HRO:206M85W/62.

[25] HRO:206M85W/182.

[26] HRO:206M85W/182.

[27] HRO:206M85W/182.

[28] HRO:206M85W/228.

[29] HRO:206M85W/86,184.

[30] HRO:206M85W/291, 292.

[31] Doughty Martin (1989) pp.191-212.

[32] HRO:206M85W/212-4.

[33] HRO:206M85W/218.

[34] HRO:206M85W/119,218.

[35] HRO:206M85W/213,215.

[36] HRO:206M85W/217.

[37] HRO:206M85W/291,292.

[38] HRO:206M85W/218.

[39] HRO 206M85W/84.

[40] HRO:W/C11/1/456,613. HRO:W/C11/2/510, 573, 726, 739, 856,and 1099.

[41] www.hants.gov.uk/hampshiretreasures/vol04/.

[42] HRO:157M89W/3/1944.

[43] HRO:26M59/499.

[44] HRO:100M97/C1/1. HRO:100M97/A9/1. HRO:44M68/F2/461. HRO:44M68/F2/464.

[45] HRO:44M68/F2/464.

[46] Doughty Martin (1989) pp.191-212.

[47] Winchester City Council planning applications.

[48] TNA: RG 14 1911 Census (Winchester)

[49] Kemble J. V. & Kirby W. S. (1994) 'Abbotts Barton Estate, Winchester. Land Use in the 16th to 20th Centuries.' *Hants Field Club 21* p17-20. Kemble J. V. H. & Kirby W. S. (1995) *The History and Development of the Abbott's Barton Estate, Winchester*. Private publication.

[50] For a detailed account of the development of suburban estates on the former Dean and Chapter lands. See Grover Christine (2008).

[51] A detailed background to the proposals and their execution is given in Short Brian (1997) *Land and society in Edwardian Britain*. Cambridge: Cambridge University Press.

[52] HRO:PL3/19/34 to 37 and PL3/19/63. The firm of Hall, Pain and Foster still operated as estate agents until recently.

[53] See Grover Richard and Grover Christine (2010) 'The origins of the British Cadastre' for more details. www.fig.net/pub/fig2010/papers/ts10f%5Cts10f_grover_3915.pdf. The paper was presented at the FIG Congress 2010 Facing the Challenges – Building the Capacity Sydney, Australia, 11-16 April 2010.

References

Afton Bethanie (1996) 'The great agricultural depression on the English chalklands: the Hampshire experience'. *Agricultural History Review* 44 pp.191-205.

Allen Mark (1999). *A Railway Revolution? A census-based analysis of the economic, social and topological effects of the coming of the railway upon the city of Winchester c1830-c1890.* Unpublished Ph.D. thesis, University of Southampton.

Allen Mark & James Tom Beaumont (2006) *The 1871 Census of Winchester (CD).* Winchester: Wessex Historical Databases.

Atkinson Tom (1963) *Elizabethan Winchester.* London: Faber and Faber.

Bailey Keith (1990) 'The Hidation of Buckinghamshire', in *Records of Buckinghamshire,* Vol. 32, pp.1-22.

Bernard G. W. (2011) 'The Dissolution of the Monasteries'. *Journal of the Historical Association.* Vol. 96 No. 324 pp.390-409

Best Geoffrey Francis Andrew (1964) *Temporal Pillars. Queen Anne's Bounty, the Ecclesiastical Commissioners, and the Church of England.* Cambridge: Cambridge University Press pp.348-380.

Bettey Joseph (1999) 'The development of water meadows in the southern counties' in Cook Hadrian and Williamson Tom *Water management in the English landscape.* Edinburgh: Edinburgh University Press pp.179-195.

Biddle Martin (1985) *Winchester in the early Middle Ages.* Winchester Studies; Vol. I. Oxford: Clarendon.

Biddle Martin et. al. (1990) *Object and economy in medieval Winchester.* Winchester Studies; Vol. 7ii. Oxford: Clarendon.

Biddle Martin and Keene Derek (2005) *Winchester about 1800.* Winchester Studies Vol. II and Historical Town Atlas IV. Whitney: Maps International.

Birch, Walter de Gray (ed.) (1892) *Liber Vitae: Register and Martyrology of New Minster and Hyde Abbey.* Winchester: Warren & Son.

Bird W. H. B. (1925) *Black Book of Winchester.* Winchester: Wykeham Press.

Bolton Clare (1991) *A Winchester Bookshop and Bindery 1729-1994.* Winchester: P & G Wells.

Bowie G. G. S. (1978) 'Watermeadows in Wessex: a re-evaluation for the period 1640-1850'. *Agricultural History Review* 35 pp.51-8.

Bowker Alfred (1902) *The King Alfred Millenary.* London: Macmillan.

Burke John (1835) *History of the Commoners of Great Britain and Ireland.* Vol. 1. London.

Bussey Sarah (2002) *Winchester voices*. Tempus Oral History Series. Stroud: Tempus.

Catholic history. www.catholic-history.org.uk/nwchs/recushandbook.htm#Penal_next.

Chapman R. W. (1952, 2nd ed.) *Jane Austen letters*. Oxford: OUP.

Clark Peter (ed.) (1981) *Country towns in pre-industrial England*. Leicester: Leicester University Press.

Collis John et al (1978) *Winchester Excavations Vol II. 1949-60*. Winchester: City of Winchester.

Cobbett William (1967) *Rural Rides*. Aylesbury: Penguin p.254. Cobbett's book was first published in 1830.

Corley T. A. B. (1975) 'Simonds' Brewery at Reading 1760-1960' in *Berks Archaeological Journal* Vol. 68 pp.77-88.

Coss Peter (2003) *The Origins of the English Gentry*. Cambridge: Cambridge University Press.

Dennis Richard (1984) *English industrial cities of the nineteenth century: a social geography*. Cambridge: Cambridge University Press.

Dickens Charles (1850) *Household Words* Vol 1 No. 8 p. 187. London: Bradbury & Evans. Found at http://www.djo.org.uk/household-words/volume-i/page-187.html.

Doubleday Arthur H. & Page William (eds.) (1973) 'Houses of Benedictine monks: New Minster, or the Abbey of Hyde', *A History of the County of Hampshire: Vol.2* pp.116-122.

Doughty Martin (1989) 'The history and archaeology of the Hyde brewery, Winchester. Part one: The archaeological survey' in *Proc. Hampshire Field Club Archaeology 45* pp.191-212.

Dyos H. J. (1961) *Victorian Suburb*. London: Leicester University Press.

Edwards Edward (ed.) (1866) *Liber Monasterii de Hyda; Chronicle of the Affairs of England, from the settlement of the Saxons to the reign of King Cnut and a Chartulary of the Abbey of Hyde, in Hampshire A.D. 455-1023*. London: Longmans, Green, Reader and Dyer.

Edward James (1858) *Statistical Table of the population, taxation, number of electors, inhabited houses, £10 householders and MPs in the United Kingdom of Great Britain and Ireland*. London: Houlston and Wright.

Epsom History. Accessed at www.epsomandewellhistoryexplorer.org.uk/MynneG.html.

Eynsham Parish Council. http://eynsham-pc.gov.uk/documents/eynsham_record_1991.pdf.

Foster R. E. (2008) 'Dissolving the Dissolute? Henry VIII and the end of English Monasticism.' *History Review*. September.

Freeman Robin (1991) *The art and architecture of Owen Browne Carter (1806-1859)*. Winchester: Hampshire County Council.

Gardner James (ed.) (1888) *Letters and Papers, Foreign and Domestic of Henry VIII* Vol. 11. www.british-history.ac.uk/source.aspx?pubid=852.

Gapper Claire, Parker Karen and Robert Edward (2002) 'Elizabethan and Jacobean Decorative features at Hyde, Winchester' in *Hampshire Studies. Proceedings Hampshire Field Club Archaeological Society.* Vol. 57 pp.59-80.

Gaskell Elizabeth (2007 paperback ed.) *Cranford and other stories.* London: Bloomsbury.

Gilmour's Directory of Winchester 1854. Accessed at http://hampshiredirectories.com/.

Grover Christine (2008) *The Suburban development of Winchester from c1850 to 1912.* Unpublished Ph.D. thesis, University of Southampton.

Grover R. and Ng'ombe A. (2012) 'Land Owners'. In: Susan J. Smith, Marja Elsinga, Lorna Fox, O'Mahony, Ong Seow Eng, Susan Wachter, Sasha Tsenkova, editors. *International Encyclopedia of Housing and Home*, Vol 4. Oxford: Elsevier. pp. 152–156.

Grover Richard and Grover Christine (2010) *The origins of the British Cadastre.* Proceeding of FIG Congress, Sydney, Australia. www.fig.net/pub/fig2010/papers/ts10f%5Cts10f_grover_3915.pdf

Habakkuk John (1994) *Marriage, debt and the estate system: English Ownership 1650-1950.* Oxford: Clarendon Press.

Hampshire County Council. www.hants.gov.uk/hampshiretreasures/vol04/.

Hampshire Observer and Winchester News (1846) *Hampshire Notes and Queries Vol III.* Winchester: Hampshire Observer Office.

Hare John (1999) *The Dissolution of the Monasteries in Hampshire.* Hampshire Papers No. 16. Winchester: Hampshire County Council.

Hasted Edward (1798) 'Parishes: Godmersham', *The History and Topographical Survey of the County of Kent:* Volume 7, pp. 319-332. www.british-history.ac.uk/report.aspx?compid=63421.

Hawkridge Audrey (1995) *Jane Austen and Hampshire.* Hampshire Papers No. 6. Winchester: Hampshire County Council. p.27.

HMSO (1835) Commissioners of Inquiry into the excise establishment, and into the management and collection of the excise revenue throughout the United Kingdom. Malt. London: His Majesty's Stationery Office.

Hornsey Ian Spencer (2003) *A history of beer and brewing.* Cambridge: Royal Society of Chemistry.

Jack Sybil (1965) 'Monastic lands in Leicestershire and their administration on the eve of dissolution' in *Leicestershire Archaeological and Historical Society Transactions* 41, pp.9-40.

James Thomas Beaumont (1993) *Winchester: a pictorial history.* Chichester: Phillimore.

James Thomas Beaumont (2007) *Winchester from prehistory to the Present*. Stroud: Tempus.

Jane Austen Society. www.jasa.net.au/japeople/parents.htm.

Jenkinson Neil (1994) *The History of Peter Symonds*. The Old Symondians Society, Winchester.

Jones E. L. (1960) 'Eighteenth-century changes in Hampshire chalkland farming'. *Agricultural History Review* 8 pp.5-19.

Keene Derek (1985) *Survey of medieval Winchester*. Winchester Studies Vols. 1 & 2 Oxford: Clarendon.

Kemble J. V. & Kirby W. S. (1994) 'Abbott's Barton Estate, Winchester. Land Use in the 16th to 20th Centuries.' *Hants Field Club* 21 pp.17-20.

Kemble J. V. H. & Kirby W. S. (1995) *The History and Development of the Abbotts Barton Estate, Winchester*. Private publication.

Kitchen G. W. (1890) *Winchester*. Historic Towns series. London: Longmans, Green & Co.

Kitchen G. W. (ed.) & Madge F. T. (1889) *Document relating to the foundation of the Chapter of Winchester AD1541-1547*. Winchester: Warren & Son.

Knowles M. D. & Hadcock R. N. (1971) *Medieval Religious Houses: England and Wales*. London: Longmans, Green & Co.p.494.

Le Faye Deirdre (1995, 3rd ed.) *Jane Austen's Letters*. Oxford: OUP.

Leigh William Austen and Knight Montague George (1911) *Chawton Manor and its owners*. London. Smith, Elder & Co.

Locke A. Audrey (1912) *In praise of Winchester*. London: Constable & Co Ltd.

Malden H. E. (1911) 'Parishes: Epsom', *A History of the County of Surrey:* Volume 3, pp.271-278.

Massey Doreen B. & Catalano Alejandrina (1978) *Capital and land: landownership by capital in Great Britain*. London: Edward Arnold.

Mingay G. E. (1976) *The Gentry. The rise and fall of a ruling class*. London: Longman

Milner John (1798) *The history and survey of the antiquities of Winchester* Vols 1 & 2. Winchester: Robbins.

Miller Sean (2001) *Charter of the New Minster, Winchester*. Anglo-Saxon Charters IX. Oxford: Oxford University Press (Published for the British Academy).

Mogg Edward (1841) *Southampton Railway and Isle of Wight guide*. London: Mogg

Mudie Robert (1838) *Hampshire Vol. 1*. Winchester: Gilmour.

Nicholas Tom (1999) 'Business and land ownership in the late nineteenth century.' *Economic History Review, New Series* Vol. 52. No. 1 pp.27-44.

Nokes Davis (1997) *Jane Austen. A life.* London: Fourth Estate Ltd.

Oxford Dictionary of National Biography. On-line.

Page William (ed.) (1908) 'The parish of Micheldever', *A History of the County of Hampshire:* Vol. 3. pp. 390-394.

Page William (ed.) (1911) 'Parishes: Kings Worthy', *A History of the County of Hampshire*: Vol. 4. pp.430-433.

Page William (ed.) (1911) 'Parishes: Steventon' *A History of the County of Hampshire:* Vol. 4. pp.171-174.

Page William (ed.) (1911) 'Parishes: Brown Candover', *A History of the County of Hampshire:* Vol. 4. pp.183-184.

Page William (ed.) (1911) 'Parishes: Mottisfont', *A History of the County of Hampshire:* Vol. 4. pp.503-510.

Page William (ed.) (1912) *A History of the County of Hampshire.* Victoria County History Vol. 5.

Parker Karen (2009) *A comparison of Winchester and Southampton house interiors and furnishings from probate inventories, 1447-1575.* Unpublished Ph.D. thesis, University of Southampton.

Plantagenet Roll of the Blood Royal. Available at Ancestry.co.uk

Pennell R. F. (1909) *Account of the Parish of Hyde.* Winchester: Gilbert.

Pigot's Directory of Hampshire 1828. Accessed at http://hampshiredirectories.com/. Available from www.historicaldirectories.org/hd/.

Poole Brenda (2000) *John Colson: a Hampshire architect of the Victorian age.* Hampshire Papers No. 20. Winchester: Hampshire County Council.

Roberts Edward (1977) *In and around Winchester.* Alresford: Laurence Oxley.

Roberts Edward (2003) *Hampshire houses 1250-1700: their dating and development.* Winchester: Hampshire County Council.

Reynolds J., Burrell C. and Dignell D. (1967) 'Durngate Mill, Winchester' *Proceedings of the Hampshire Field Club and Archaeological Society.* Vol. 24 pp.103-12. Also printed by Millbrook Press Limited: Southampton.

Rosen Adrienne (1975) *Economic and social aspects of the history of Winchester 1520-1670.* Unpublished D.Phil, University of Oxford.

Rosen Adrienne (1981) 'Winchester in transition 1580-1700' in Clark Peter (ed.) *Country towns in pre-industrial England.* pp.144-185. Leicester: Leicester University Press.

Rowse A. L. (1965) 'Thomas Wriothesley. First Earl of Southampton' *The Huntington Library Quarterly* Vol. 28. No. 2. pp.105-129. California: University of California Press.

Rumble Alexander (2001) *Property and piety in early medieval Winchester*. Winchester Studies; Vol. 4iii. Oxford: Clarendon.

Sadler's Directory of Hampshire 1784. Accessed at http://hampshiredirectories.com/.

Sharples Joseph (2004) *Liverpool*. Pevsner Architectural Guides. London: Yale.

Short Brian (1997) *Land and society in Edwardian Britain*. Cambridge: Cambridge University Press.

Simpson Alfred William Brian (1961) *An Introduction to the History of the Land Law*. London: Oxford University Press.

Smith Mark (ed.) (2004) *Doing the duty of the Parish: Survey of the Church*. Hampshire Record Series Vol. XVII. Winchester: Hampshire County Council.

Slater's Hampshire Directory 1784. http://hampshiredirectories.com/.

Tomalin Claire (1997) *Jane Austen. A life*. London: Penguin.

Turner Alex Paul (1993) *Socio-economic aspects of non-local stone buildings in Winchester 1500-1800*. Unpublished M.Phil, University of Southampton.

Turner Michael (2004) 'Agriculture, 1860-1914' in Floud, Roderick & Johnson, Paul (eds.) (2004) *Cambridge Economic History of Modern Britain Vol. 2. 1860-1939*. Cambridge: Cambridge University Press.

Warner Richard (1795) *Collections for the History of Hampshire and the Bishopric of Winchester*. Vol. 1. London: Warner (self-published).

Warren & Sons (1902) *Shilling Guide to Winchester 1902*. Winchester: Warrens.

Warren T. W. (ed.) (1903) *Winchester Illustrated*. Winchester: Warren's Library.

Watson Sydney (n.d. but after 1892) *On active service. The story of the Soldiers' Home Winchester*. London: Partridge & Co.

Wells C. W. and Charles (1961) *The Story of St Bartholomew's Hyde*. Ramsgate: Graham Cumming.

West Downs Society. Memories of the Herbert/Brymer Era 1897-1922. www.westdowns.com/cornhist.htm.

White (1859) *History of Hampshire*. www.genealogysupplies.com/index.php.

Wilson Derek (2001) *In the Lion's Court. Power, Ambition and Sudden Death in the Reign of Henry VIII*. London: Hutchinson. p.410.

Winchester Museums Service (2003) *Hyde Abbey last resting place of Alfred the Great*. Winchester: Winchester City Council.

Woodward G. W. O. (1966) *Dissolution of the Monasteries*. London: Blandford Press Ltd.

Vancouver Charles (1810) *General view of the agriculture of Hampshire including the Isle of Wight*. London: Richard Phillips.

Youings Joyce (1971) *The Dissolution of the Monasteries*. London: George Allen & Unwin

Yates P. (2007 2nd ed.) *Time Gentlemen Please. The story of Winchester's pubs, breweries and hotels past and present*. Winchester: City of Winchester Trust.

Yorke Barbara (1999) The *King Alfred Millenary in Winchester, 1901*. Hampshire Papers No. 17. Winchester: Hampshire County Council.

Primary Sources:

Census: The National Archives (TNA) Public Record Office

HO 107/1674	1851 Census (Winchester).
RG9/691-693	1861 Census (Winchester).
RG10/ 1209-1212	1871 Census (Winchester).
RG11/1231-1233	1881 Census (Winchester).
RG12/936-938	1891 Census (Winchester).
RG13/1081-1083	1901 Census (Winchester).
RG4	1911 Census (Winchester).

Hampshire Record Office (main collections):

13M85W/	Simonds Family Papers.
39M89/E/B	Knight Collection.
206M85W/	Winchester Brewery collection.
67M92W/	Faithfull and Gardner of Winchester, Solicitors.
W/C11/1&2	Winchester Building plans.

Maps:

Ordnance Survey	Winchester: 1st Edition 1873, 2nd Edition 1897 and 3rd Edition 1909.
HRO:3M46/1	Map by Godson.
HRO:13M85W/32	Map by Hogben.
HRO:W/K4/1/15/1	Map by William Godson in 1767.
HRO: 4506W/1	Printed map of Winchester c1800.
HRO:W/F5/1/10	Part of Barton Farm and Hyde Abbey Farm.
HRO:PC 562/18&19	1769 Freehold Estates belonging to Thomas Knight, Abbots Barton Uplands.

General Collections (number after M indicate year acquired):

44M68/F2/461	1920 Conveyance of 52 Hyde Abbey Rd.
44M68/F2/464	1967 Purchase of St Bartholomew's Diocesan Maternity Home.
44M69/E18/1/94	1789 Plans of the Bridewell.

44M69/G3/679	1788 Bridewell Calendar Easter Sessions.
44M69/93/992	1823 New Prison or County Bridewell Michaelmas Sessions.
44M69/K1/16	1818 Rules and order for Government of Gaol and Bridewell or House of Correction of County of Southampton 1818.
11M70/C3/2	1824-26 Hyde Abbey School Pupil Fees.
55M8/W/PW2	1830 Churchwarden Book for Hyde (Book 38B).
38M48/220	1891 Plans for Fyfhyde.
38M48/223	1900 Abbots Barton Estate.
38M48/229	1884 Building lease for Park Road.
5M53/319	1531 Lands in Segensworth, Charke and Lee Britten in Titchfield.
44M68/F2/461	1881 52 Hyde Abbey Rd (4 Garfield Terrace).
11M70/C3/1	1807-28 Hyde Abbey School Accounts.
11M70/C3/2	1824 Hyde Abbey School Pupil Fees.
14M70/12	1926 Conveyance of 7 King Alfred Terrace.
55M81W/PO3	1794-1814 Poor Relief Parish of St Bartholomew.
55M81W/PO5	1820-1832 Weekly relief Book Parish of St Bartholomew.
48M84W/167	1934 Sale of 1 Victoria Road, 34-37 Hyde Abbey Road and 41-46 Andover Road (all leasehold).
48M84W/168	1920 Sale of 53 Hyde Abbey Road (leasehold).
48M84W/359	1920 Sale of 14 Victoria Road (leasehold).
48M84W/379	1924 Sale of 9 Thurloe Place.
283M87W	1872 1 North Walls St Peter's Villa/ Winchester Refuge.
144M89W/1	1835 Release of house garden and land in Hyde St.
149M89/R4/6032	1665-1757 Bundle of papers relating to mills and meadows between Abbots Worthy and Winchester.
34M91W/771	1866 Anthony Edmund's Charity.
117M91/SP203	1950 Sale of 1 Hyde St.
92M95/F2/1/19	1819 Report on Bridewell by Baring, chairman.
92M95/F2/1/44-46	1828 Letters from Bridewell keeper.
92M95/F2/1/14	1825 Letter from Rev. John Old Zillwood, Chaplain to Baring.
100M97/A9/1	1928-1938 Maternity Rescue Home.
100M97/C1/1	1915-1972 Winchester Diocesan Union for Preventative and Rescue Work.
H/CS2/2/75-76	1856 Property in North Walls.
Q22/1/1/271	1799 -1831 Land Tax for St Bartholomew's Hyde.
W/C1/5/273	Correspondence relating to development of the Oxlease Estate between H S Frampton, A Frampton, and Lemon, city engineers.

Index

Abbey Farm, xii, 1, 5, 19, 28-38, 51, 66-73, 74, 76, 80, 84, 85, 87-93, 102-111, 196, 240, 241, 242

Abbots Barton Farm, 1, 27, 46, 47, 70, 81, 89-90, 105, 135, 138, 142, 157, 159, 161, 164, 238, 239

Abbots Barton Dairy, **86**

Abbots Barton Farmhouse, **87**, 93, 94, 146

Abbotts Barton House, 158, **159**, 235, 238

Abbots Worthy, 21, 22, 36, 41, 43, 70, 80, 91

Alswitha Terrace, 218, **219**

Andover Road, 8, 20, 25, 45, 89, 107, 140, 142, 167, 171, 172, 173,174, 201, 202, 205, 206, 207, 235, 239, 245, 247, 248

Andover Terrace, 204, 205, 206, 207

Arthur Road, 208, 210, 211, 212, 224, 247, 248

Austen
    Edward, xii, 47, 51, 66-71, **68**, 72, 102, 111, 116, 127, 135, 136, 241, 242
    Family, 66, **67**,
    Jane, 47, 66, 67, 69, 71, 133, 135

Barton Farm, xi, 19, 39, 64, 65, 70, 73, 76, 80, 82, 83, 84, 86, 87, 88, 93, 94, 103, 126, **137**, 147, 152, 190, 225, 237

Baverstock, 71, 135-137

Bedford Duke of, xii, 22, 48, 51, 63-66, 70-73, 82-86, 89, 91, 93, 105, 107, 111, 116, 191, 226, 240

Bethell family, 19, 20, 26-34, 41, 44-46, 226, 240

Birinus Road, 208, 211, 214, 247

Bishop of Winchester, 6, 7, 8, 11, 12, 13, 24, 45, 48, 101, 103, 109

Bowker family, 109, 144, 145, 158, 167, 173, 177, 179, 185, 224, 233, 245-247

Brewery, 29, 105, 110, 115, 125, 129, 130, 149-155
    Hyde, 126, 131, 132, 147, 157, 158, 225, 227-230, 237
    Winchester, 222, 223, 230-233, 237-238, 241

Bridewell, xi, 109, 113, 115, 116, 118, 119-124, 132, 133, 147, 148, 187, 190, 220, 240, 242

Brockway Alfred and Aaron, 173, 185, 198, 199, 203, 206

Carter
    Family,176, 189, 191, 192, 203, 205, 206, 247
    Lewis, 174, 206, 233, 246

Chaundler family, 1, 13, 19, 26, 27, 39-44, 46, 49, 109, 240

Chawton, xii, 47, 50, 55, 59, 69, 70, 71, 135, 240

Clerke family, 1, 21, 26, 27, 34, 35-37, 44, 45, 46, 62, 80, 129, 223, 240

Conygary Estate, 168, 187, 188, 208-**213**, 233

Corham, Roger, 13, 20, 27, 40, 41, 42, 44, 45, 46,

Cromwell
      Thomas, 1, 9, 10, 11, 12, 13, 14
      Oliver, 26, 43
Dean and Chapter, 13, 20, 24, 28, 45, 46, 70, 111, 135, 139, 149, 156, 162, 187, 201, 203, 222, 223, 234, 241
Deane
      Arthur Elliot, 187, 188, 208, 210, 212, 214, 217, 230, 242
      Charles March, 145, 147, 208, 211, 212, 214, 217
      Family, 208, 220
      Thomas, 69, 102, 115, 126, 127, 129, 130, 147, 155, 188, 190, 208, 223, 241
Dissolution, 11-14
Doswell family, 94, 115, 129, 130, 225
Durngate Mills, **24**, **48**, 50, 83, 84, 85, 87, 101, 102, 103, 156, 234, 237
Eagles Field, 187, 201-207, 223, 233, 241
Edington Road, 183
Egbert Road, 208, 210, 211, 212, 224, 225, **247**, **248**
Firmstone Rev., 146, 222, 224, 234, 247
Fletcher Nathaniel and Mary, 129
Frampton
      Alfred, 208, 210, 211, 212, 214, 217
      Family, 242, 247
      Henry, 148, 189, 203, 206, 208, 212, 233
      Henry Swift, 210, 212, 217, 233
Gallows Field, 89, 90, 94, 98, 101, 104, 140
Gallows Hill Development, 163, 164, **172**, 173-184, 185
Godmersham, xii, 47, 51, 58, 59, 61, 69, 70, 71, 93, 102, 240
Godwin family, 127, 130, 149, 205
Gover family, 120, 123, 142, 143, 147, 171, 185, 197, 198
Gradeige family, 131, 147, 148, 223, 224
Highfield Lodge, 142, 143, 146, 184, 245
Hinton family, 58, 61, 71, 135, 136, 137
hops, 76, 77, 78, 89, 101, 105, 125, 129, 157
Hughes and Green, 208, 210, 211, 212, 233
Hussey Thomas, 43, 49
Hyde Abbey, xi, xii, 1, 3-6, 8-19, 21, 22, 24, 28, 29, 34, 39, 41, 44, 46
Hyde Abbey Gateway, 4, **15**, **16**, **22**, 29, 113
Hyde Abbey Road, 165, 173, 174, 187, 196-200, **197**, **200**, 220, 233, 234, 235, 236, 238, 248
Hyde Abbey School, 116-118, 132, 226
Hyde Church Lane, 25, 44, 111, 113, 224, 234, 247
Hyde Church Path, 113,
Hyde Churchyard, 15, **20**, 115, 146, 147, 225, 248
Hyde Close, 8, 44, 201, **202**, 203, **207**, 223, 224, 226, 233, 235, 247, 228

Hyde House, 28, 29, **30**, **31**, 32, **33**, 34, 35, 42, 44, 91, 93, 110, 111, 113, 226

Hyde Lodge, **143**, 144, 145, 168, 236, 246

Hyde Street, xi, 3, 6, 7, 8, 19, 20, 25, 26, 28, 29, 35, 42, 44-5, 46, 91, 109-115, 125, 126, 127, 128, 129, **131**, 132, 133, **134**, 145-148, 155, **157**, **191**, 192, 222-226, 227, 231, 232, 234, 235, 237, 239, 241, 243, 247, 248

Hyde Tavern, 126, **154**, 222, 247

King Alfred Place, **105**, 113, 147, 153, 187, 190, 191, **192**, **193**, 199, 210, 218, 220, 225, 233, 234, 237, 247, 248

King Alfred Terrace, **218**

Knight,

    Bulstrode Peachey, 51, 54, 55, **56**, 71, 89

    Broadnax-May Thomas (the elder), 51, 58, 59, 60, **61**, 66, **67**, 69, 71, 72, 73, 83, 84, 85, 86, 91, 93, 99, 100, 101, 103, 107, 111, 136, 226, 240, 241

    Catherine, 51, 66, 67, 69, 70, 71, 102, 116, 127, 135

    Elizabeth (née Martin), xii, 47, 50, 51, 53, 54, 55, **56,** 57, 58, 59, 61, 70, 71, 89, 106, 133, 135, 136, 137, 157, 240, 241

    Thomas (the younger), 51, 60, 66, 67, **68**, 69, 70, 71, 101, 111, 115, 116, 119, 126, 135, 136, 218, 240

Knights of Chawton Family Tree, **54**

Lankhills, 144, 145, 162, 167, 169, 179, 224, 234, 235, 236, 245, 247

Law suit, 133, 135-137

Lewkenor family, xii, 26, 47, 50, 51, 52, 53, 54, 55, 59, 70, 71

Lewkenor Family Tree, **53**

Limekilns, 43, 94, 140, 163

Limekilns Development, 171, **172**, 183, 185

Mackadam Lucy, 37, 62, 63

Macklin family, 146, 206, 208, 210, 211, 212, 217, 233, 248

malthouse, 5, 19, 20, 34, 40, 43, 49, 76, 91, 93, 103, 115, 125, 126, 129, 130, 132, 151, 155, 156, 225, 226, 232, 243

Malthouse Nos. 1, 2, or 3, 126, 127, **128,** 129, **131**, 149, 152, 153, 222, 227

Martin family, 47, 50, 51, 53, 54, **56**, 71, 136

May Family Tree, **60**

May, John (Coopers Arms), 147, 149, 153, 154, 155

Micklam,

    Thomas, 174, 175, 183, 185, 196, 197, 198, 199, 200

    Mrs, 233, 234, 246, 248

Monks Road, 20, 208, 211, 214, 217, 247

Morecroft James, 37, 62, 63, 64, 89, 91

Moss Richard, 225, 227, 228, 230, 241

Muller Mary, 155, 227, 228, 232, 241

Mynne Anne, xii, 43, 49, 50, 51, 70, 240

Mynne Lady Anne (Lewkenor) **52**, 53

Mynne Family Tree, **52**

New Minster, 3, 6, 239

North Walls, xi, 50, 87, 142, 148, 153, 194, 195, 196, 220, 222, 227, 238

Northbrook Lord, 22, 162, 187, 188, 190, 201, 203, 205, 233, 241, 242, 248

Nunnaminster, 11

Nuns Road, 211, 214, 247

Nuns Walk, **6**, 87, 94, 183, 208

Nuns Walk (road), 208, 211, 214, 217, 247

Old Hop Garden, 76, 94, 98, 101, 104, 140, 163, 164, 171

Old Hop Garden Development, 167- 170, 183, 185

Oxlease Estate, 187, 208, 209, 210, 211, 214-**217**, 233

Oxlease Little and Great, 19

Page Richard, 115, 225

Page Robert, 126, 127, 130

Park Road, 140, **165**, **166**, **168**, 171, **172**, 173-182, 183, 184, 185, 188, 196, 198, 224, 233, 234, 235, 236, 239, 246, 247, 248

Paulet family, 11, 13, 26, 27, 40, 41, 42, 201

Pyle Nicholas, 126, 127, 129, 132, 149, 241

Priors Barton Farm, St Cross. 70, 135, 156, 225

railway, xii, 25, 101, 125, 133, 138, 139, 140, 141, 142, 144, 145, 146, 147, 157, 162, 163, 164, 167, 168, 173, 174, 190, 230, 242

Refuge (Home for Fallen Women), xii, 194, 195, **196**, 197, 199, 236

Richards

Family, 218, 226, 237, 248

Rev Charles (father), 102, 103, 109, 111, 115, 116, 118, 127, 132, 223

Rev Charles (son), 115, 118, 223, 226

Russell family, 21, 22, 23, 63, 66, 91, 107, 111

Sandys family, 13, 34, 41, 42

Sawyer Ashton, 179, 233, 245, 246

Saxon Road, 113, **209**, 210, 211, 212, 230, 247, 248

Shearman family, 176, 189, 212, 218, 220, 248

sheep, xii 47, 74, 75, 76, 79, 80, 103, 105, 107, 138, 157, 162

Sheep Fair Field, 145, 179

Shenton family, 198, 199, 206, 230, 233, 248

Simonds

Family, 74, 135, 145, 146, 155, 157, 158, 159, 169, 170, 222, 228, 233, 234, 238, 246

William, xii, 70, 74, 103, 107, 133, 135-147, 149, 155-156, 157, 159, 241, 242

William Barrow, xi, xii, 133, 142, 145, 148, 158 – 186, **186**, 187, 188, 190, 191, 196, 197, 198, 220, 222, 223, 224, 225, 227, 234, 235, 238, 241, 242, 243, 246

William Barrow Family Tree, **160**

Simonds of Reading,

Brewery, 70, 125, 227, **229**, **231**

Blackall, 70, 155, 228

Brewery in Winchester, 149-155, 157

James, 147, 155, 227

St Bartholomew's

Church, **2**, 3, 4, 15, 25, 35, 87, **109**, 153, 179, 225, 237

Parish, 13, 41, 93, 115, 118, 129, 139, 201, 208

Parishioners, 8, 20, 28, 45

Vicar, 14, 39, 64, 118, 132, 248

St Cross

Hospital, 40, 203

Parish, 12, 70, 74, 103, 135, 139, 140, 156, 158, 228, 230

St John's Hospital, 8, 20, 28, 45, 139, 147, 162, 203

St John's Parish, 62, 102, 103, 129

St Johns Street, 43, 129, 149, 153

Stockbridge Road, 8, 45

Stopher Thomas, 184, 203, 205, 210, 211, 212, 217, 218, 232

Swan Lane, 7, 8, 20, 25, 45, 107, 111, 113, 115, 124, 125, 126, **130**, **131**, 145, 147, 149, 151, 152, **202**, 222, 223, 227, 234, 248

Thurloe Place, 202, 203, 204, 205, 206, 207, 224, 247

Turnpikes, 106-108, 139

Uplands, 89, 93, **94**, **95**, 98, 140, 173, 185, 234, 239, 242, 245

Victoria Road, 111, 202, 203, 205, 206, 207, 223, 233, 235, 247, 248

Waldron family, 73, 84, 85, 86, 91, 126, 127

water meadows, xii, 19, 24, **38**, 47, 48, 61, 64, 70, 72, 73, 74, 75, 79-86, **81**, 87, 89, 91, 93, 94, 101, 105, 161, 162, 196, 220, **221**, 238, 240

White Swan, 126, 129, 130, **132**, 149, 222, 227, 237, 248

Winchester College, 8, 13, 20, 24, 28, 29, 39, 45, 46, 69, 75, 107, 109, 116, 139, 143, 159, 169, 171, 186, 194, 203, 243

Winnall, 75, 80, 84, 87, 101, 145, 162

Woodward, William, 47, 51, 55, 59, 71, 136

Worthy Lane, 8, 20, 25, 44, 107, 224, 241

Worthy Road, 8, 20, 25, 44, 45, 89, 93, 94, 111, 113, 140, 142, 163, 167, **168**, **169**, **170**, 173, 176, 179, 201, 202, 205, 207, 212, 224, 236, 246, 247

Worthy Road Development, **169**, **170**, 183, **184**

Wriothesley- Russell Family Tree, **23**

Wriothesley Thomas, xi, xii, 11, 12, 13, 14, 19, 21, 22, 24, 28, 39, 63, 66, 71, 91, 240, 243

Wriothesley family, 34, 41, 66

Wyeth

Hugh, 167, 169, 176, 185, 237

James, 147, 148, 155, 232